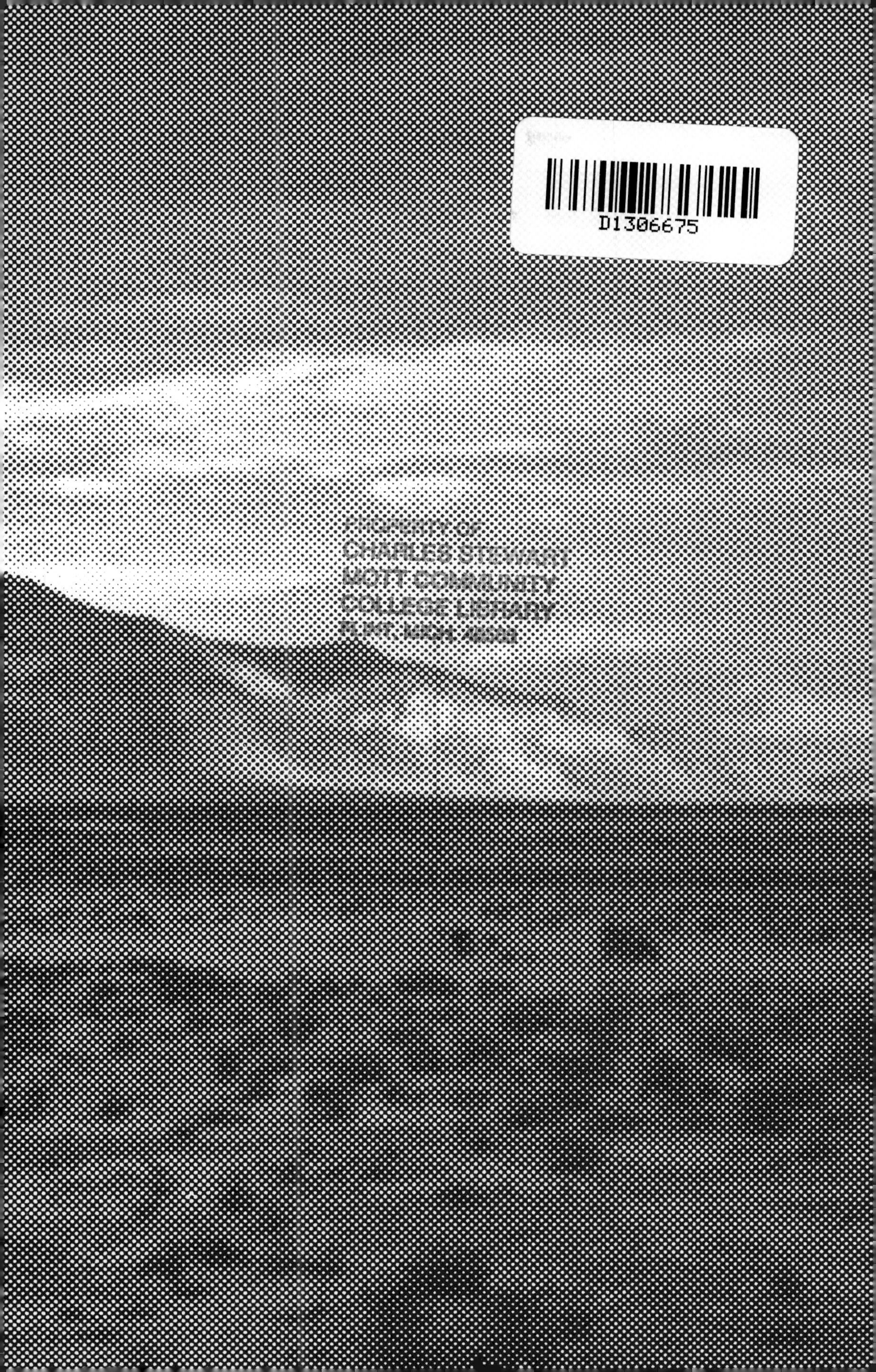

fallout

J. ROBERT OPPENHEIMER, LEO SZILARD, AND THE POLITICAL SCIENCE OF THE ATOMIC BOMB

Jim Ottaviani, Janine Johnston, Steve Lieber, Vince Locke, Bernie Mireault, and Jeff Parker with Chris Kemple, Eddy Newell, and Robin Thompson

other books about scientists from G.T. Labs

SAFECRACKER: A TWO-FISTED SCIENCE COMIC
TWO-FISTED SCIENCE
WILD PERSON IN THE WOODS
DIGNIFYING SCIENCE
"TALKING" ORANGUTANS IN BORNEO

science fiction

Though not a work of history, this book isn't entirely fiction either. We've fabricated some details in service of the story, but the characters said and did (most of) the things you'll read. And as the notes and references will indicate, many of the quotes and incidents that you'll think most likely to be made up are the best documented facts.

FALLOUT: J. ROBERT OPPENHEIMER, LEO SZILARD, AND THE POLITICAL SCIENCE OF THE ATOMIC BOMB

First Edition: October 2001

ISBN 0-9660106-3-9
Library of Congress Control Number: 2001091068

 Special thanks to my alert editors, patient family and friends, and the Godfathers.

A General Tektronics Labs production.

G.T. Labs
P.O. Box 8145
Ann Arbor, MI 48107

info@gt-labs.com
www.gt-labs.com

5 4 3 2 1

contents

prologue
(1996)

I made the great mistake of feeling relieved of my responsibility ... the chance to show the world that science can stop a terrible war without killing a single person was lost.
—Edward Teller, *New York Times*, December 28, 1970

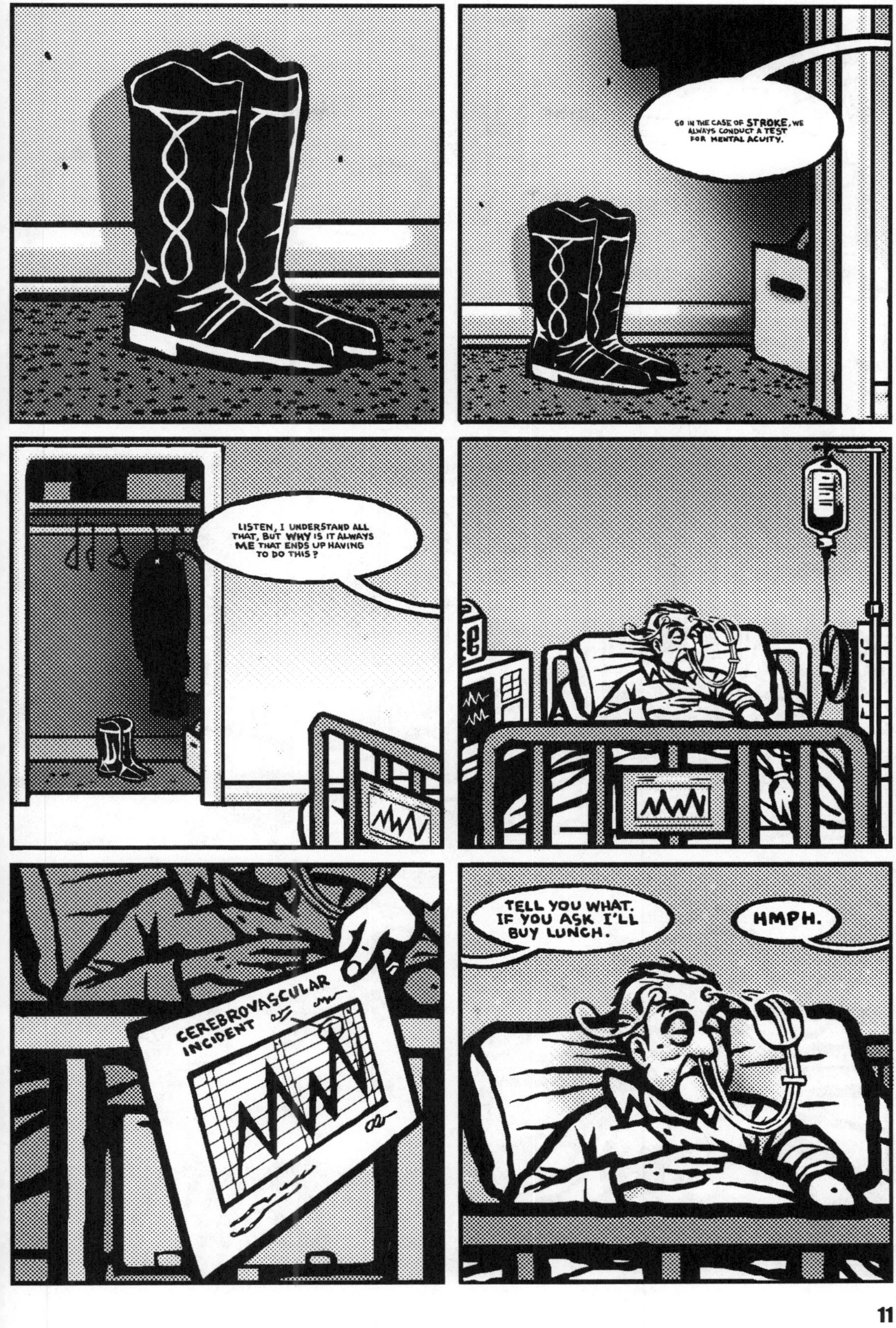
SO IN THE CASE OF STROKE, WE ALWAYS CONDUCT A TEST FOR MENTAL ACUITY.
LISTEN, I UNDERSTAND ALL THAT, BUT WHY IS IT ALWAYS ME THAT ENDS UP HAVING TO DO THIS?
CEREBROVASCULAR INCIDENT
TELL YOU WHAT. IF YOU ASK I'LL BUY LUNCH.
HMPH.

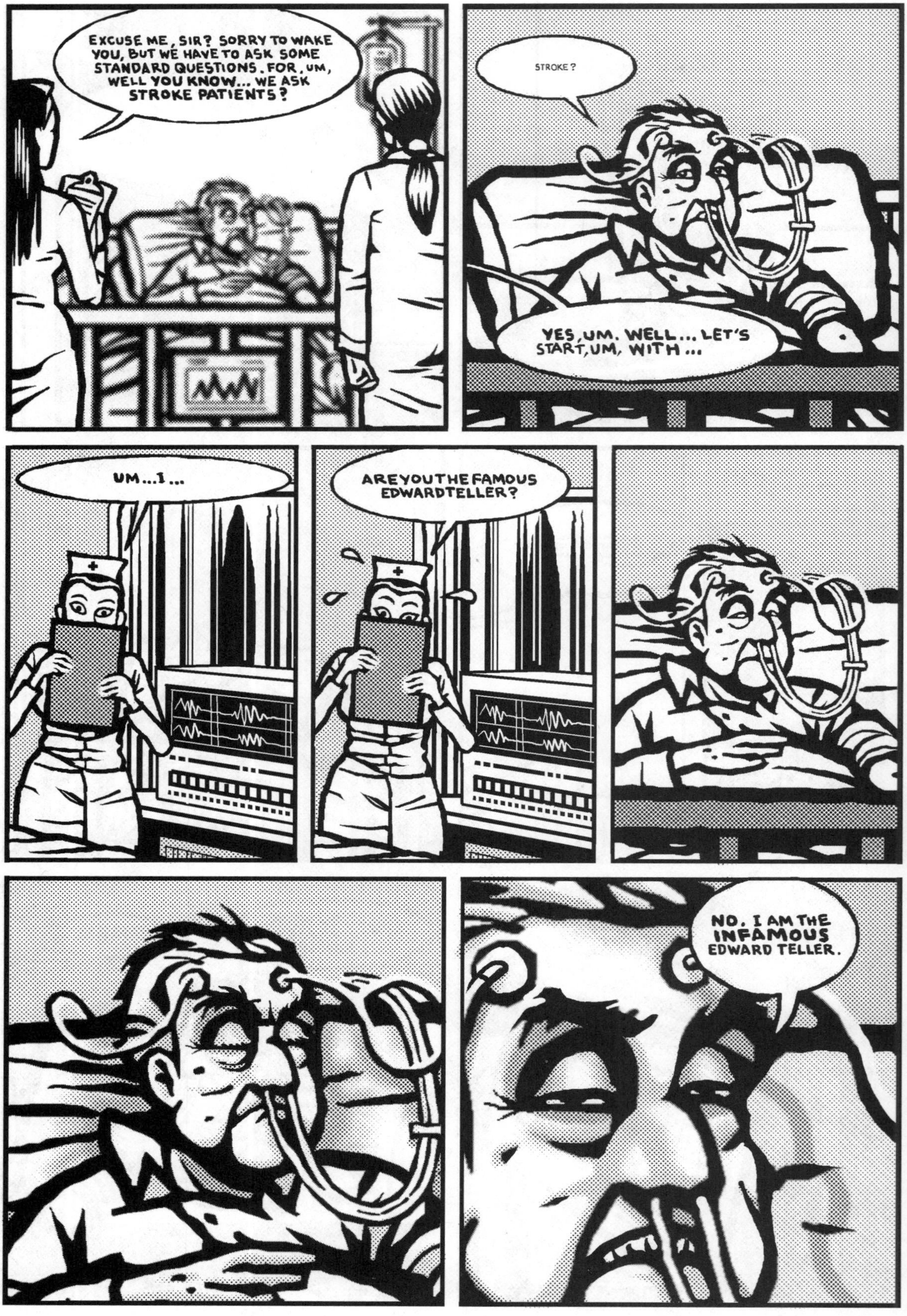
EXCUSE ME, SIR? SORRY TO WAKE YOU, BUT WE HAVE TO ASK SOME STANDARD QUESTIONS. FOR, UM, WELL YOU KNOW... WE ASK STROKE PATIENTS?
STROKE?
YES, UM. WELL... LET'S START, UM, WITH...
UM...I...
AREYOUTHEFAMOUS EDWARDTELLER?
NO. I AM THE INFAMOUS EDWARD TELLER.

A FEW MORE QUESTIONS DR
MY NAME IS NOT STRANGELOVE.
I WASN'T
I DON'T KNOW ABOUT STRANGELOVE.
I'M NOT INTERESTED IN STRANGELOVE.
ope 2100
15:10 TEMP
SYS MEAN DIA
124 88 59
I SEE.
ope 2100
15:10 TEMP
SYS MEAN
124 88

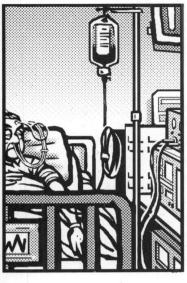

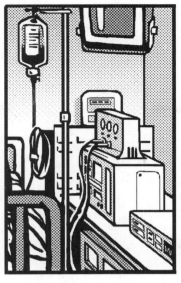

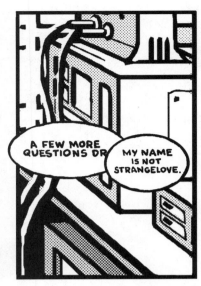

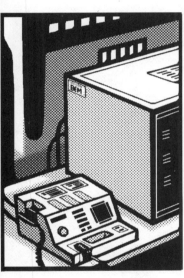

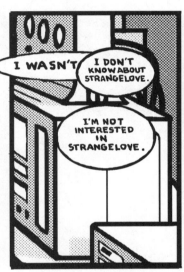

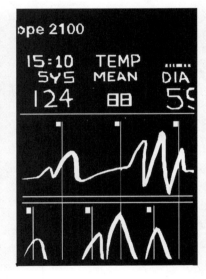

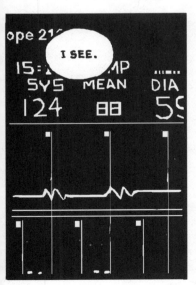

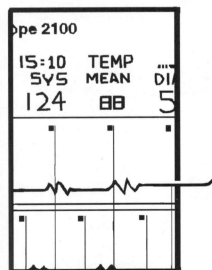

birth

(1932-1939)

Zerstöre nicht, was Du nicht erschaffen kannst.
        —Zehn Gebote von Leo Szilard, 30. Oktober 1940
[Do not destroy what you cannot create.
        —Ten Commandments by Leo Szilard, 30 October 1940]

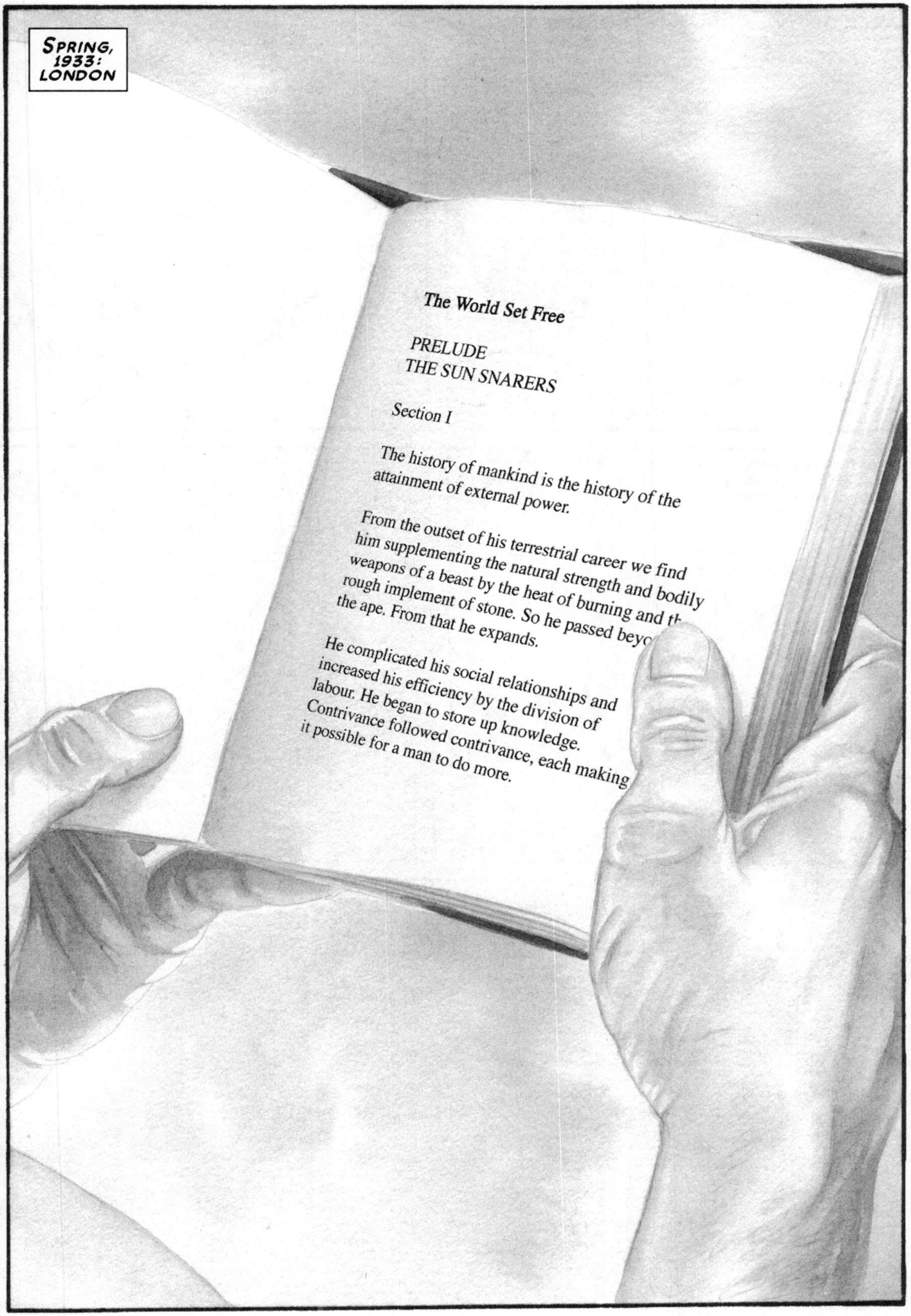
SPRING, 1933: LONDON
The World Set Free
PRELUDE
THE SUN SNARERS
Section I
The history of mankind is the history of the attainment of external power.
From the outset of his terrestrial career we find him supplementing the natural strength and bodily weapons of a beast by the heat of burning and th rough implement of stone. So he passed beyo the ape. From that he expands.
He complicated his social relationships and increased his efficiency by the division of labour. He began to store up knowledge. Contrivance followed contrivance, each making it possible for a man to do more.

So slowly, by human standards, did humanity gather itself together out of the dim intimations of the beast. And that first glimmering of speculation, that first story of achievement, that story-teller bright-eyed and flushed under his matted hair, gesticulating to his gaping, incredulous listener, gripping his wrist to keep him attentive, was the most marvellous beginning this world has ever seen. It doomed the mammoths, and it began the setting of that snare that shall catch the sun.

So slowly, by human standards, did humanity gather itself together out of the dim intimations of the beast.

And that first glimmering of speculation, that first story of achievement, that story-teller bright-eyed and flushed under his matted hair,

gesticulating to his gaping, incredulous listener, gripping his wrist to keep him attentive, was the most marvellous beginning this world has ever seen.

GERMANY ELECTS NEW CHANCELLOR

KNOCK KNOCK

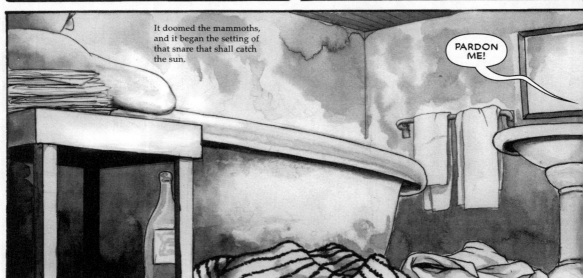

It doomed the mammoths, and it began the setting of that snare that shall catch the sun.

PARDON ME!

ERR... ARE YOU ALL RIGHT DR. SZILARD?
YES YES, QUITE FINE, THANK YOU.
WELL...
...IT'S JUST THAT YOU'VE BEEN IN THERE FOR, WELL...
THREE HOURS.
IS IT NOON ALREADY?!
I WILL BE LATE FOR AN APPOINTMENT!
THANK YOU SO KINDLY FOR INTERRUPTING ME--I WILL BE OUT IN A MOMENT.

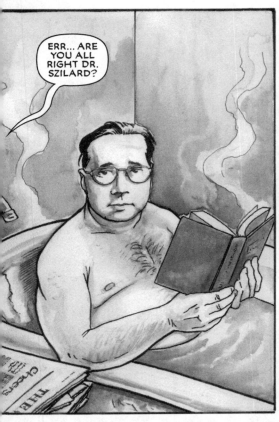

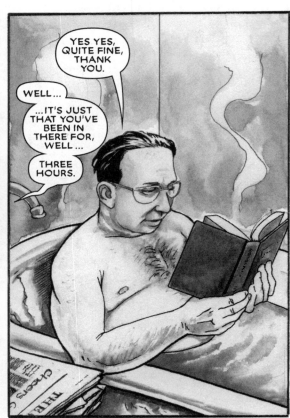

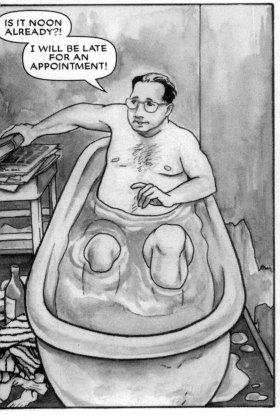

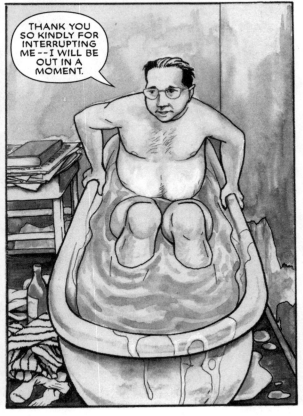

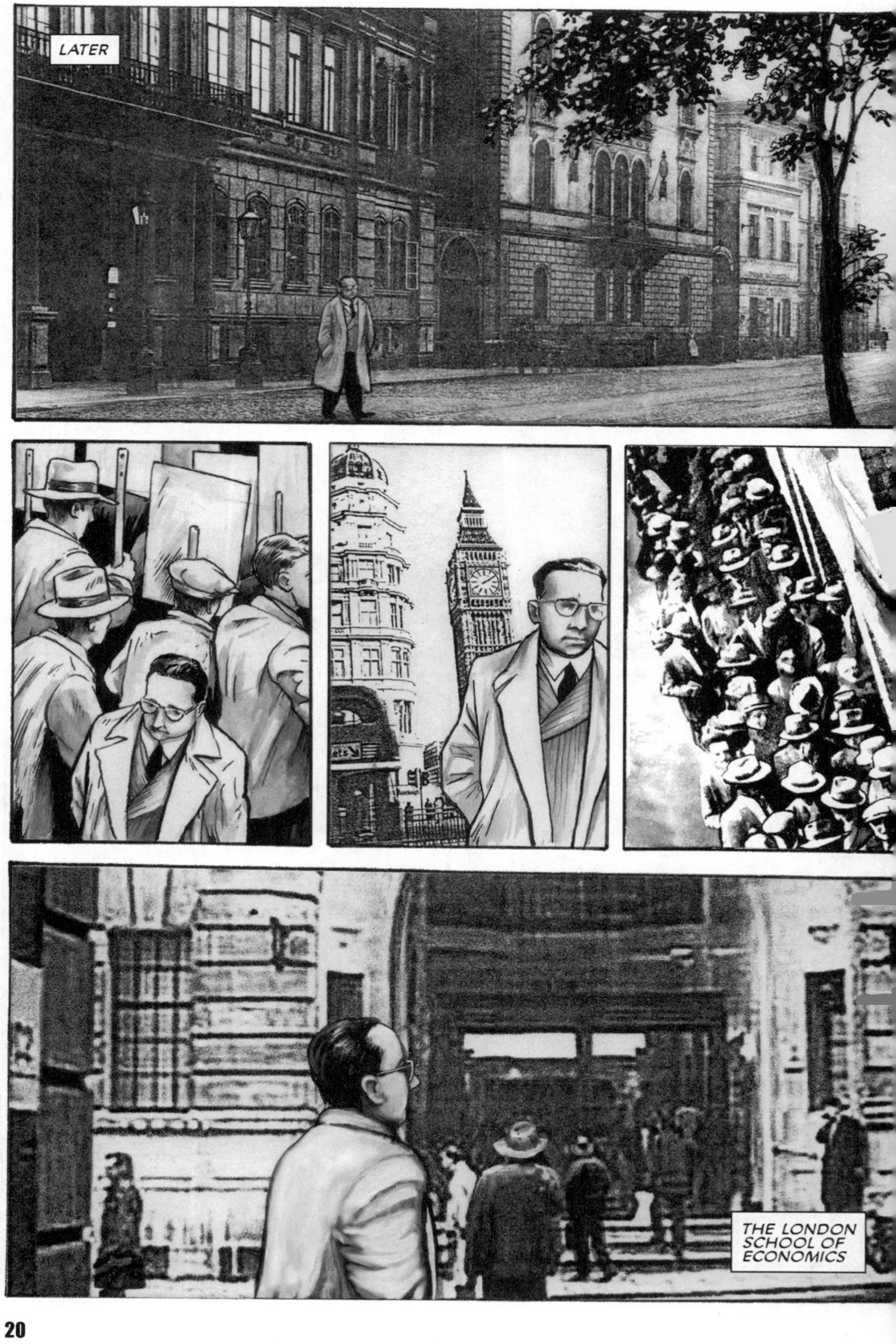
LATER
THE LONDON SCHOOL OF ECONOMICS

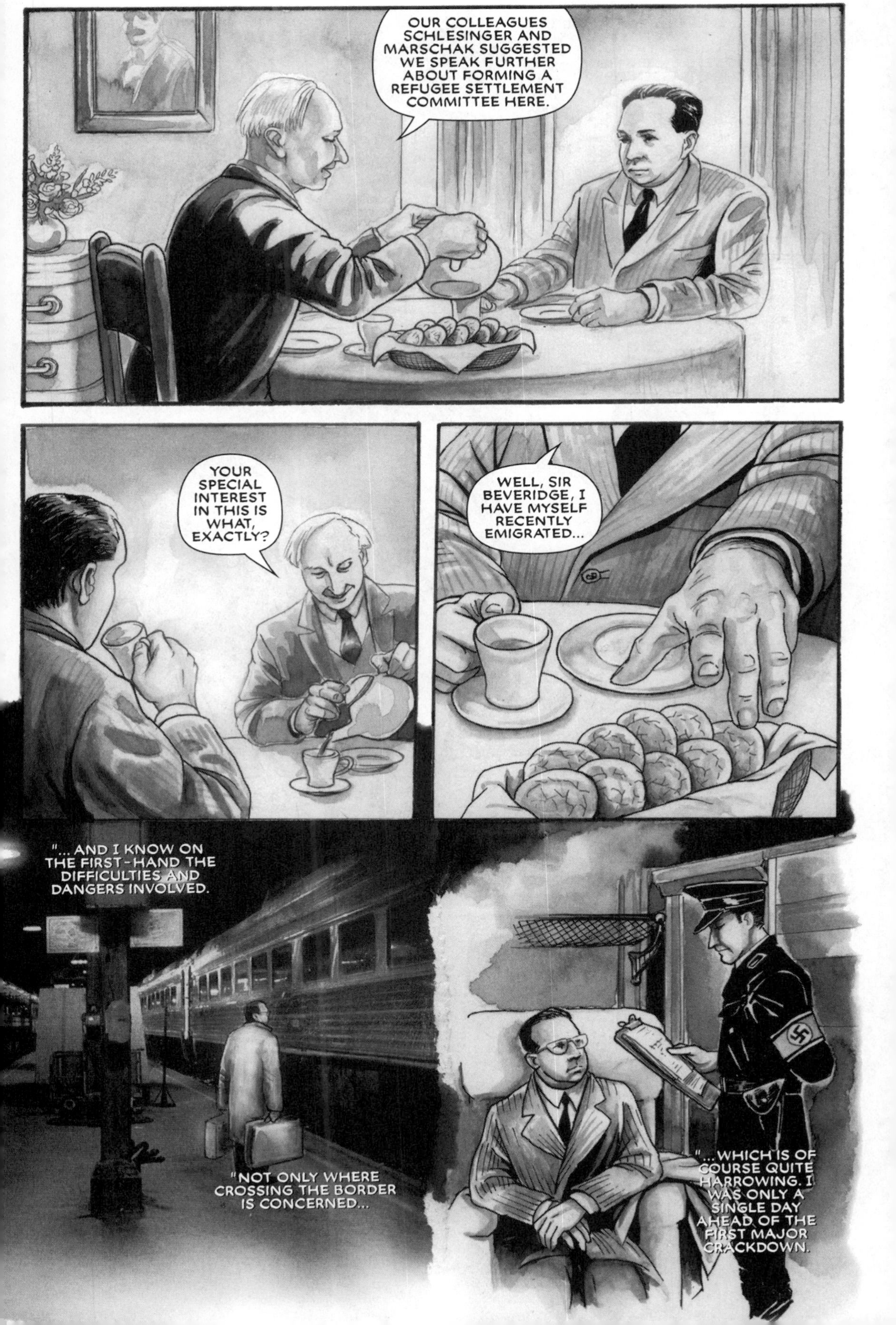
OUR COLLEAGUES SCHLESINGER AND MARSCHAK SUGGESTED WE SPEAK FURTHER ABOUT FORMING A REFUGEE SETTLEMENT COMMITTEE HERE.
YOUR SPECIAL INTEREST IN THIS IS WHAT, EXACTLY?
WELL, SIR BEVERIDGE, I HAVE MYSELF RECENTLY EMIGRATED...
"...AND I KNOW ON THE FIRST-HAND THE DIFFICULTIES AND DANGERS INVOLVED.
"NOT ONLY WHERE CROSSING THE BORDER IS CONCERNED...
"...WHICH IS OF COURSE QUITE HARROWING. I WAS ONLY A SINGLE DAY AHEAD OF THE FIRST MAJOR CRACKDOWN.

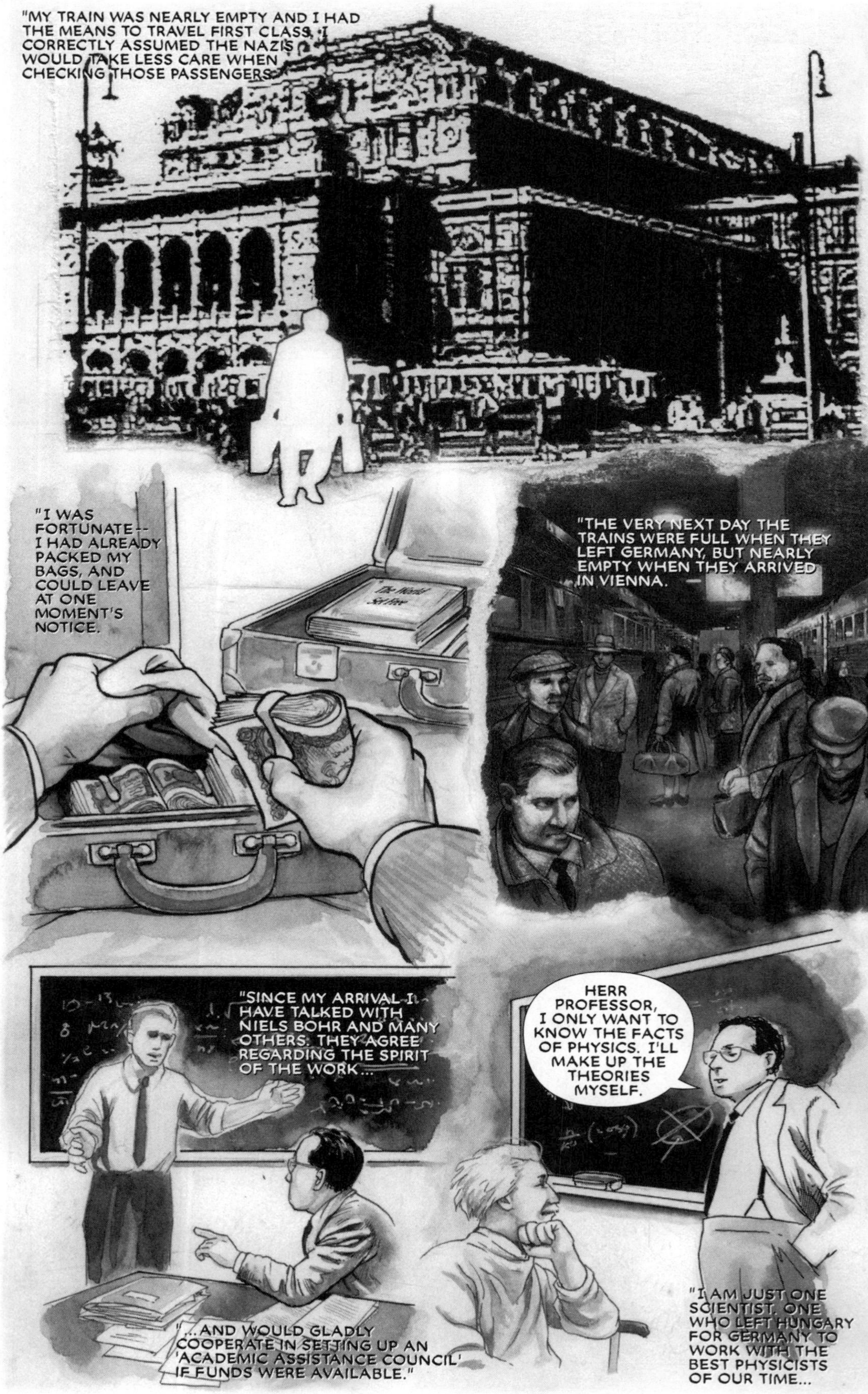
"MY TRAIN WAS NEARLY EMPTY AND I HAD THE MEANS TO TRAVEL FIRST CLASS. I CORRECTLY ASSUMED THE NAZIS WOULD TAKE LESS CARE WHEN CHECKING THOSE PASSENGERS.
"I WAS FORTUNATE-- I HAD ALREADY PACKED MY BAGS, AND COULD LEAVE AT ONE MOMENT'S NOTICE.
"THE VERY NEXT DAY THE TRAINS WERE FULL WHEN THEY LEFT GERMANY, BUT NEARLY EMPTY WHEN THEY ARRIVED IN VIENNA.
"SINCE MY ARRIVAL I HAVE TALKED WITH NIELS BOHR AND MANY OTHERS. THEY AGREE REGARDING THE SPIRIT OF THE WORK...
"...AND WOULD GLADLY COOPERATE IN SETTING UP AN 'ACADEMIC ASSISTANCE COUNCIL' IF FUNDS WERE AVAILABLE."
HERR PROFESSOR, I ONLY WANT TO KNOW THE FACTS OF PHYSICS. I'LL MAKE UP THE THEORIES MYSELF.
"I AM JUST ONE SCIENTIST. ONE WHO LEFT HUNGARY FOR GERMANY TO WORK WITH THE BEST PHYSICISTS OF OUR TIME...

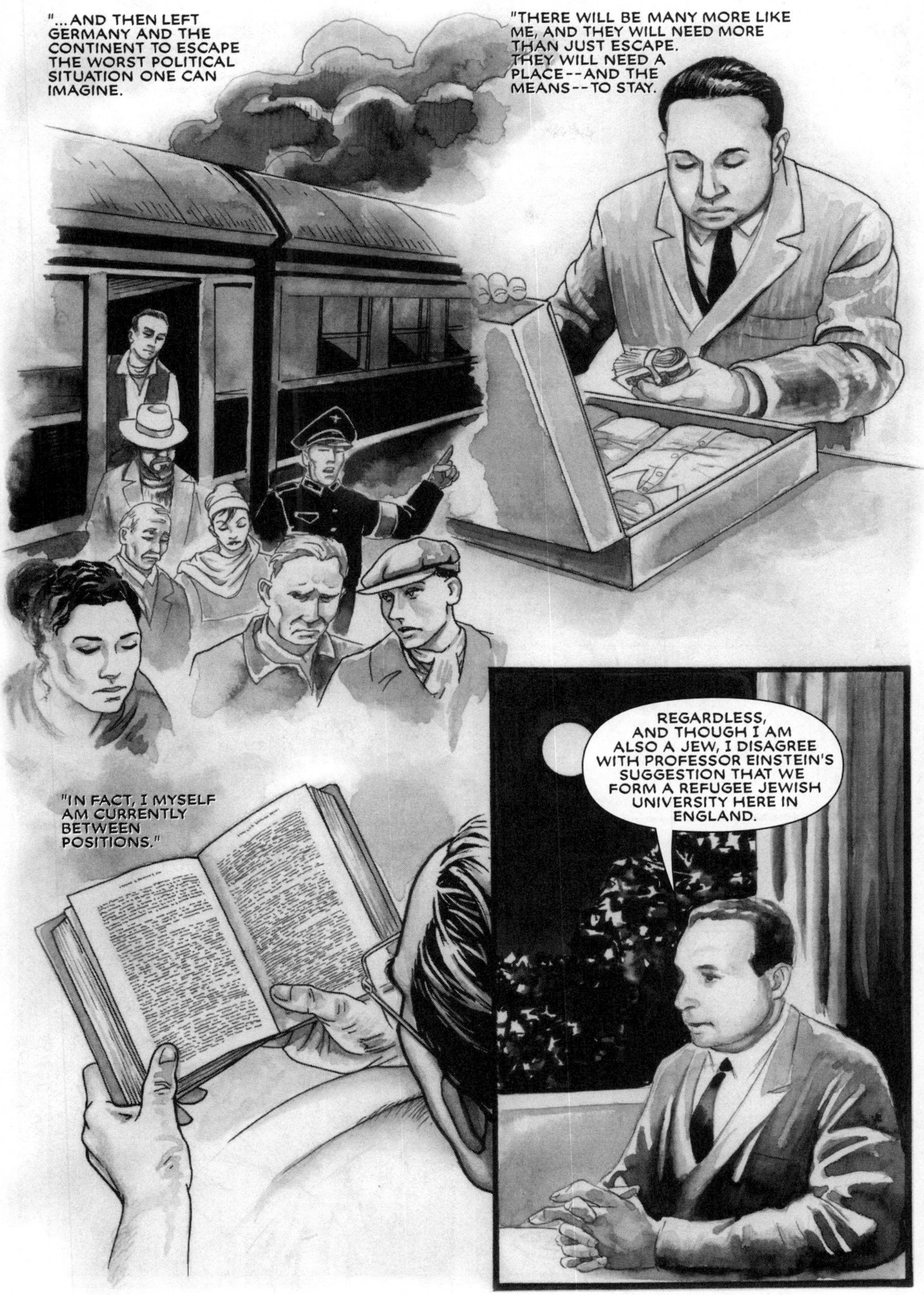
"...AND THEN LEFT GERMANY AND THE CONTINENT TO ESCAPE THE WORST POLITICAL SITUATION ONE CAN IMAGINE.
"THERE WILL BE MANY MORE LIKE ME, AND THEY WILL NEED MORE THAN JUST ESCAPE. THEY WILL NEED A PLACE--AND THE MEANS--TO STAY.
"IN FACT, I MYSELF AM CURRENTLY BETWEEN POSITIONS."
REGARDLESS, AND THOUGH I AM ALSO A JEW, I DISAGREE WITH PROFESSOR EINSTEIN'S SUGGESTION THAT WE FORM A REFUGEE JEWISH UNIVERSITY HERE IN ENGLAND.

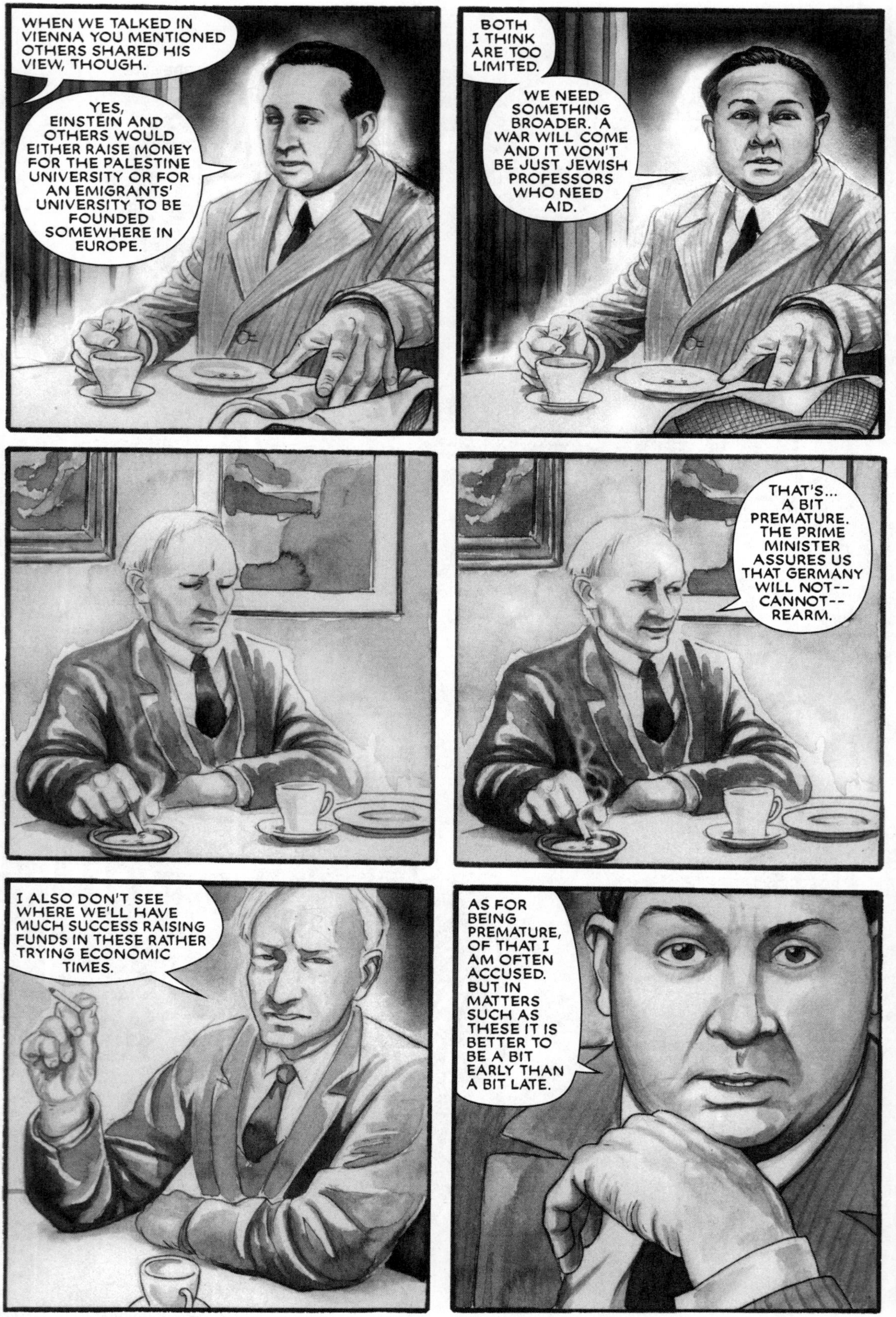
WHEN WE TALKED IN VIENNA YOU MENTIONED OTHERS SHARED HIS VIEW, THOUGH.
YES, EINSTEIN AND OTHERS WOULD EITHER RAISE MONEY FOR THE PALESTINE UNIVERSITY OR FOR AN EMIGRANTS' UNIVERSITY TO BE FOUNDED SOMEWHERE IN EUROPE.
BOTH I THINK ARE TOO LIMITED.
WE NEED SOMETHING BROADER. A WAR WILL COME AND IT WON'T BE JUST JEWISH PROFESSORS WHO NEED AID.
THAT'S... A BIT PREMATURE. THE PRIME MINISTER ASSURES US THAT GERMANY WILL NOT-- CANNOT-- REARM.
I ALSO DON'T SEE WHERE WE'LL HAVE MUCH SUCCESS RAISING FUNDS IN THESE RATHER TRYING ECONOMIC TIMES.
AS FOR BEING PREMATURE, OF THAT I AM OFTEN ACCUSED. BUT IN MATTERS SUCH AS THESE IT IS BETTER TO BE A BIT EARLY THAN A BIT LATE.

REGARDING OUR PROSPECT FOR SUCCESS, I WOULD SAY THIS: WHEN A CHILD I READ A BOOK CALLED *THE TRAGEDY OF MAN.* FROM IT I LEARNED VERY LITTLE...

...PERHAPS I WAS *PREMATURE* IN READING IT.

BUT I DID LEARN THIS: IT IS NOT NECESSARY TO SUCCEED IN ORDER TO PERSEVERE.

IF SCIENCE CANNOT YET SAVE THE WORLD, PERHAPS WE SCIENTISTS CAN SAVE SOME OF IT.

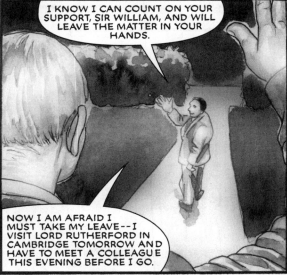

I KNOW I CAN COUNT ON YOUR SUPPORT, SIR WILLIAM, AND WILL LEAVE THE MATTER IN YOUR HANDS.

NOW I AM AFRAID I MUST TAKE MY LEAVE--I VISIT LORD RUTHERFORD IN CAMBRIDGE TOMORROW AND HAVE TO MEET A COLLEAGUE THIS EVENING BEFORE I GO.

Rutherford ran the world-renowned Cavendish Laboratory in Cambridge, where James Chadwick discovered the neutron.

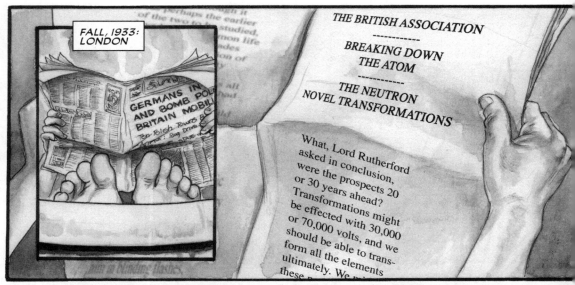

FALL, 1933: LONDON

THE BRITISH ASSOCIATION

BREAKING DOWN
THE ATOM

THE NEUTRON
NOVEL TRANSFORMATIONS

What, Lord Rutherford asked in conclusion, were the prospects 20 or 30 years ahead? Transformations might be effected with 30,000 or 70,000 volts, and we should be able to transform all the elements ultimately. We ...
these ...

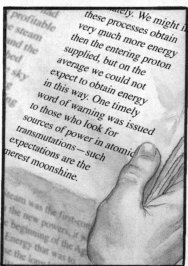

...ately. We might in these processes obtain very much more energy then the entering proton supplied, but on the average we could not expect to obtain energy in this way. One timely word of warning was issued to those who look for sources of power in atomic transmutations—such expectations are the merest moonshine.

...eam was the first ...
... the new power ...
... beginning of the A ...
... Energy that was to ...
... the lone ...

RUTHERFORD IS AN EXPERT IN NUCLEAR PHYSICS.

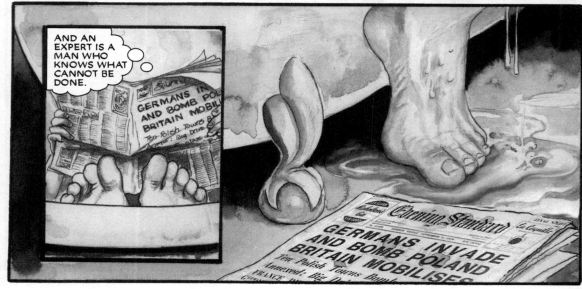

AND AN EXPERT IS A MAN WHO KNOWS WHAT CANNOT BE DONE.

Evening Standard
GERMANS INVADE
AND BOMB POLAND
BRITAIN MOBILISES

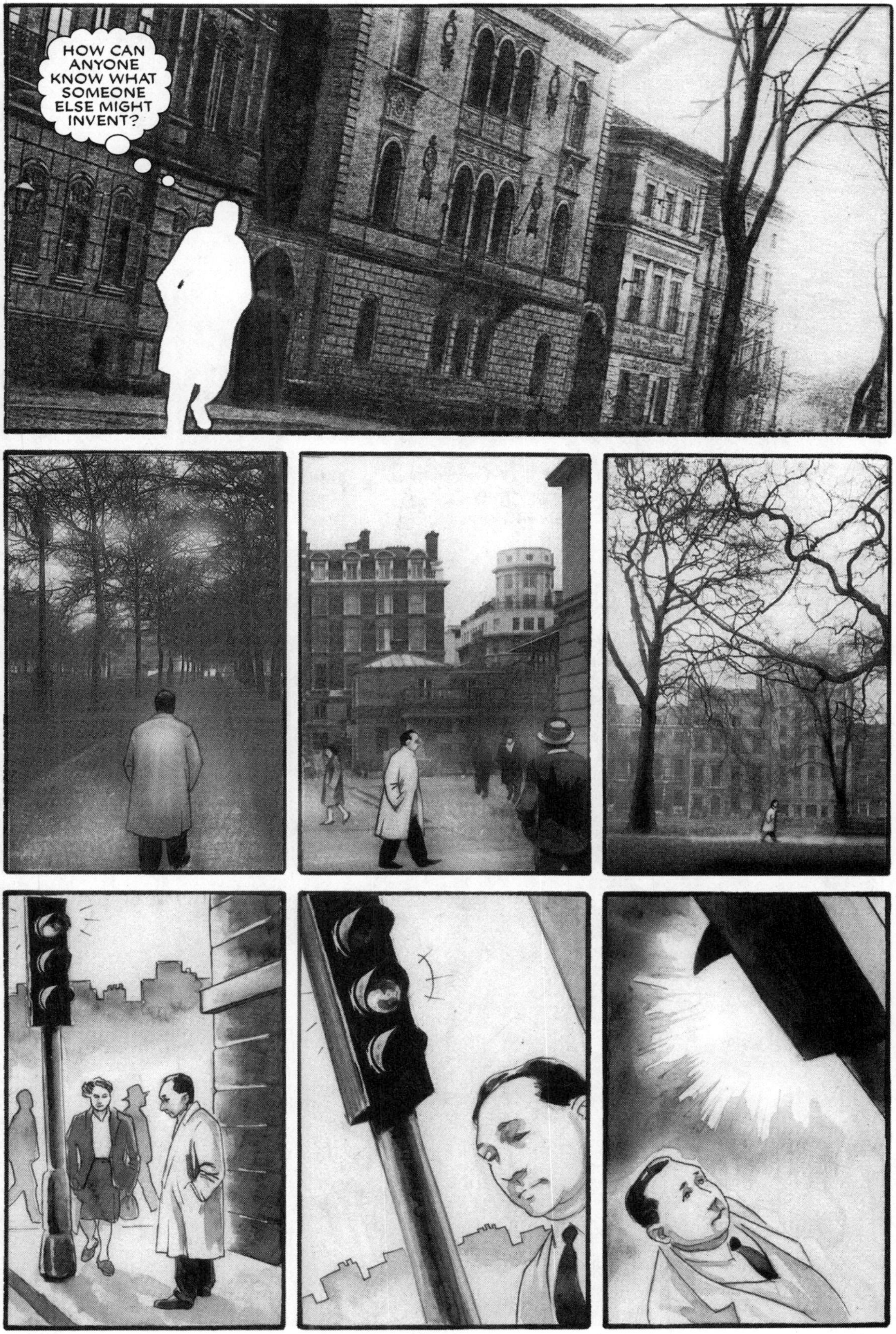
HOW CAN ANYONE KNOW WHAT SOMEONE ELSE MIGHT INVENT?

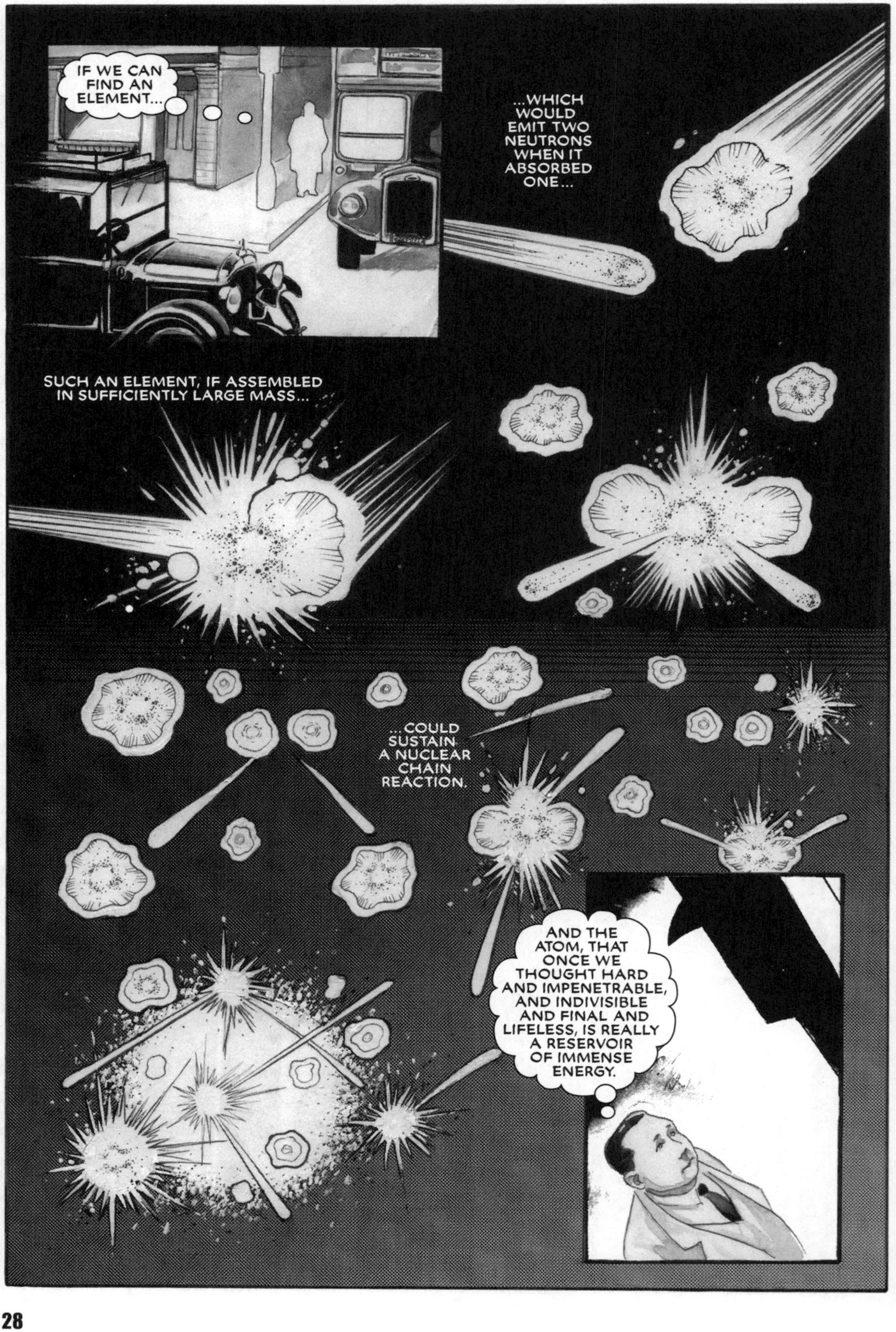
IF WE CAN FIND AN ELEMENT...
...WHICH WOULD EMIT TWO NEUTRONS WHEN IT ABSORBED ONE...
SUCH AN ELEMENT, IF ASSEMBLED IN SUFFICIENTLY LARGE MASS...
...COULD SUSTAIN A NUCLEAR CHAIN REACTION.
AND THE ATOM, THAT ONCE WE THOUGHT HARD AND IMPENETRABLE, AND INDIVISIBLE AND FINAL AND LIFELESS, IS REALLY A RESERVOIR OF IMMENSE ENERGY.

"And the frightful armoured monsters that had hooted and smoked and thundered about the world for four awful decades were swept away to the dealers in old metal, and the highways thronged with light and clean and shimmering shapes of silvered steel."

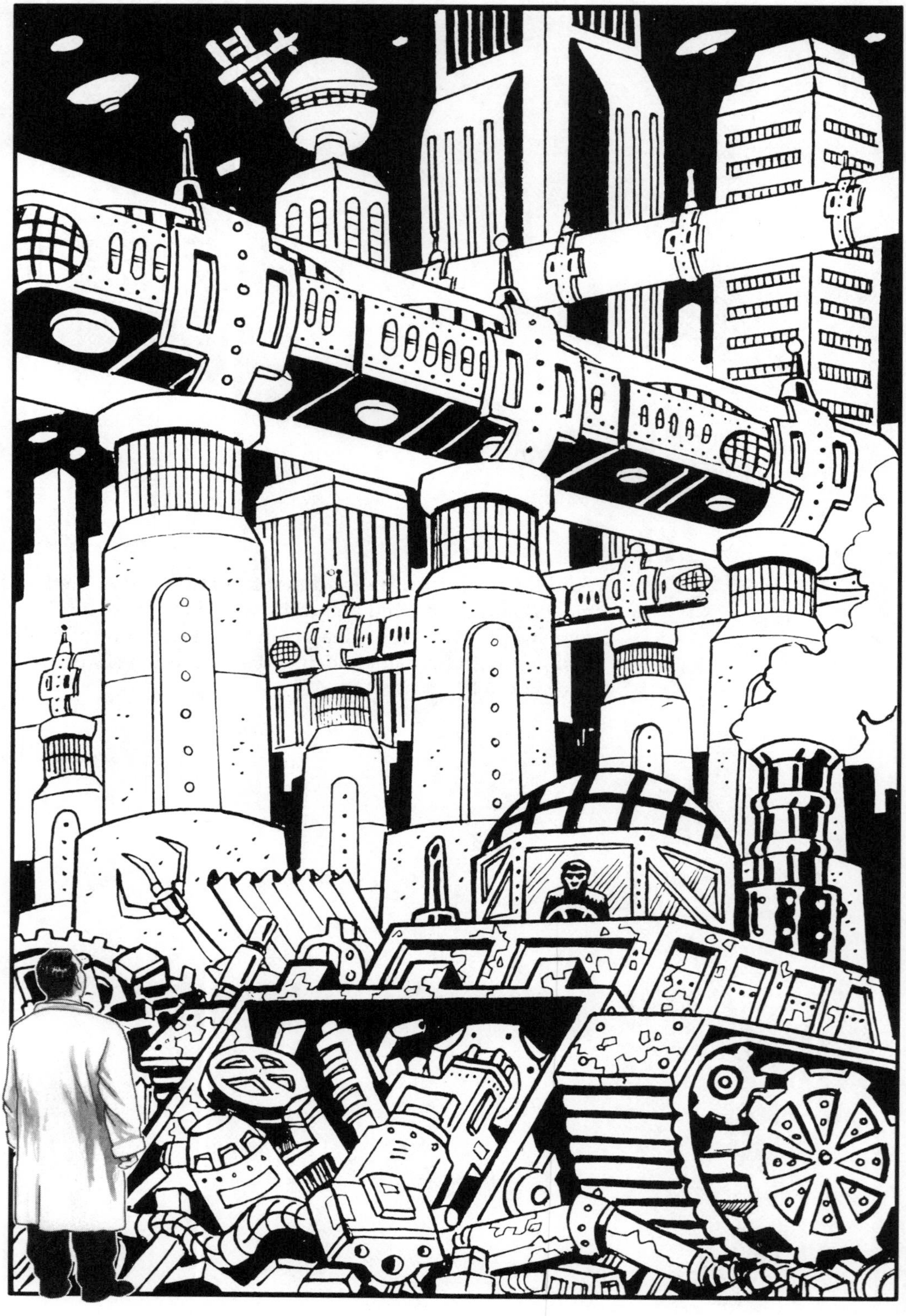

"Then came the epoch of the Leap into the Air, where the new atomic aeroplane became indeed a mania; every one of means was frantic to possess a thing so controllable, so secure and so free from the dust and danger of the road, and in France alone in the year 1943 thirty thousand of these new aeroplanes were manufactured and licensed, and soared humming softly into the sky.

"The glaring factories working night and day, the glittering new vehicles swinging noiselessly along the roads, the flights of dragon-flies that swooped and soared and circled in the air…"

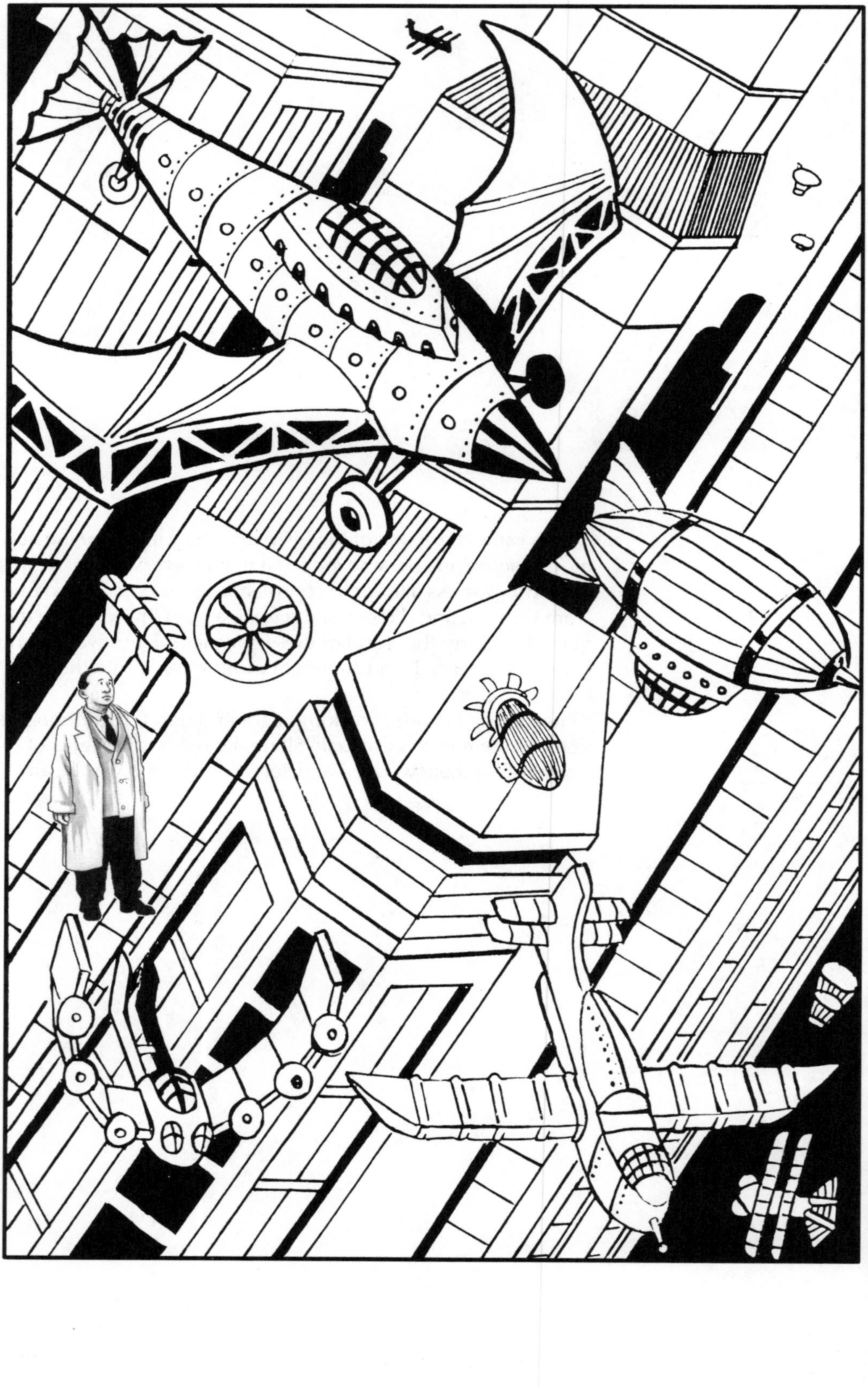

"The insanitary horse and the plebeian bicycle had been banished from the roadway, which was now of a resilient, glass-like surface, spotlessly clean; and the foot passenger was restricted to a narrow vestige of the ancient footpath on either side of the track and forbidden at the risk of a fine, if he survived, to cross the roadway. People descended from their automobiles upon this pavement and went through the lower shops to the lifts and stairs to the new ways for pedestrians, the Rows, that ran along the front of the houses at the level of the first story, and, being joined by frequent bridges, gave the newer parts of London a curiously Venetian appearance. In some streets there were upper and even third-story Rows. For most of the day and all night the shop windows were lit by electric light, and many establishments had made, as it were, canals of public footpaths through their premises in order to increase their window space."

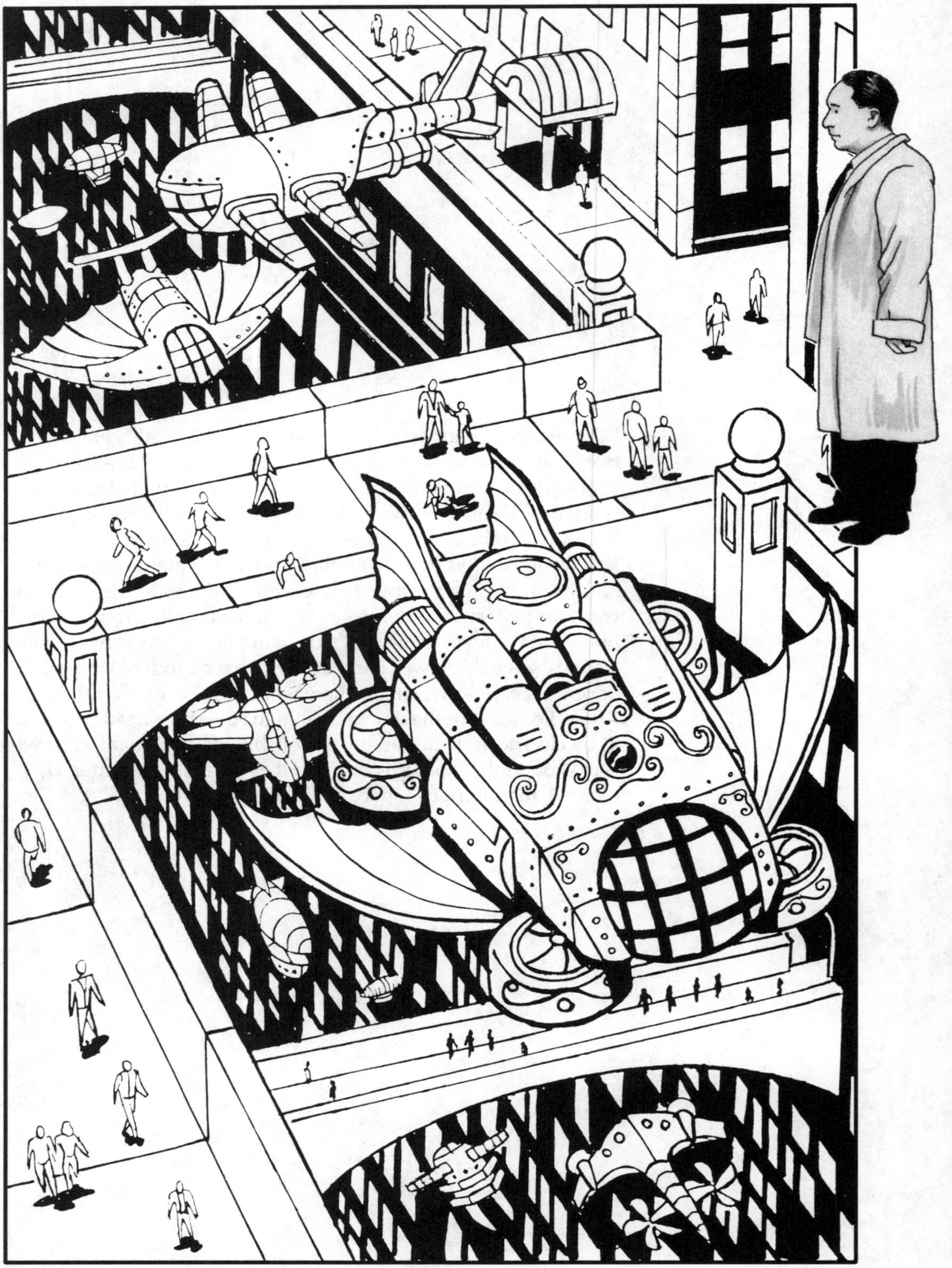

"In the centre was a garden raised on arches lit by festoons of lights and connected with the Rows by eight graceful bridges, beneath which hummed the interlacing streams of motor traffic, pulsating as the current alternated between east and west and north and south. Above rose great frontages of intricate rather than beautiful reinforced porcelain, studded with lights, barred by bold illuminated advertisements, and glowing with reflections. There were the two historical music halls of this place, the Shakespeare Memorial Theatre, in which the municipal players revolved perpetually through the cycle of Shakespeare's plays, and four other great houses of refreshment and entertainment whose pinnacles streamed up into the blue obscurity of the night. The south side of the square was in dark contrast to the others; it was still being rebuilt, and a lattice of steel bars surmounted by the frozen gestures of monstrous cranes rose over the excavated sites of vanished Victorian buildings.

"And I became aware of something very sensational that had been flashed upon the transparencies at the newspaper kiosks at the corners of the square. Forgetting for a moment my penniless condition, I made my way over a bridge to buy a paper, for in those days the papers, which were printed upon thin sheets of metallic foil, were sold at determinate points by specially licensed purveyors."

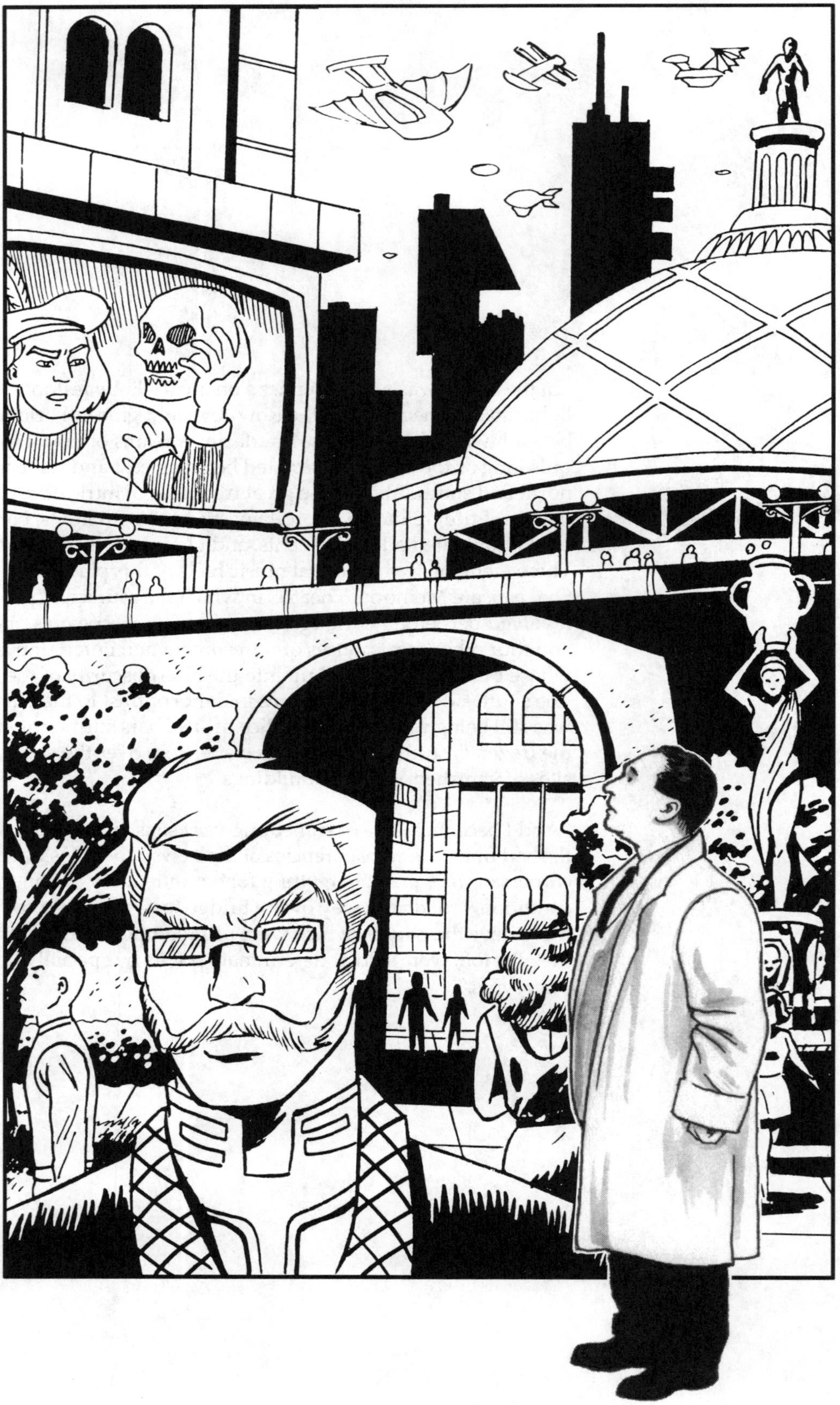

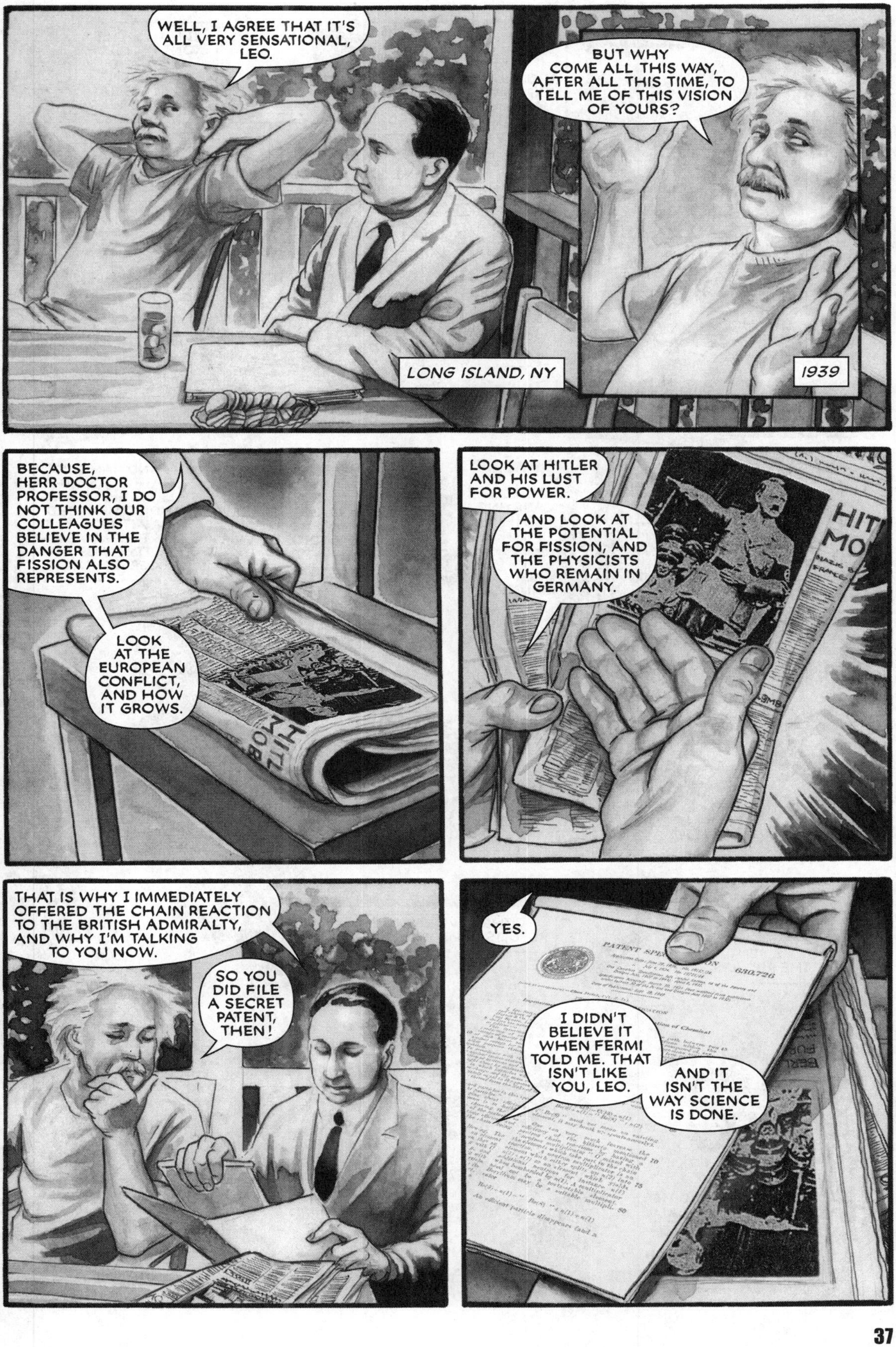
WELL, I AGREE THAT IT'S ALL VERY SENSATIONAL, LEO.
BUT WHY COME ALL THIS WAY, AFTER ALL THIS TIME, TO TELL ME OF THIS VISION OF YOURS?
LONG ISLAND, NY
1939
BECAUSE, HERR DOCTOR PROFESSOR, I DO NOT THINK OUR COLLEAGUES BELIEVE IN THE DANGER THAT FISSION ALSO REPRESENTS.
LOOK AT THE EUROPEAN CONFLICT, AND HOW IT GROWS.
LOOK AT HITLER AND HIS LUST FOR POWER.
AND LOOK AT THE POTENTIAL FOR FISSION, AND THE PHYSICISTS WHO REMAIN IN GERMANY.
THAT IS WHY I IMMEDIATELY OFFERED THE CHAIN REACTION TO THE BRITISH ADMIRALTY, AND WHY I'M TALKING TO YOU NOW.
SO YOU DID FILE A SECRET PATENT, THEN!
YES.
I DIDN'T BELIEVE IT WHEN FERMI TOLD ME. THAT ISN'T LIKE YOU, LEO.
AND IT ISN'T THE WAY SCIENCE IS DONE.

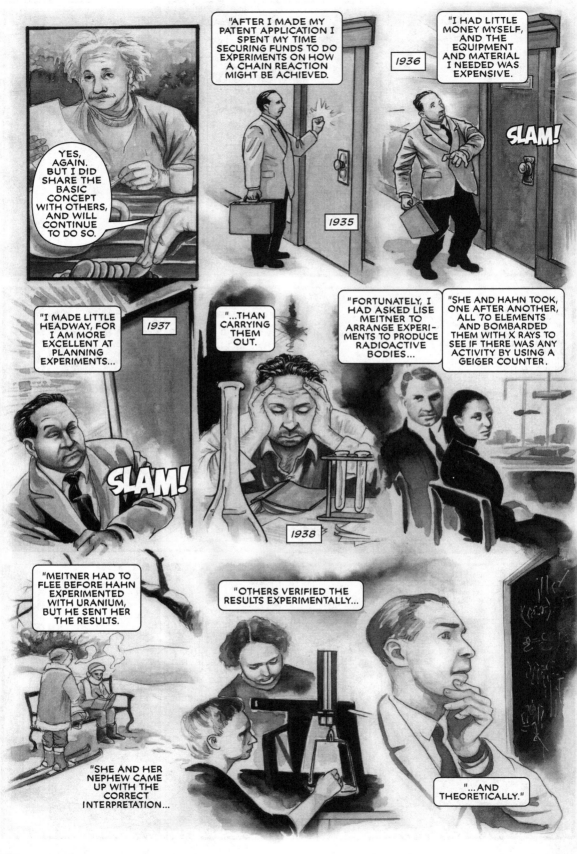

"AFTER I MADE MY PATENT APPLICATION I SPENT MY TIME SECURING FUNDS TO DO EXPERIMENTS ON HOW A CHAIN REACTION MIGHT BE ACHIEVED."

1936

"I HAD LITTLE MONEY MYSELF, AND THE EQUIPMENT AND MATERIAL I NEEDED WAS EXPENSIVE.

SLAM!

YES, AGAIN. BUT I DID SHARE THE BASIC CONCEPT WITH OTHERS, AND WILL CONTINUE TO DO SO.

1935

"I MADE LITTLE HEADWAY, FOR I AM MORE EXCELLENT AT PLANNING EXPERIMENTS...

1937

"...THAN CARRYING THEM OUT.

"FORTUNATELY, I HAD ASKED LISE MEITNER TO ARRANGE EXPERIMENTS TO PRODUCE RADIOACTIVE BODIES...

"SHE AND HAHN TOOK, ONE AFTER ANOTHER, ALL 70 ELEMENTS AND BOMBARDED THEM WITH X RAYS TO SEE IF THERE WAS ANY ACTIVITY BY USING A GEIGER COUNTER.

SLAM!

1938

"MEITNER HAD TO FLEE BEFORE HAHN EXPERIMENTED WITH URANIUM, BUT HE SENT HER THE RESULTS.

"OTHERS VERIFIED THE RESULTS EXPERIMENTALLY...

"SHE AND HER NEPHEW CAME UP WITH THE CORRECT INTERPRETATION...

"...AND THEORETICALLY."

38

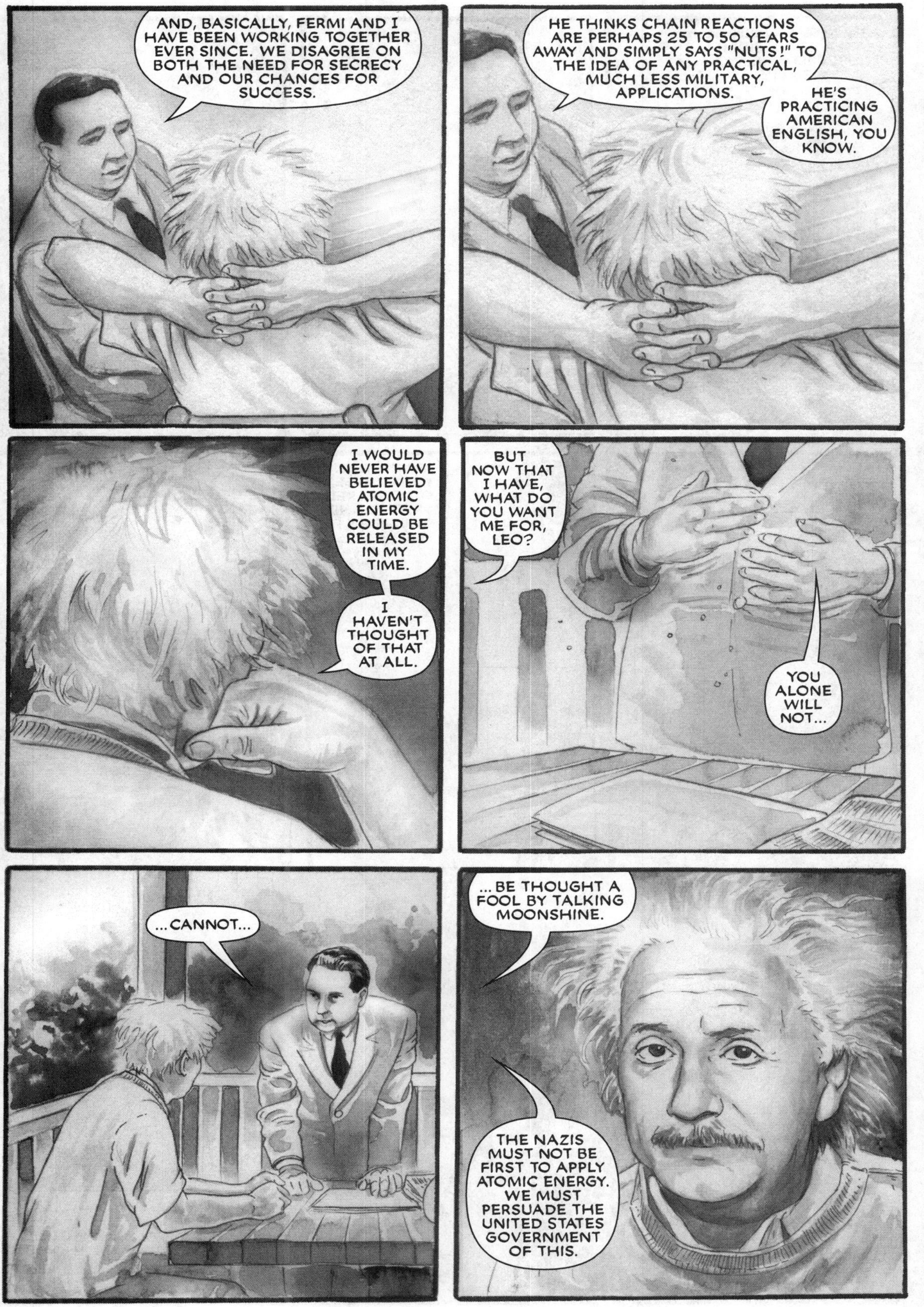
AND, BASICALLY, FERMI AND I HAVE BEEN WORKING TOGETHER EVER SINCE. WE DISAGREE ON BOTH THE NEED FOR SECRECY AND OUR CHANCES FOR SUCCESS.
HE THINKS CHAIN REACTIONS ARE PERHAPS 25 TO 50 YEARS AWAY AND SIMPLY SAYS "NUTS!" TO THE IDEA OF ANY PRACTICAL, MUCH LESS MILITARY, APPLICATIONS.
HE'S PRACTICING AMERICAN ENGLISH, YOU KNOW.
I WOULD NEVER HAVE BELIEVED ATOMIC ENERGY COULD BE RELEASED IN MY TIME.
I HAVEN'T THOUGHT OF THAT AT ALL.
BUT NOW THAT I HAVE, WHAT DO YOU WANT ME FOR, LEO?
YOU ALONE WILL NOT...
...CANNOT...
...BE THOUGHT A FOOL BY TALKING MOONSHINE.
THE NAZIS MUST NOT BE FIRST TO APPLY ATOMIC ENERGY. WE MUST PERSUADE THE UNITED STATES GOVERNMENT OF THIS.

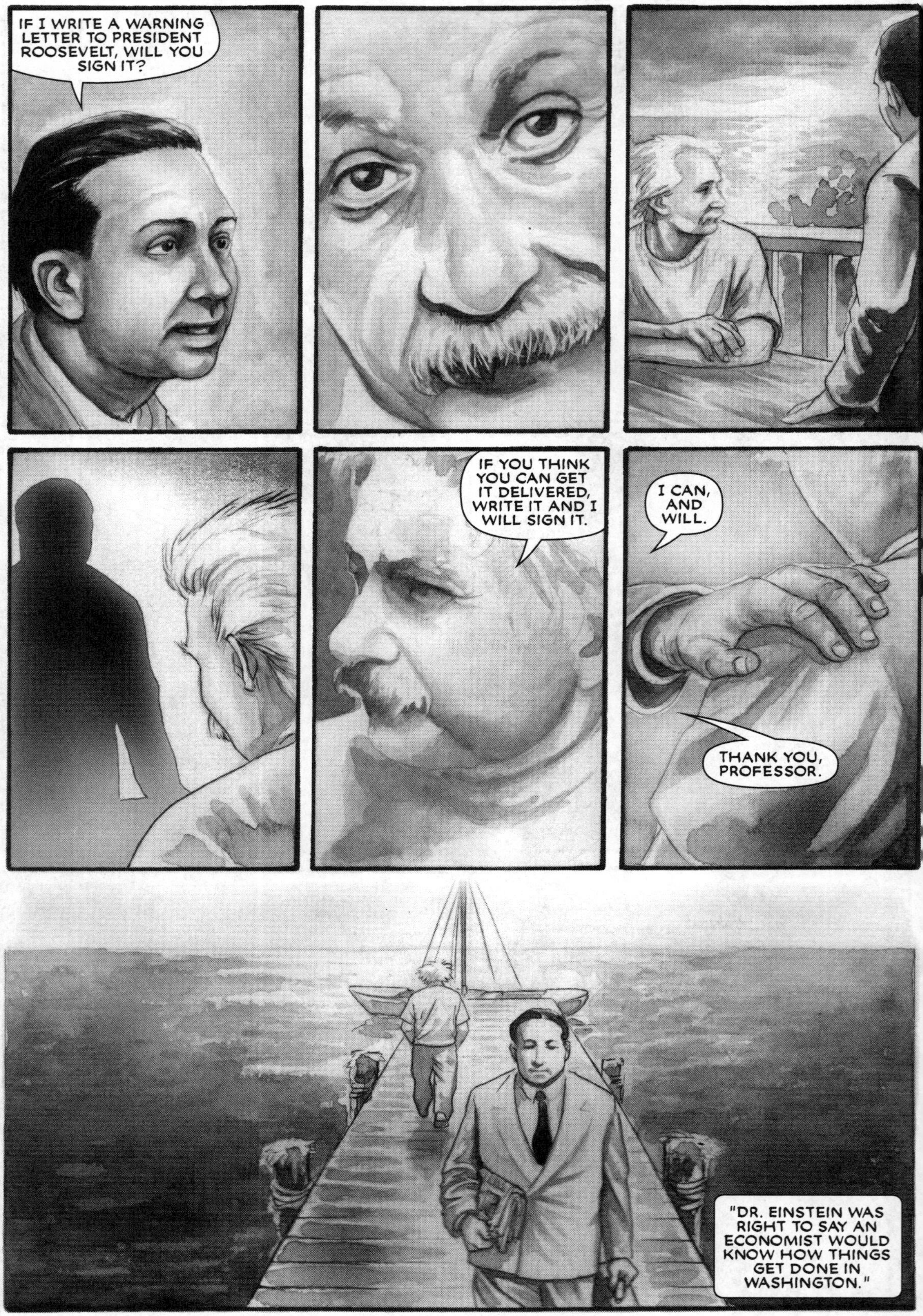

IF I WRITE A WARNING LETTER TO PRESIDENT ROOSEVELT, WILL YOU SIGN IT?
IF YOU THINK YOU CAN GET IT DELIVERED, WRITE IT AND I WILL SIGN IT.
I CAN, AND WILL.
THANK YOU, PROFESSOR.
"DR. EINSTEIN WAS RIGHT TO SAY AN ECONOMIST WOULD KNOW HOW THINGS GET DONE IN WASHINGTON."

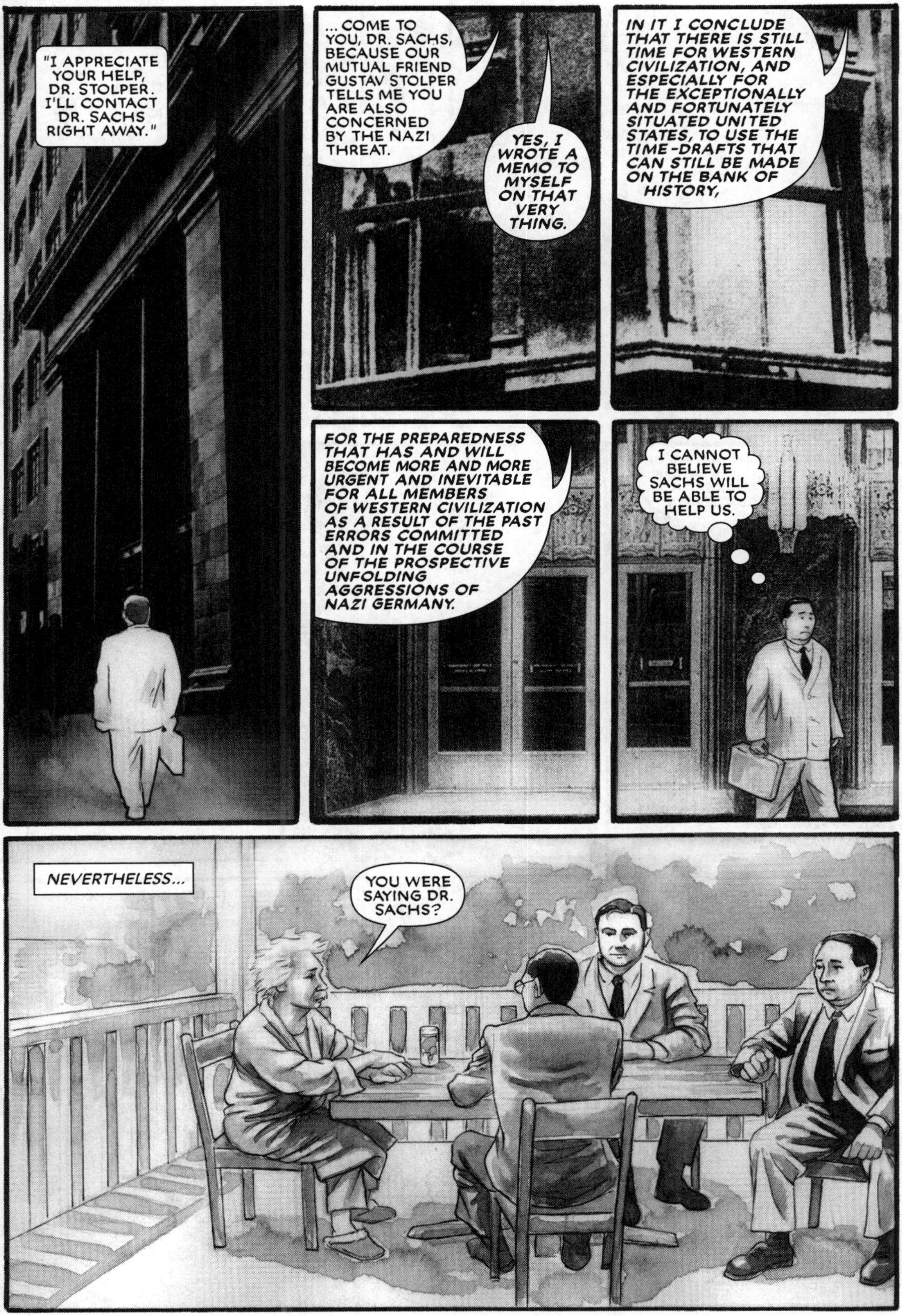
"I APPRECIATE YOUR HELP, DR. STOLPER. I'LL CONTACT DR. SACHS RIGHT AWAY."
... COME TO YOU, DR. SACHS, BECAUSE OUR MUTUAL FRIEND GUSTAV STOLPER TELLS ME YOU ARE ALSO CONCERNED BY THE NAZI THREAT.
YES, I WROTE A MEMO TO MYSELF ON THAT VERY THING.
IN IT I CONCLUDE THAT THERE IS STILL TIME FOR WESTERN CIVILIZATION, AND ESPECIALLY FOR THE EXCEPTIONALLY AND FORTUNATELY SITUATED UNITED STATES, TO USE THE TIME-DRAFTS THAT CAN STILL BE MADE ON THE BANK OF HISTORY,
FOR THE PREPAREDNESS THAT HAS AND WILL BECOME MORE AND MORE URGENT AND INEVITABLE FOR ALL MEMBERS OF WESTERN CIVILIZATION AS A RESULT OF THE PAST ERRORS COMMITTED AND IN THE COURSE OF THE PROSPECTIVE UNFOLDING AGGRESSIONS OF NAZI GERMANY.
I CANNOT BELIEVE SACHS WILL BE ABLE TO HELP US.
NEVERTHELESS...
YOU WERE SAYING DR. SACHS?

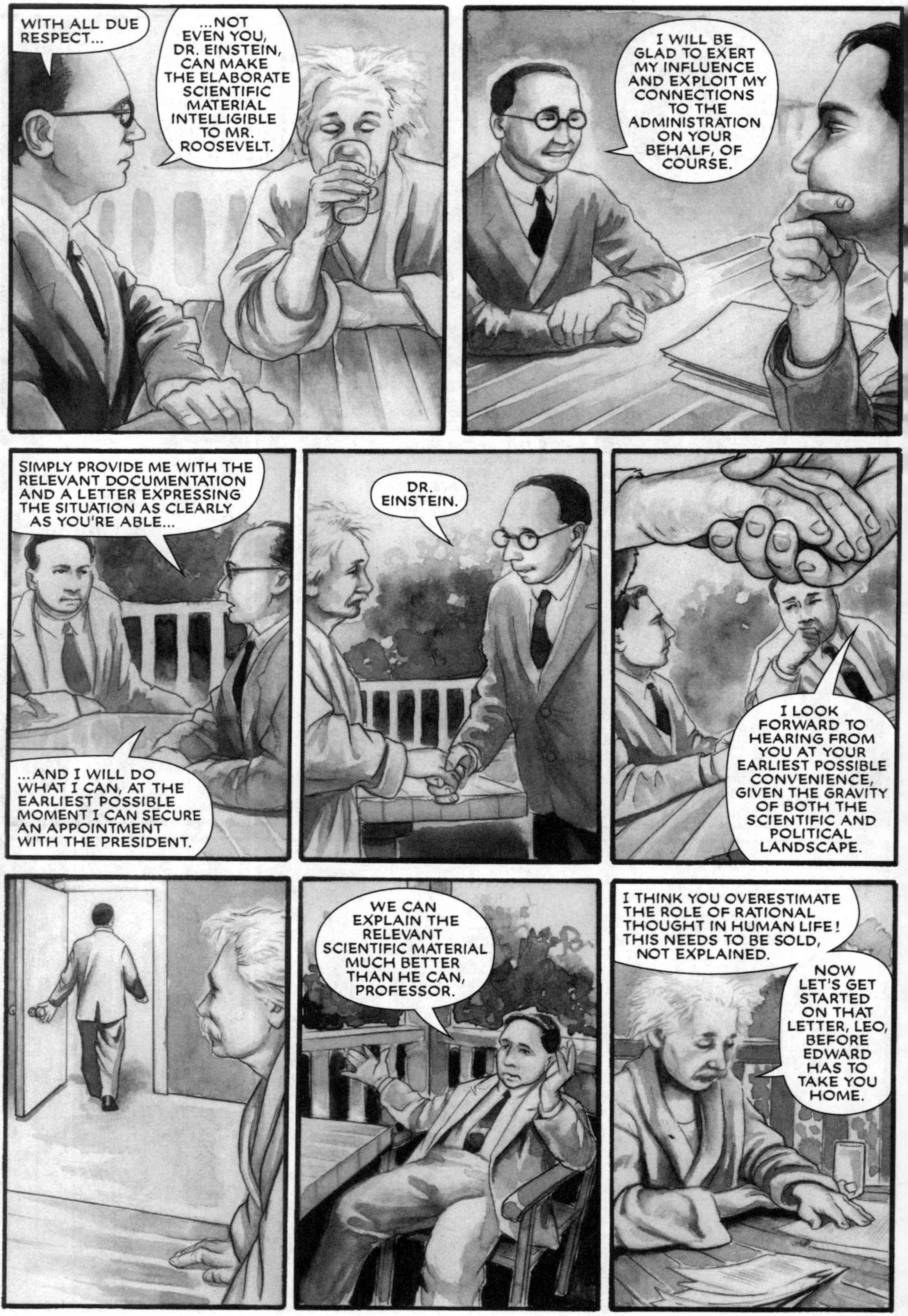
WITH ALL DUE RESPECT...
...NOT EVEN YOU, DR. EINSTEIN, CAN MAKE THE ELABORATE SCIENTIFIC MATERIAL INTELLIGIBLE TO MR. ROOSEVELT.
I WILL BE GLAD TO EXERT MY INFLUENCE AND EXPLOIT MY CONNECTIONS TO THE ADMINISTRATION ON YOUR BEHALF, OF COURSE.
SIMPLY PROVIDE ME WITH THE RELEVANT DOCUMENTATION AND A LETTER EXPRESSING THE SITUATION AS CLEARLY AS YOU'RE ABLE...
...AND I WILL DO WHAT I CAN, AT THE EARLIEST POSSIBLE MOMENT I CAN SECURE AN APPOINTMENT WITH THE PRESIDENT.
DR. EINSTEIN.
I LOOK FORWARD TO HEARING FROM YOU AT YOUR EARLIEST POSSIBLE CONVENIENCE, GIVEN THE GRAVITY OF BOTH THE SCIENTIFIC AND POLITICAL LANDSCAPE.
WE CAN EXPLAIN THE RELEVANT SCIENTIFIC MATERIAL MUCH BETTER THAN HE CAN, PROFESSOR.
I THINK YOU OVERESTIMATE THE ROLE OF RATIONAL THOUGHT IN HUMAN LIFE! THIS NEEDS TO BE SOLD, NOT EXPLAINED.
NOW LET'S GET STARTED ON THAT LETTER, LEO, BEFORE EDWARD HAS TO TAKE YOU HOME.

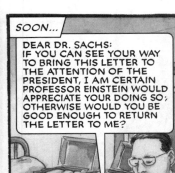

SOON...

DEAR DR. SACHS:
IF YOU CAN SEE YOUR WAY TO BRING THIS LETTER TO THE ATTENTION OF THE PRESIDENT, I AM CERTAIN PROFESSOR EINSTEIN WOULD APPRECIATE YOUR DOING SO; OTHERWISE WOULD YOU BE GOOD ENOUGH TO RETURN THE LETTER TO ME?

A LONG WAR

LATER...

DEAR PROFESSOR:
LAST WEEK WIGNER AND I VISITED DR. SACHS, WHO ADMITTED THAT HE IS STILL HOLDING YOUR LETTER. THERE IS A DISTINCT POSSIBILITY THAT HE WILL BE OF NO USE TO US.

STATE OF SIEGE

EVEN LATER...

...IF THIS IS THE CASE, WE MUST PUT THE MATTER IN SOMEONE ELSE'S HANDS. ENCLOSED IS THE TALK BY LINDBERGH WHICH YOU HAVE PERHAPS NOT READ. I AM AFRAID HE IS IN FACT NOT OUR MAN.

NAZIS THREATEN FRENCH BO...

HIS DISCUSSION ABOUT THE NEUTRALITY LAW IS ON A PITIFUL LEVEL. AND YET ONE BECOMES KINDLY DISPOSED TOWARDS LINDBERGH FOR HE AT LEAST EMITS HUMAN SOUNDS.

AND SO, FINALLY...

...ENGAGE IN A MENTAL PROJECTION FROM THE NORMAL COURSE OF RESEARCH-DEVELOPMENT TO THE IMPACT OF A MERE SCIENTIFIC POSSIBILITY UPON THE NATIONAL DEFENSE,

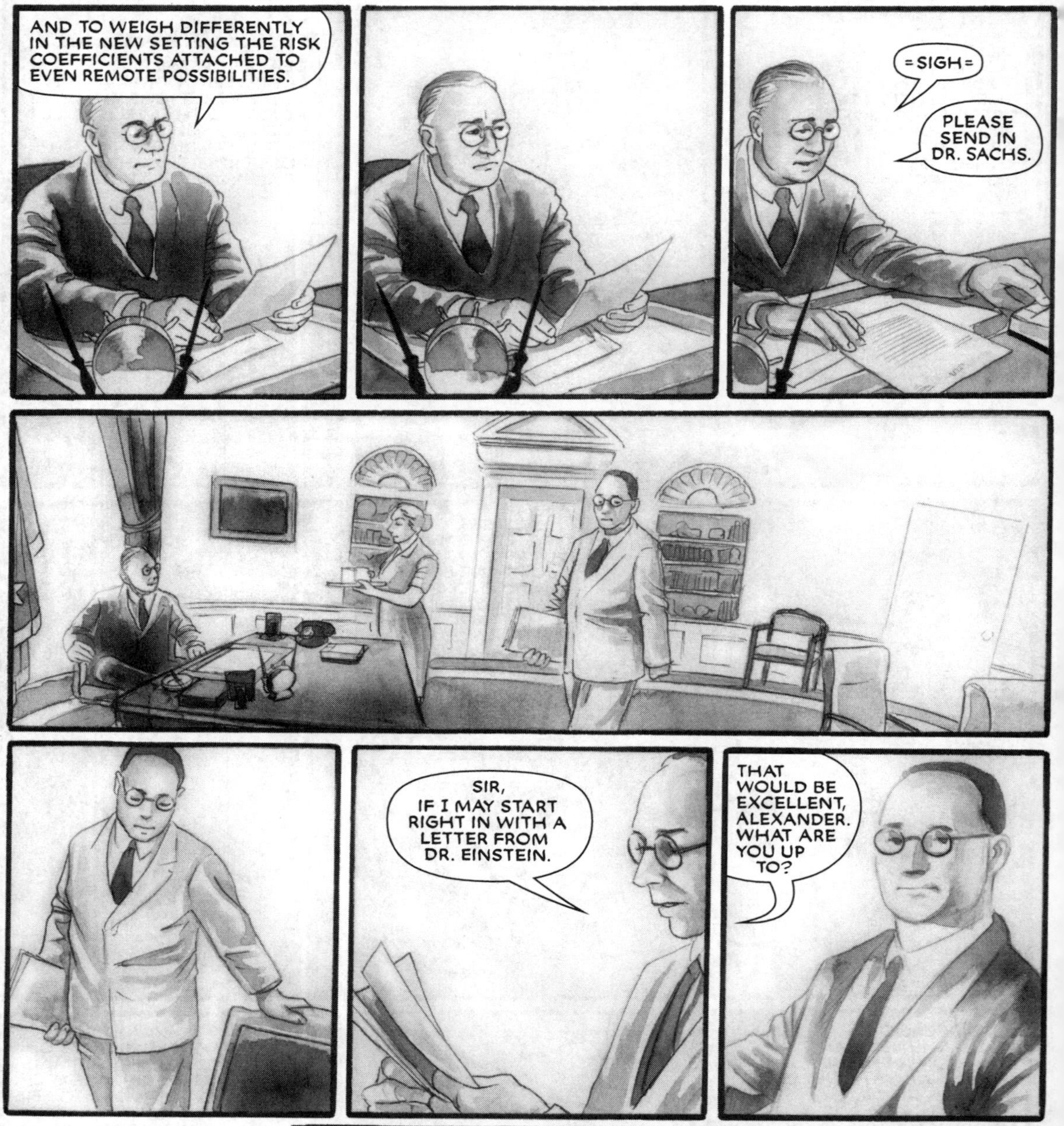
AND TO WEIGH DIFFERENTLY IN THE NEW SETTING THE RISK COEFFICIENTS ATTACHED TO EVEN REMOTE POSSIBILITIES.
= SIGH =
PLEASE SEND IN DR. SACHS.
SIR, IF I MAY START RIGHT IN WITH A LETTER FROM DR. EINSTEIN.
THAT WOULD BE EXCELLENT, ALEXANDER. WHAT ARE YOU UP TO?

“Mr. President…

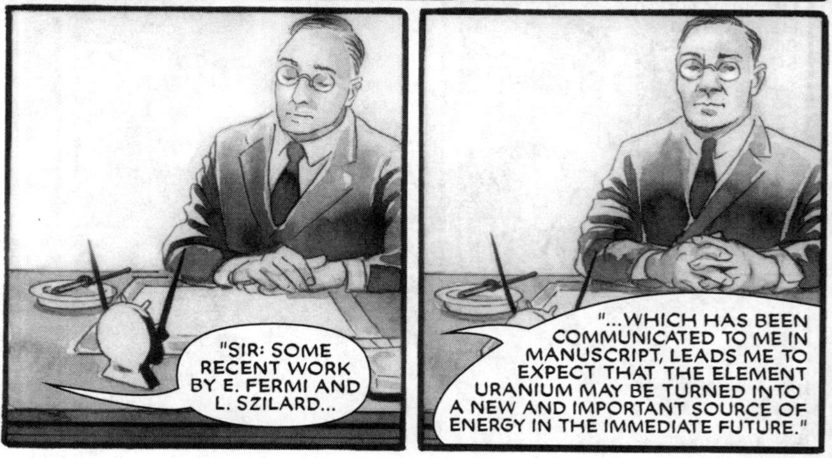
"SIR: SOME RECENT WORK BY E. FERMI AND L. SZILARD...
"...WHICH HAS BEEN COMMUNICATED TO ME IN MANUSCRIPT, LEADS ME TO EXPECT THAT THE ELEMENT URANIUM MAY BE TURNED INTO A NEW AND IMPORTANT SOURCE OF ENERGY IN THE IMMEDIATE FUTURE."

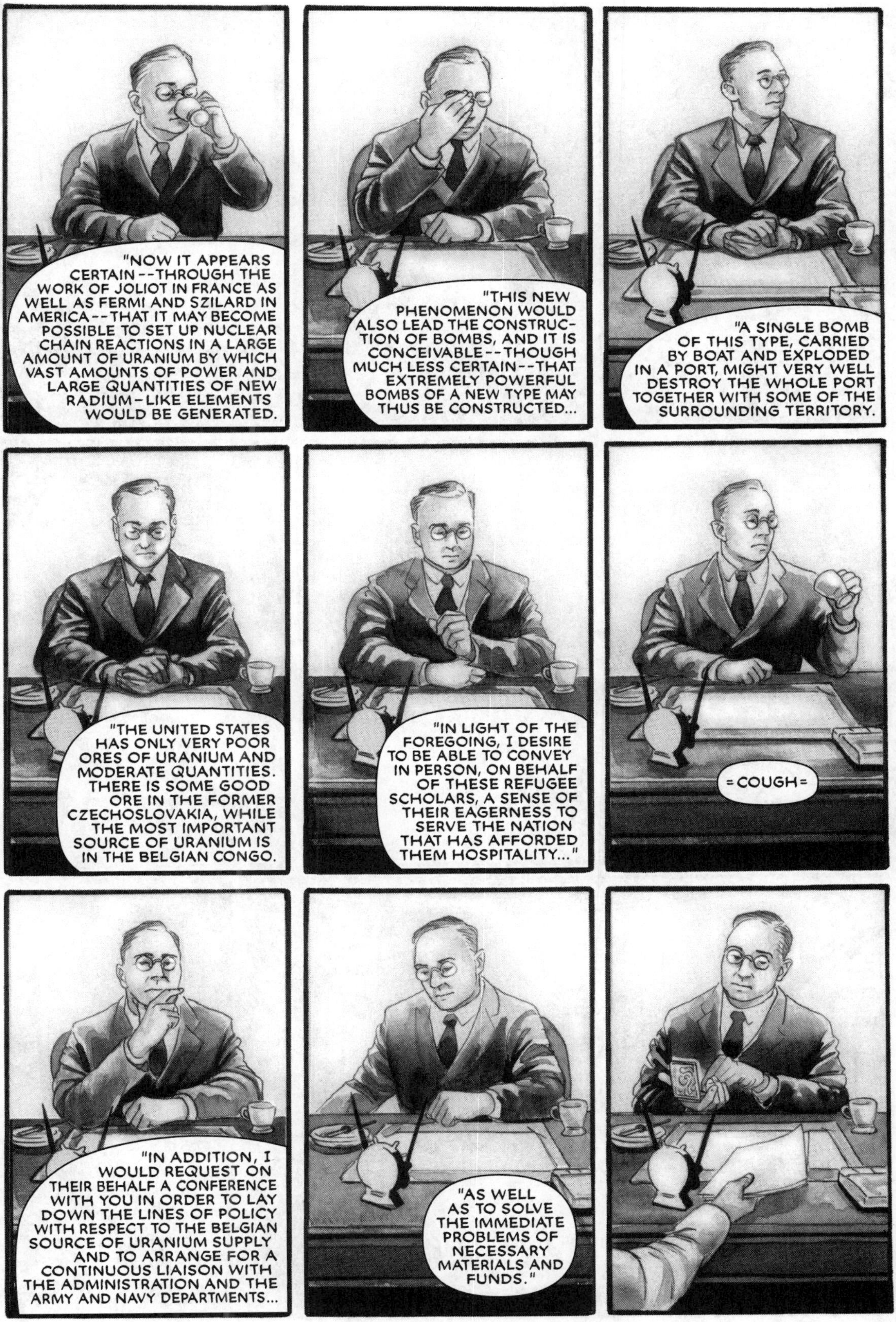
"NOW IT APPEARS CERTAIN--THROUGH THE WORK OF JOLIOT IN FRANCE AS WELL AS FERMI AND SZILARD IN AMERICA--THAT IT MAY BECOME POSSIBLE TO SET UP NUCLEAR CHAIN REACTIONS IN A LARGE AMOUNT OF URANIUM BY WHICH VAST AMOUNTS OF POWER AND LARGE QUANTITIES OF NEW RADIUM-LIKE ELEMENTS WOULD BE GENERATED.
"THIS NEW PHENOMENON WOULD ALSO LEAD THE CONSTRUCTION OF BOMBS, AND IT IS CONCEIVABLE--THOUGH MUCH LESS CERTAIN--THAT EXTREMELY POWERFUL BOMBS OF A NEW TYPE MAY THUS BE CONSTRUCTED...
"A SINGLE BOMB OF THIS TYPE, CARRIED BY BOAT AND EXPLODED IN A PORT, MIGHT VERY WELL DESTROY THE WHOLE PORT TOGETHER WITH SOME OF THE SURROUNDING TERRITORY.
"THE UNITED STATES HAS ONLY VERY POOR ORES OF URANIUM AND MODERATE QUANTITIES. THERE IS SOME GOOD ORE IN THE FORMER CZECHOSLOVAKIA, WHILE THE MOST IMPORTANT SOURCE OF URANIUM IS IN THE BELGIAN CONGO.
"IN LIGHT OF THE FOREGOING, I DESIRE TO BE ABLE TO CONVEY IN PERSON, ON BEHALF OF THESE REFUGEE SCHOLARS, A SENSE OF THEIR EAGERNESS TO SERVE THE NATION THAT HAS AFFORDED THEM HOSPITALITY..."
=COUGH=
"IN ADDITION, I WOULD REQUEST ON THEIR BEHALF A CONFERENCE WITH YOU IN ORDER TO LAY DOWN THE LINES OF POLICY WITH RESPECT TO THE BELGIAN SOURCE OF URANIUM SUPPLY AND TO ARRANGE FOR A CONTINUOUS LIAISON WITH THE ADMINISTRATION AND THE ARMY AND NAVY DEPARTMENTS...
"AS WELL AS TO SOLVE THE IMMEDIATE PROBLEMS OF NECESSARY MATERIALS AND FUNDS."

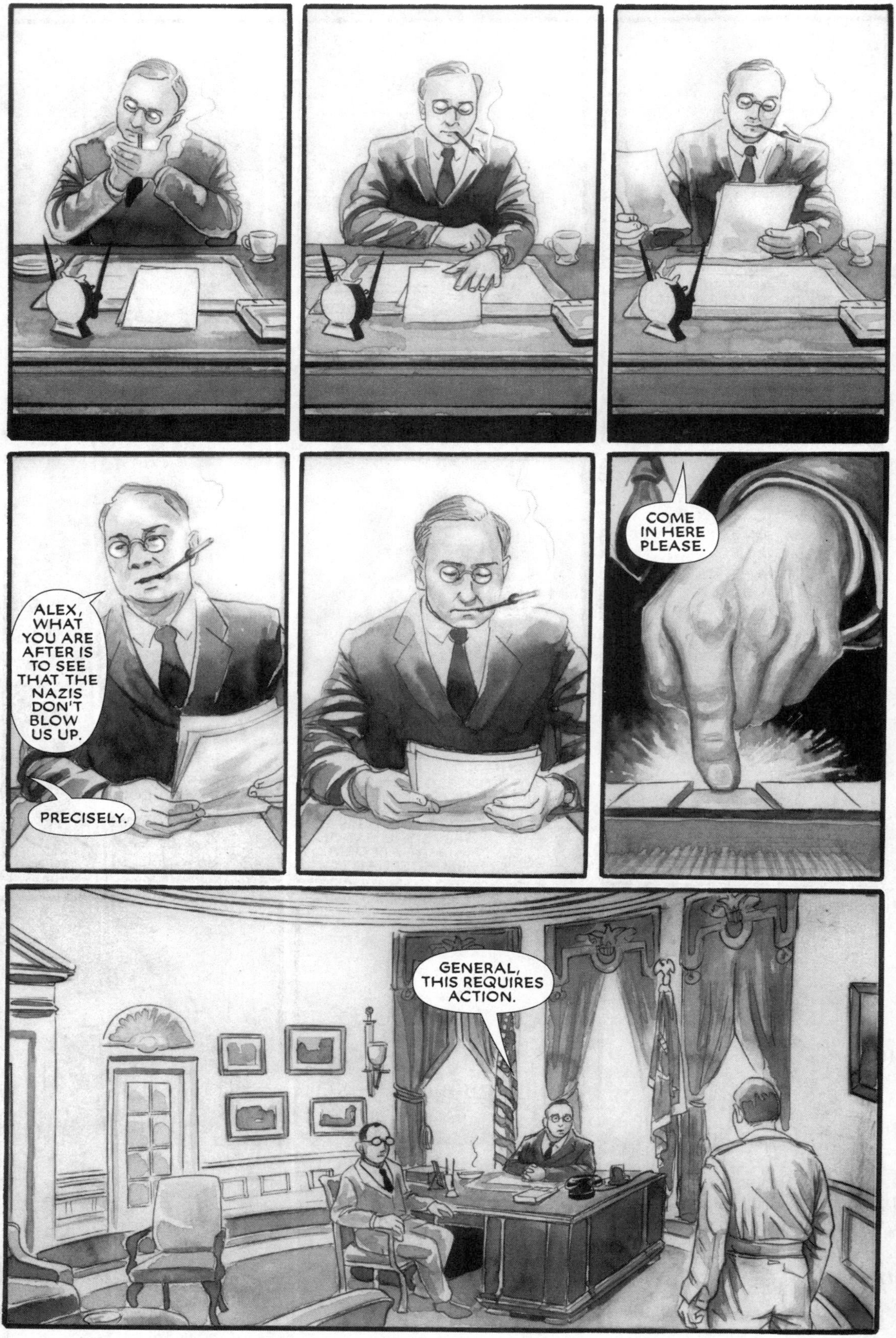
ALEX, WHAT YOU ARE AFTER IS TO SEE THAT THE NAZIS DON'T BLOW US UP.
PRECISELY.
COME IN HERE PLEASE.
GENERAL, THIS REQUIRES ACTION.

interlude

A great truth is a truth whose opposite is also a great truth.
　　　　　　　　　　　—a favorite saying of Niels Bohr

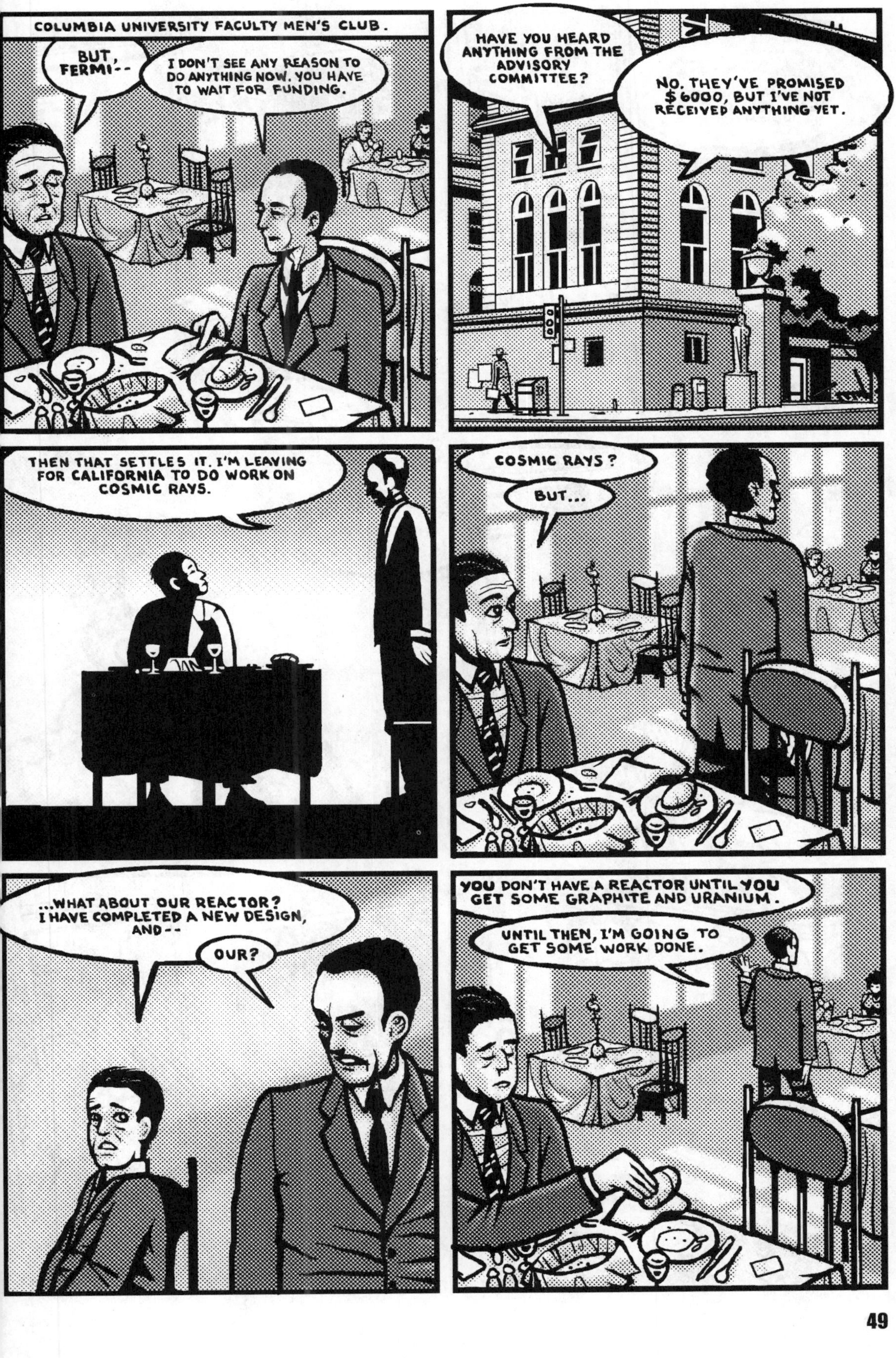
COLUMBIA UNIVERSITY FACULTY MEN'S CLUB.
BUT, FERMI--
I DON'T SEE ANY REASON TO DO ANYTHING NOW. YOU HAVE TO WAIT FOR FUNDING.
HAVE YOU HEARD ANYTHING FROM THE ADVISORY COMMITTEE?
NO. THEY'VE PROMISED $6000, BUT I'VE NOT RECEIVED ANYTHING YET.
THEN THAT SETTLES IT. I'M LEAVING FOR CALIFORNIA TO DO WORK ON COSMIC RAYS.
COSMIC RAYS?
BUT...
...WHAT ABOUT OUR REACTOR? I HAVE COMPLETED A NEW DESIGN, AND--
OUR?
YOU DON'T HAVE A REACTOR UNTIL YOU GET SOME GRAPHITE AND URANIUM.
UNTIL THEN, I'M GOING TO GET SOME WORK DONE.

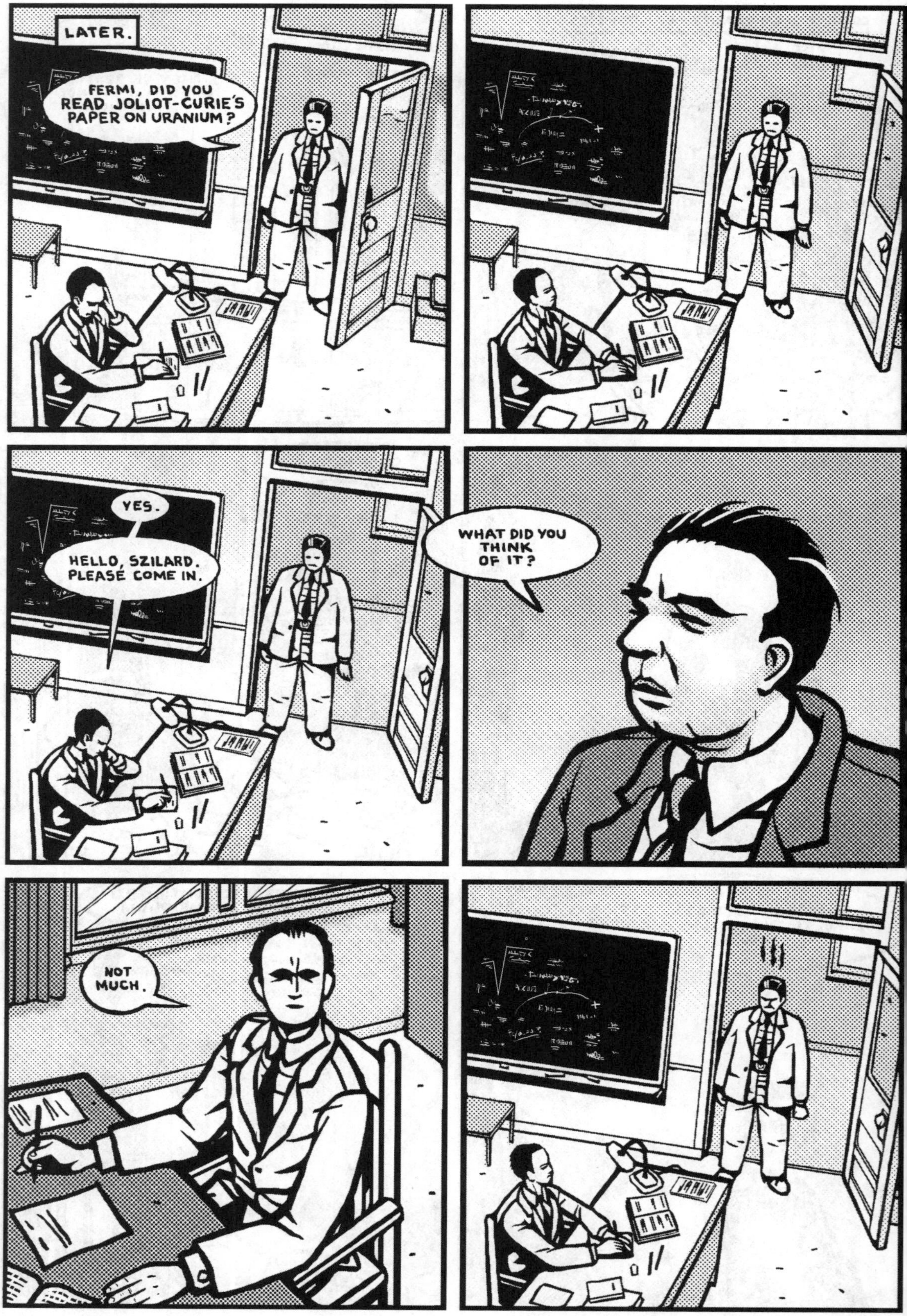
LATER.
FERMI, DID YOU READ JOLIOT-CURIE'S PAPER ON URANIUM?
YES.
HELLO, SZILARD. PLEASE COME IN.
WHAT DID YOU THINK OF IT?
NOT MUCH.

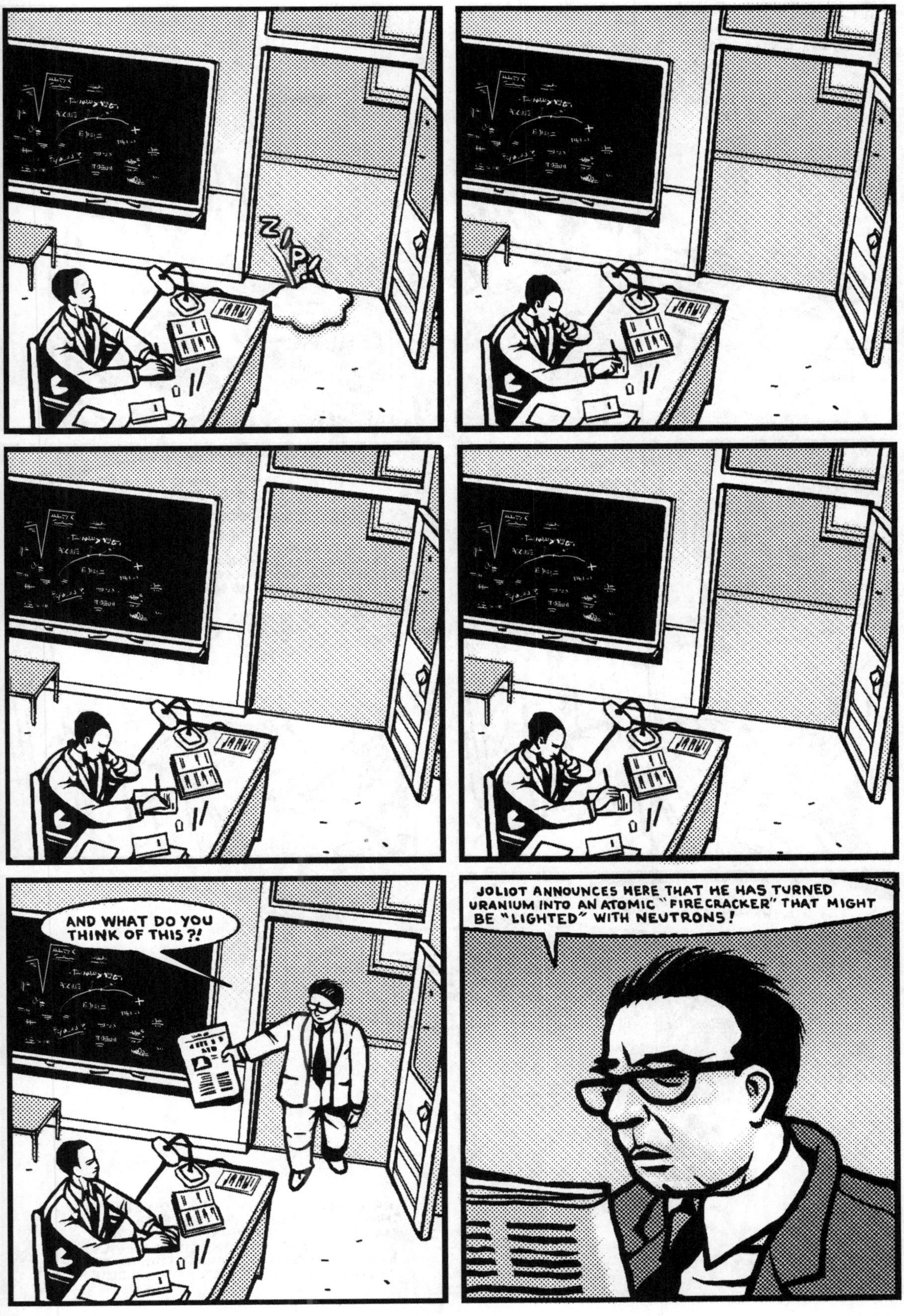
ZIP!
AND WHAT DO YOU THINK OF THIS?!
JOLIOT ANNOUNCES HERE THAT HE HAS TURNED URANIUM INTO AN ATOMIC "FIRECRACKER" THAT MIGHT BE "LIGHTED" WITH NEUTRONS!

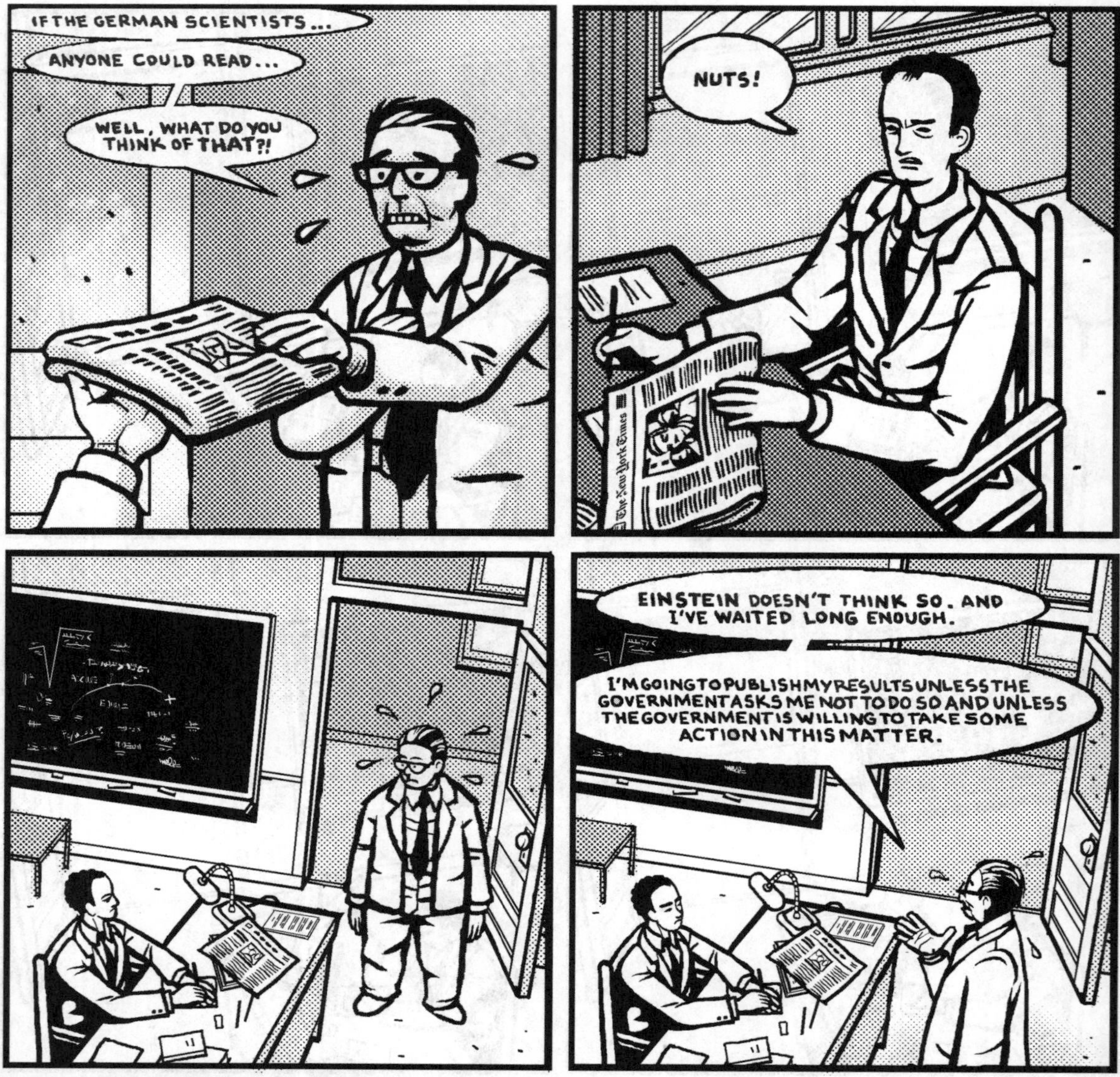
IF THE GERMAN SCIENTISTS...
ANYONE COULD READ...
WELL, WHAT DO YOU THINK OF THAT?!
NUTS!
EINSTEIN DOESN'T THINK SO. AND I'VE WAITED LONG ENOUGH.
I'M GOING TO PUBLISH MY RESULTS UNLESS THE GOVERNMENT ASKS ME NOT TO DO SO AND UNLESS THE GOVERNMENT IS WILLING TO TAKE SOME ACTION IN THIS MATTER.

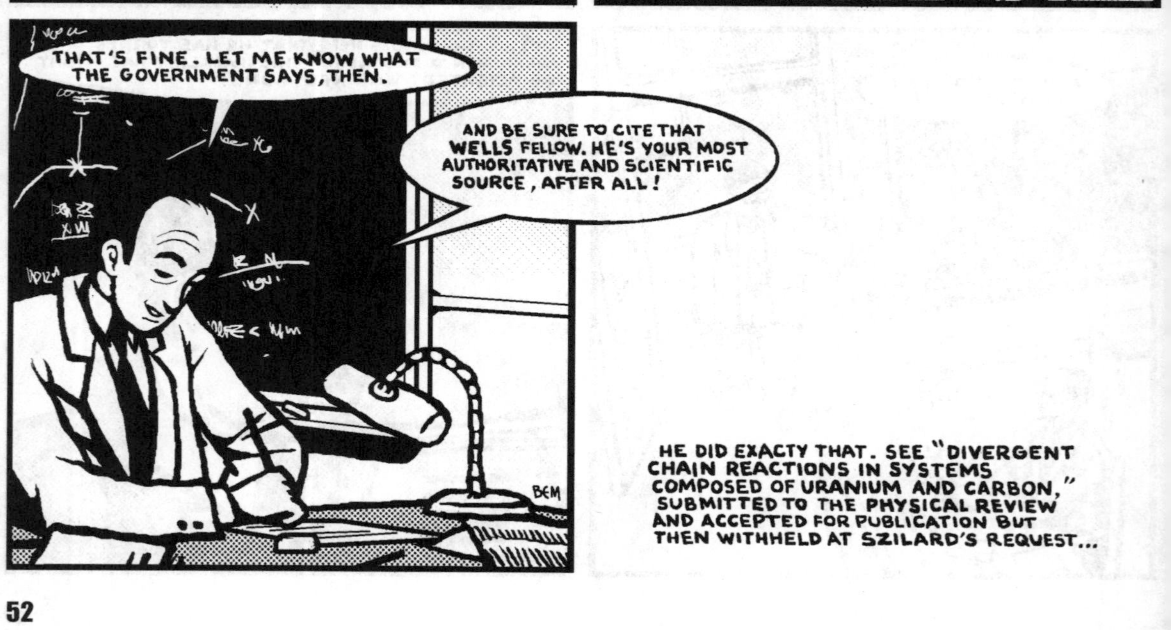
THAT'S FINE. LET ME KNOW WHAT THE GOVERNMENT SAYS, THEN.
AND BE SURE TO CITE THAT WELLS FELLOW. HE'S YOUR MOST AUTHORITATIVE AND SCIENTIFIC SOURCE, AFTER ALL!
BEM

HE DID EXACTY THAT. SEE "DIVERGENT CHAIN REACTIONS IN SYSTEMS COMPOSED OF URANIUM AND CARBON," SUBMITTED TO THE PHYSICAL REVIEW AND ACCEPTED FOR PUBLICATION BUT THEN WITHHELD AT SZILARD'S REQUEST...

school

(1942)

One of the things that worries us is that none of the people in our field are publishing work in the *Physical Review* for the very good reason that they are not doing anything that can be published. … We have often wondered whether your great talent for physics and for burlesque could not appropriately be put to use by your publishing some work in the names of a few of the men… It would give you a chance to express in the most appropriate way possible your evaluation of their qualities and you would have a delicious opportunity to argue with yourself in the public press.

—J. Robert Oppenheimer in a 1943 letter to Wolfgang Pauli

Although I would be glad to be helpful in the suggested way, I am afraid I should publish the few things which I have at present to say with my own name to prove to the "money-givers" that after all I am [giving them] something for their money, fearing their sense of burlesque to be rather underdeveloped…

—Pauli, in reply

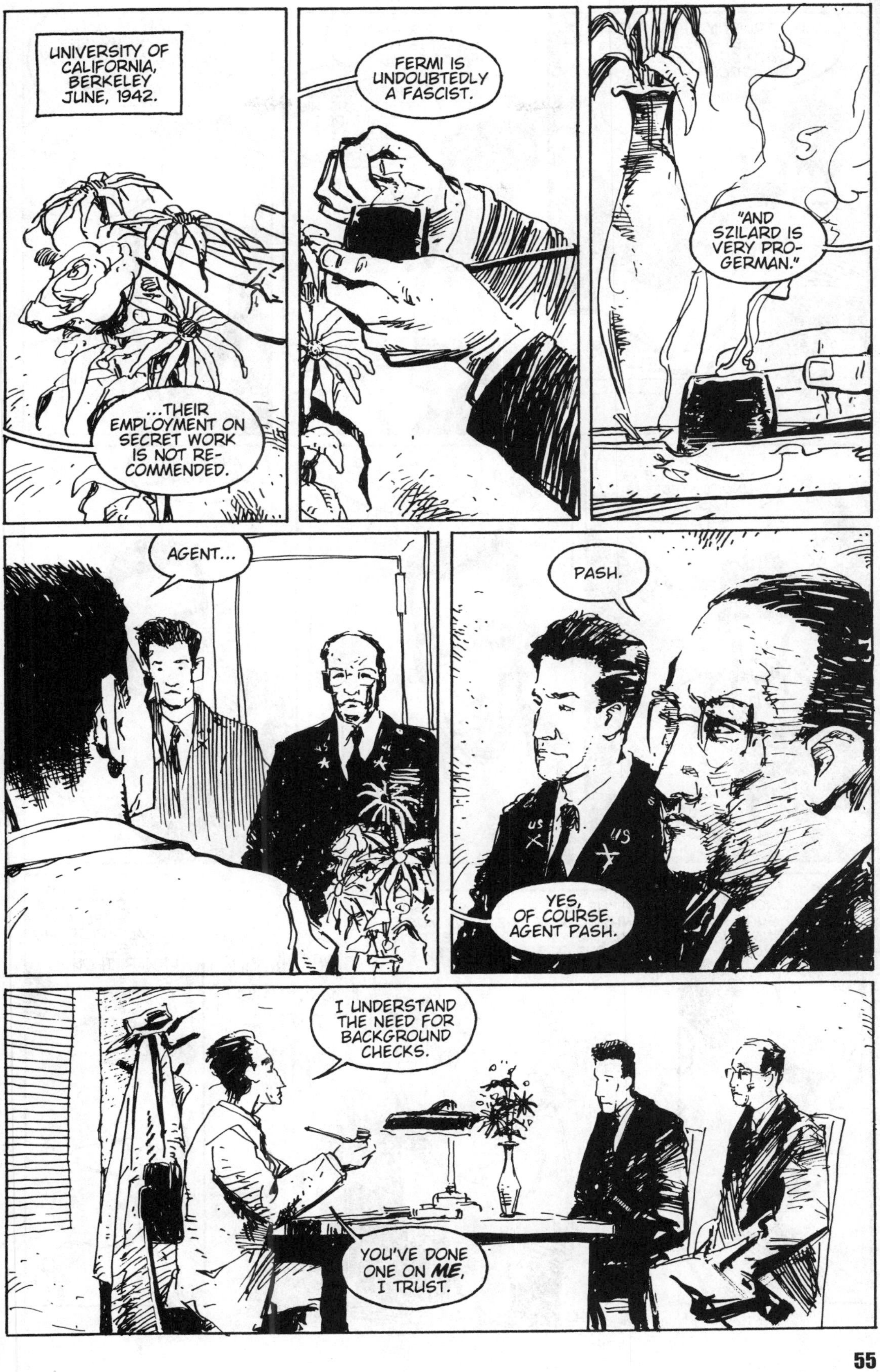
UNIVERSITY OF CALIFORNIA, BERKELEY JUNE, 1942.
...THEIR EMPLOYMENT ON SECRET WORK IS NOT RE-COMMENDED.
FERMI IS UNDOUBTEDLY A FASCIST.
"AND SZILARD IS VERY PRO-GERMAN."
AGENT...
PASH.
YES, OF COURSE. AGENT PASH.
I UNDERSTAND THE NEED FOR BACKGROUND CHECKS.
YOU'VE DONE ONE ON *ME*, I TRUST.

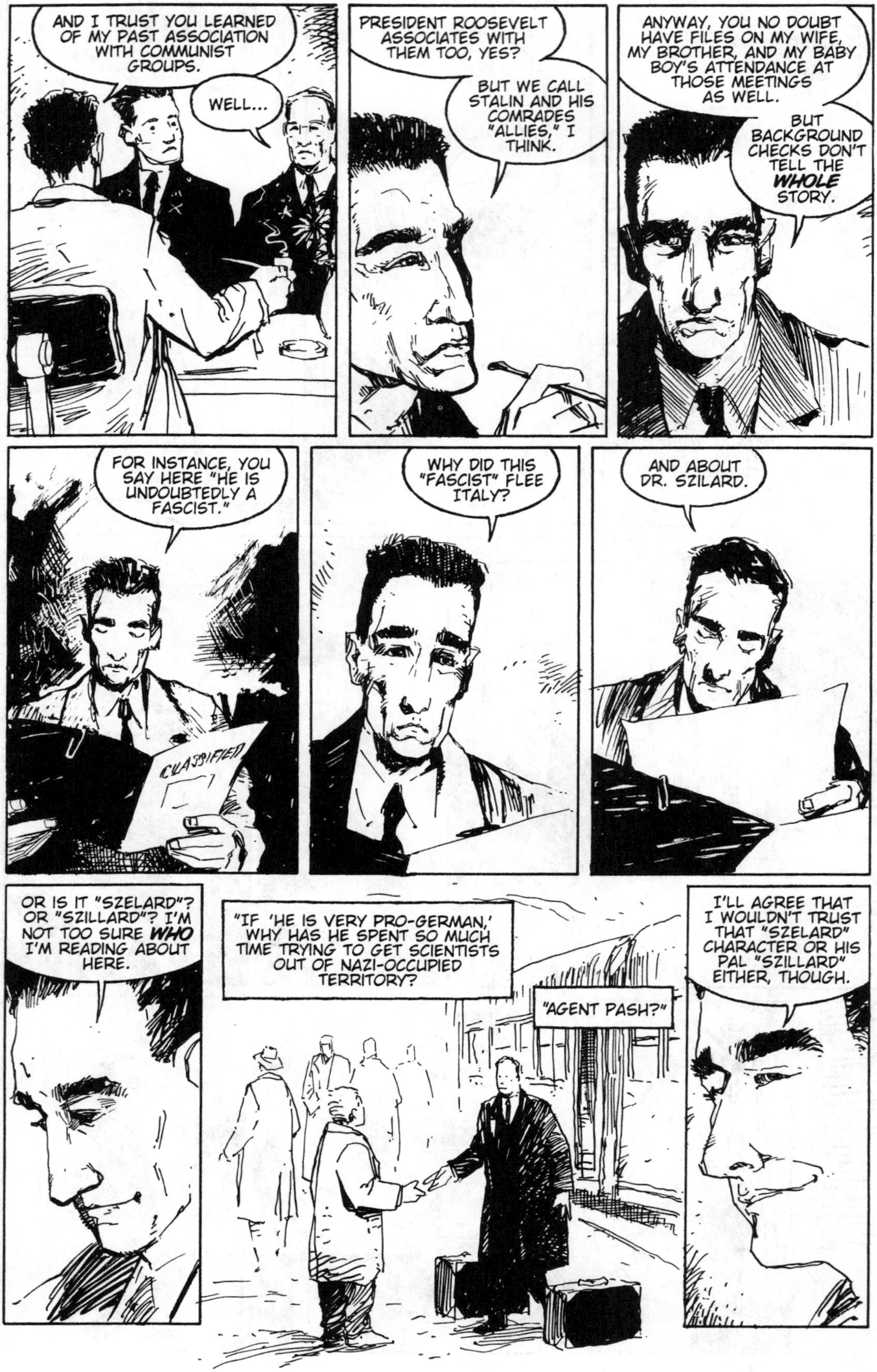
AND I TRUST YOU LEARNED OF MY PAST ASSOCIATION WITH COMMUNIST GROUPS.
WELL...
PRESIDENT ROOSEVELT ASSOCIATES WITH THEM TOO, YES?
BUT WE CALL STALIN AND HIS COMRADES "ALLIES," I THINK.
ANYWAY, YOU NO DOUBT HAVE FILES ON MY WIFE, MY BROTHER, AND MY BABY BOY'S ATTENDANCE AT THOSE MEETINGS AS WELL.
BUT BACKGROUND CHECKS DON'T TELL THE WHOLE STORY.
FOR INSTANCE, YOU SAY HERE "HE IS UNDOUBTEDLY A FASCIST."
CLASSIFIED
WHY DID THIS "FASCIST" FLEE ITALY?
AND ABOUT DR. SZILARD.
OR IS IT "SZELARD"? OR "SZILLARD"? I'M NOT TOO SURE WHO I'M READING ABOUT HERE.
"IF 'HE IS VERY PRO-GERMAN,' WHY HAS HE SPENT SO MUCH TIME TRYING TO GET SCIENTISTS OUT OF NAZI-OCCUPIED TERRITORY?
"AGENT PASH?"
I'LL AGREE THAT I WOULDN'T TRUST THAT "SZELARD" CHARACTER OR HIS PAL "SZILLARD" EITHER, THOUGH.

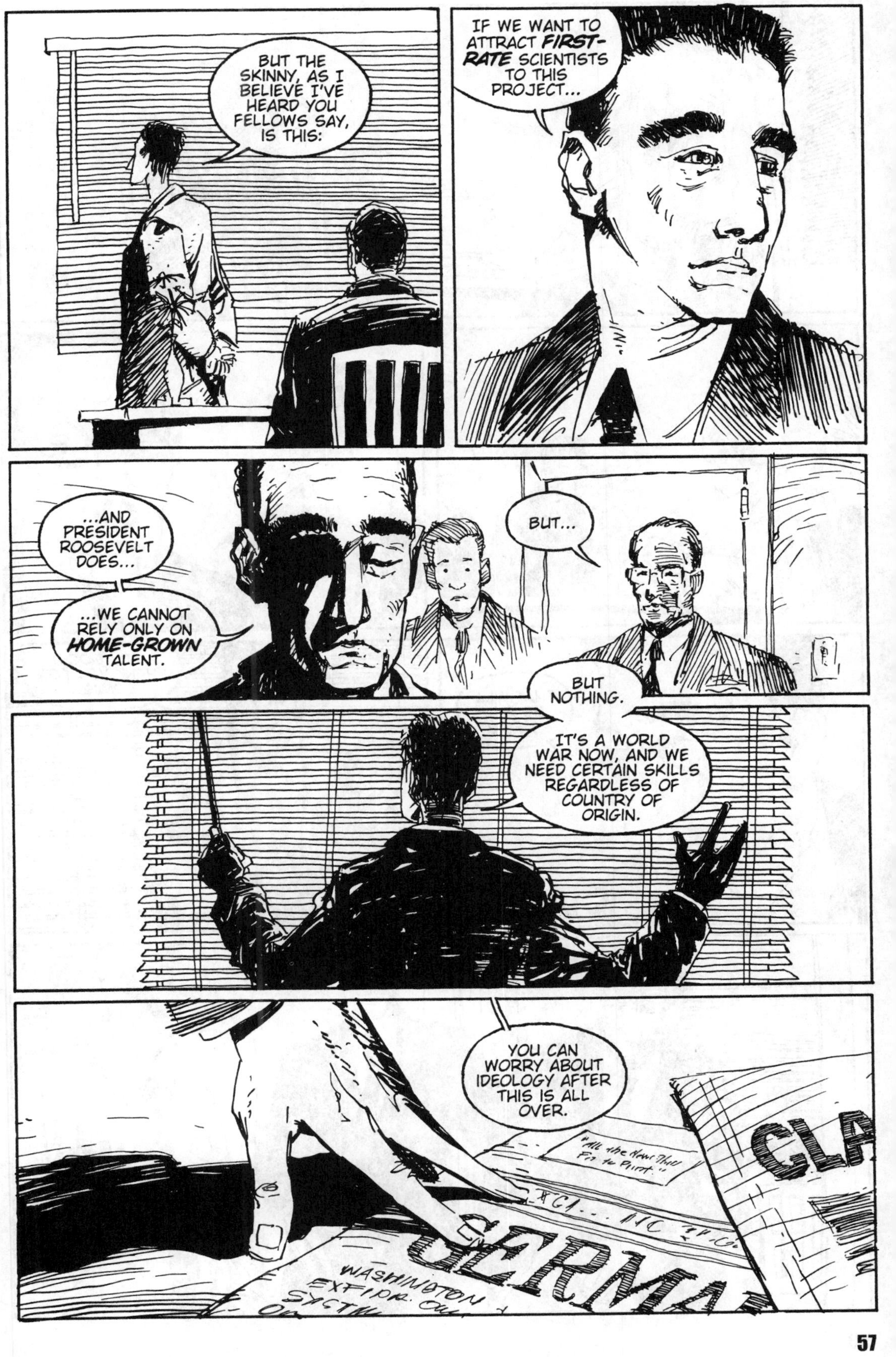
BUT THE SKINNY, AS I BELIEVE I'VE HEARD YOU FELLOWS SAY, IS THIS:
IF WE WANT TO ATTRACT **FIRST-RATE** SCIENTISTS TO THIS PROJECT...
...AND PRESIDENT ROOSEVELT DOES...
...WE CANNOT RELY ONLY ON ***HOME-GROWN*** TALENT.
BUT...
BUT NOTHING.
IT'S A WORLD WAR NOW, AND WE NEED CERTAIN SKILLS REGARDLESS OF COUNTRY OF ORIGIN.
YOU CAN WORRY ABOUT IDEOLOGY AFTER THIS IS ALL OVER.

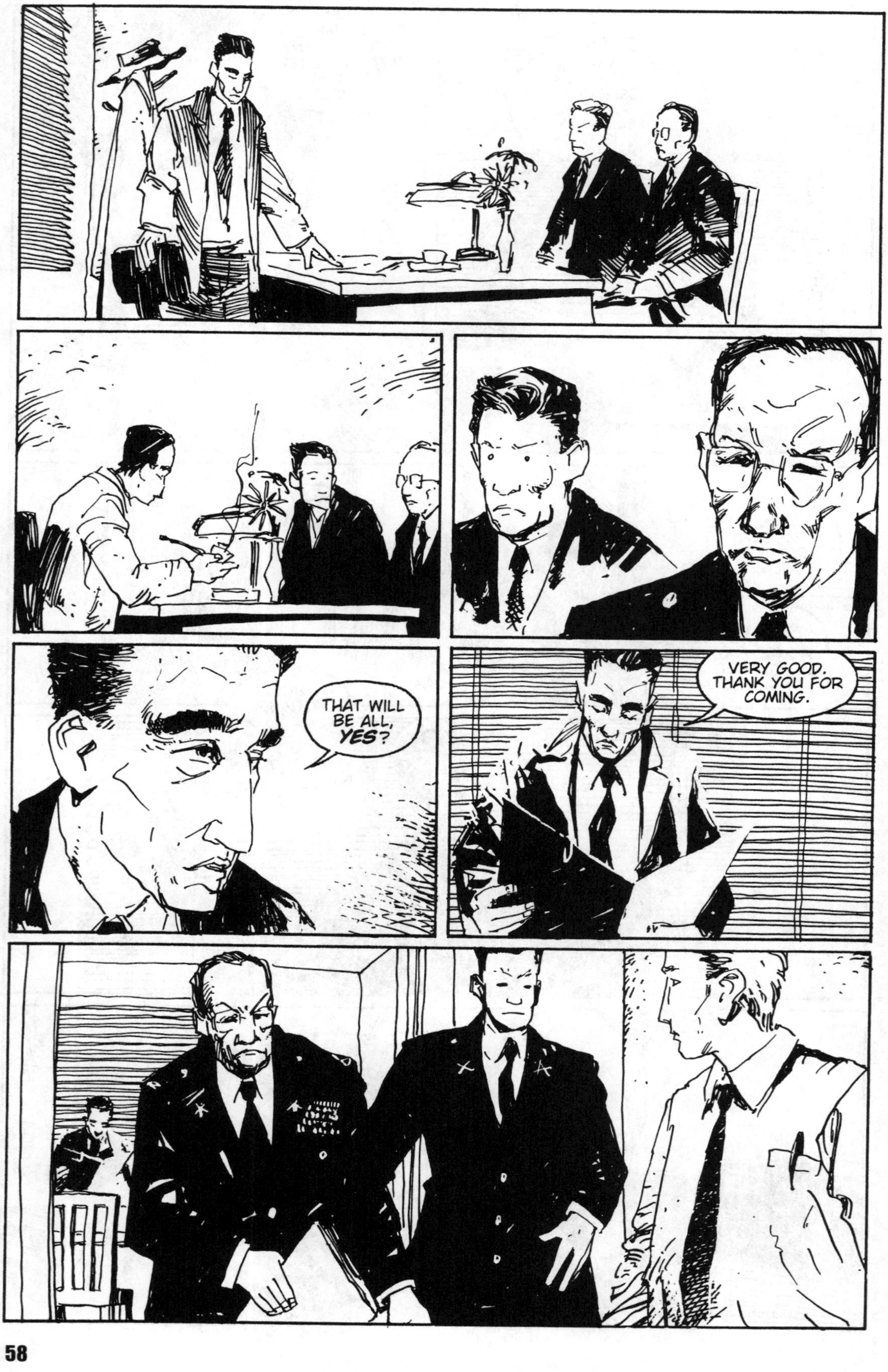
THAT WILL BE ALL, *YES*?
VERY GOOD. THANK YOU FOR COMING.

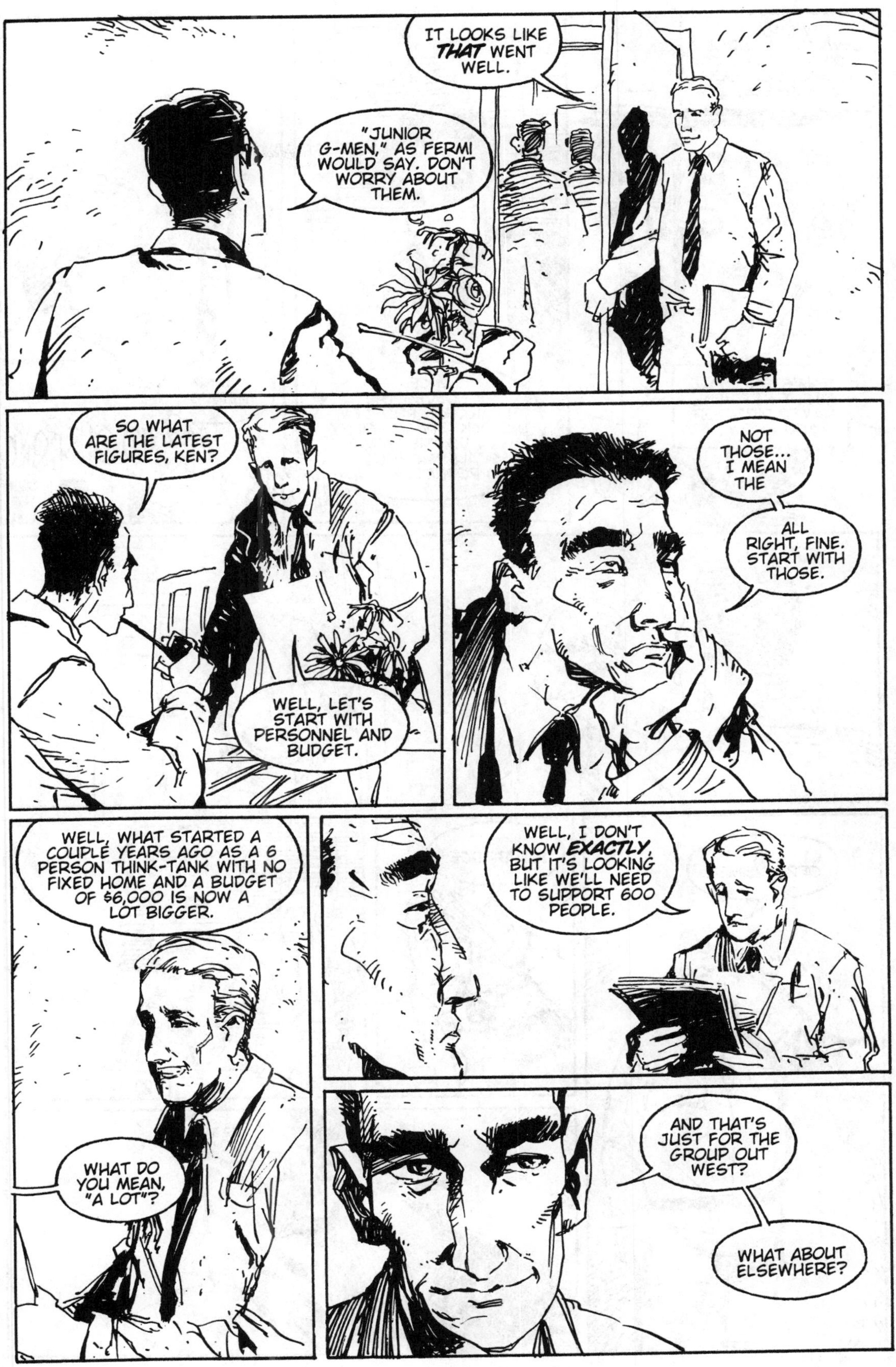
IT LOOKS LIKE *THAT* WENT WELL.
"JUNIOR G-MEN," AS FERMI WOULD SAY. DON'T WORRY ABOUT THEM.
SO WHAT ARE THE LATEST FIGURES, KEN?
WELL, LET'S START WITH PERSONNEL AND BUDGET.
NOT THOSE... I MEAN THE
ALL RIGHT, FINE. START WITH THOSE.
WELL, WHAT STARTED A COUPLE YEARS AGO AS A 6 PERSON THINK-TANK WITH NO FIXED HOME AND A BUDGET OF $6,000 IS NOW A LOT BIGGER.
WHAT DO YOU MEAN, "A LOT"?
WELL, I DON'T KNOW *EXACTLY*, BUT IT'S LOOKING LIKE WE'LL NEED TO SUPPORT 600 PEOPLE.
AND THAT'S JUST FOR THE GROUP OUT WEST?
WHAT ABOUT ELSEWHERE?

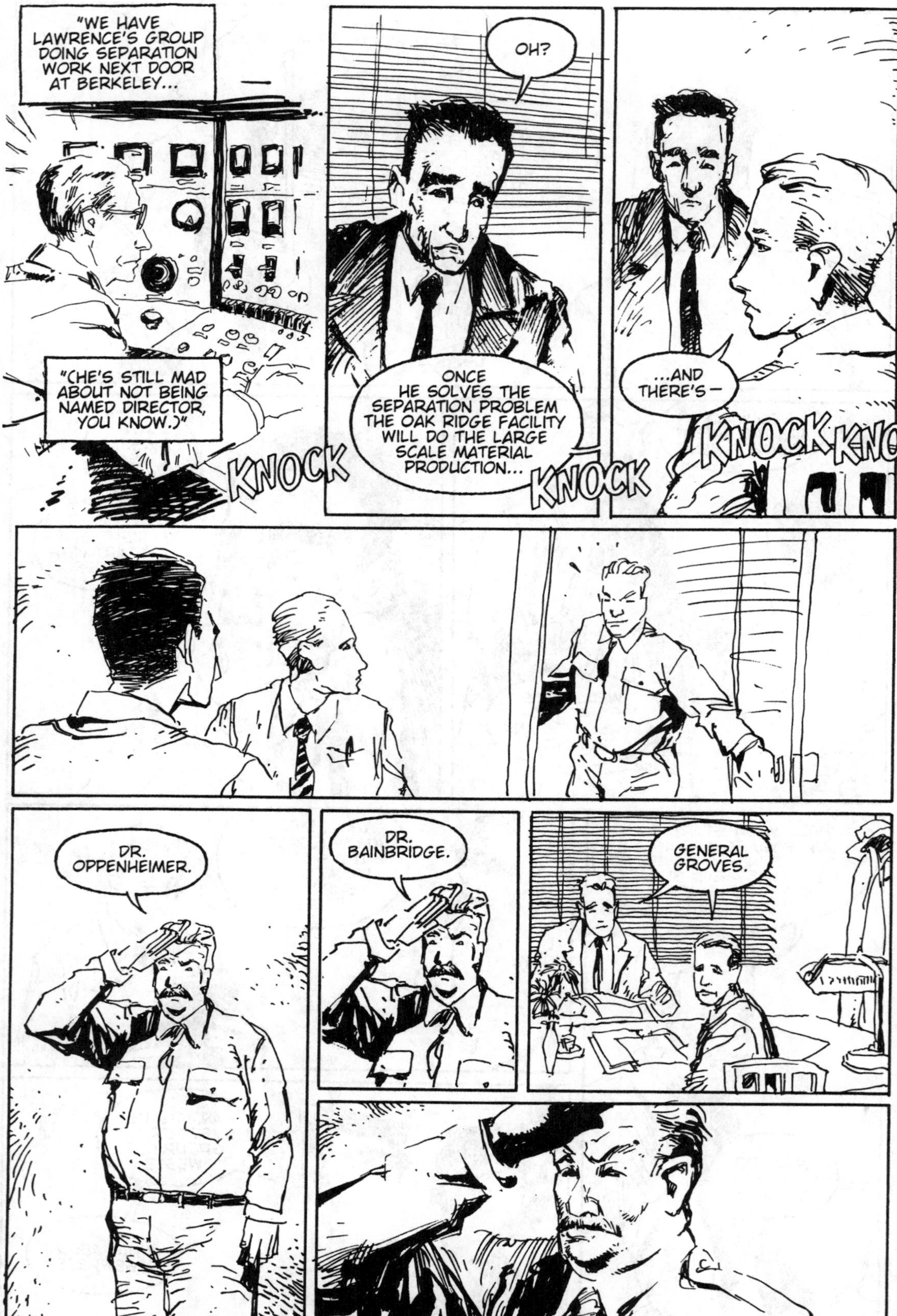
"WE HAVE LAWRENCE'S GROUP DOING SEPARATION WORK NEXT DOOR AT BERKELEY...
"(HE'S STILL MAD ABOUT NOT BEING NAMED DIRECTOR, YOU KNOW.)"
KNOCK
OH?
ONCE HE SOLVES THE SEPARATION PROBLEM THE OAK RIDGE FACILITY WILL DO THE LARGE SCALE MATERIAL PRODUCTION...
KNOCK
...AND THERE'S—
KNOCK
DR. OPPENHEIMER.
DR. BAINBRIDGE.
GENERAL GROVES.

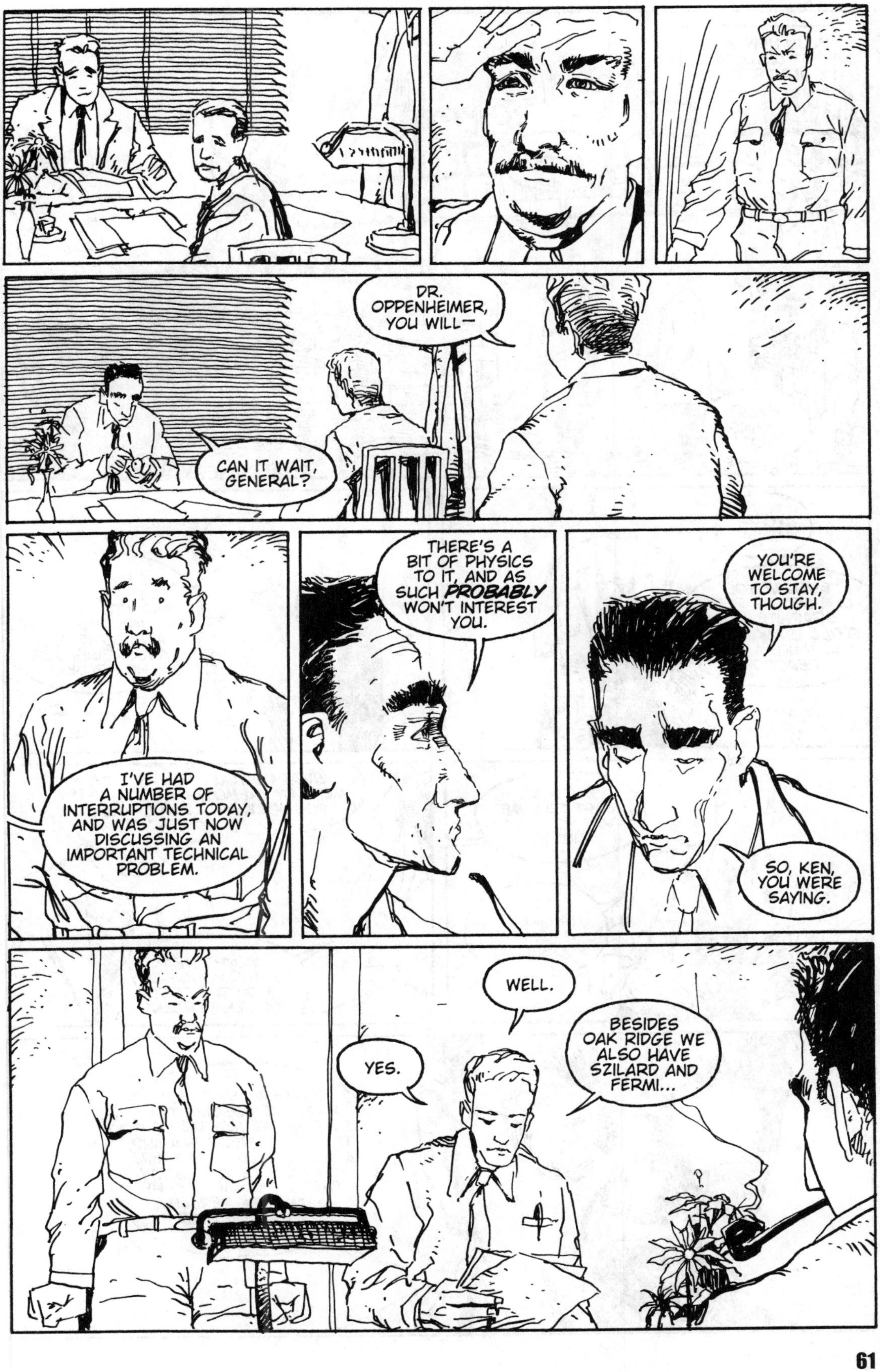
DR. OPPENHEIMER, YOU WILL—
CAN IT WAIT, GENERAL?
I'VE HAD A NUMBER OF INTERRUPTIONS TODAY, AND WAS JUST NOW DISCUSSING AN IMPORTANT TECHNICAL PROBLEM.
THERE'S A BIT OF PHYSICS TO IT, AND AS SUCH PROBABLY WON'T INTEREST YOU.
YOU'RE WELCOME TO STAY, THOUGH.
SO, KEN, YOU WERE SAYING.
WELL.
YES.
BESIDES OAK RIDGE WE ALSO HAVE SZILARD AND FERMI...

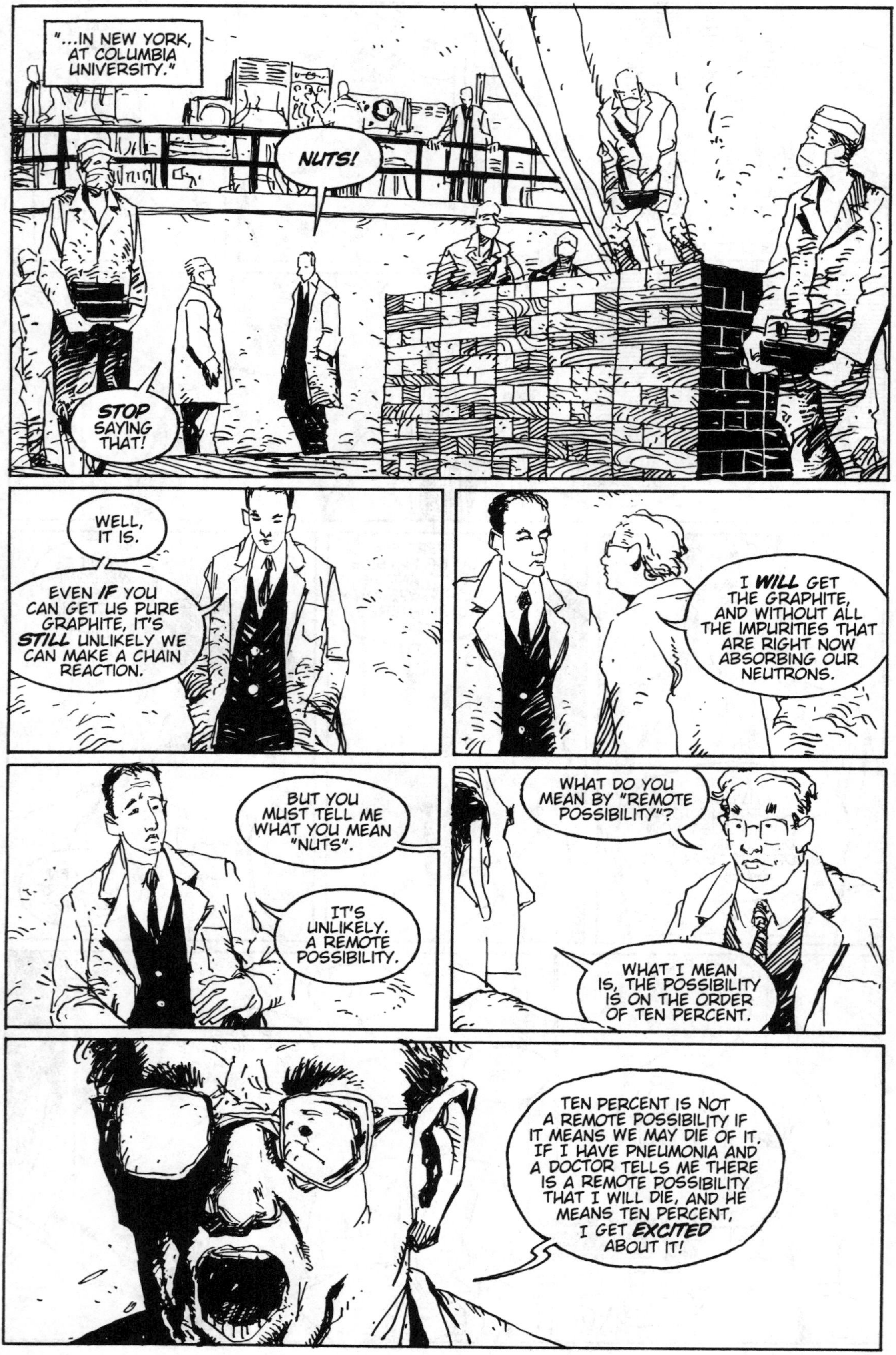

"...IN NEW YORK, AT COLUMBIA UNIVERSITY."
NUTS!
STOP SAYING THAT!
WELL, IT IS.
EVEN IF YOU CAN GET US PURE GRAPHITE, IT'S STILL UNLIKELY WE CAN MAKE A CHAIN REACTION.
I WILL GET THE GRAPHITE, AND WITHOUT ALL THE IMPURITIES THAT ARE RIGHT NOW ABSORBING OUR NEUTRONS.
BUT YOU MUST TELL ME WHAT YOU MEAN "NUTS".
IT'S UNLIKELY. A REMOTE POSSIBILITY.
WHAT DO YOU MEAN BY "REMOTE POSSIBILITY"?
WHAT I MEAN IS, THE POSSIBILITY IS ON THE ORDER OF TEN PERCENT.
TEN PERCENT IS NOT A REMOTE POSSIBILITY IF IT MEANS WE MAY DIE OF IT. IF I HAVE PNEUMONIA AND A DOCTOR TELLS ME THERE IS A REMOTE POSSIBILITY THAT I WILL DIE, AND HE MEANS TEN PERCENT, I GET EXCITED ABOUT IT!

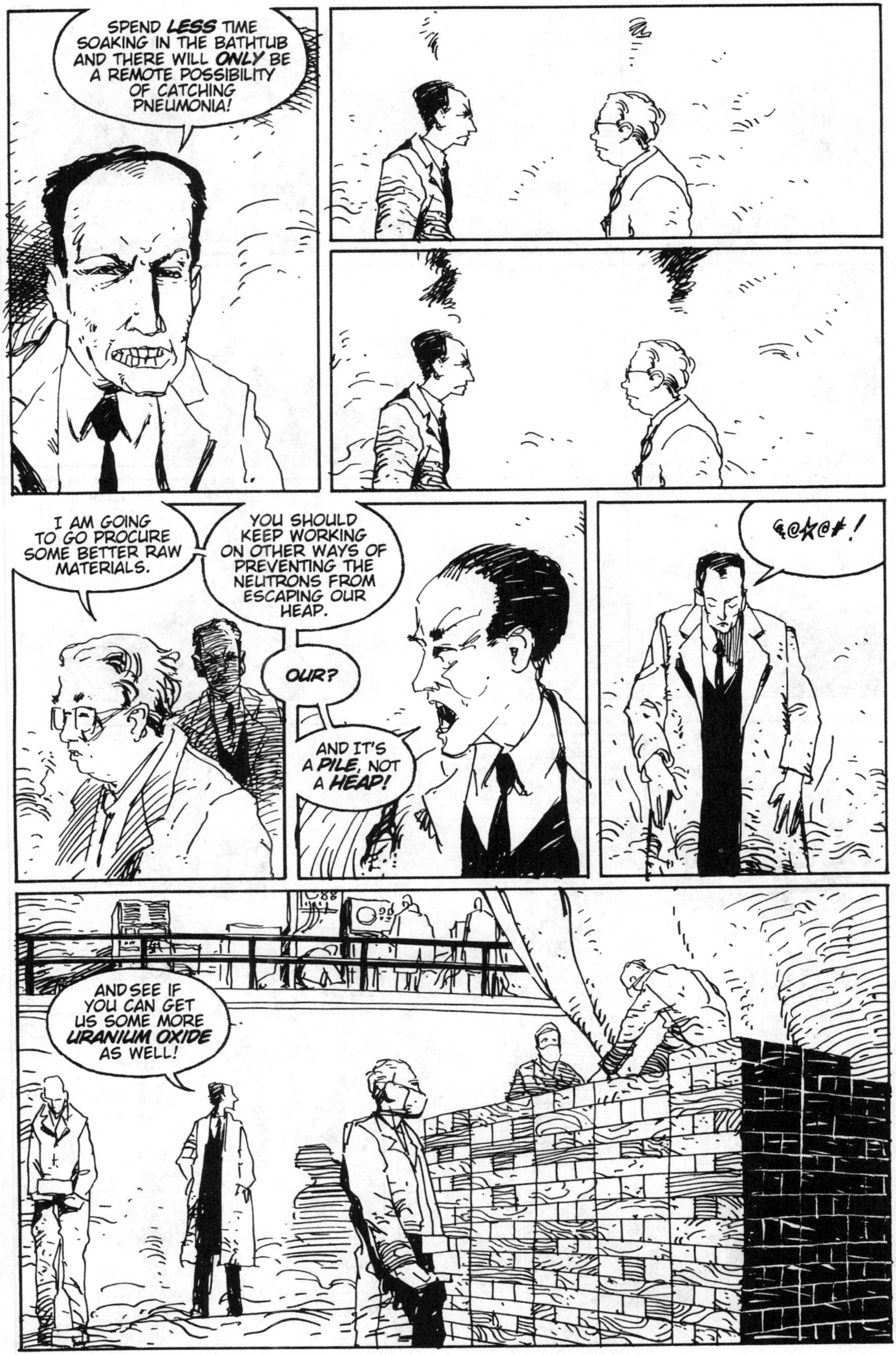

SPEND LESS TIME SOAKING IN THE BATHTUB AND THERE WILL ONLY BE A REMOTE POSSIBILITY OF CATCHING PNEUMONIA!
I AM GOING TO GO PROCURE SOME BETTER RAW MATERIALS.
YOU SHOULD KEEP WORKING ON OTHER WAYS OF PREVENTING THE NEUTRONS FROM ESCAPING OUR HEAP.
OUR?
AND IT'S A PILE, NOT A HEAP!
&@☆@#!
AND SEE IF YOU CAN GET US SOME MORE URANIUM OXIDE AS WELL!

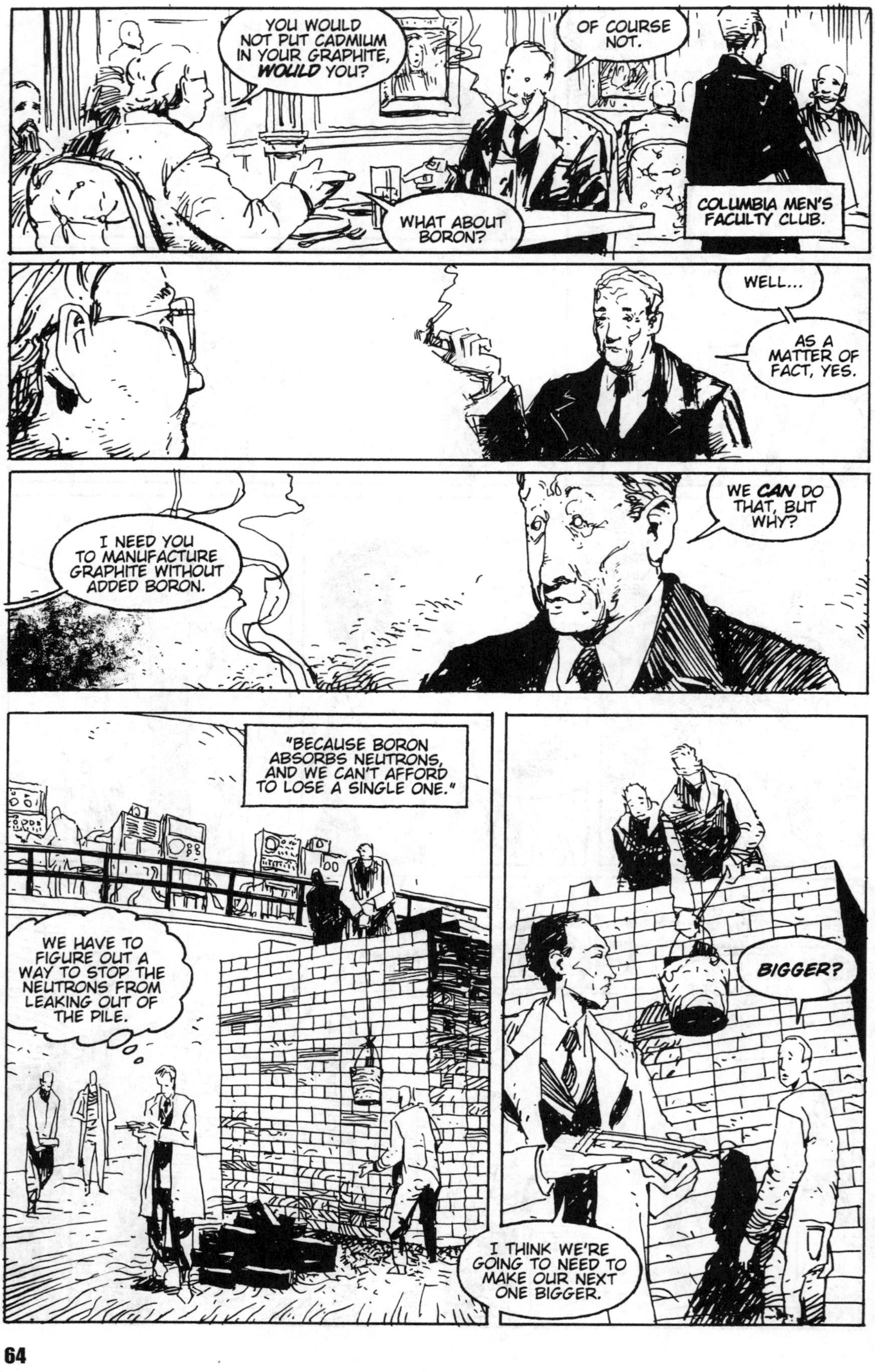

YOU WOULD NOT PUT CADMIUM IN YOUR GRAPHITE, WOULD YOU?
OF COURSE NOT.
WHAT ABOUT BORON?
COLUMBIA MEN'S FACULTY CLUB.
WELL...
AS A MATTER OF FACT, YES.
I NEED YOU TO MANUFACTURE GRAPHITE WITHOUT ADDED BORON.
WE CAN DO THAT, BUT WHY?
"BECAUSE BORON ABSORBS NEUTRONS, AND WE CAN'T AFFORD TO LOSE A SINGLE ONE."
WE HAVE TO FIGURE OUT A WAY TO STOP THE NEUTRONS FROM LEAKING OUT OF THE PILE.
I THINK WE'RE GOING TO NEED TO MAKE OUR NEXT ONE BIGGER.
BIGGER?

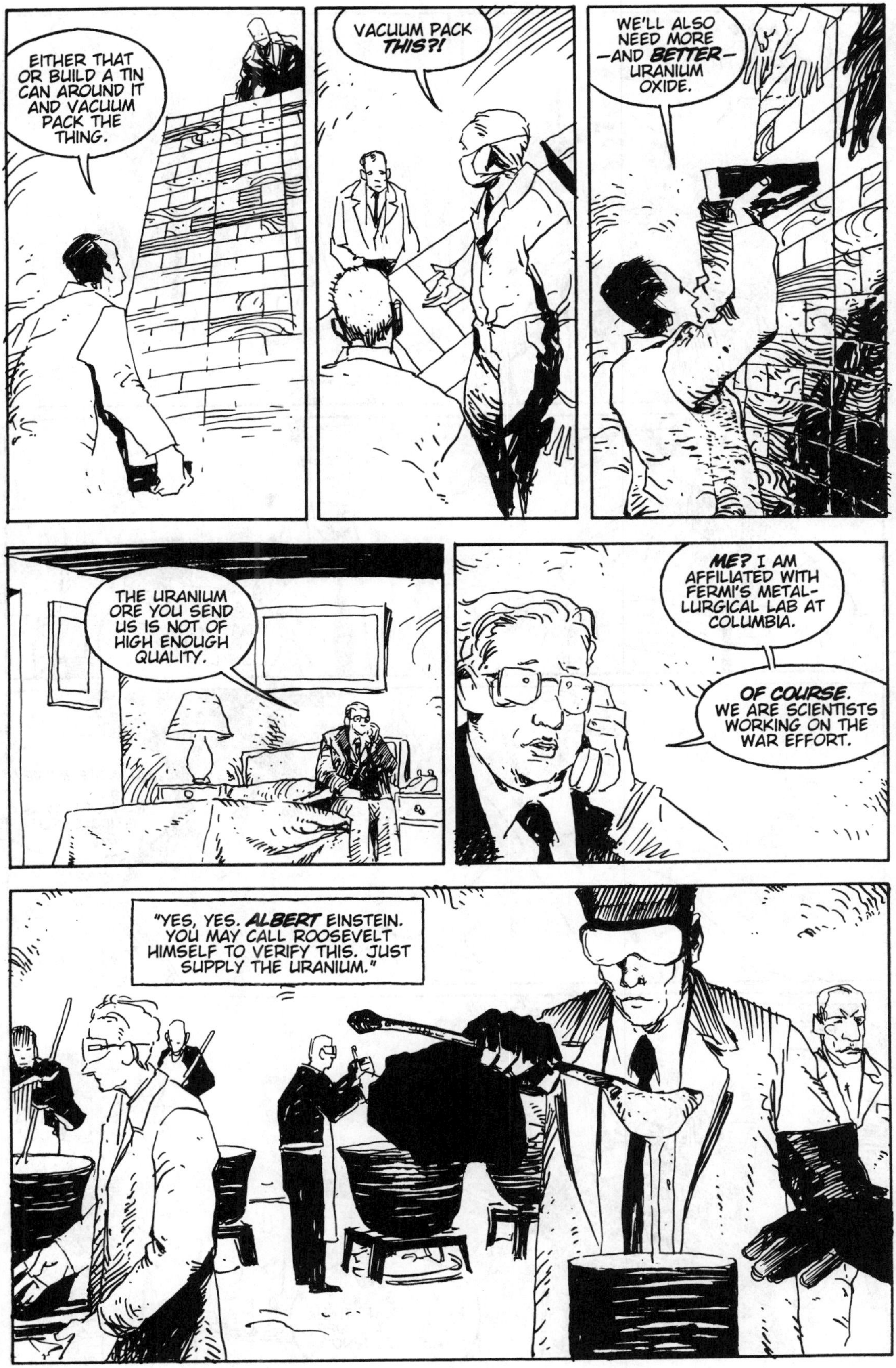
EITHER THAT OR BUILD A TIN CAN AROUND IT AND VACUUM PACK THE THING.
VACUUM PACK THIS?!
WE'LL ALSO NEED MORE —AND BETTER— URANIUM OXIDE.
THE URANIUM ORE YOU SEND US IS NOT OF HIGH ENOUGH QUALITY.
ME? I AM AFFILIATED WITH FERMI'S METAL-LURGICAL LAB AT COLUMBIA.
OF COURSE. WE ARE SCIENTISTS WORKING ON THE WAR EFFORT.
"YES, YES. ALBERT EINSTEIN. YOU MAY CALL ROOSEVELT HIMSELF TO VERIFY THIS. JUST SUPPLY THE URANIUM."

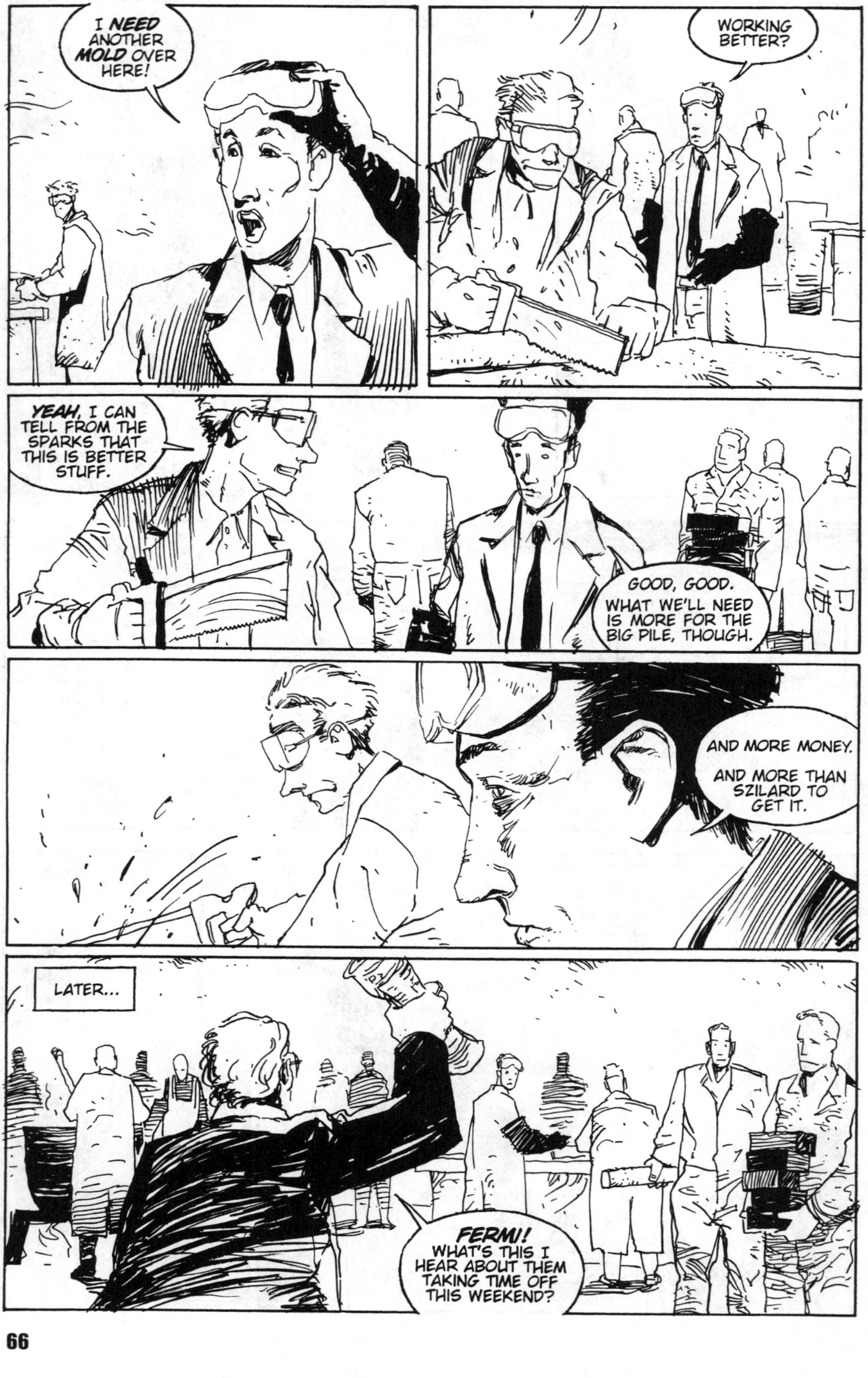

I NEED ANOTHER MOLD OVER HERE!
WORKING BETTER?
YEAH, I CAN TELL FROM THE SPARKS THAT THIS IS BETTER STUFF.
GOOD, GOOD.
WHAT WE'LL NEED IS MORE FOR THE BIG PILE, THOUGH.
AND MORE MONEY.
AND MORE THAN SZILARD TO GET IT.
LATER...
FERMI! WHAT'S THIS I HEAR ABOUT THEM TAKING TIME OFF THIS WEEKEND?

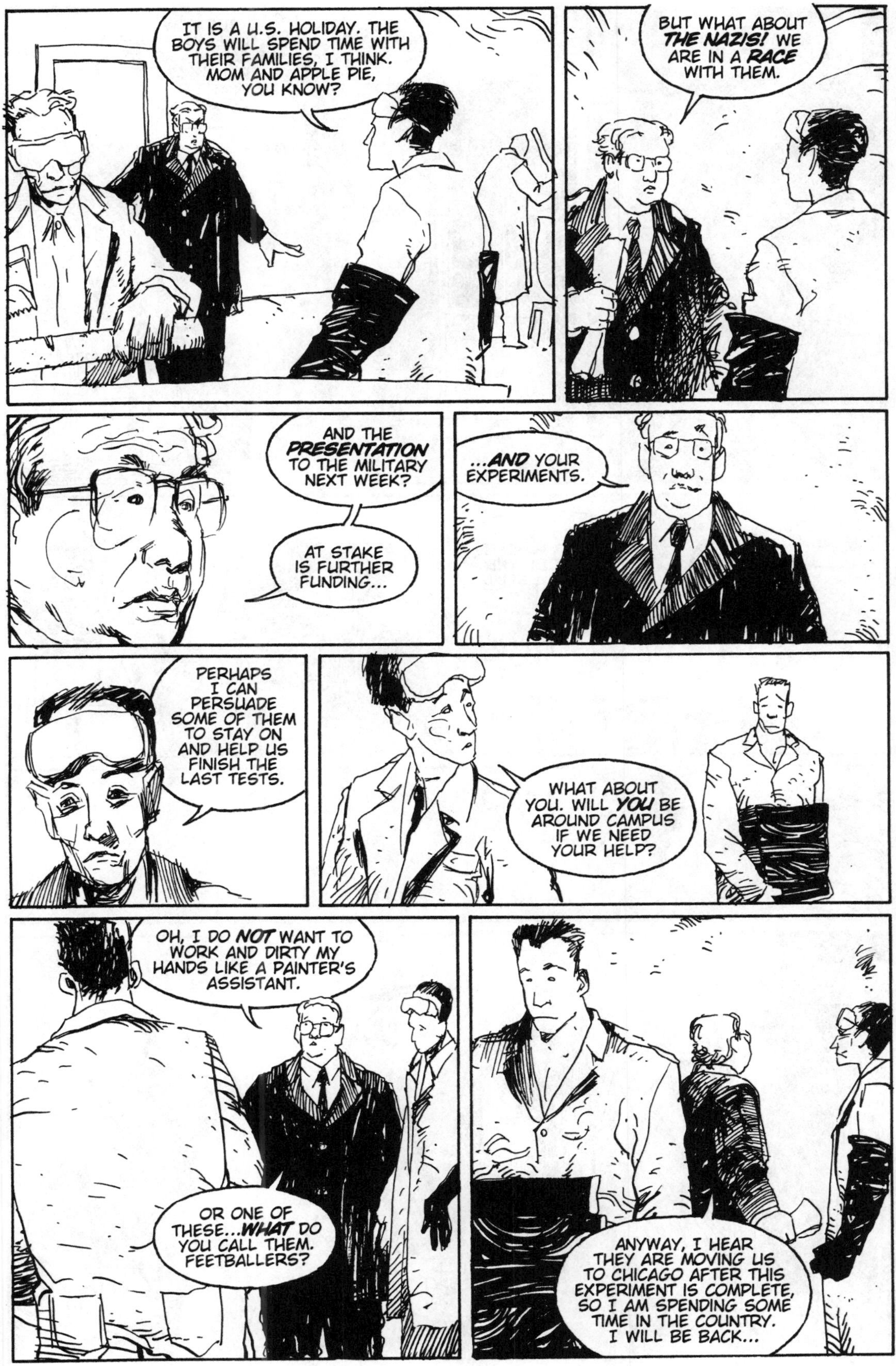
IT IS A U.S. HOLIDAY. THE BOYS WILL SPEND TIME WITH THEIR FAMILIES, I THINK. MOM AND APPLE PIE, YOU KNOW?
BUT WHAT ABOUT THE NAZIS! WE ARE IN A RACE WITH THEM.
AND THE PRESENTATION TO THE MILITARY NEXT WEEK?
AT STAKE IS FURTHER FUNDING...
...AND YOUR EXPERIMENTS.
PERHAPS I CAN PERSUADE SOME OF THEM TO STAY ON AND HELP US FINISH THE LAST TESTS.
WHAT ABOUT YOU. WILL YOU BE AROUND CAMPUS IF WE NEED YOUR HELP?
OH, I DO NOT WANT TO WORK AND DIRTY MY HANDS LIKE A PAINTER'S ASSISTANT.
OR ONE OF THESE...WHAT DO YOU CALL THEM. FEETBALLERS?
ANYWAY, I HEAR THEY ARE MOVING US TO CHICAGO AFTER THIS EXPERIMENT IS COMPLETE, SO I AM SPENDING SOME TIME IN THE COUNTRY. I WILL BE BACK...

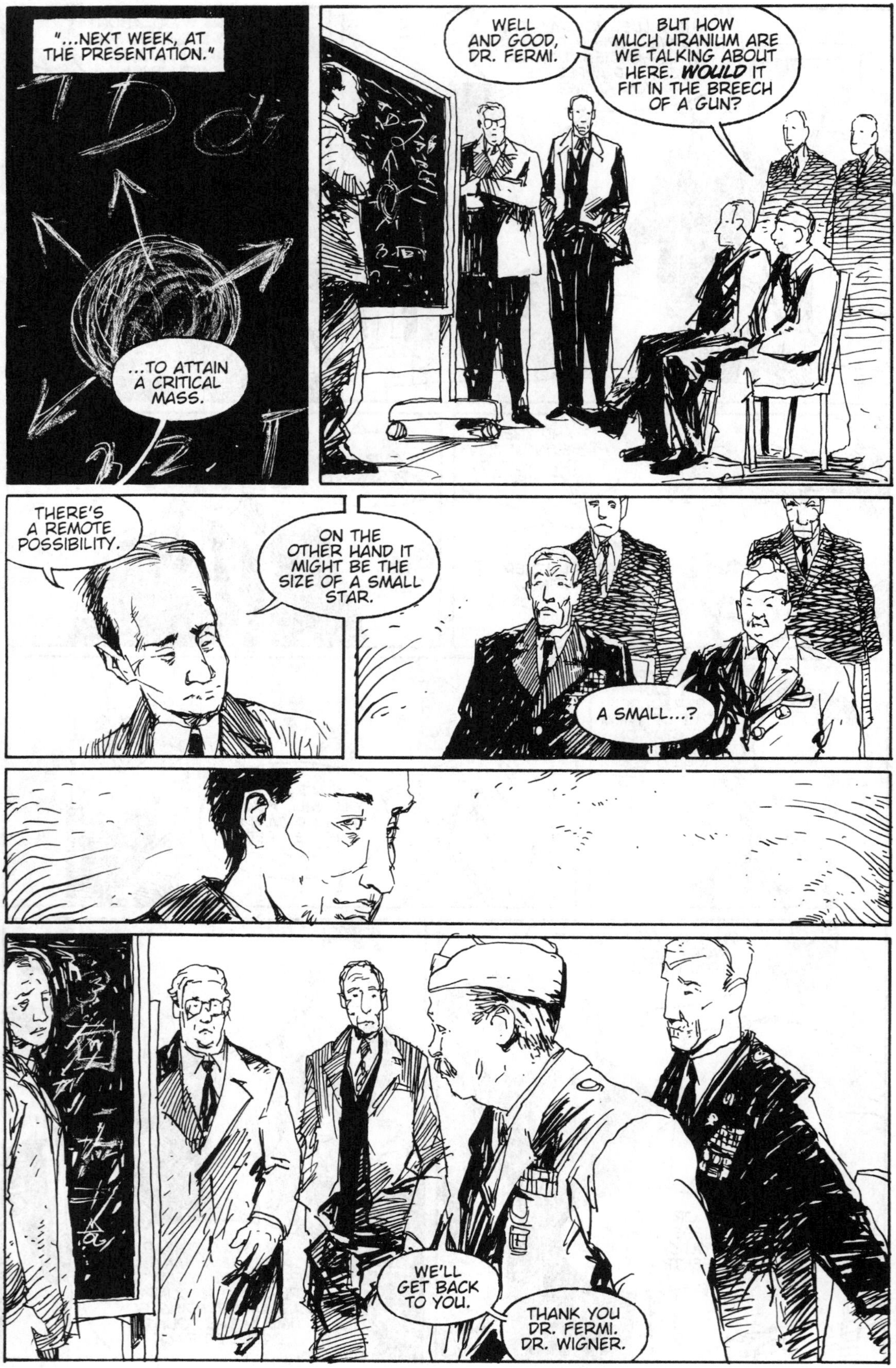
"...NEXT WEEK, AT THE PRESENTATION."
...TO ATTAIN A CRITICAL MASS.
WELL AND GOOD, DR. FERMI.
BUT HOW MUCH URANIUM ARE WE TALKING ABOUT HERE. WOULD IT FIT IN THE BREECH OF A GUN?
THERE'S A REMOTE POSSIBILITY.
ON THE OTHER HAND IT MIGHT BE THE SIZE OF A SMALL STAR.
A SMALL...?
WE'LL GET BACK TO YOU.
THANK YOU DR. FERMI. DR. WIGNER.

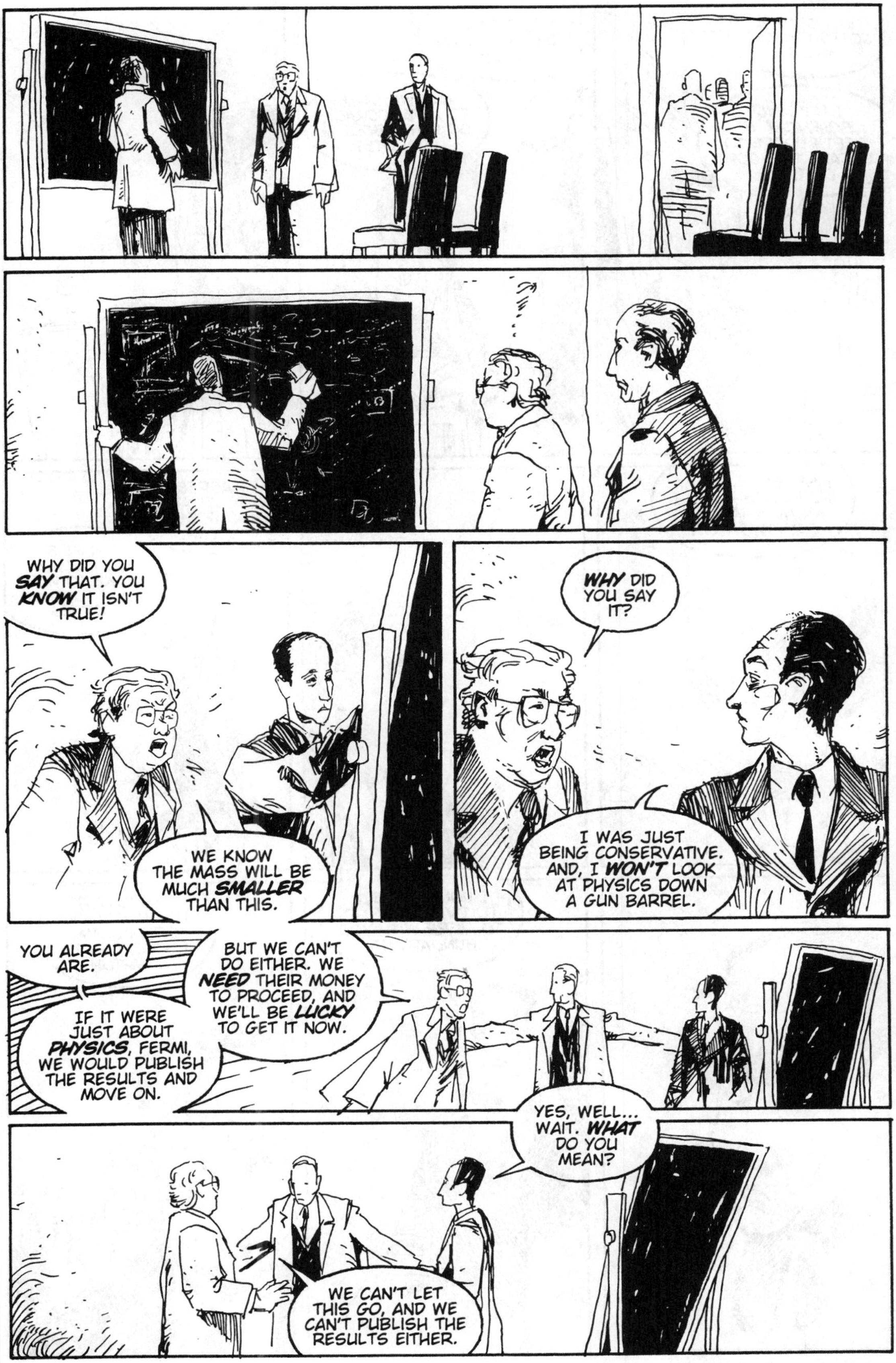
WHY DID YOU SAY THAT. YOU KNOW IT ISN'T TRUE!
WE KNOW THE MASS WILL BE MUCH SMALLER THAN THIS.
WHY DID YOU SAY IT?
I WAS JUST BEING CONSERVATIVE. AND, I WON'T LOOK AT PHYSICS DOWN A GUN BARREL.
YOU ALREADY ARE.
IF IT WERE JUST ABOUT PHYSICS, FERMI, WE WOULD PUBLISH THE RESULTS AND MOVE ON.
BUT WE CAN'T DO EITHER. WE NEED THEIR MONEY TO PROCEED, AND WE'LL BE LUCKY TO GET IT NOW.
YES, WELL... WAIT. WHAT DO YOU MEAN?
WE CAN'T LET THIS GO, AND WE CAN'T PUBLISH THE RESULTS EITHER.

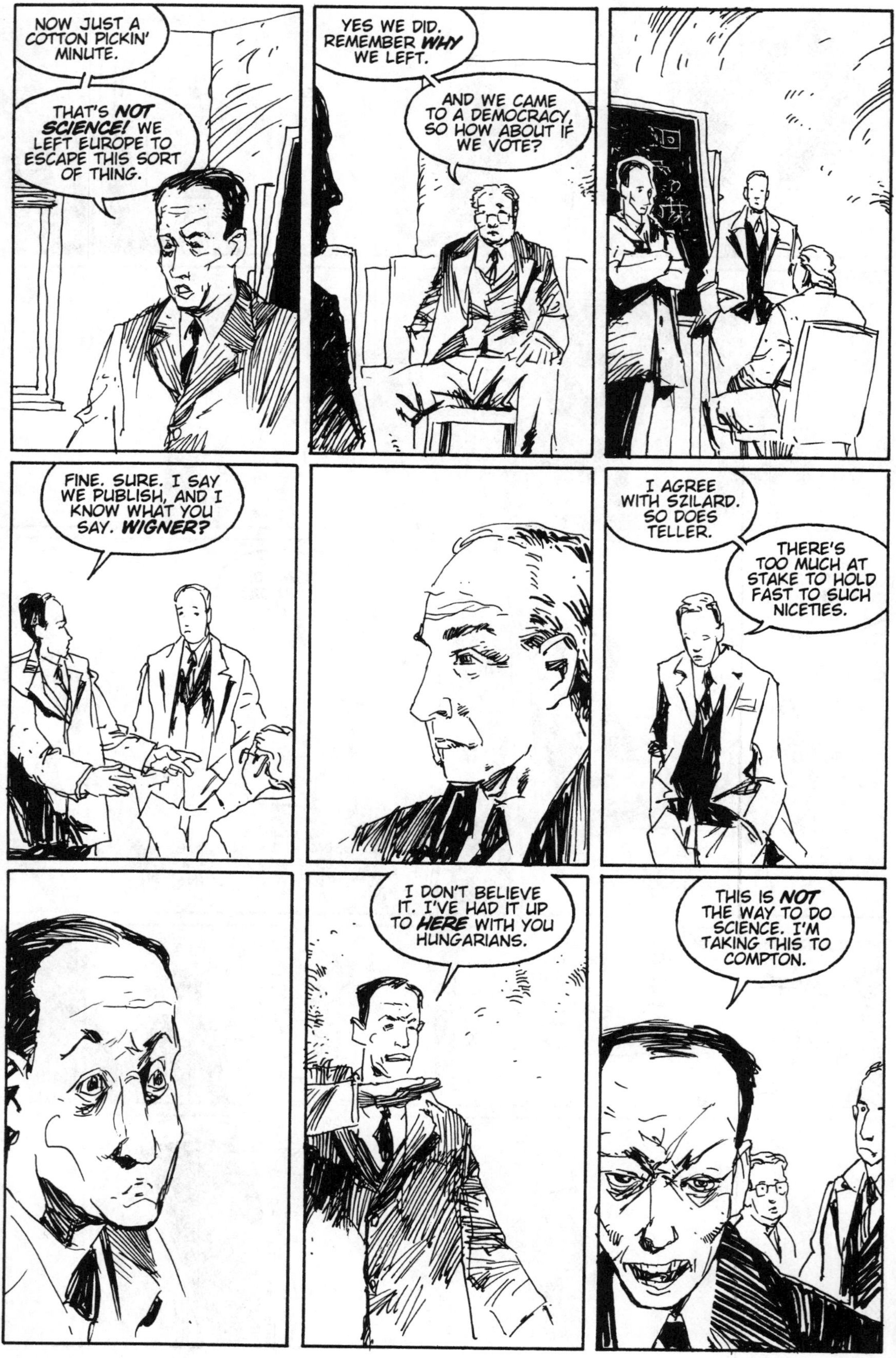
NOW JUST A COTTON PICKIN' MINUTE.
THAT'S NOT SCIENCE! WE LEFT EUROPE TO ESCAPE THIS SORT OF THING.
YES WE DID. REMEMBER WHY WE LEFT.
AND WE CAME TO A DEMOCRACY, SO HOW ABOUT IF WE VOTE?
FINE. SURE. I SAY WE PUBLISH, AND I KNOW WHAT YOU SAY. WIGNER?
I AGREE WITH SZILARD. SO DOES TELLER.
THERE'S TOO MUCH AT STAKE TO HOLD FAST TO SUCH NICETIES.
I DON'T BELIEVE IT. I'VE HAD IT UP TO HERE WITH YOU HUNGARIANS.
THIS IS NOT THE WAY TO DO SCIENCE. I'M TAKING THIS TO COMPTON.

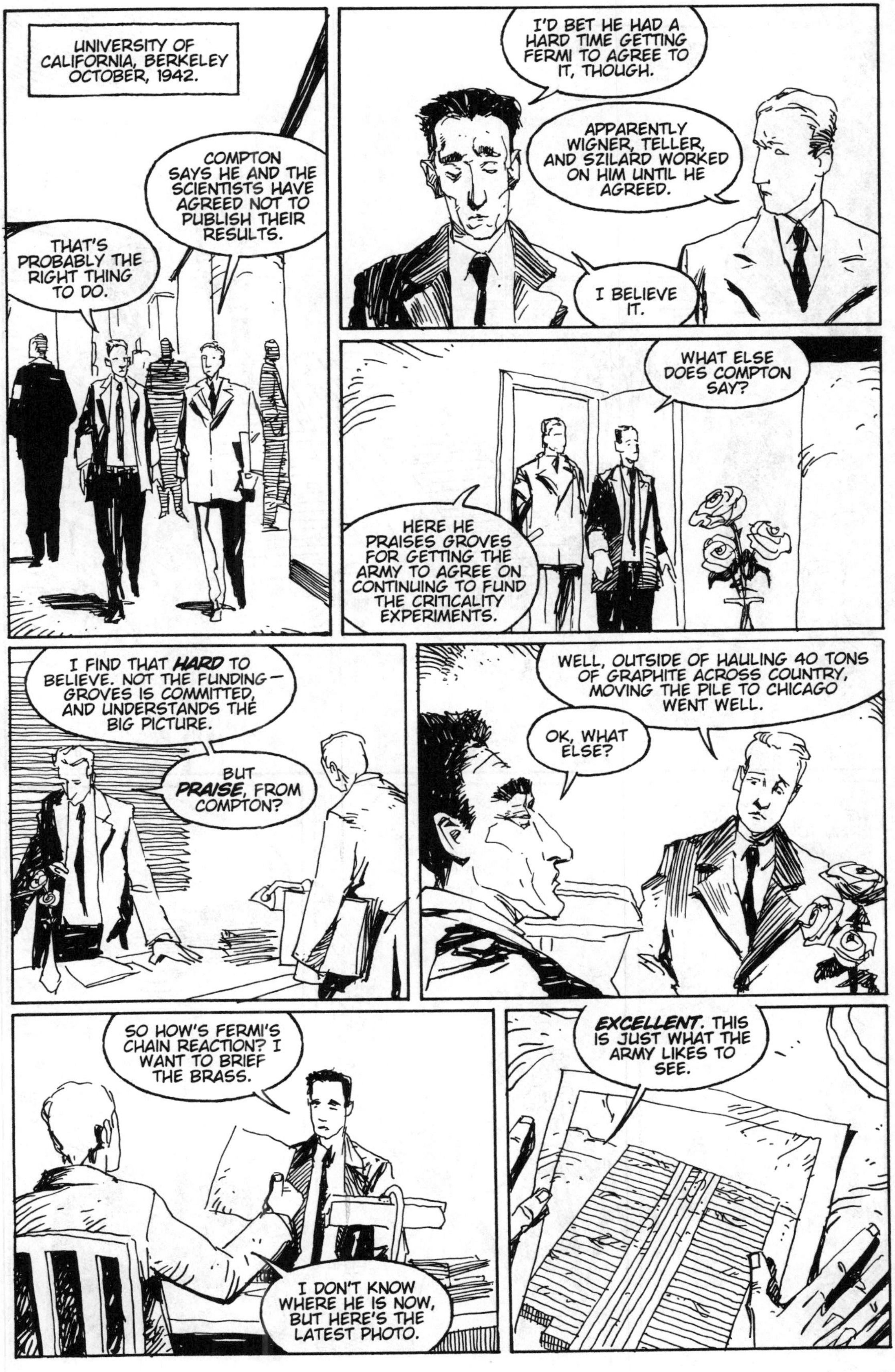
UNIVERSITY OF CALIFORNIA, BERKELEY OCTOBER, 1942.
COMPTON SAYS HE AND THE SCIENTISTS HAVE AGREED NOT TO PUBLISH THEIR RESULTS.
THAT'S PROBABLY THE RIGHT THING TO DO.
I'D BET HE HAD A HARD TIME GETTING FERMI TO AGREE TO IT, THOUGH.
APPARENTLY WIGNER, TELLER, AND SZILARD WORKED ON HIM UNTIL HE AGREED.
I BELIEVE IT.
WHAT ELSE DOES COMPTON SAY?
HERE HE PRAISES GROVES FOR GETTING THE ARMY TO AGREE ON CONTINUING TO FUND THE CRITICALITY EXPERIMENTS.
I FIND THAT HARD TO BELIEVE. NOT THE FUNDING— GROVES IS COMMITTED, AND UNDERSTANDS THE BIG PICTURE.
BUT PRAISE, FROM COMPTON?
WELL, OUTSIDE OF HAULING 40 TONS OF GRAPHITE ACROSS COUNTRY, MOVING THE PILE TO CHICAGO WENT WELL.
OK, WHAT ELSE?
SO HOW'S FERMI'S CHAIN REACTION? I WANT TO BRIEF THE BRASS.
I DON'T KNOW WHERE HE IS NOW, BUT HERE'S THE LATEST PHOTO.
EXCELLENT. THIS IS JUST WHAT THE ARMY LIKES TO SEE.

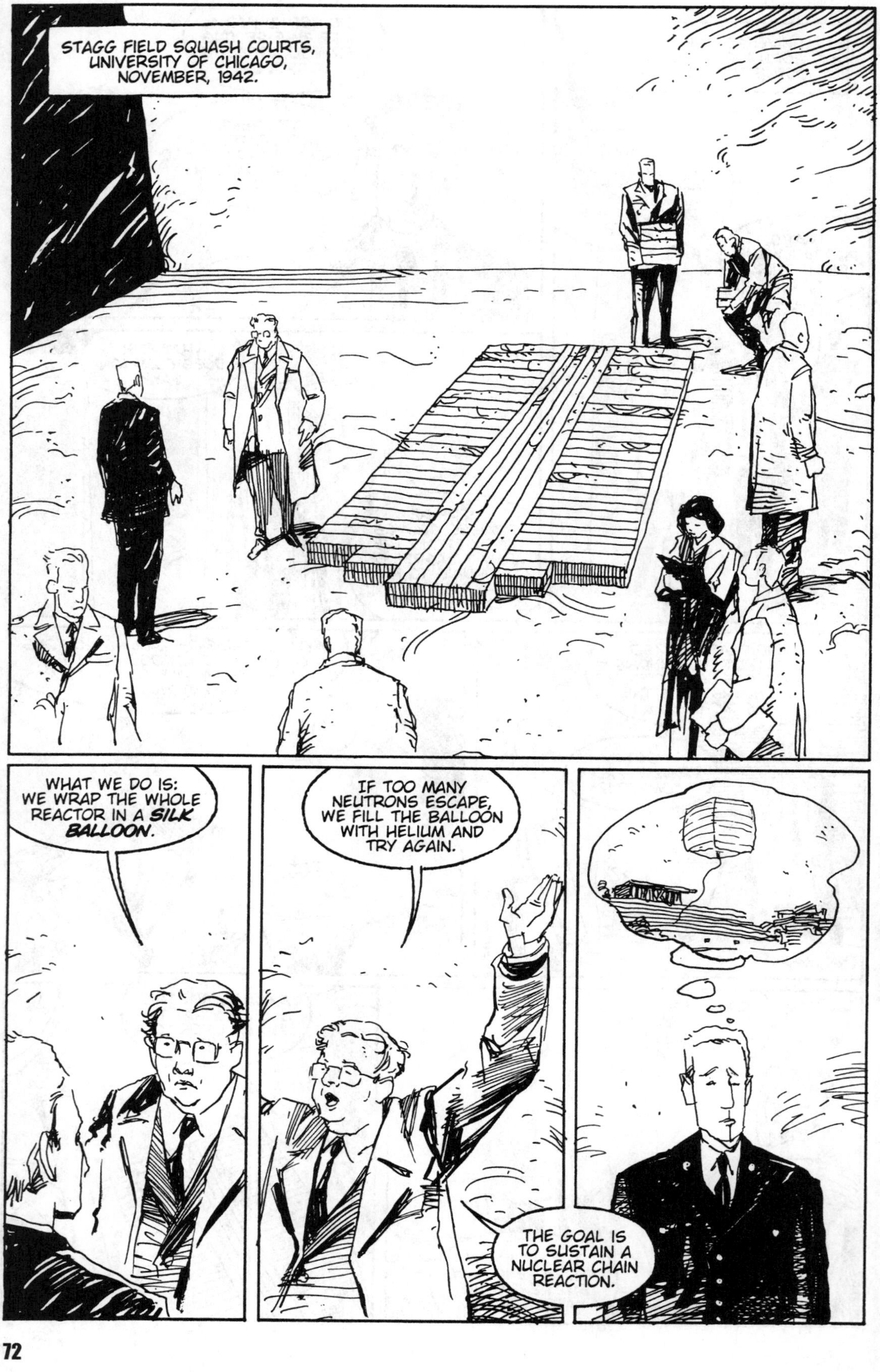
STAGG FIELD SQUASH COURTS, UNIVERSITY OF CHICAGO, NOVEMBER, 1942.
WHAT WE DO IS: WE WRAP THE WHOLE REACTOR IN A SILK BALLOON.
IF TOO MANY NEUTRONS ESCAPE, WE FILL THE BALLOON WITH HELIUM AND TRY AGAIN.
THE GOAL IS TO SUSTAIN A NUCLEAR CHAIN REACTION.

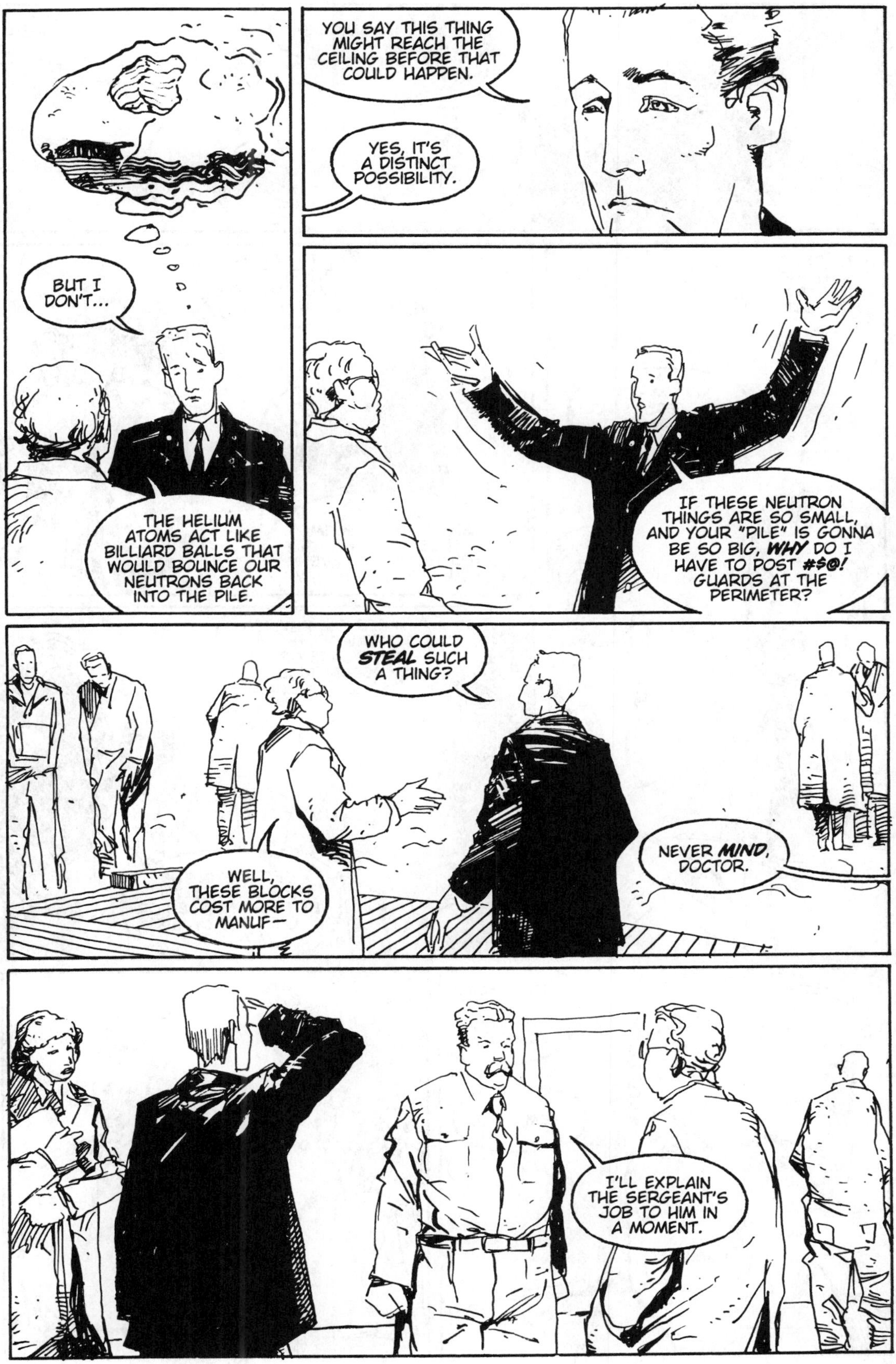
YOU SAY THIS THING MIGHT REACH THE CEILING BEFORE THAT COULD HAPPEN.
YES, IT'S A DISTINCT POSSIBILITY.
BUT I DON'T...
THE HELIUM ATOMS ACT LIKE BILLIARD BALLS THAT WOULD BOUNCE OUR NEUTRONS BACK INTO THE PILE.
IF THESE NEUTRON THINGS ARE SO SMALL, AND YOUR "PILE" IS GONNA BE SO BIG, WHY DO I HAVE TO POST #$@! GUARDS AT THE PERIMETER?
WHO COULD STEAL SUCH A THING?
WELL, THESE BLOCKS COST MORE TO MANUF—
NEVER MIND, DOCTOR.
I'LL EXPLAIN THE SERGEANT'S JOB TO HIM IN A MOMENT.

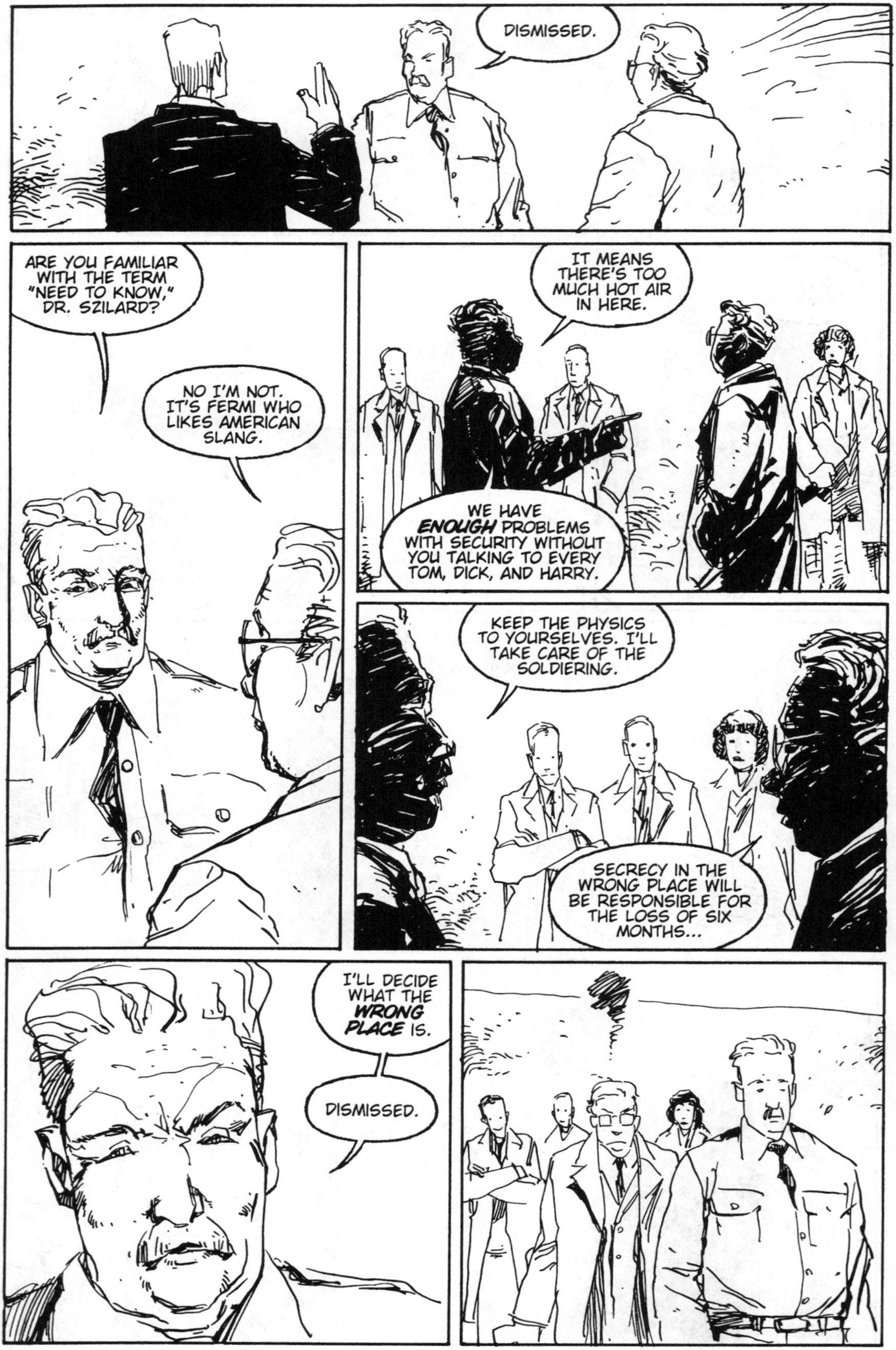
DISMISSED.
ARE YOU FAMILIAR WITH THE TERM "NEED TO KNOW," DR. SZILARD?
NO I'M NOT. IT'S FERMI WHO LIKES AMERICAN SLANG.
IT MEANS THERE'S TOO MUCH HOT AIR IN HERE.
WE HAVE ENOUGH PROBLEMS WITH SECURITY WITHOUT YOU TALKING TO EVERY TOM, DICK, AND HARRY.
KEEP THE PHYSICS TO YOURSELVES. I'LL TAKE CARE OF THE SOLDIERING.
SECRECY IN THE WRONG PLACE WILL BE RESPONSIBLE FOR THE LOSS OF SIX MONTHS...
I'LL DECIDE WHAT THE WRONG PLACE IS.
DISMISSED.

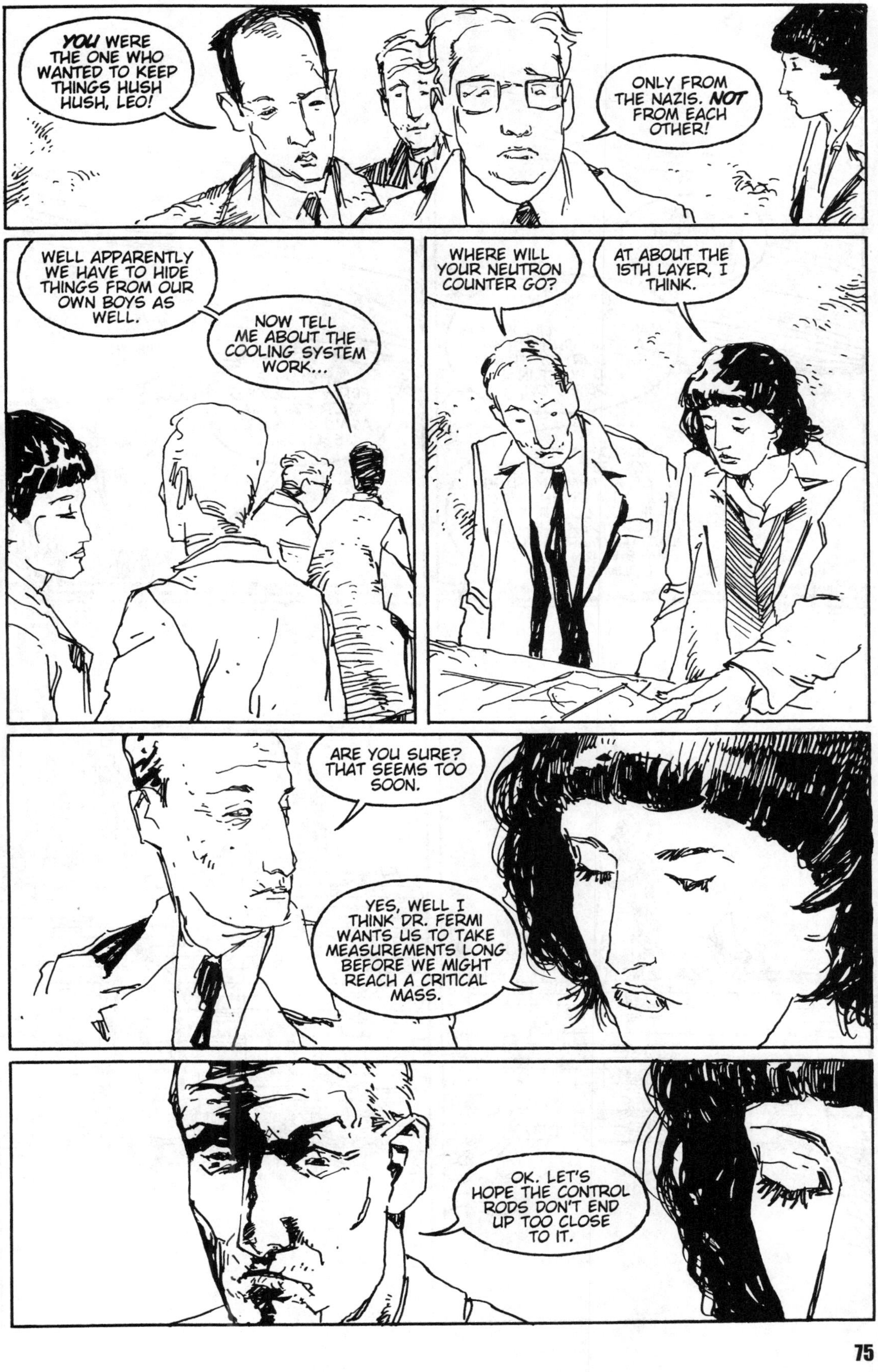
YOU WERE THE ONE WHO WANTED TO KEEP THINGS HUSH HUSH, LEO!
ONLY FROM THE NAZIS. NOT FROM EACH OTHER!
WELL APPARENTLY WE HAVE TO HIDE THINGS FROM OUR OWN BOYS AS WELL.
NOW TELL ME ABOUT THE COOLING SYSTEM WORK...
WHERE WILL YOUR NEUTRON COUNTER GO?
AT ABOUT THE 15TH LAYER, I THINK.
ARE YOU SURE? THAT SEEMS TOO SOON.
YES, WELL I THINK DR. FERMI WANTS US TO TAKE MEASUREMENTS LONG BEFORE WE MIGHT REACH A CRITICAL MASS.
OK. LET'S HOPE THE CONTROL RODS DON'T END UP TOO CLOSE TO IT.

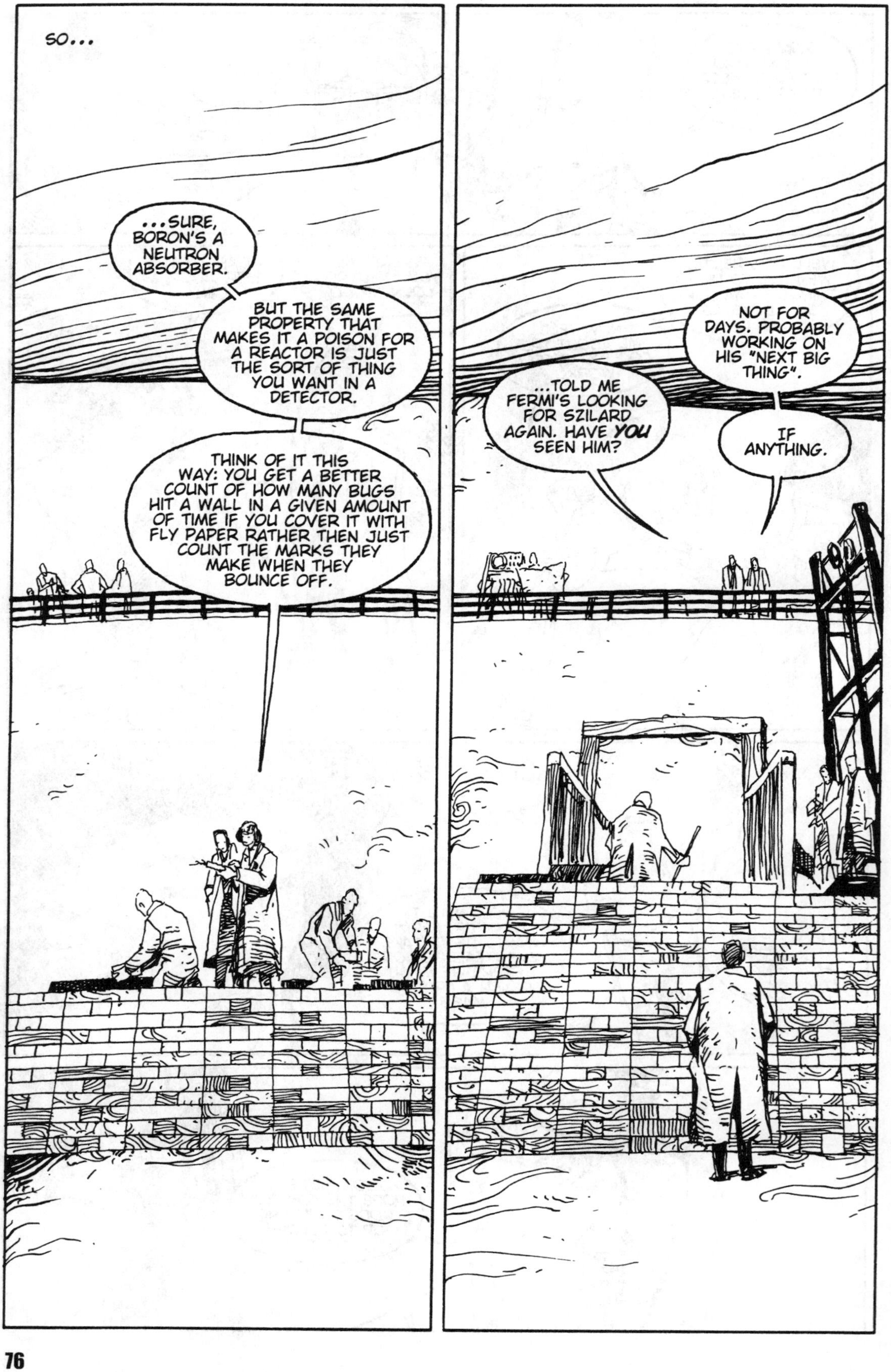
SO...
...SURE, BORON'S A NEUTRON ABSORBER.
BUT THE SAME PROPERTY THAT MAKES IT A POISON FOR A REACTOR IS JUST THE SORT OF THING YOU WANT IN A DETECTOR.
THINK OF IT THIS WAY: YOU GET A BETTER COUNT OF HOW MANY BUGS HIT A WALL IN A GIVEN AMOUNT OF TIME IF YOU COVER IT WITH FLY PAPER RATHER THEN JUST COUNT THE MARKS THEY MAKE WHEN THEY BOUNCE OFF.
...TOLD ME FERMI'S LOOKING FOR SZILARD AGAIN. HAVE YOU SEEN HIM?
NOT FOR DAYS. PROBABLY WORKING ON HIS "NEXT BIG THING".
IF ANYTHING.

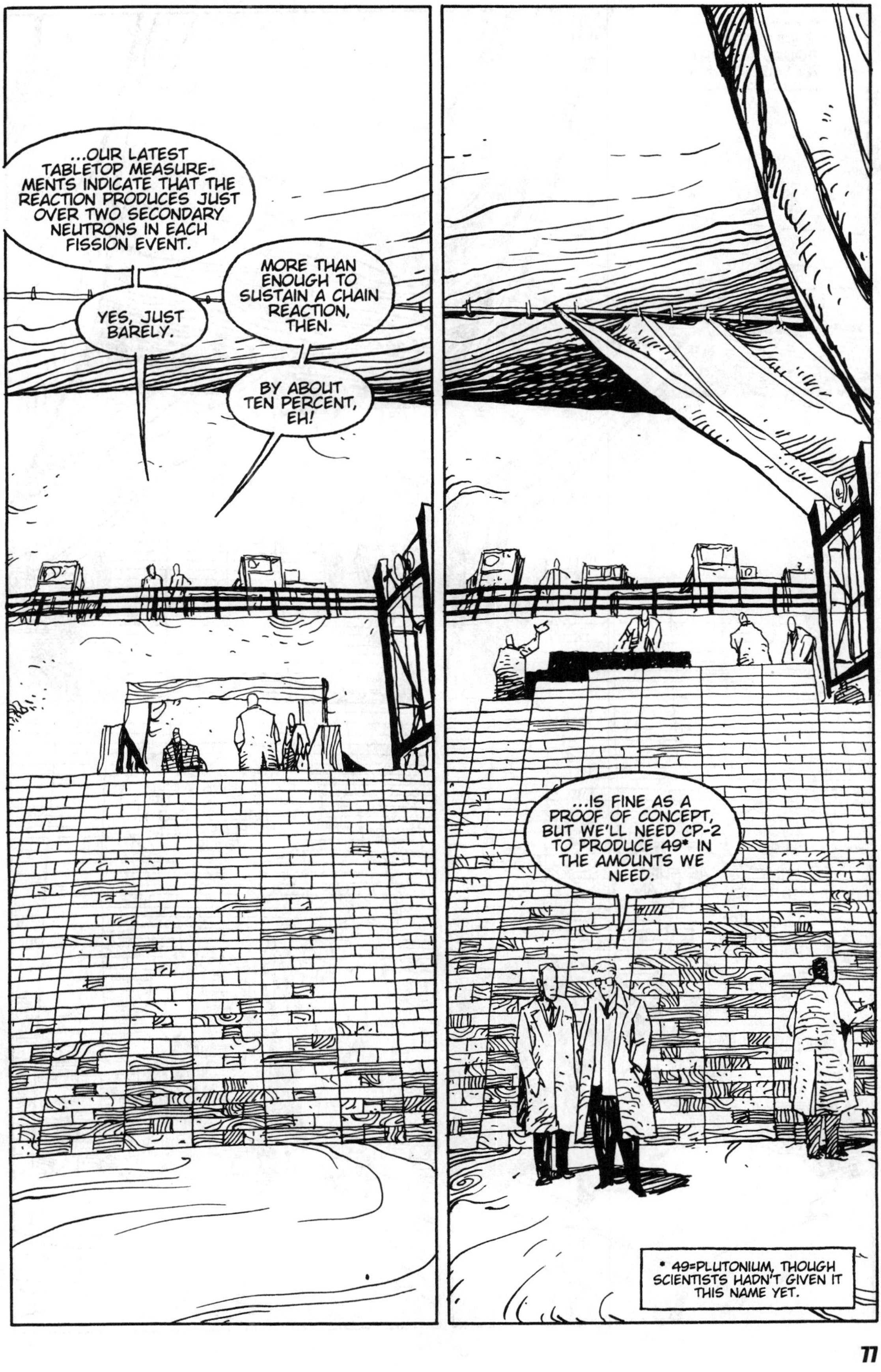
...OUR LATEST TABLETOP MEASUREMENTS INDICATE THAT THE REACTION PRODUCES JUST OVER TWO SECONDARY NEUTRONS IN EACH FISSION EVENT.
YES, JUST BARELY.
MORE THAN ENOUGH TO SUSTAIN A CHAIN REACTION, THEN.
BY ABOUT TEN PERCENT, EH!
...IS FINE AS A PROOF OF CONCEPT, BUT WE'LL NEED CP-2 TO PRODUCE 49* IN THE AMOUNTS WE NEED.
* 49=PLUTONIUM, THOUGH SCIENTISTS HADN'T GIVEN IT THIS NAME YET.

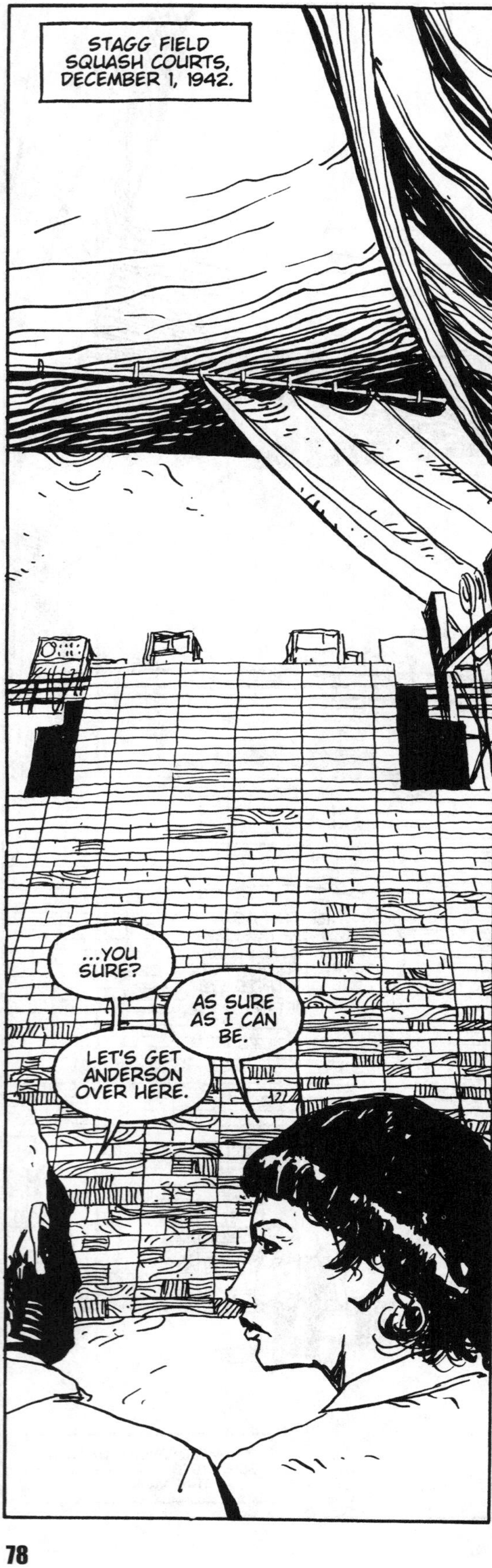
STAGG FIELD SQUASH COURTS, DECEMBER 1, 1942.
...YOU SURE?
AS SURE AS I CAN BE.
LET'S GET ANDERSON OVER HERE.

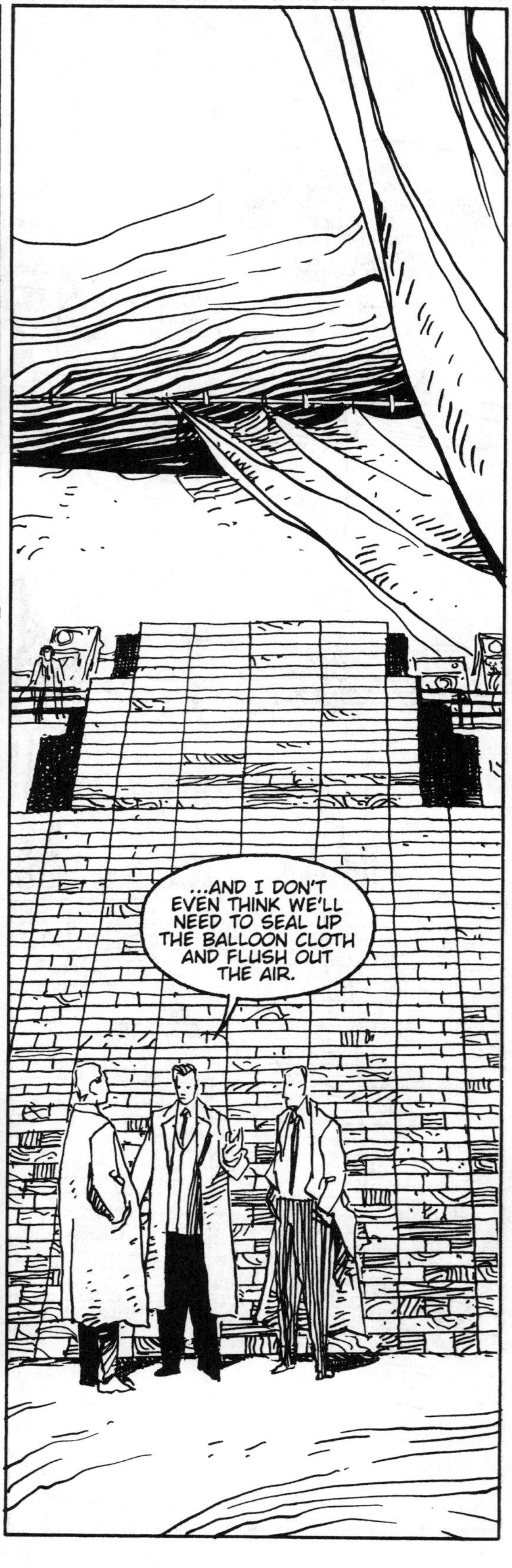
...AND I DON'T EVEN THINK WE'LL NEED TO SEAL UP THE BALLOON CLOTH AND FLUSH OUT THE AIR.

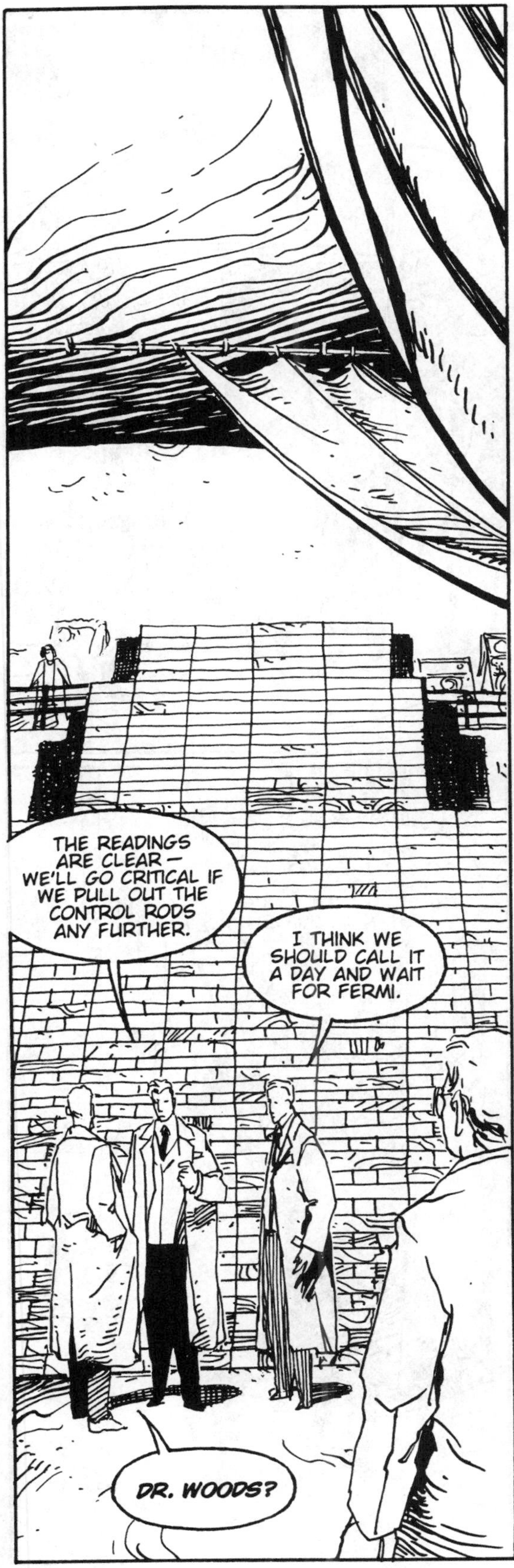
THE READINGS ARE CLEAR — WE'LL GO CRITICAL IF WE PULL OUT THE CONTROL RODS ANY FURTHER.
I THINK WE SHOULD CALL IT A DAY AND WAIT FOR FERMI.
DR. WOODS?

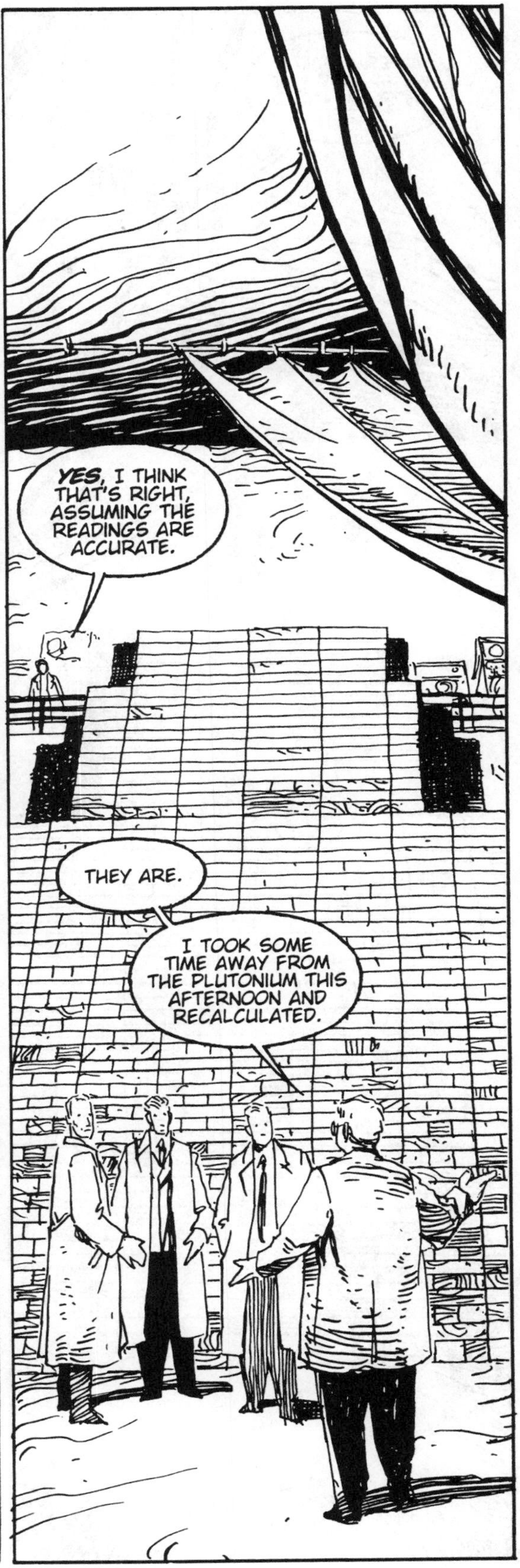
YES, I THINK THAT'S RIGHT, ASSUMING THE READINGS ARE ACCURATE.
THEY ARE.
I TOOK SOME TIME AWAY FROM THE PLUTONIUM THIS AFTERNOON AND RECALCULATED.

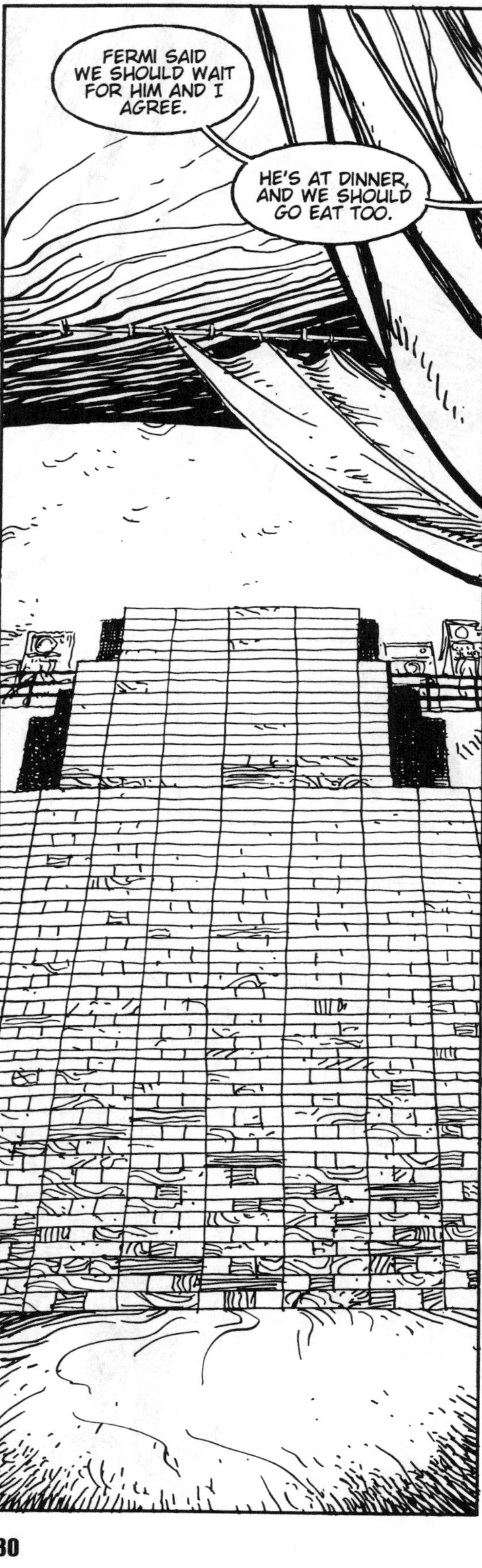
FERMI SAID WE SHOULD WAIT FOR HIM AND I AGREE.
HE'S AT DINNER, AND WE SHOULD GO EAT TOO.

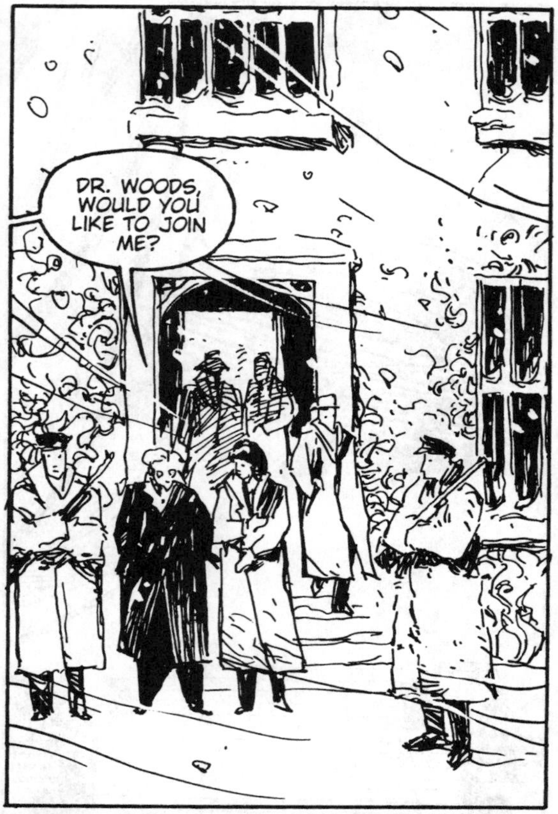
DR. WOODS, WOULD YOU LIKE TO JOIN ME?

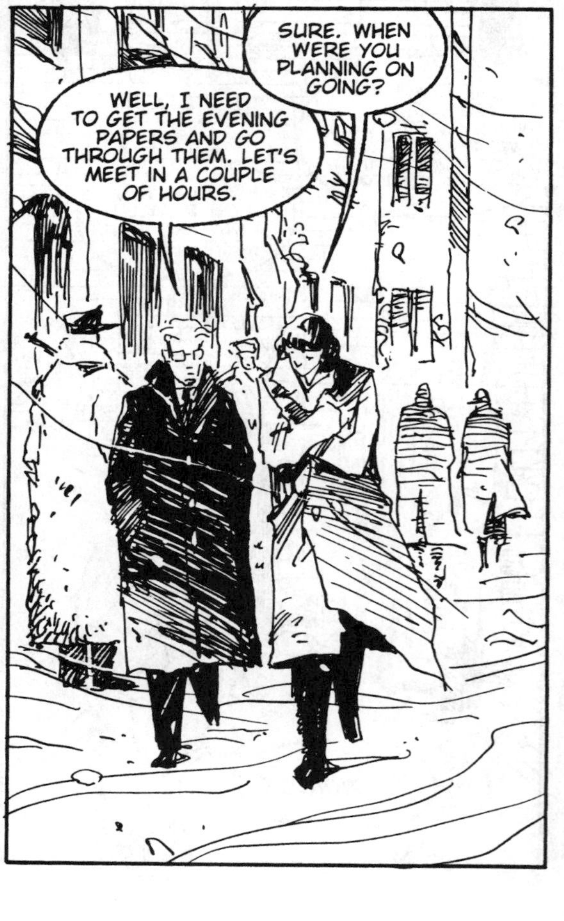
SURE. WHEN WERE YOU PLANNING ON GOING?
WELL, I NEED TO GET THE EVENING PAPERS AND GO THROUGH THEM. LET'S MEET IN A COUPLE OF HOURS.

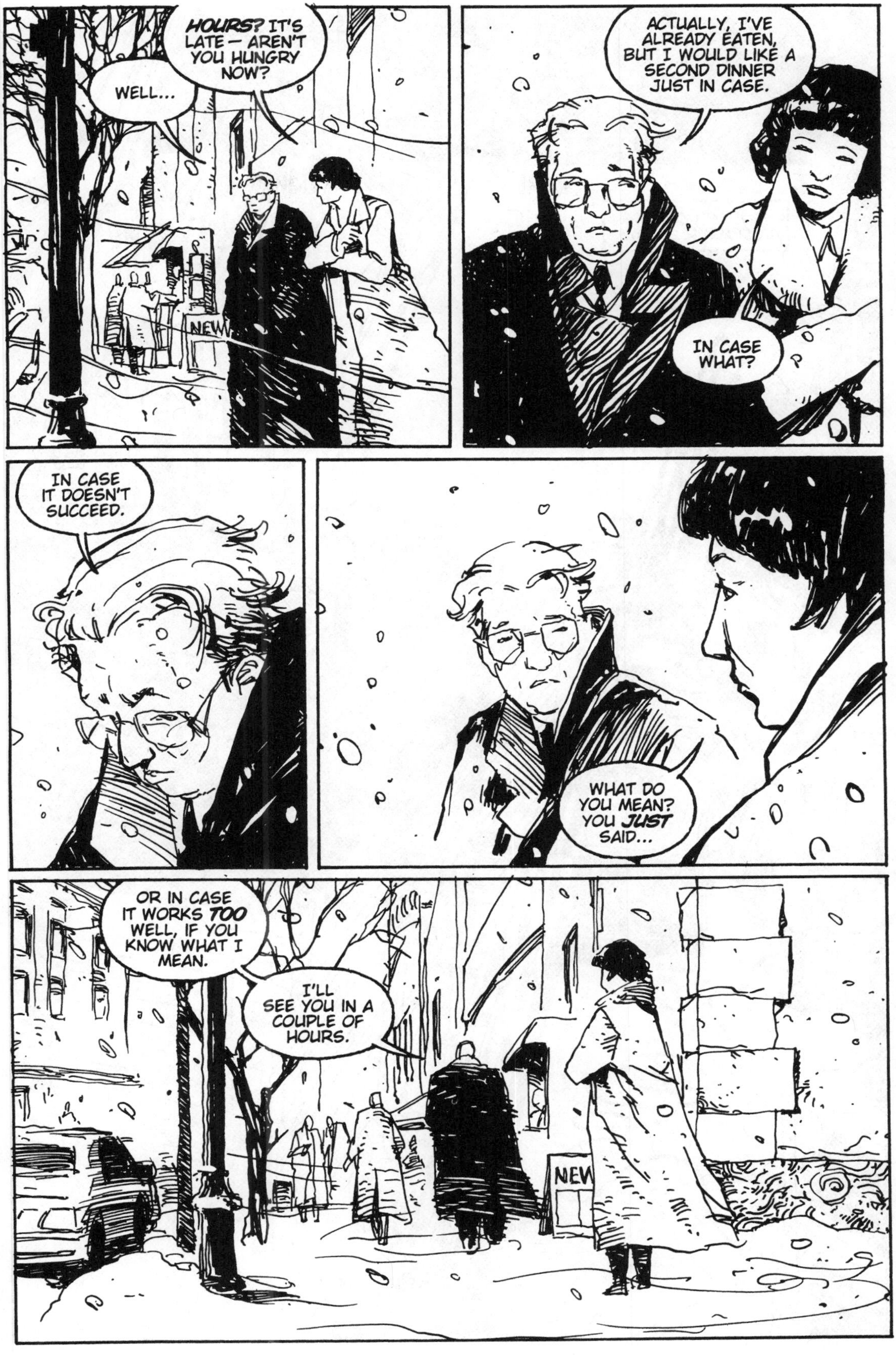
WELL...
HOURS? IT'S LATE — AREN'T YOU HUNGRY NOW?
NEW
ACTUALLY, I'VE ALREADY EATEN, BUT I WOULD LIKE A SECOND DINNER JUST IN CASE.
IN CASE WHAT?
IN CASE IT DOESN'T SUCCEED.
WHAT DO YOU MEAN? YOU JUST SAID...
OR IN CASE IT WORKS TOO WELL, IF YOU KNOW WHAT I MEAN.
I'LL SEE YOU IN A COUPLE OF HOURS.
NEW

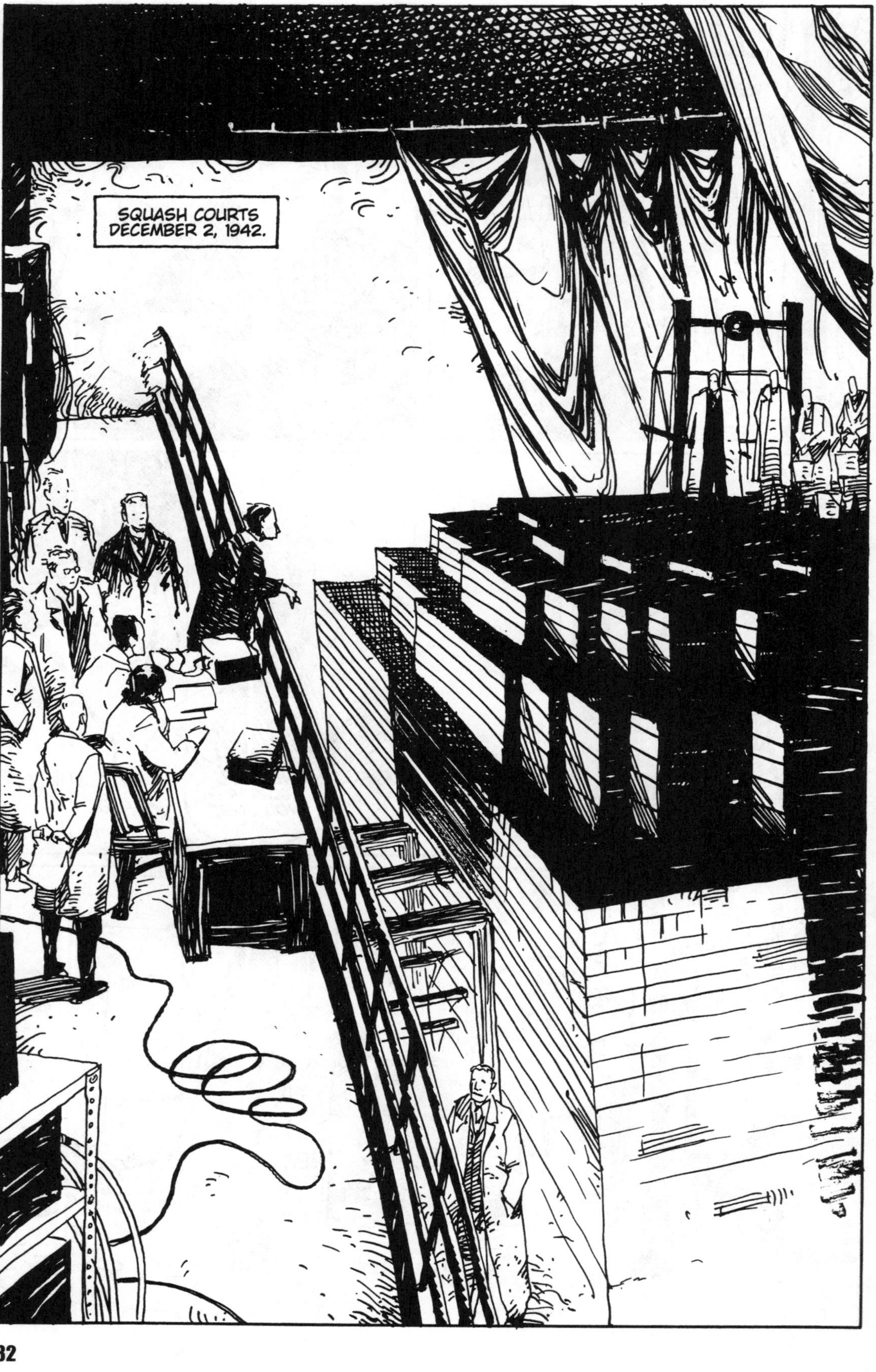
SQUASH COURTS
DECEMBER 2, 1942.

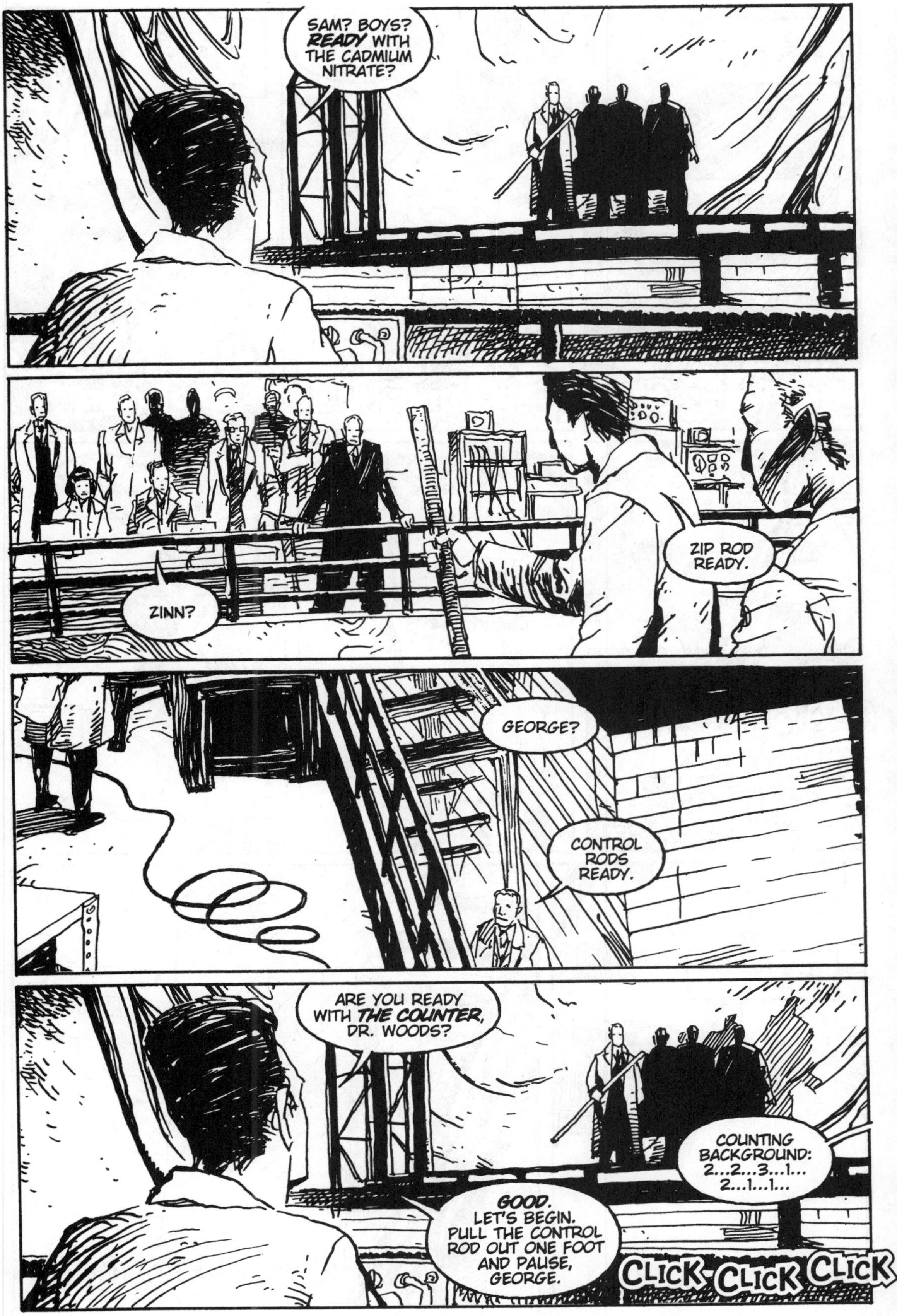
SAM? BOYS? READY WITH THE CADMIUM NITRATE?
ZIP ROD READY.
ZINN?
GEORGE?
CONTROL RODS READY.
ARE YOU READY WITH THE COUNTER, DR. WOODS?
COUNTING BACKGROUND: 2...2...3...1... 2...1...1...
GOOD. LET'S BEGIN. PULL THE CONTROL ROD OUT ONE FOOT AND PAUSE, GEORGE.
CLICK CLICK CLICK

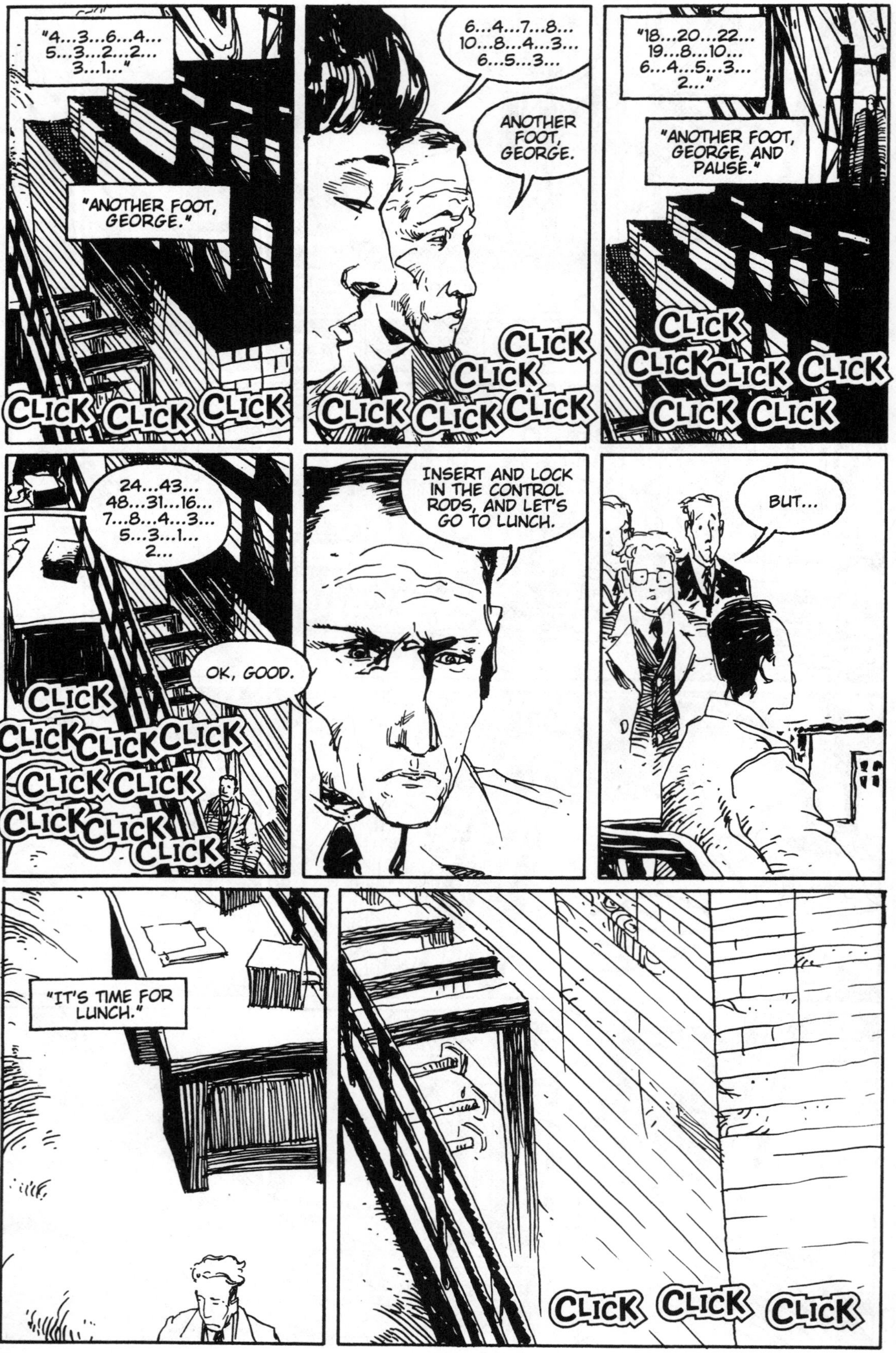
"4...3...6...4...
5...3...2...2...
3...1..."
"ANOTHER FOOT,
GEORGE."
CLICK CLICK CLICK
6...4...7...8...
10...8...4...3...
6...5...3...
ANOTHER
FOOT,
GEORGE.
CLICK CLICK CLICK CLICK CLICK
"18...20...22...
19...8...10...
6...4...5...3...
2..."
"ANOTHER FOOT,
GEORGE, AND
PAUSE."
CLICK CLICK CLICK CLICK CLICK CLICK
24...43...
48...31...16...
7...8...4...3...
5...3...1...
2...
OK, GOOD.
CLICK CLICK CLICK CLICK CLICK CLICK CLICK CLICK CLICK
INSERT AND LOCK
IN THE CONTROL
RODS, AND LET'S
GO TO LUNCH.
BUT...
"IT'S TIME FOR
LUNCH."
CLICK CLICK CLICK

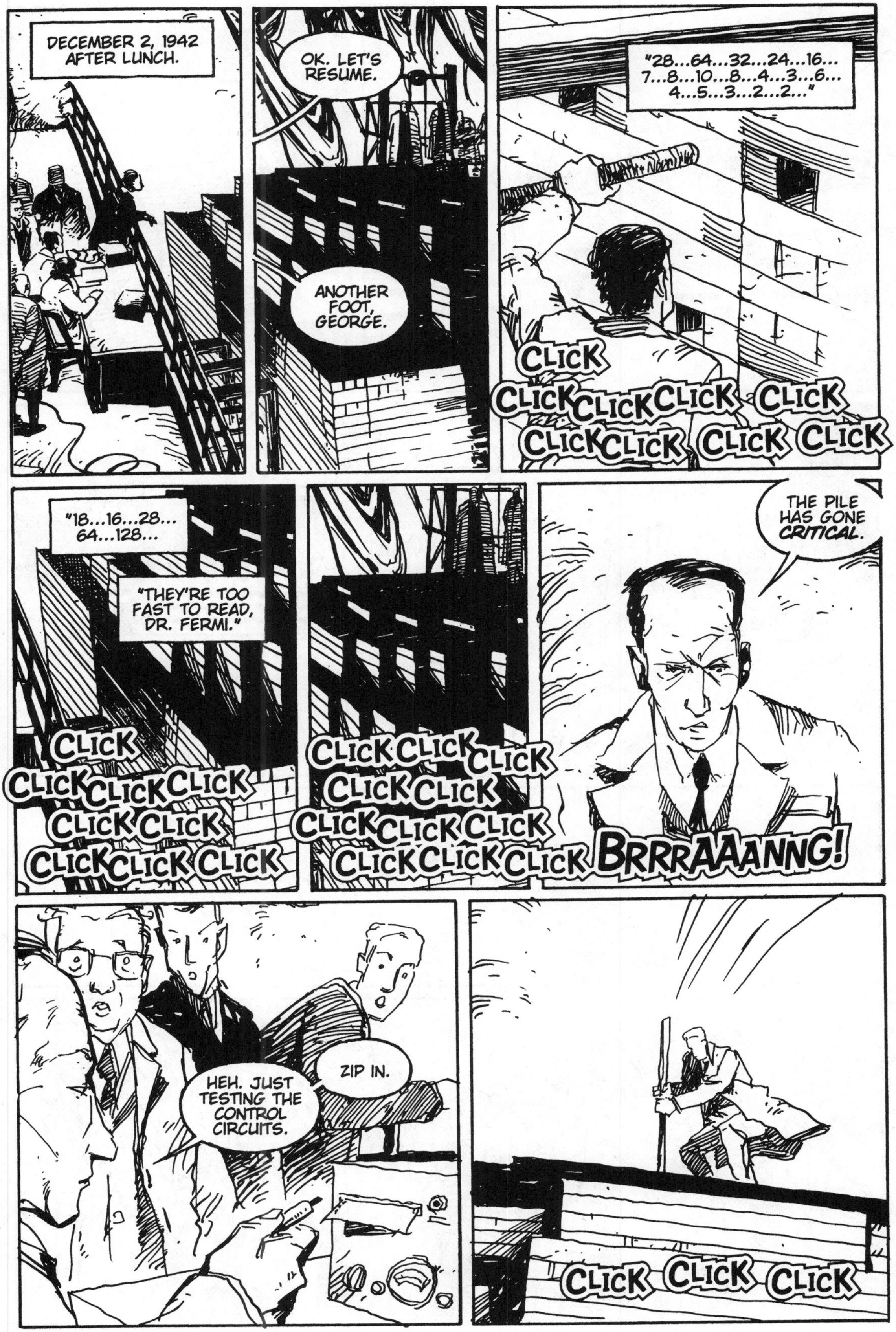

DECEMBER 2, 1942
AFTER LUNCH.
OK. LET'S RESUME.
ANOTHER FOOT, GEORGE.
"28...64...32...24...16...
7...8...10...8...4...3...6...
4...5...3...2...2..."
CLICK
CLICK CLICK CLICK CLICK
CLICK CLICK CLICK CLICK
"18...16...28...
64...128...
"THEY'RE TOO FAST TO READ, DR. FERMI."
CLICK
CLICK CLICK CLICK
CLICK CLICK
CLICK CLICK CLICK
CLICK CLICK CLICK
CLICK CLICK
CLICK CLICK CLICK
CLICK CLICK CLICK
THE PILE HAS GONE *CRITICAL*.
BRRRAAANNG!
HEH. JUST TESTING THE CONTROL CIRCUITS.
ZIP IN.
CLICK CLICK CLICK

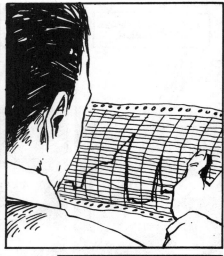

COME ON UP HERE, FELLAS. AND BRING SOME PAPER CUPS.

POP!

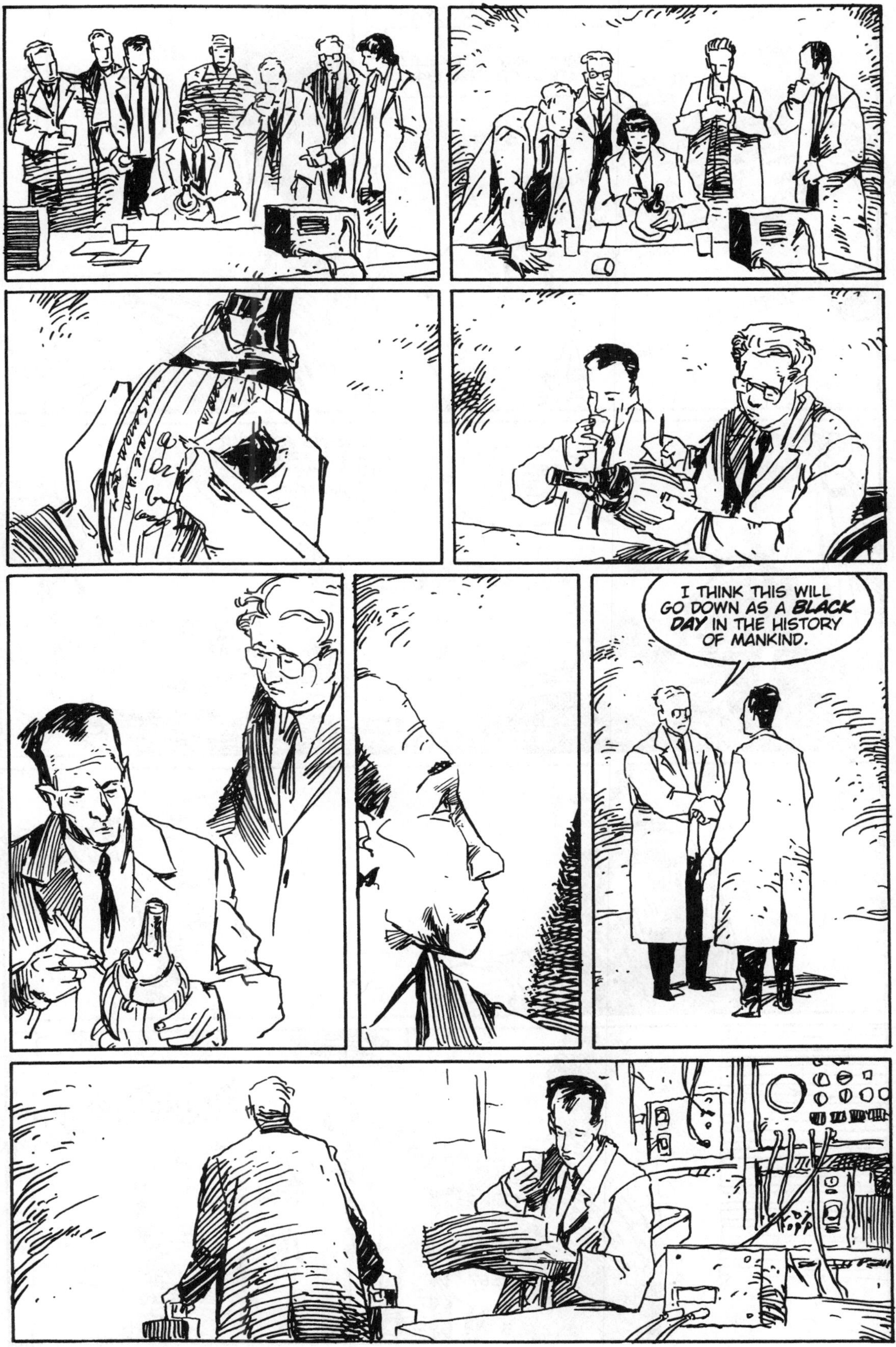
I THINK THIS WILL GO DOWN AS A BLACK DAY IN THE HISTORY OF MANKIND.

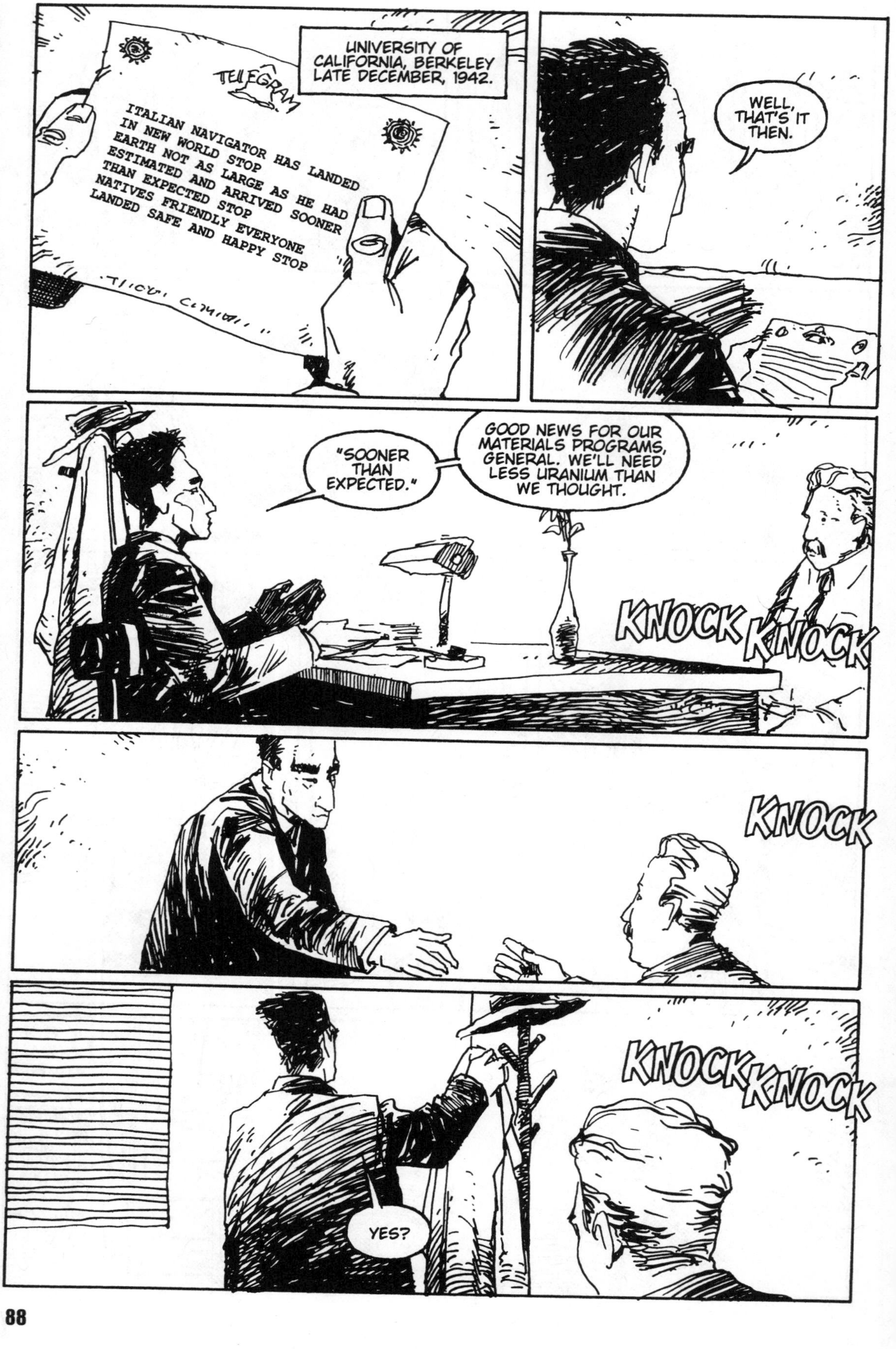
UNIVERSITY OF CALIFORNIA, BERKELEY LATE DECEMBER, 1942.
TELEGRAM
ITALIAN NAVIGATOR HAS LANDED IN NEW WORLD STOP EARTH NOT AS LARGE AS HE HAD ESTIMATED AND ARRIVED SOONER THAN EXPECTED STOP NATIVES FRIENDLY EVERYONE LANDED SAFE AND HAPPY STOP
WELL, THAT'S IT THEN.
"SOONER THAN EXPECTED."
GOOD NEWS FOR OUR MATERIALS PROGRAMS, GENERAL. WE'LL NEED LESS URANIUM THAN WE THOUGHT.
KNOCK KNOCK
KNOCK
KNOCK KNOCK
YES?

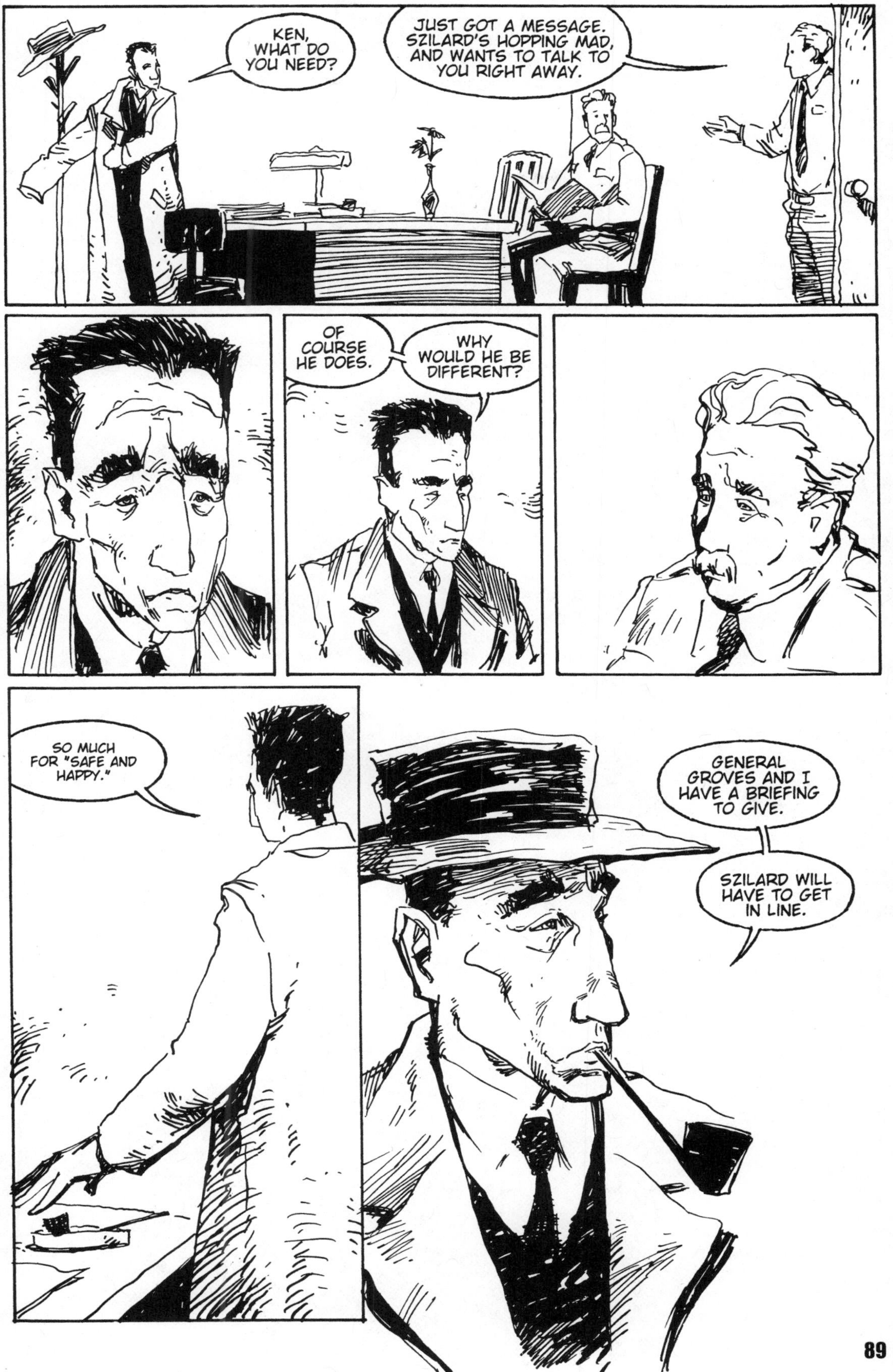
KEN, WHAT DO YOU NEED?
JUST GOT A MESSAGE. SZILARD'S HOPPING MAD, AND WANTS TO TALK TO YOU RIGHT AWAY.
OF COURSE HE DOES.
WHY WOULD HE BE DIFFERENT?
SO MUCH FOR "SAFE AND HAPPY."
GENERAL GROVES AND I HAVE A BRIEFING TO GIVE.
SZILARD WILL HAVE TO GET IN LINE.

interlude

A Los Alamos Primer

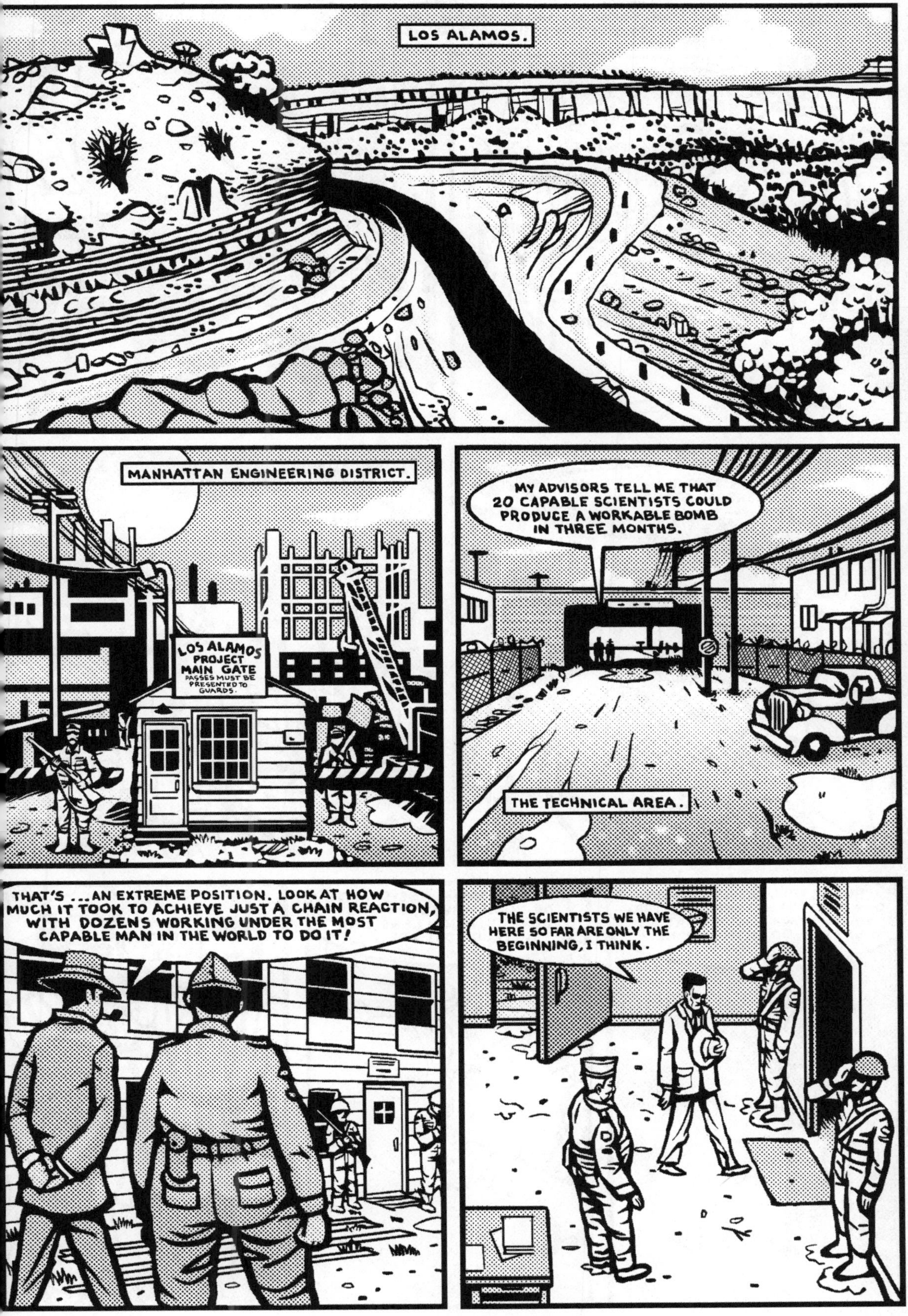
LOS ALAMOS.
MANHATTAN ENGINEERING DISTRICT.
LOS ALAMOS PROJECT MAIN GATE PASSES MUST BE PRESENTED TO GUARDS.
MY ADVISORS TELL ME THAT 20 CAPABLE SCIENTISTS COULD PRODUCE A WORKABLE BOMB IN THREE MONTHS.
THE TECHNICAL AREA.
THAT'S ...AN EXTREME POSITION. LOOK AT HOW MUCH IT TOOK TO ACHIEVE JUST A CHAIN REACTION, WITH DOZENS WORKING UNDER THE MOST CAPABLE MAN IN THE WORLD TO DO IT!
THE SCIENTISTS WE HAVE HERE SO FAR ARE ONLY THE BEGINNING, I THINK.

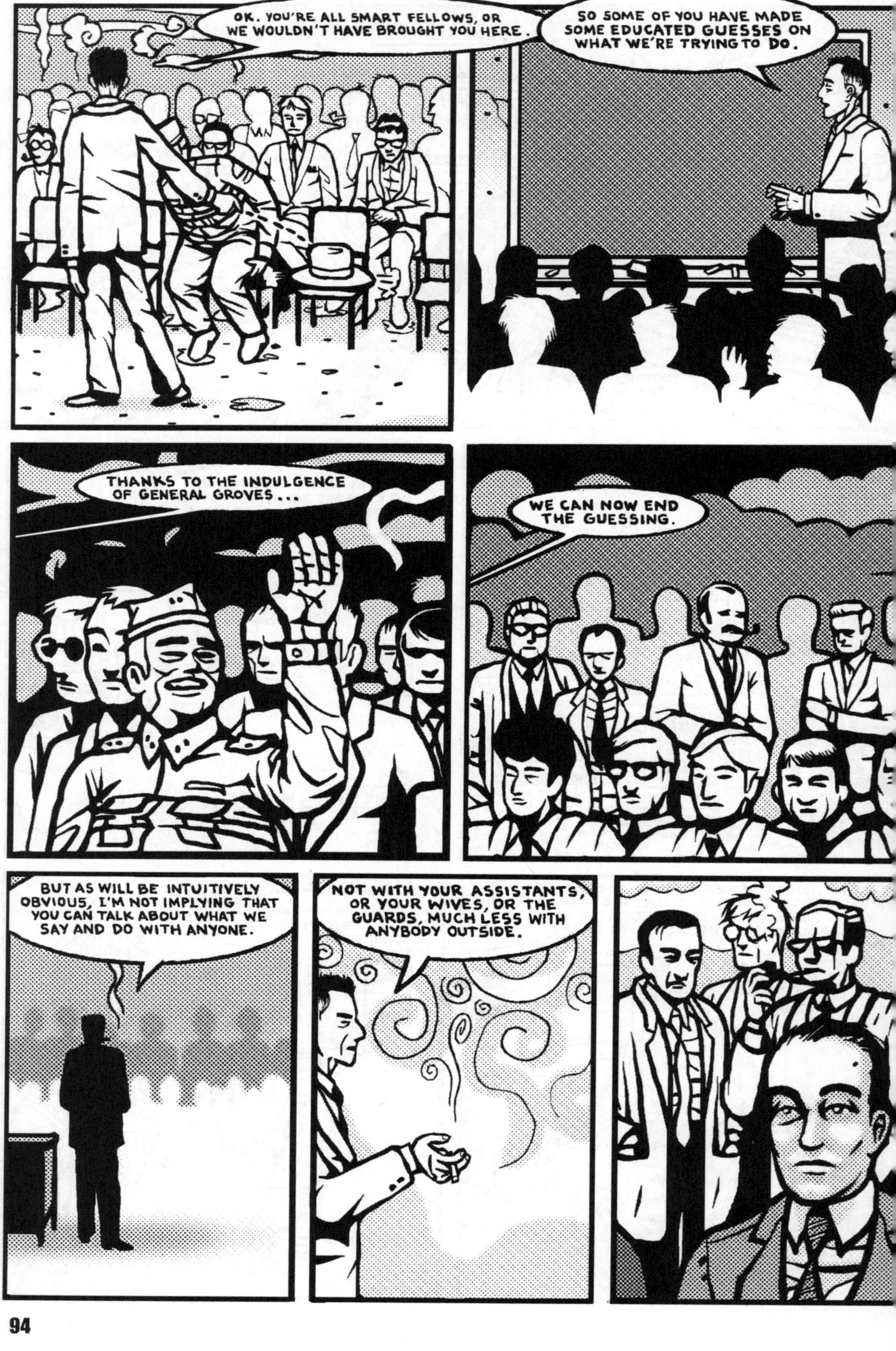
OK. YOU'RE ALL SMART FELLOWS, OR WE WOULDN'T HAVE BROUGHT YOU HERE.
SO SOME OF YOU HAVE MADE SOME EDUCATED GUESSES ON WHAT WE'RE TRYING TO DO.
THANKS TO THE INDULGENCE OF GENERAL GROVES...
WE CAN NOW END THE GUESSING.
BUT AS WILL BE INTUITIVELY OBVIOUS, I'M NOT IMPLYING THAT YOU CAN TALK ABOUT WHAT WE SAY AND DO WITH ANYONE.
NOT WITH YOUR ASSISTANTS, OR YOUR WIVES, OR THE GUARDS, MUCH LESS WITH ANYBODY OUTSIDE.

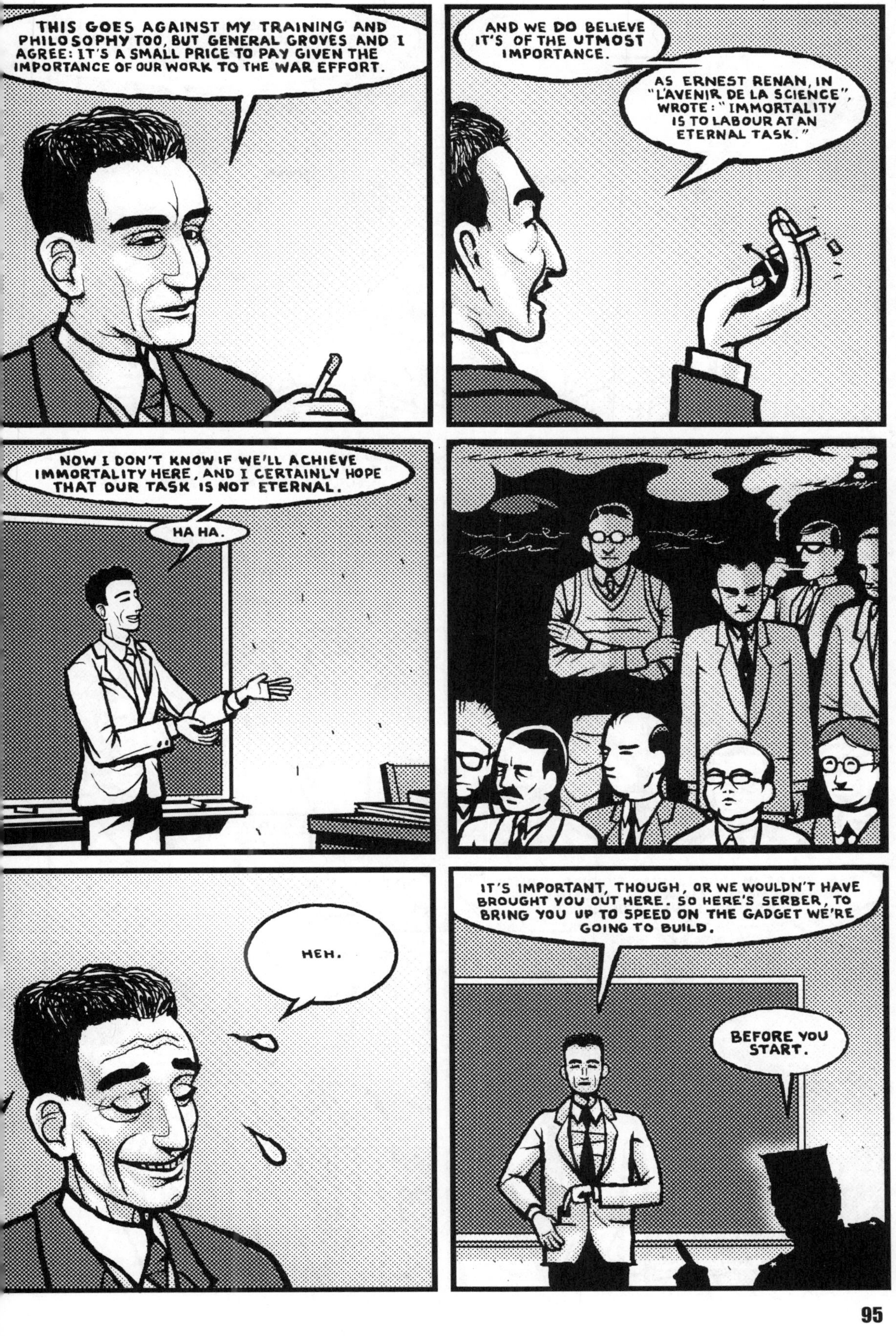
THIS GOES AGAINST MY TRAINING AND PHILOSOPHY TOO, BUT GENERAL GROVES AND I AGREE: IT'S A SMALL PRICE TO PAY GIVEN THE IMPORTANCE OF OUR WORK TO THE WAR EFFORT.
AND WE DO BELIEVE IT'S OF THE UTMOST IMPORTANCE.
AS ERNEST RENAN, IN "L'AVENIR DE LA SCIENCE", WROTE: "IMMORTALITY IS TO LABOUR AT AN ETERNAL TASK."
NOW I DON'T KNOW IF WE'LL ACHIEVE IMMORTALITY HERE, AND I CERTAINLY HOPE THAT OUR TASK IS NOT ETERNAL.
HA HA.
HEH.
IT'S IMPORTANT, THOUGH, OR WE WOULDN'T HAVE BROUGHT YOU OUT HERE. SO HERE'S SERBER, TO BRING YOU UP TO SPEED ON THE GADGET WE'RE GOING TO BUILD.
BEFORE YOU START.

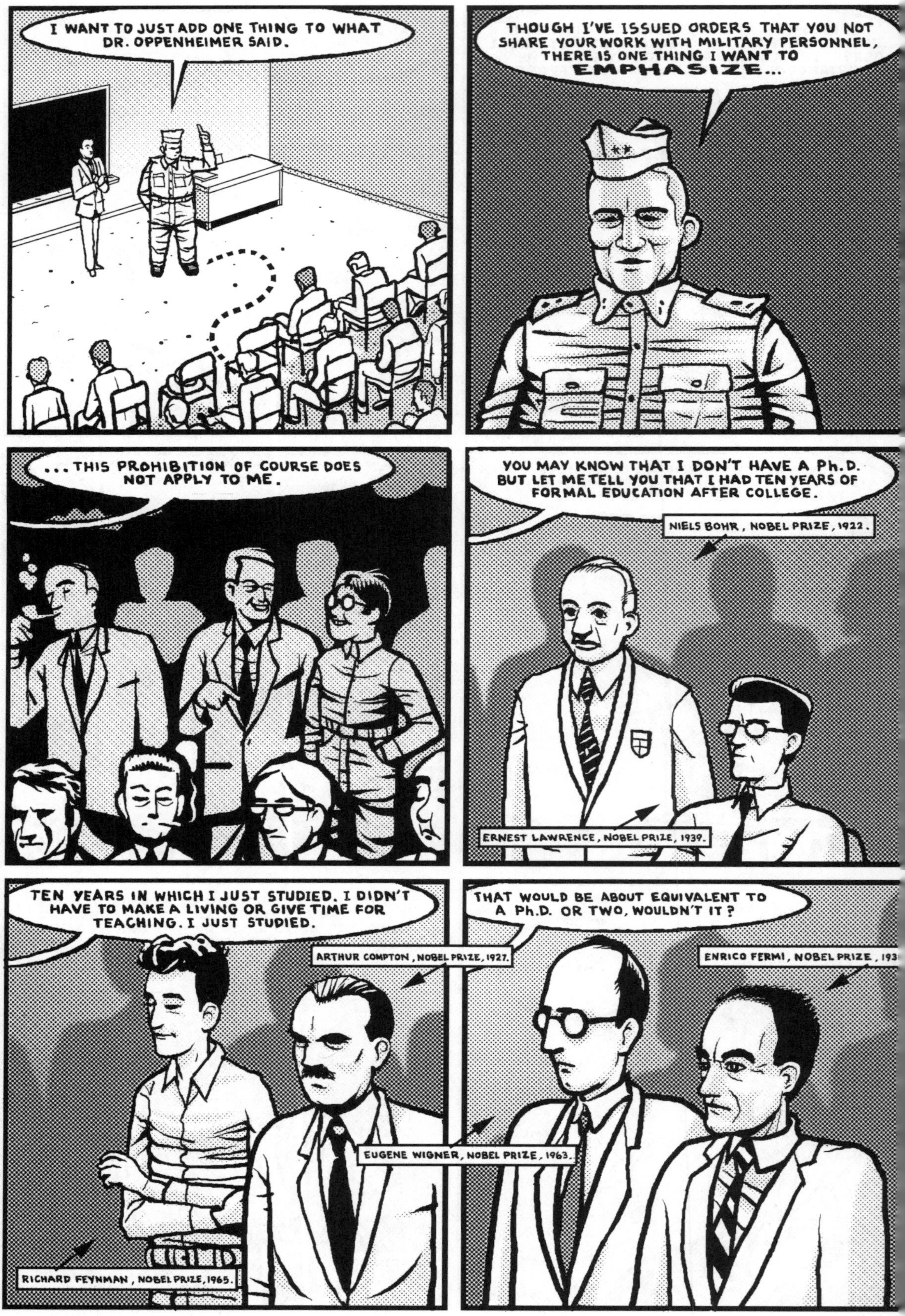
I WANT TO JUST ADD ONE THING TO WHAT DR. OPPENHEIMER SAID.
THOUGH I'VE ISSUED ORDERS THAT YOU NOT SHARE YOUR WORK WITH MILITARY PERSONNEL, THERE IS ONE THING I WANT TO EMPHASIZE...
...THIS PROHIBITION OF COURSE DOES NOT APPLY TO ME.
YOU MAY KNOW THAT I DON'T HAVE A Ph.D. BUT LET ME TELL YOU THAT I HAD TEN YEARS OF FORMAL EDUCATION AFTER COLLEGE.
NIELS BOHR, NOBEL PRIZE, 1922.
ERNEST LAWRENCE, NOBEL PRIZE, 1939.
TEN YEARS IN WHICH I JUST STUDIED. I DIDN'T HAVE TO MAKE A LIVING OR GIVE TIME FOR TEACHING. I JUST STUDIED.
ARTHUR COMPTON, NOBEL PRIZE, 1927.
RICHARD FEYNMAN, NOBEL PRIZE, 1965.
THAT WOULD BE ABOUT EQUIVALENT TO A Ph.D. OR TWO, WOULDN'T IT?
ENRICO FERMI, NOBEL PRIZE, 193
EUGENE WIGNER, NOBEL PRIZE, 1963.

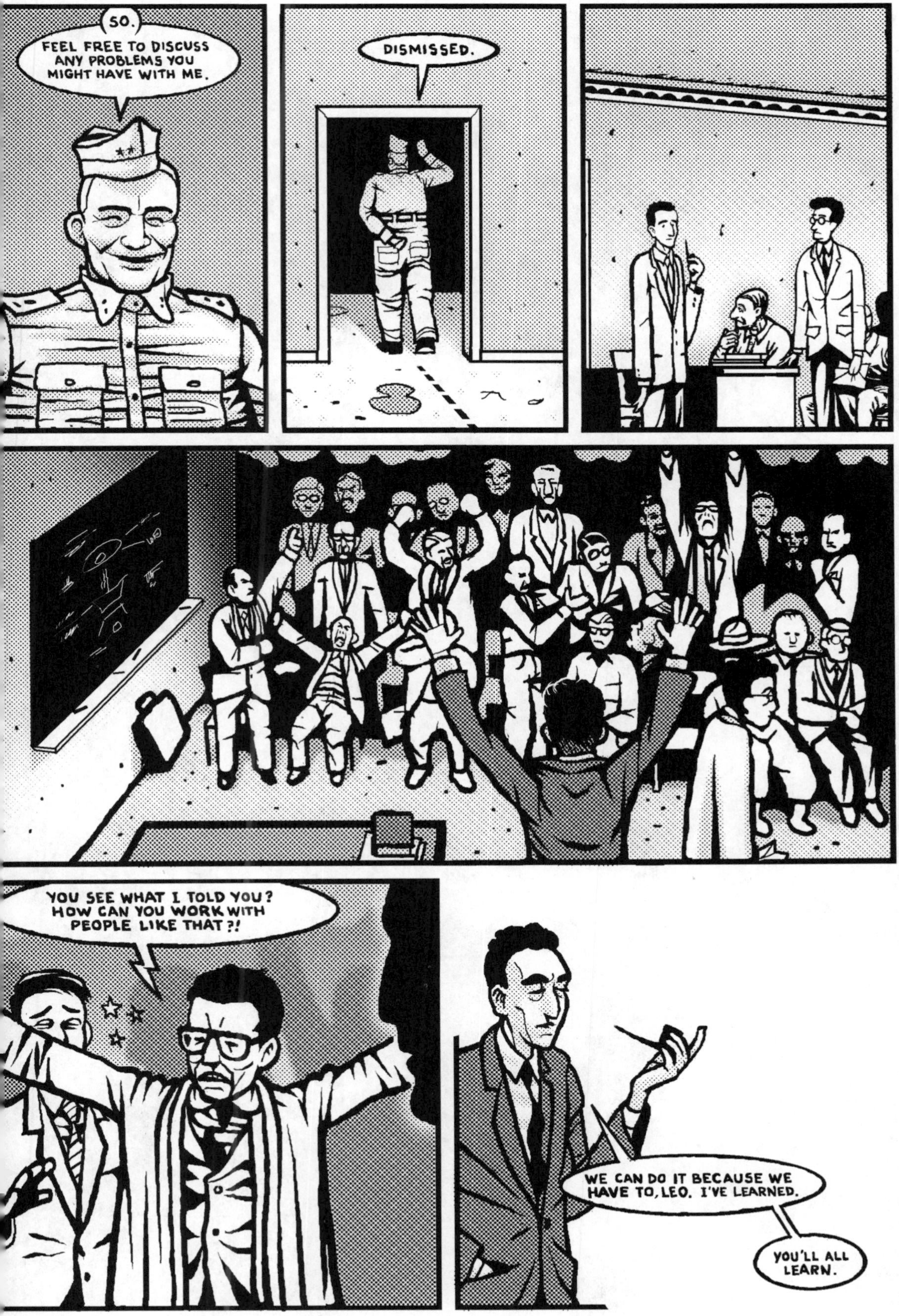
SO.
FEEL FREE TO DISCUSS ANY PROBLEMS YOU MIGHT HAVE WITH ME.
DISMISSED.
YOU SEE WHAT I TOLD YOU? HOW CAN YOU WORK WITH PEOPLE LIKE THAT?!
WE CAN DO IT BECAUSE WE HAVE TO, LEO. I'VE LEARNED.
YOU'LL ALL LEARN.

work
(1945)

Some people claim to have wondered at the time about the future of mankind. I didn't. We were at war and the damned thing worked.
　　—Norris Bradbury, quoted in *The Day the Sun Rose Twice*

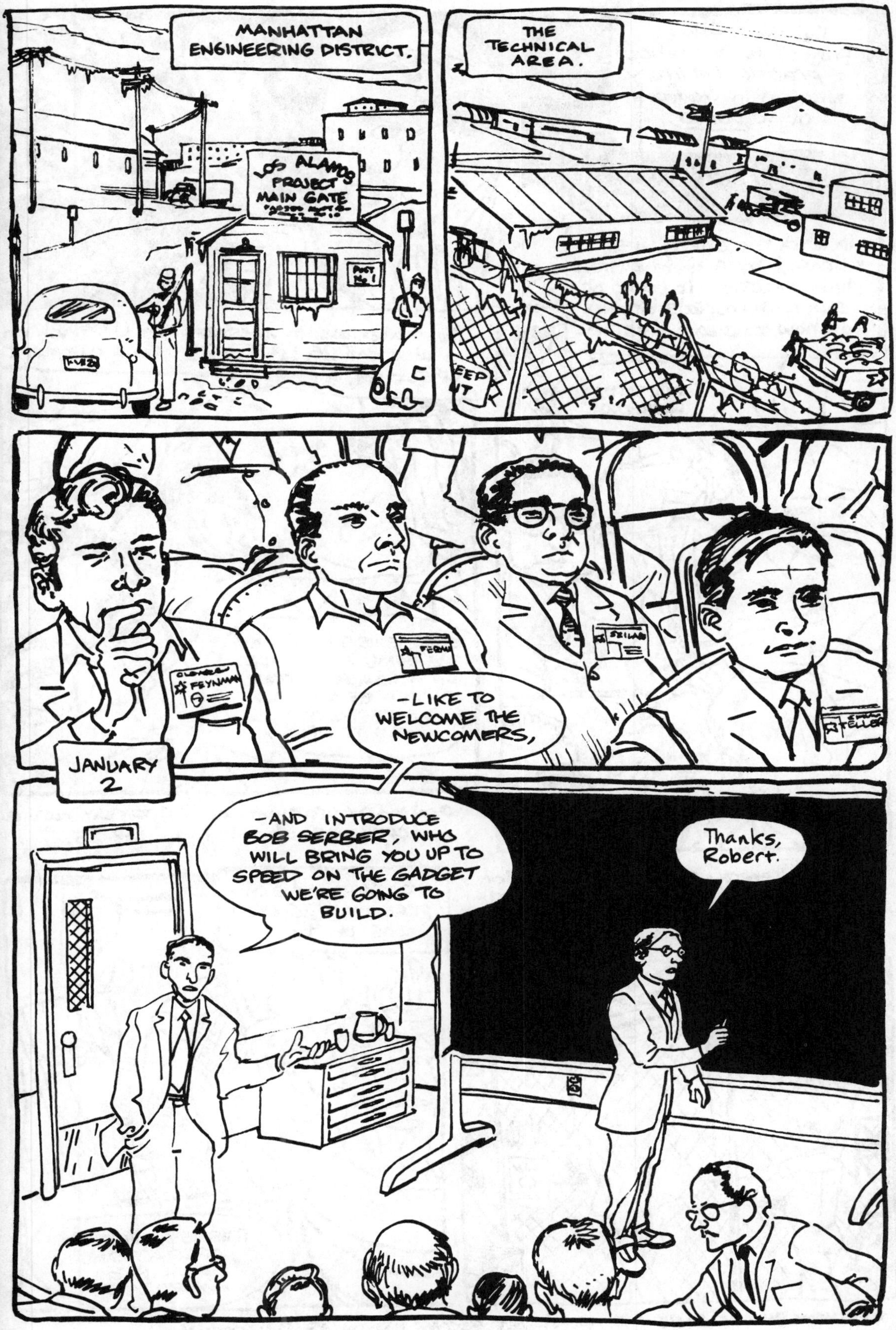
MANHATTAN ENGINEERING DISTRICT.
LOS ALAMOS PROJECT MAIN GATE
THE TECHNICAL AREA.
FEYNMAN
TELLER
-LIKE TO WELCOME THE NEWCOMERS,
JANUARY 2
-AND INTRODUCE BOB SERBER, WHO WILL BRING YOU UP TO SPEED ON THE GADGET WE'RE GOING TO BUILD.
Thanks, Robert.

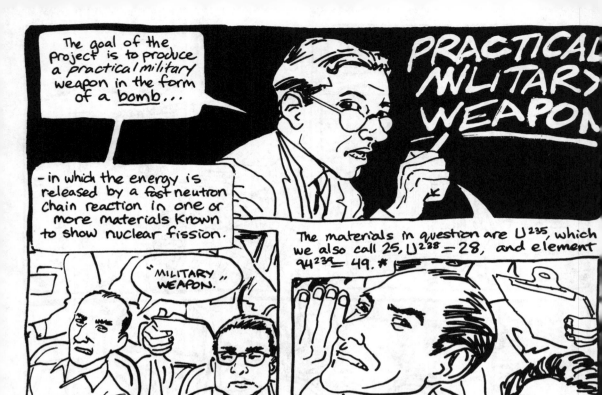

The goal of the project is to produce a *practical military* weapon in the form of a <u>bomb</u>...

PRACTICAL MILITARY WEAPON

- in which the energy is released by a *fast neutron chain reaction* in one or more materials known to show nuclear fission.

"MILITARY WEAPON."

The materials in question are U^{235}, which we also call 25, U^{238} = 28, and element 94^{239} = 49. *

EVEN IF WE BROUGHT 'EM THE BOMB READY-MADE ON A SILVER PLATTER THERE'D BE A 50-50 CHANCE THEY'D MESS IT UP.

"Ordinary uranium as it occurs in nature contains about 1/140 of 25."

"The direct energy release in the fission process is considerably more than 10,000,000 times the heat of reaction per atom in ordinary explosions."

"So, 2 pounds of uranium = 20,000 tons of t.n.t."

THIS IS A *MILITARY OPERATION,* DURING WARTIME.

*ELEMENT 94 WAS SO NEW IT HADN'T YET BECOME KNOWN AS PLUTONIUM.

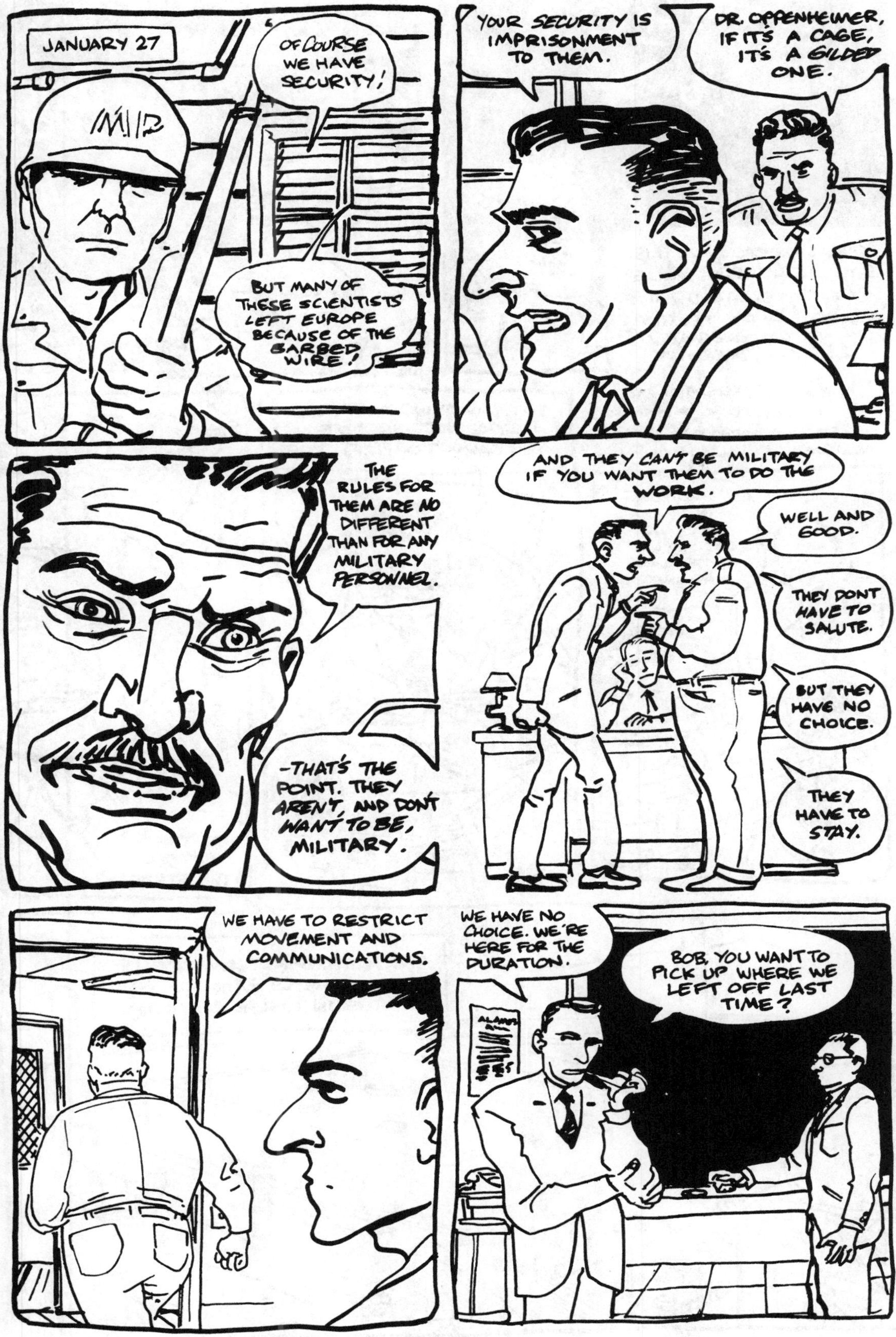
JANUARY 27
OF COURSE WE HAVE SECURITY!
BUT MANY OF THESE SCIENTISTS LEFT EUROPE BECAUSE OF THE BARBED WIRE!
YOUR SECURITY IS IMPRISONMENT TO THEM.
DR. OPPENHEIMER, IF IT'S A CAGE, IT'S A GILDED ONE.
THE RULES FOR THEM ARE NO DIFFERENT THAN FOR ANY MILITARY PERSONNEL.
-THAT'S THE POINT. THEY AREN'T, AND DON'T WANT TO BE, MILITARY.
AND THEY CAN'T BE MILITARY IF YOU WANT THEM TO DO THE WORK.
WELL AND GOOD.
THEY DONT HAVE TO SALUTE.
BUT THEY HAVE NO CHOICE.
THEY HAVE TO STAY.
WE HAVE TO RESTRICT MOVEMENT AND COMMUNICATIONS.
WE HAVE NO CHOICE. WE'RE HERE FOR THE DURATION.
BOB, YOU WANT TO PICK UP WHERE WE LEFT OFF LAST TIME?

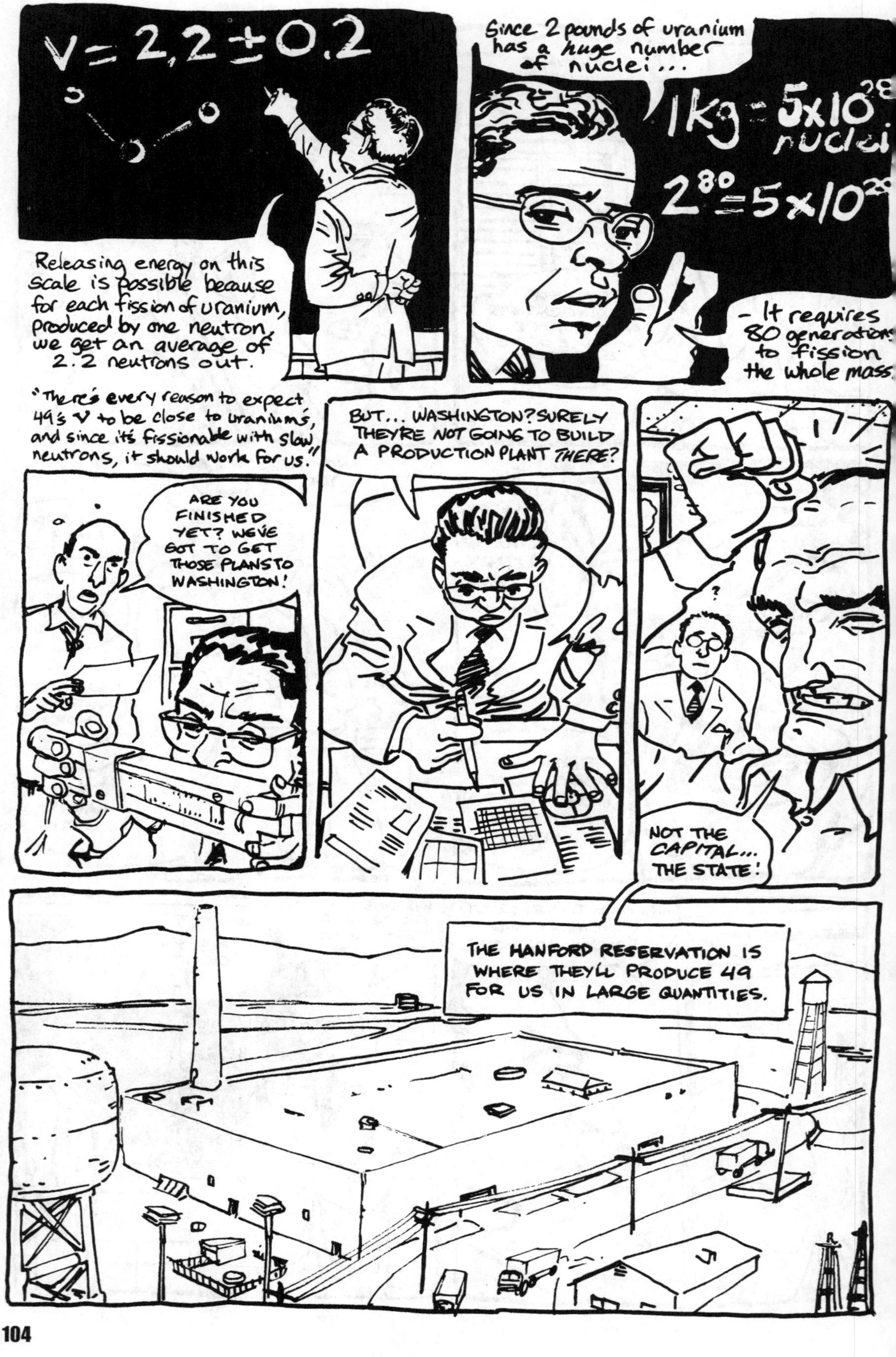
V=2,2±0.2
Releasing energy on this scale is possible because for each fission of uranium, produced by one neutron, we get an average of 2.2 neutrons out.
Since 2 pounds of uranium has a huge number of nuclei...
1kg = 5x10^28 nuclei
2^80 = 5x10^28
- It requires 80 generations to fission the whole mass.
"There's every reason to expect 49's V to be close to uranium's, and since it's fissionable with slow neutrons, it should work for us."
ARE YOU FINISHED YET? WE'VE GOT TO GET THOSE PLANS TO WASHINGTON!
BUT... WASHINGTON? SURELY THEY'RE NOT GOING TO BUILD A PRODUCTION PLANT THERE?
NOT THE CAPITAL... THE STATE!
THE HANFORD RESERVATION IS WHERE THEY'LL PRODUCE 49 FOR US IN LARGE QUANTITIES.

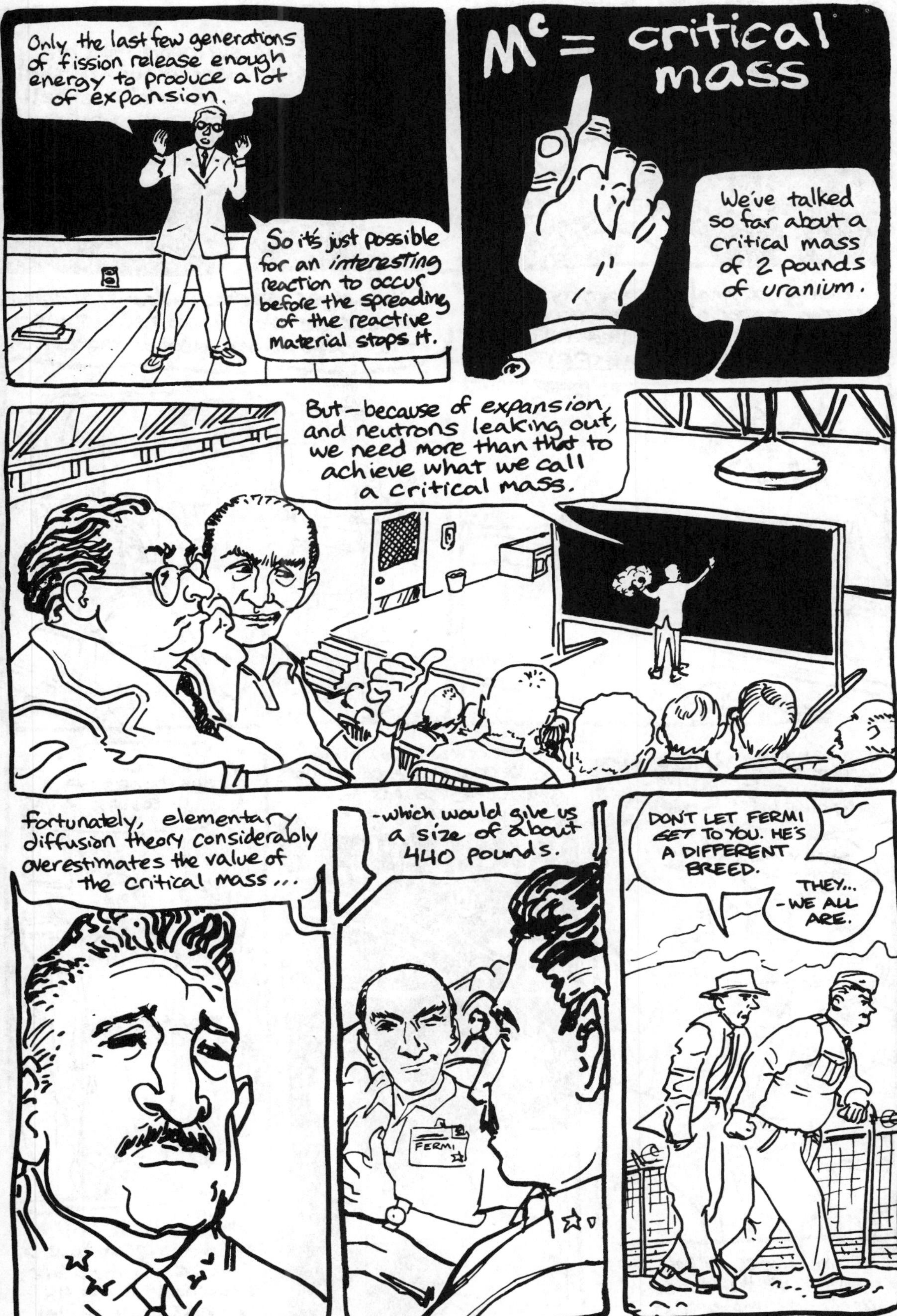
Only the last few generations of fission release enough energy to produce a lot of expansion.
So it's just possible for an *interesting* reaction to occur before the spreading of the reactive material stops it.
Mc = critical mass
We've talked so far about a critical mass of 2 pounds of uranium.
But—because of expansion, and neutrons leaking out, we need more than that to achieve what we call a critical mass.
fortunately, elementary diffusion theory considerably overestimates the value of the critical mass...
-which would give us a size of about 440 pounds.
FERMI
DON'T LET FERMI GET TO YOU. HE'S A DIFFERENT BREED.
THEY... -WE ALL ARE.

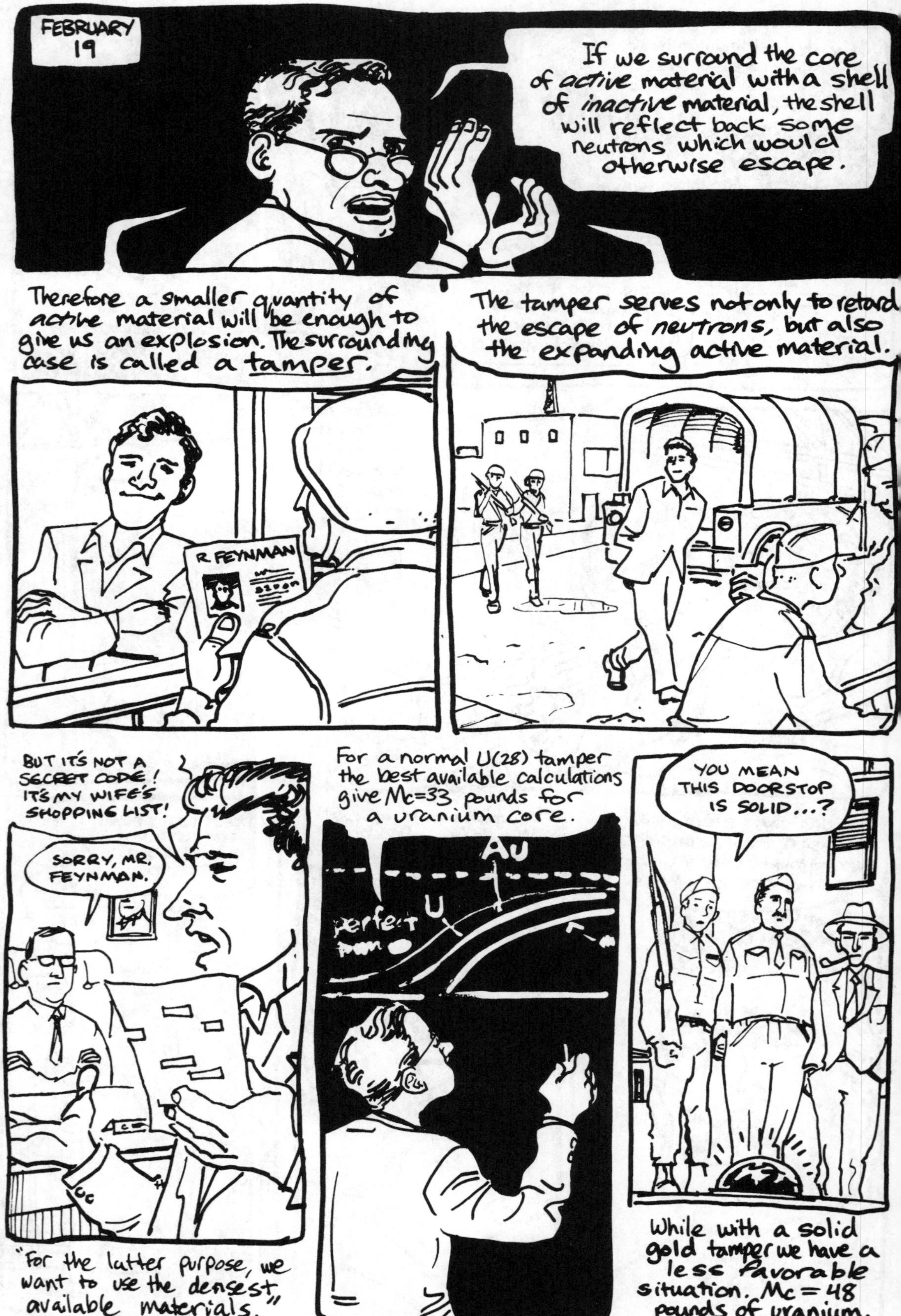
FEBRUARY 19
If we surround the core of active material with a shell of inactive material, the shell will reflect back some neutrons which would otherwise escape.
Therefore a smaller quantity of active material will be enough to give us an explosion. The surrounding case is called a tamper.
The tamper serves not only to retard the escape of neutrons, but also the expanding active material.
R FEYNMAN
BUT IT'S NOT A SECRET CODE! IT'S MY WIFE'S SHOPPING LIST!
SORRY, MR. FEYNMAN.
"For the latter purpose, we want to use the densest available materials."
For a normal U(28) tamper the best available calculations give Mc=33 pounds for a uranium core.
AU
U
YOU MEAN THIS DOORSTOP IS SOLID...?
While with a solid gold tamper we have a less favorable situation. Mc = 48 pounds of uranium.

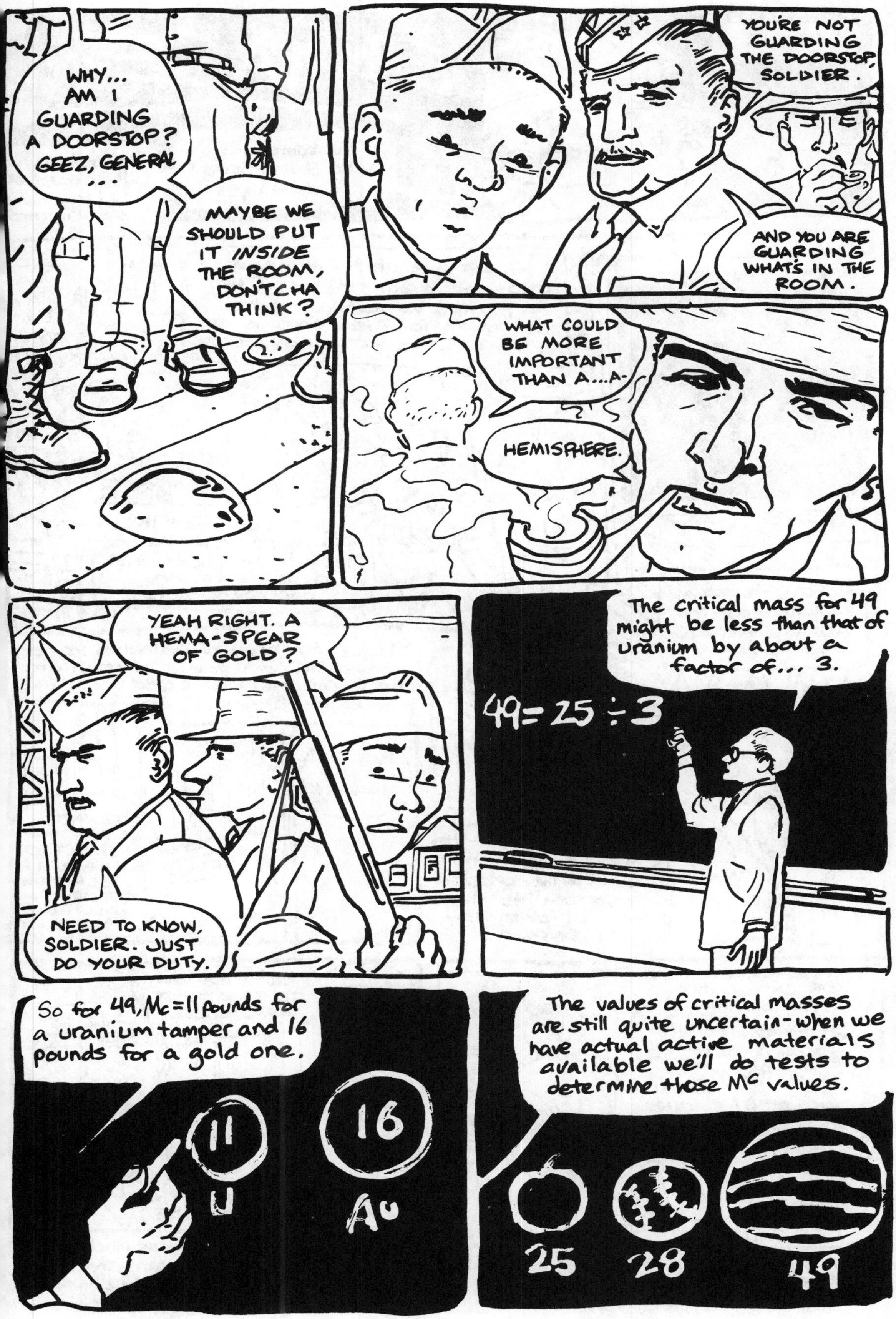
WHY... AM I GUARDING A DOORSTOP? GEEZ, GENERAL ...
MAYBE WE SHOULD PUT IT INSIDE THE ROOM, DON'TCHA THINK?
YOU'RE NOT GUARDING THE DOORSTOP, SOLDIER.
AND YOU ARE GUARDING WHAT'S IN THE ROOM.
WHAT COULD BE MORE IMPORTANT THAN A...A-
HEMISPHERE.
YEAH RIGHT. A HEMA-SPEAR OF GOLD?
NEED TO KNOW, SOLDIER. JUST DO YOUR DUTY.
The critical mass for 49 might be less than that of uranium by about a factor of... 3.
49= 25 ÷ 3
So for 49, Mc=11 pounds for a uranium tamper and 16 pounds for a gold one.
11
U
16
Au
The values of critical masses are still quite uncertain- when we have actual active materials available we'll do tests to determine those Mc values.
25
28
49

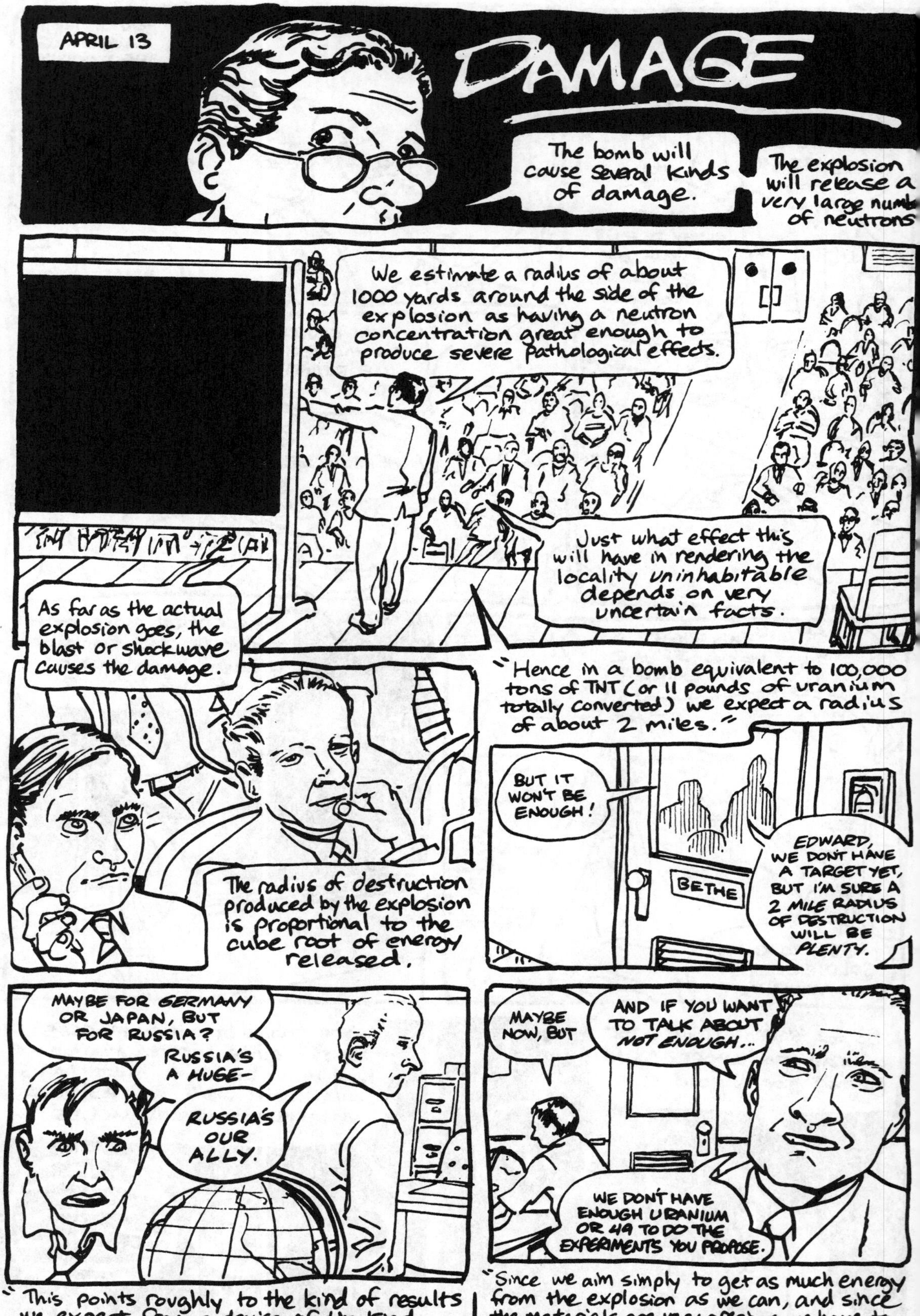

APRIL 13
DAMAGE
The bomb will cause several kinds of damage.
The explosion will release a very large numb of neutrons
We estimate a radius of about 1000 yards around the side of the explosion as having a neutron concentration great enough to produce severe pathological effects.
Just what effect this will have in rendering the locality uninhabitable depends on very uncertain facts.
As far as the actual explosion goes, the blast or shockwave causes the damage.
The radius of destruction produced by the explosion is proportional to the cube root of energy released.
"Hence in a bomb equivalent to 100,000 tons of TNT (or 11 pounds of uranium totally converted) we expect a radius of about 2 miles."
BUT IT WON'T BE ENOUGH!
BETHE
EDWARD, WE DON'T HAVE A TARGET YET, BUT I'M SURE A 2 MILE RADIUS OF DESTRUCTION WILL BE PLENTY.
MAYBE FOR GERMANY OR JAPAN, BUT FOR RUSSIA?
RUSSIA'S A HUGE-
RUSSIA'S OUR ALLY.
MAYBE NOW, BUT
AND IF YOU WANT TO TALK ABOUT NOT ENOUGH...
WE DON'T HAVE ENOUGH URANIUM OR 49 TO DO THE EXPERIMENTS YOU PROPOSE.
"This points roughly to the kind of results we expect from a device of the kind we hope to make."
"Since we aim simply to get as much energy from the explosion as we can, and since the materials are very precious, we have to do this with very high efficiency."

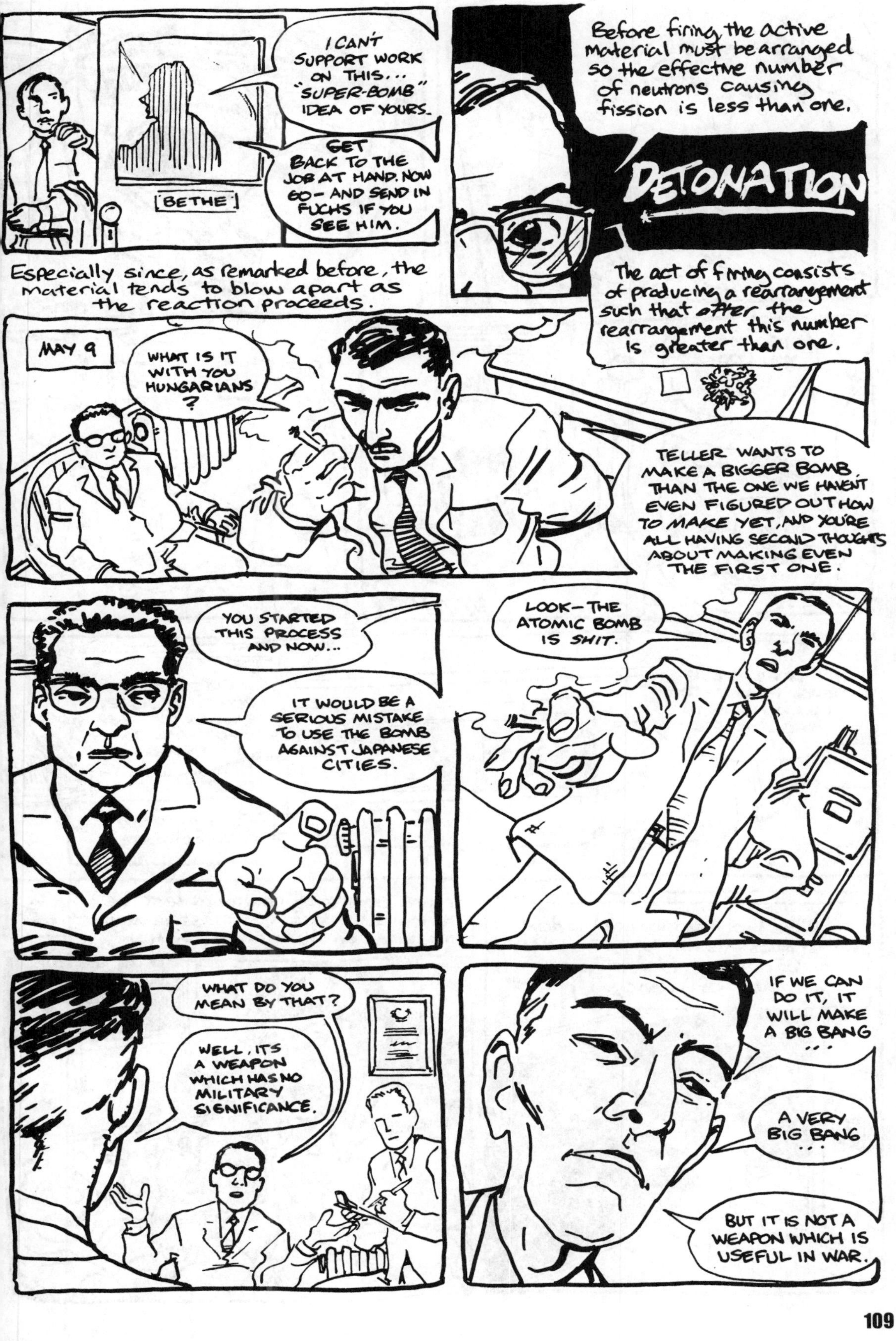
I CAN'T SUPPORT WORK ON THIS... "SUPER-BOMB" IDEA OF YOURS.
GET BACK TO THE JOB AT HAND. NOW GO— AND SEND IN FUCHS IF YOU SEE HIM.
BETHE
Before firing the active material must be arranged so the effective number of neutrons causing fission is less than one.
DETONATION
The act of firing consists of producing a rearrangement such that after the rearrangement this number is greater than one.
Especially since, as remarked before, the material tends to blow apart as the reaction proceeds.
MAY 9
WHAT IS IT WITH YOU HUNGARIANS?
TELLER WANTS TO MAKE A BIGGER BOMB THAN THE ONE WE HAVEN'T EVEN FIGURED OUT HOW TO MAKE YET, AND YOU'RE ALL HAVING SECOND THOUGHTS ABOUT MAKING EVEN THE FIRST ONE.
YOU STARTED THIS PROCESS AND NOW...
IT WOULD BE A SERIOUS MISTAKE TO USE THE BOMB AGAINST JAPANESE CITIES.
LOOK— THE ATOMIC BOMB IS *SHIT*.
WHAT DO YOU MEAN BY THAT?
WELL, ITS A WEAPON WHICH HAS NO MILITARY SIGNIFICANCE.
IF WE CAN DO IT, IT WILL MAKE A BIG BANG...
A VERY BIG BANG...
BUT IT IS NOT A WEAPON WHICH IS USEFUL IN WAR.

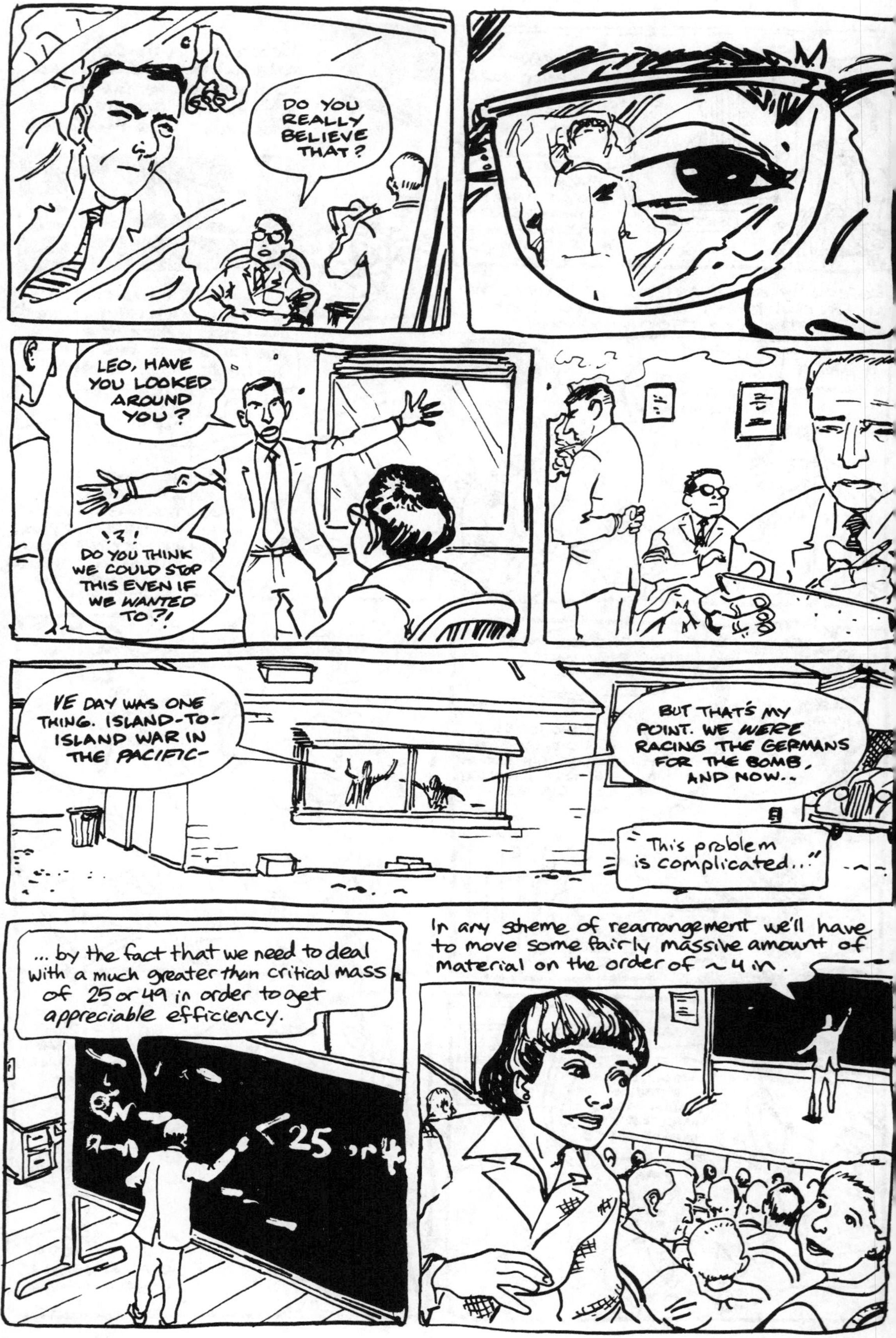
DO YOU REALLY BELIEVE THAT?
LEO, HAVE YOU LOOKED AROUND YOU?
!?! DO YOU THINK WE COULD STOP THIS EVEN IF WE WANTED TO?!
VE DAY WAS ONE THING. ISLAND-TO-ISLAND WAR IN THE PACIFIC-
BUT THAT'S MY POINT. WE WERE RACING THE GERMANS FOR THE BOMB, AND NOW..
"This problem is complicated..."
... by the fact that we need to deal with a much greater than critical mass of 25 or 49 in order to get appreciable efficiency.
< 25 or 4
In any scheme of rearrangement we'll have to move some fairly massive amount of material on the order of ~4 in.

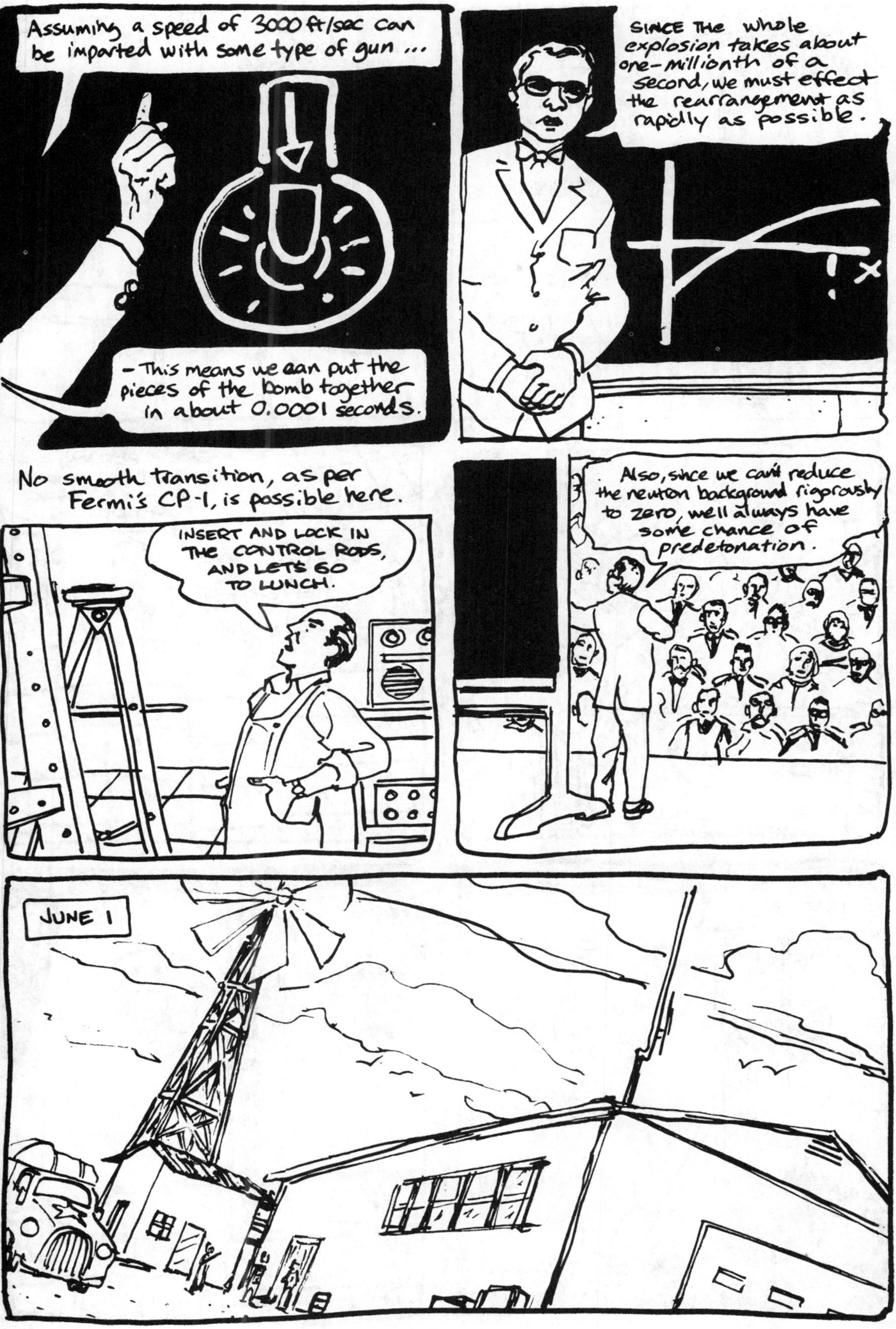

Assuming a speed of 3000 ft/sec can be imparted with some type of gun ...
– This means we can put the pieces of the bomb together in about 0.0001 seconds.
SINCE THE whole explosion takes about one-millionth of a second, we must effect the rearrangement as rapidly as possible.
No smooth transition, as per Fermi's CP-1, is possible here.
INSERT AND LOCK IN THE CONTROL RODS, AND LET'S GO TO LUNCH.
Also, since we can't reduce the neutron background rigorously to zero, we'll always have some chance of predetonation.
JUNE 1

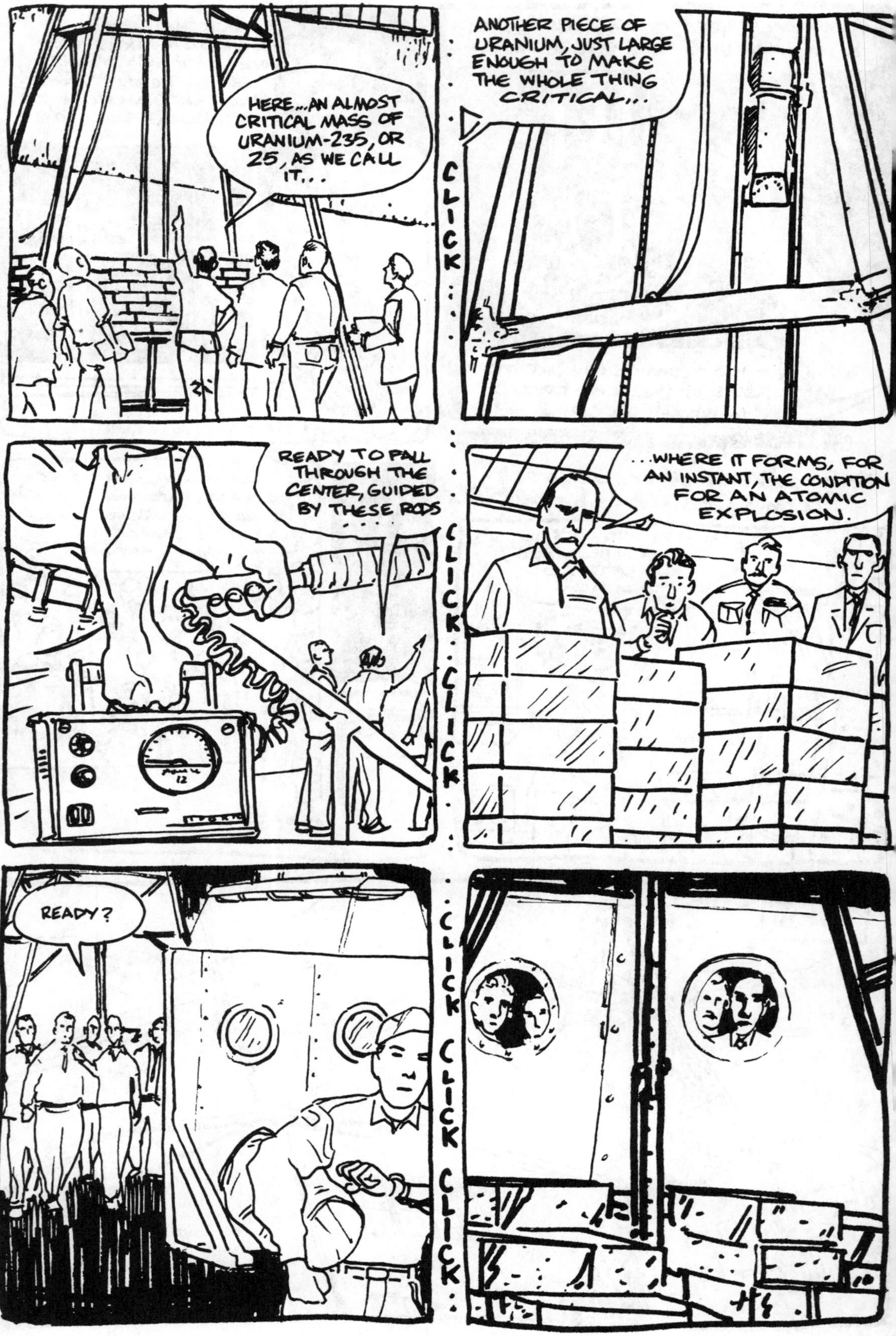
HERE...AN ALMOST CRITICAL MASS OF URANIUM-235, OR 25, AS WE CALL IT...
ANOTHER PIECE OF URANIUM, JUST LARGE ENOUGH TO MAKE THE WHOLE THING CRITICAL...
CLICK
READY TO FALL THROUGH THE CENTER, GUIDED BY THESE RODS
...WHERE IT FORMS, FOR AN INSTANT, THE CONDITION FOR AN ATOMIC EXPLOSION.
CLICK CLICK CLICK
READY?
CLICK CLICK CLICK

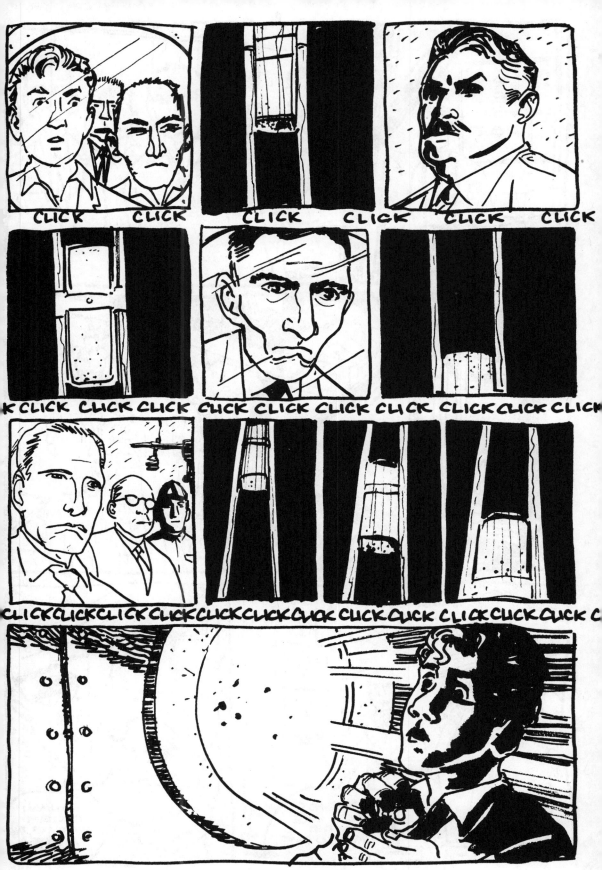

CLICK   CLICK   CLICK   CLICK   CLICK   CLICK

K CLICK CLICK CLICK   CLICK CLICK CLICK   CLICK   CLICK CLICK CLICK

CLICK CLICK CLICK CLICK CLICK CLICK CLICK CLICK CLICK CLICK CLICK CLICK C

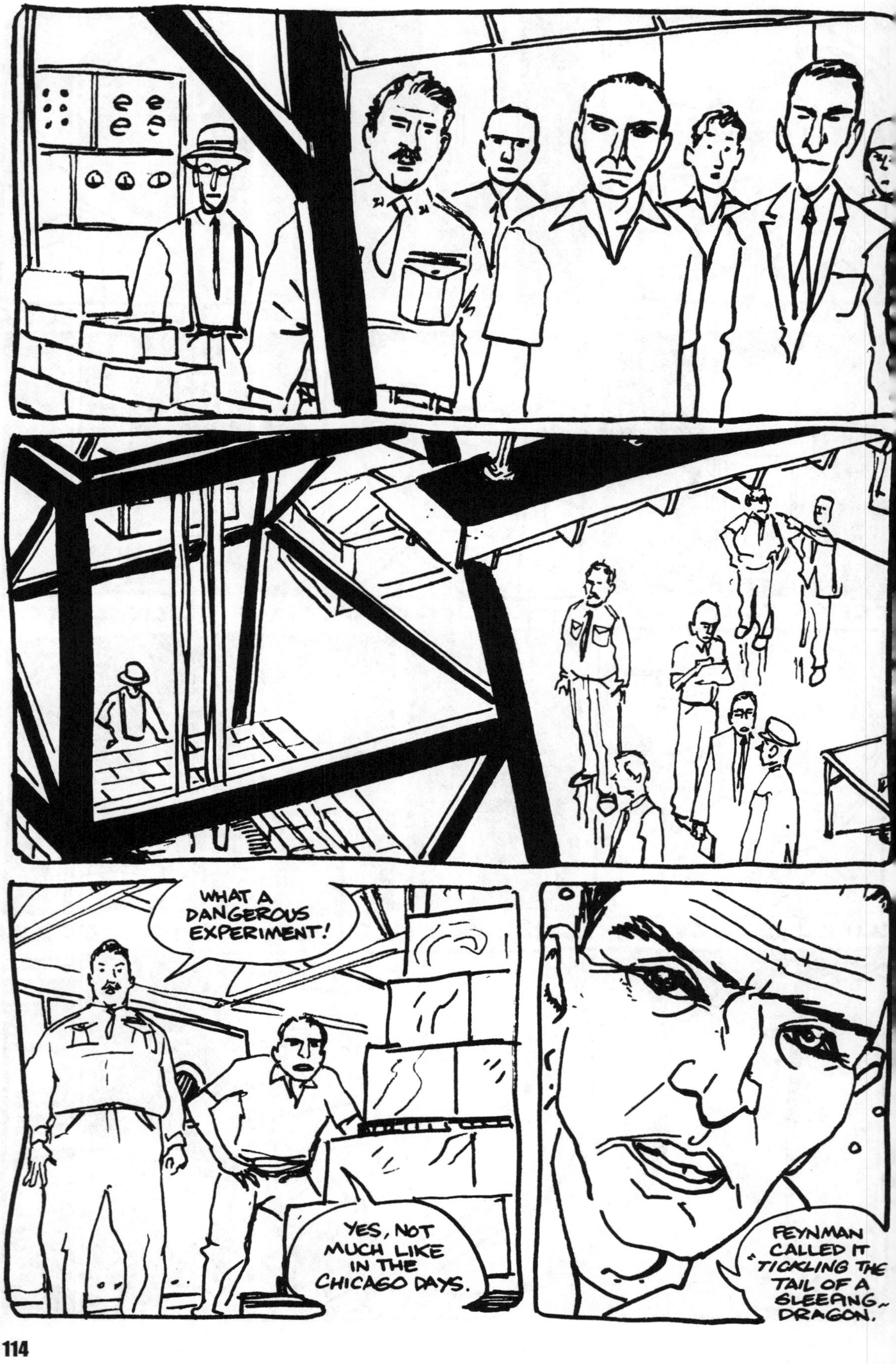
WHAT A DANGEROUS EXPERIMENT!
YES, NOT MUCH LIKE IN THE CHICAGO DAYS.
FEYNMAN CALLED IT "TICKLING THE TAIL OF A SLEEPING DRAGON."

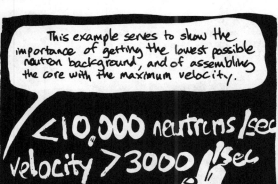

This example serves to show the importance of getting the lowest possible neutron background, and of assembling the core with the maximum velocity.

<10,000 neutrons/sec

velocity >3000 /sec

JUNE 16

28 gives 15 neutrons/
25 gives 150 " kg·sec
49 gives 500 "

Both are difficult — we have concerns about spontaneous fission and *nuclear* reactions... And a uranium tamper makes things worse.

"49 will be difficult to work with from the standpoint of neutron background whereas uranium (25) without 28 tamper will not be very difficult."

"Fortunately, if by bad luck or if the neutron background is very high, the bomb goes off *prematurely* and we get a *fizzle*."

"Calculations show it will generate the equivalent of about 60 tons of TNT — enough energy to completely...

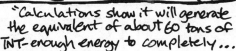

"DESTROY ITSELF..."

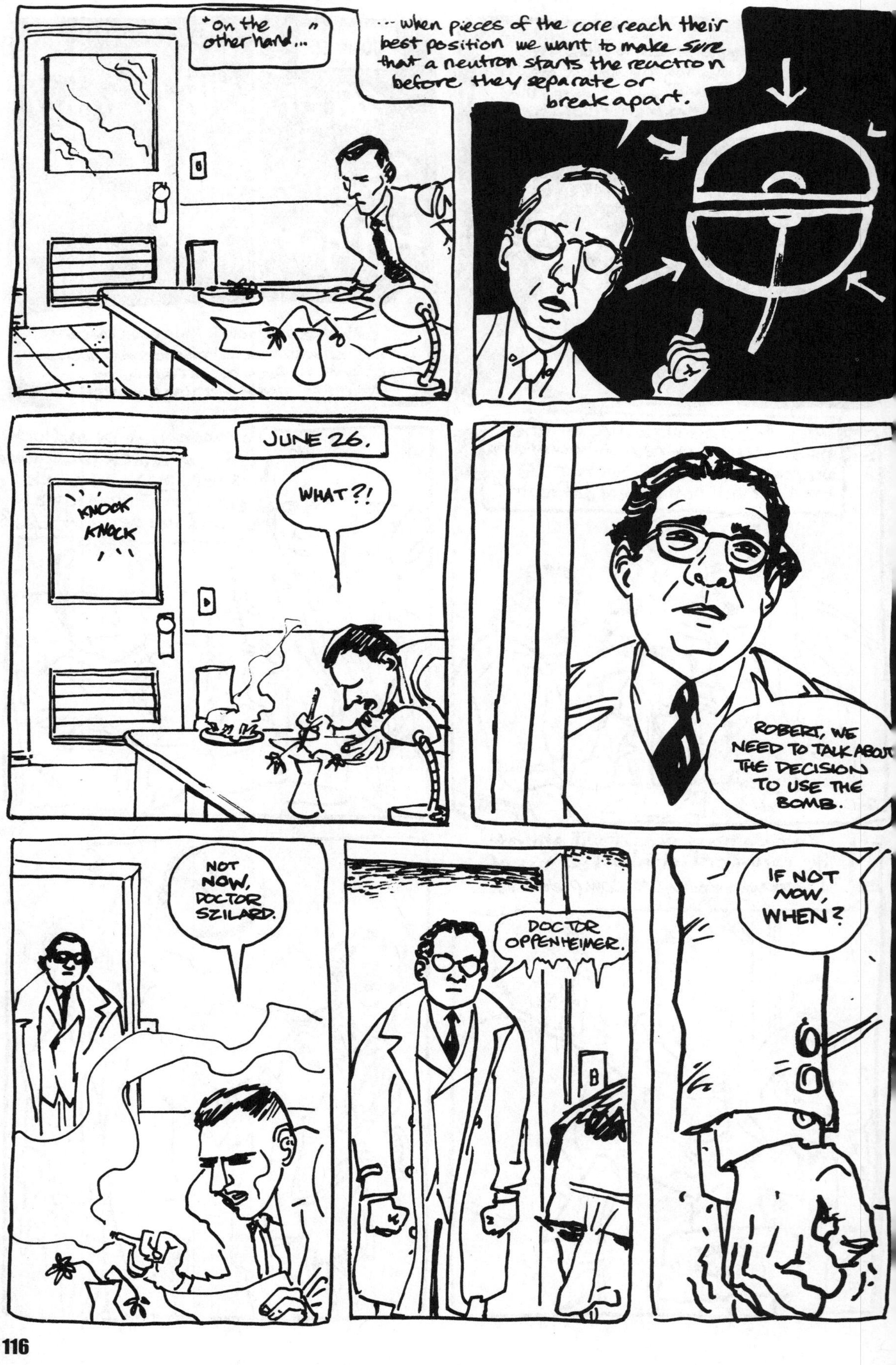
"On the other hand..."
...when pieces of the core reach their best position we want to make sure that a neutron starts the reaction before they separate or break apart.
JUNE 26.
KNOCK KNOCK
WHAT?!
ROBERT, WE NEED TO TALK ABOUT THE DECISION TO USE THE BOMB.
NOT NOW, DOCTOR SZILARD.
DOCTOR OPPENHEIMER.
IF NOT NOW, WHEN?

AFTER WE KNOW WE ACTUALLY HAVE A BOMB TO TALK ABOUT.

YOU'RE CONFIDENT. YOU'RE CONFIDENT OR YOU WOULDN'T BE SO ANXIOUS. LOOK.

LISTEN.

WE'RE NOW SAYING THAT INDIVIDUAL GERMANS SHARE GUILT FOR ACTS GERMANY COMMITTED SINCE THEY DIDN'T *PROTEST* THOSE ACTS.

THEIR DEFENSE— THAT PROTESTING WOULDN'T HAVE MADE A DIFFERENCE ... IS *UNACCEPTABLE* TO US, EVEN THOUGH THEY WOULD'VE RISKED LIFE AND LIBERTY TO MAKE THEIR PROTEST. ... WE CAN RAISE OUR VOICES NOW, WITHOUT ANY SUCH RISK.

WELL, OTHER THAN THE DISPLEASURE OF THOSE IN CHARGE OF OUR WORK ON "ATOMIC POWER".

THOSE SAME PEOPLE, OUR AIR FORCE, HAVE BOMBED TOKYO IN THE SAME MANNER OF THE GERMANS IN ENGLAND.

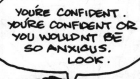

OUR USE OF ATOMIC BOMBS IN THIS WAR WOULD CARRY THE WORLD MUCH FURTHER ON A PATH OF RUTHLESSNESS.

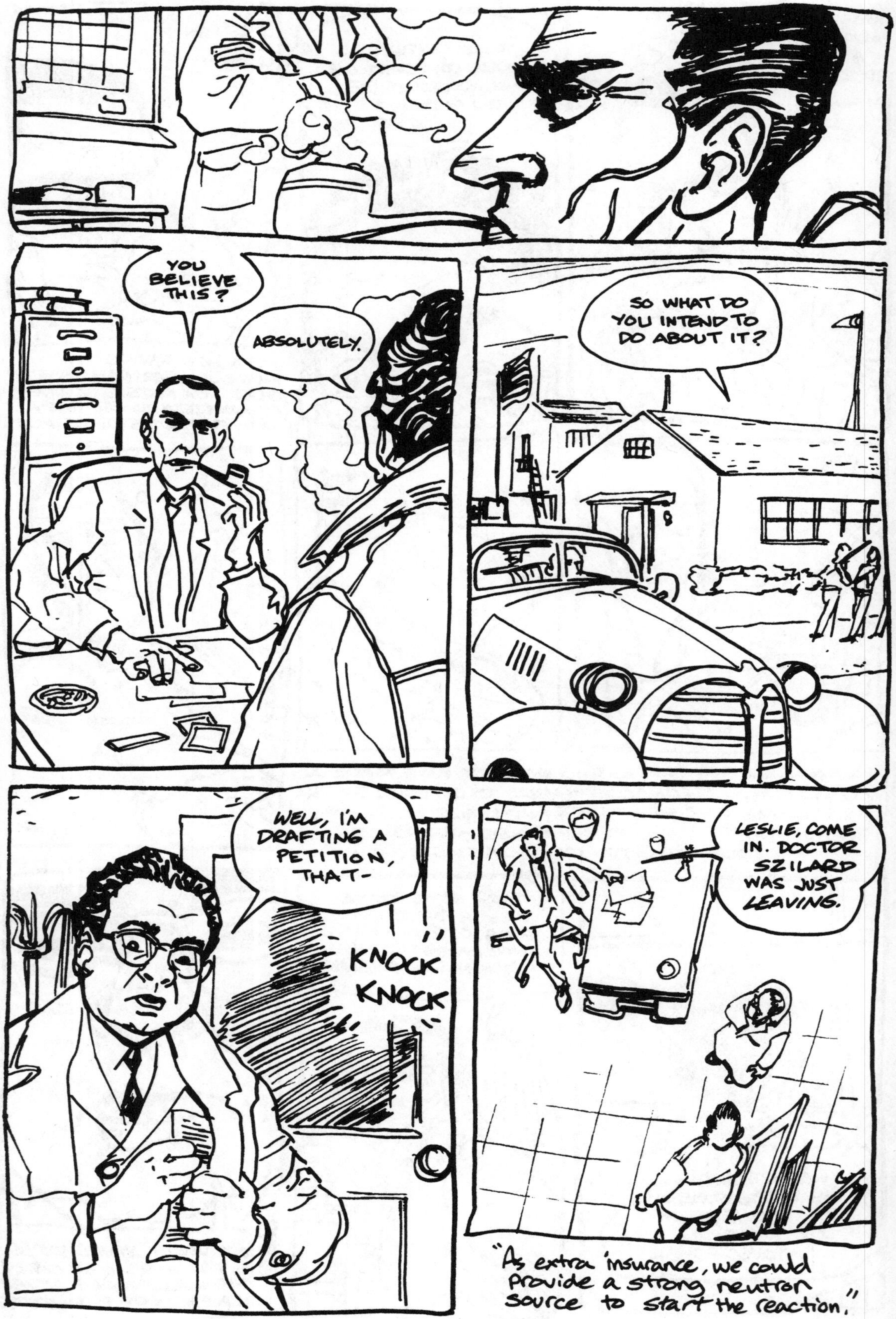
YOU BELIEVE THIS?
ABSOLUTELY.
SO WHAT DO YOU INTEND TO DO ABOUT IT?
WELL, I'M DRAFTING A PETITION, THAT-
"KNOCK KNOCK"
LESLIE, COME IN. DOCTOR SZILARD WAS JUST LEAVING.
"As extra insurance, we could provide a strong neutron source to start the reaction."

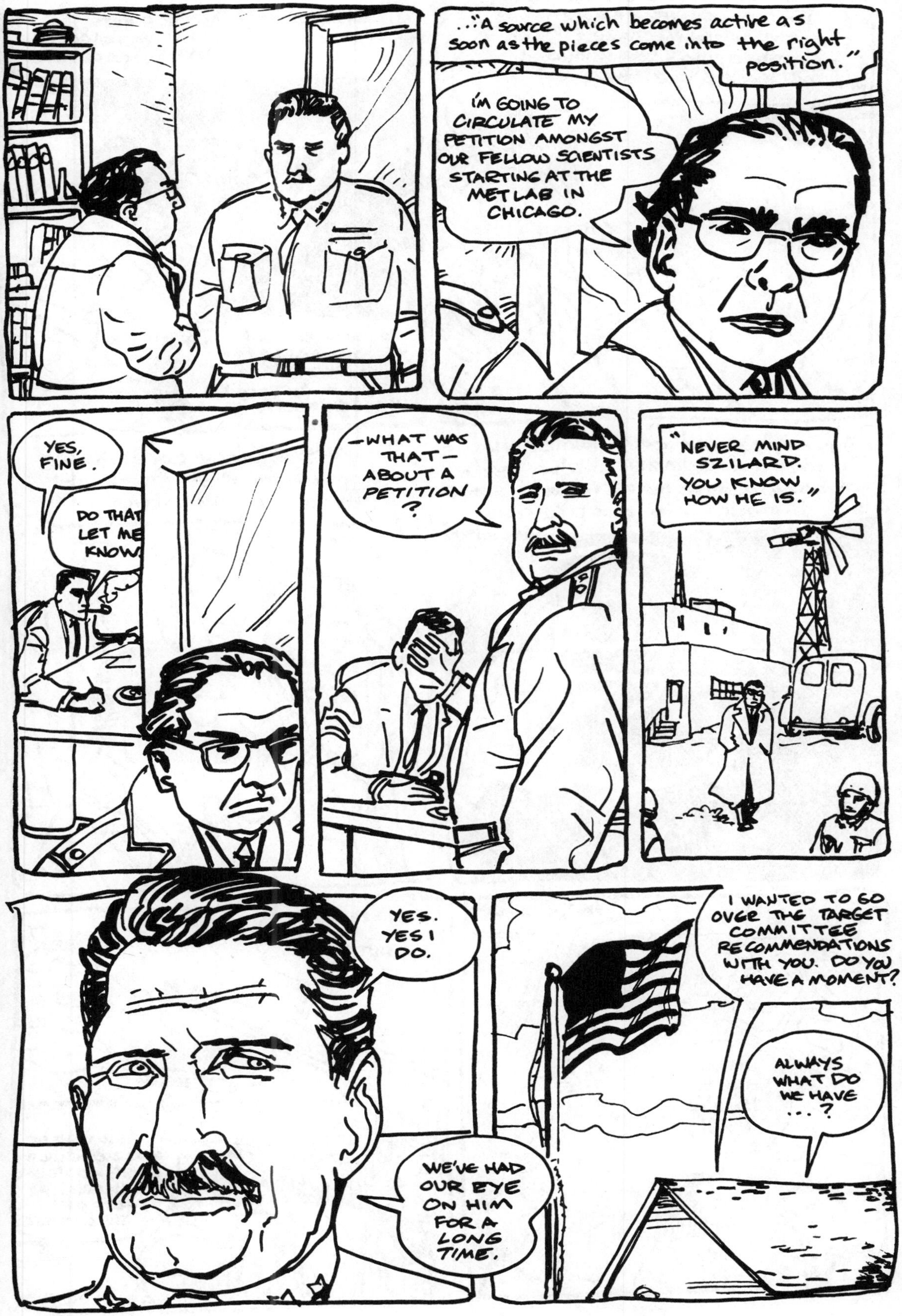
..."A source which becomes active as soon as the pieces come into the right position."
I'M GOING TO CIRCULATE MY PETITION AMONGST OUR FELLOW SCIENTISTS STARTING AT THE METLAB IN CHICAGO.
YES, FINE.
DO THAT LET ME KNOW
—WHAT WAS THAT— ABOUT A PETITION?
"NEVER MIND SZILARD. YOU KNOW HOW HE IS."
YES. YES I DO.
WE'VE HAD OUR EYE ON HIM FOR A LONG TIME.
I WANTED TO GO OVER THE TARGET COMMITTEE RECOMMENDATIONS WITH YOU. DO YOU HAVE A MOMENT?
ALWAYS WHAT DO WE HAVE ...?

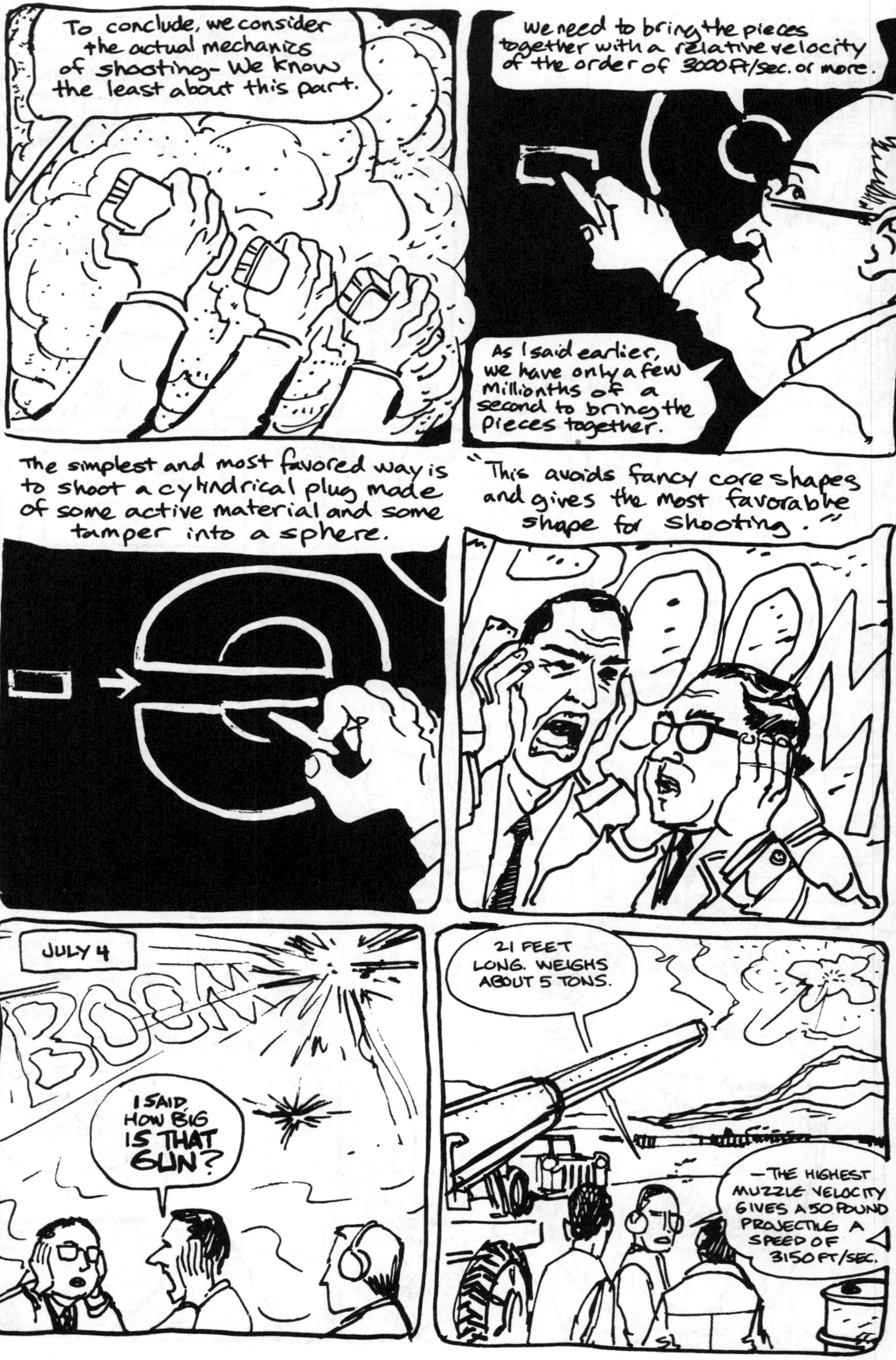
To conclude, we consider the actual mechanics of shooting- We know the least about this part.
We need to bring the pieces together with a relative velocity of the order of 3000 ft/sec. or more.
As I said earlier, we have only a few Millionths of a second to bring the pieces together.
The simplest and most favored way is to shoot a cylindrical plug made of some active material and some tamper into a sphere.
"This avoids fancy core shapes and gives the most favorable shape for shooting."
JULY 4
BOOM
I SAID, HOW BIG IS THAT GUN?
21 FEET LONG. WEIGHS ABOUT 5 TONS.
—THE HIGHEST MUZZLE VELOCITY GIVES A 50 POUND PROJECTILE A SPEED OF 3150 FT/SEC.

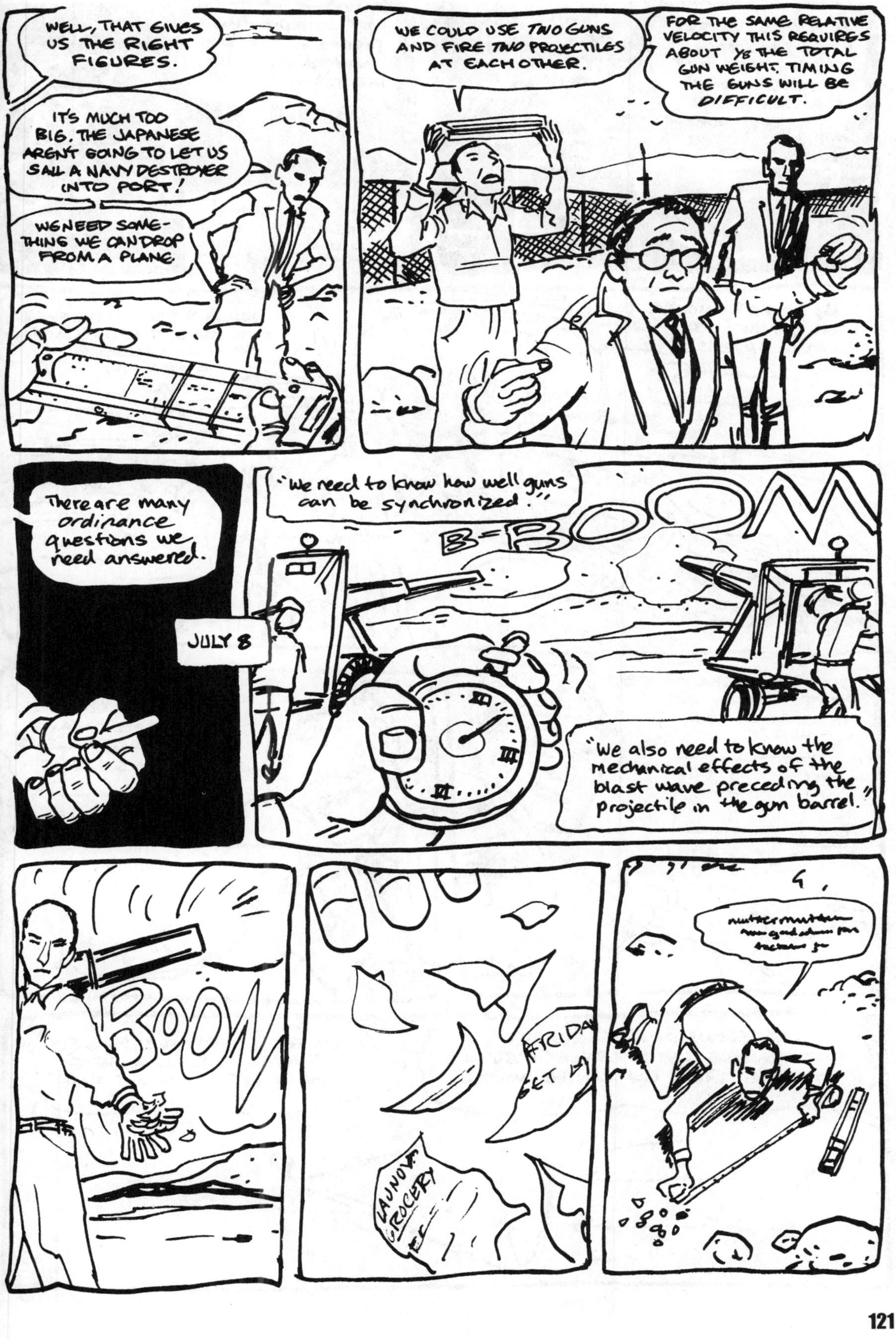

WELL, THAT GIVES US THE RIGHT FIGURES.
IT'S MUCH TOO BIG. THE JAPANESE AREN'T GOING TO LET US SAIL A NAVY DESTROYER INTO PORT!
WE NEED SOMETHING WE CAN DROP FROM A PLANE.
WE COULD USE TWO GUNS AND FIRE TWO PROJECTILES AT EACH OTHER.
FOR THE SAME RELATIVE VELOCITY THIS REQUIRES ABOUT 1/8 THE TOTAL GUN WEIGHT. TIMING THE GUNS WILL BE DIFFICULT.
There are many ordinance questions we need answered.
JULY 8
"We need to know how well guns can be synchronized."
B-BOOOM
"We also need to know the mechanical effects of the blast wave preceding the projectile in the gun barrel."
BOOM
FRIDAY
GROCERY

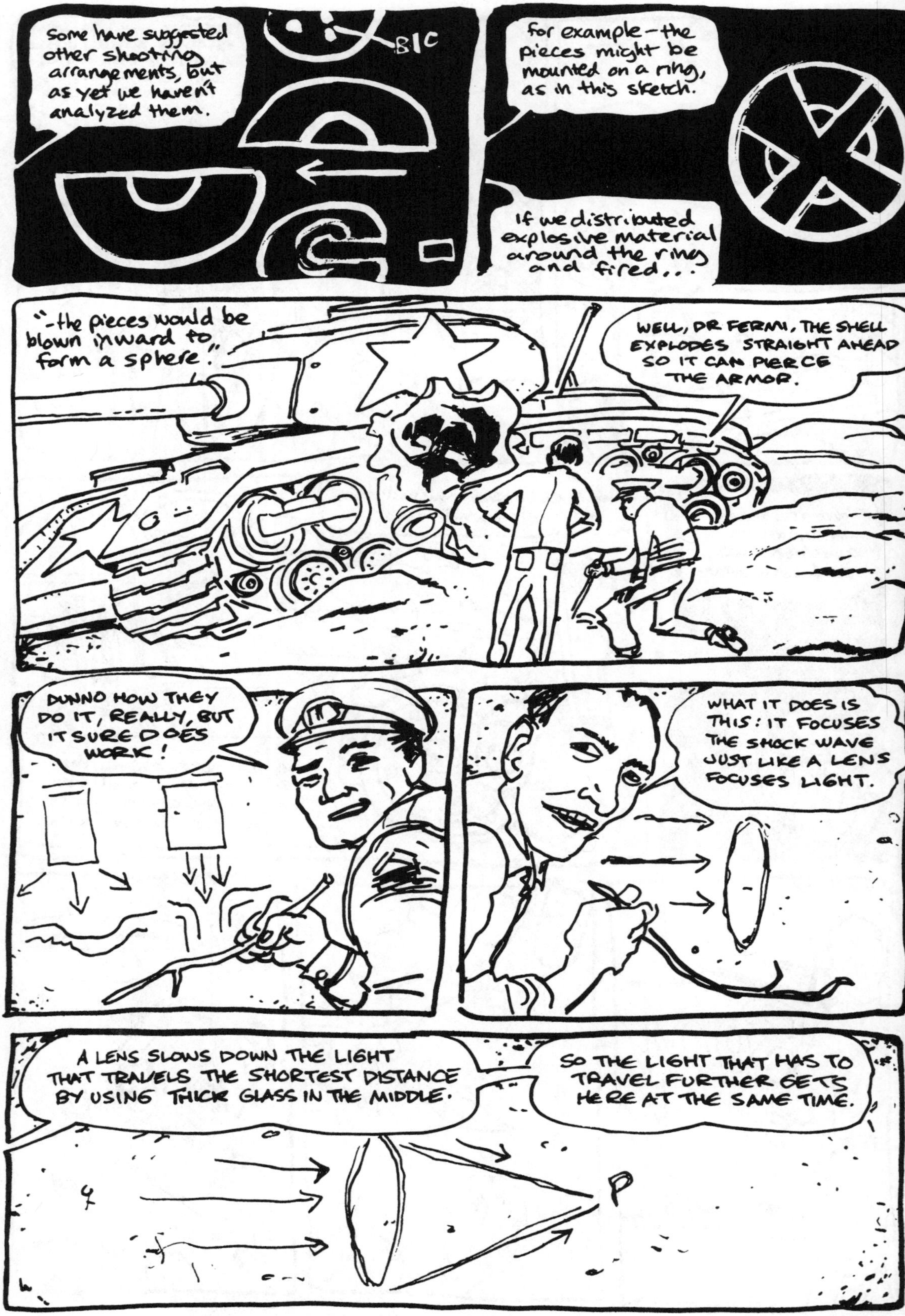

Some have suggested other shooting arrangements, but as yet we haven't analyzed them.
BIC
for example — the pieces might be mounted on a ring, as in this sketch.
If we distributed explosive material around the ring and fired . .
"-the pieces would be blown inward to form a sphere".
WELL, DR FERMI, THE SHELL EXPLODES STRAIGHT AHEAD SO IT CAN PIERCE THE ARMOR.
DUNNO HOW THEY DO IT, REALLY, BUT IT SURE DOES WORK!
WHAT IT DOES IS THIS: IT FOCUSES THE SHOCK WAVE JUST LIKE A LENS FOCUSES LIGHT.
A LENS SLOWS DOWN THE LIGHT THAT TRAVELS THE SHORTEST DISTANCE BY USING THICK GLASS IN THE MIDDLE.
SO THE LIGHT THAT HAS TO TRAVEL FURTHER GETS HERE AT THE SAME TIME.
P

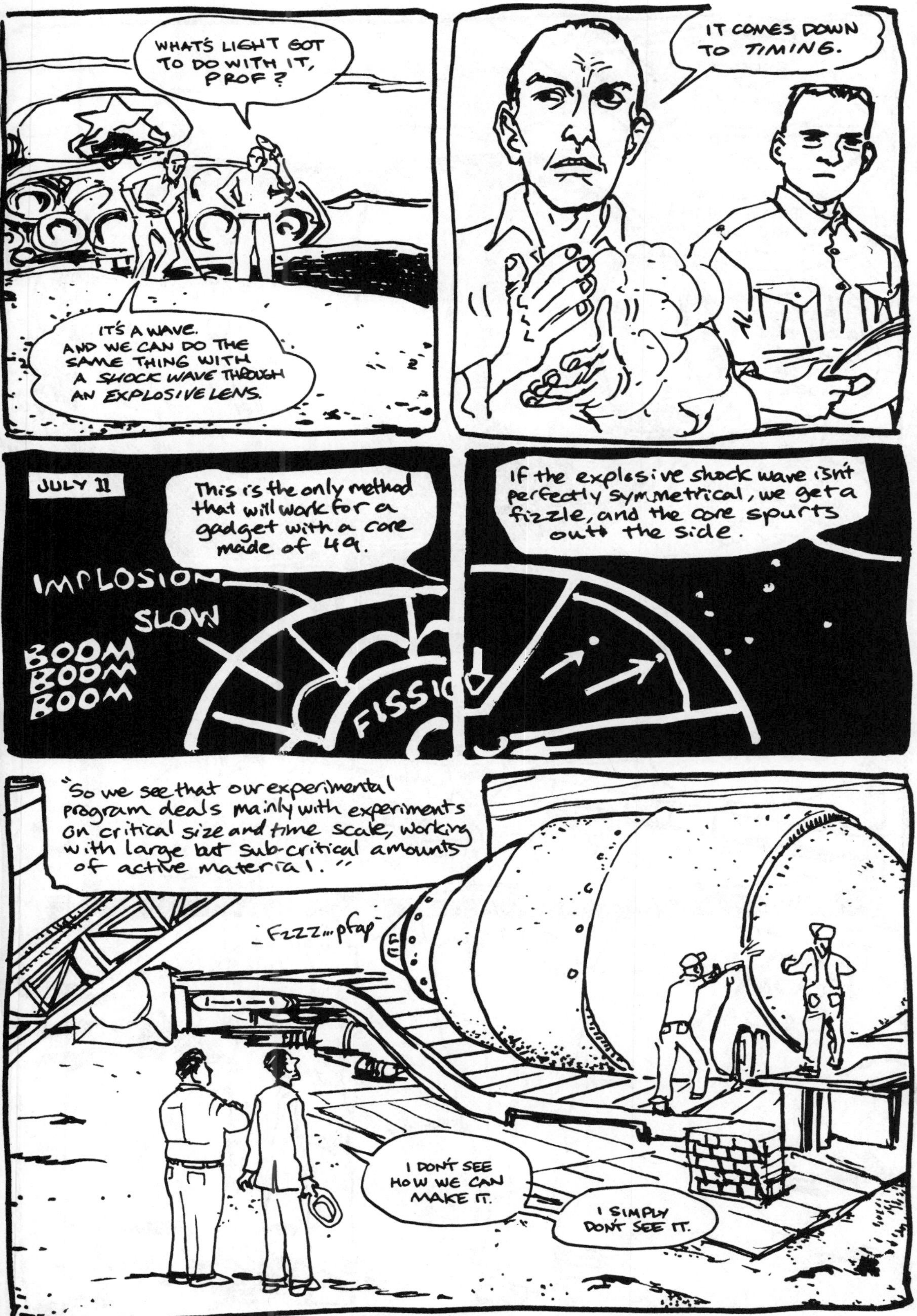
WHAT'S LIGHT GOT TO DO WITH IT, PROF?
IT'S A WAVE. AND WE CAN DO THE SAME THING WITH A SHOCK WAVE THROUGH AN EXPLOSIVE LENS.
IT COMES DOWN TO TIMING.
JULY 11
This is the only method that will work for a gadget with a core made of 49.
IMPLOSION
SLOW
BOOM BOOM BOOM
FISSIO
If the explosive shock wave isn't perfectly symmetrical, we get a fizzle, and the core spurts outt the side.
"So we see that our experimental program deals mainly with experiments on critical size and time scale, working with large but sub-critical amounts of active material."
Fzzz...pfap
I DON'T SEE HOW WE CAN MAKE IT.
I SIMPLY DON'T SEE IT.

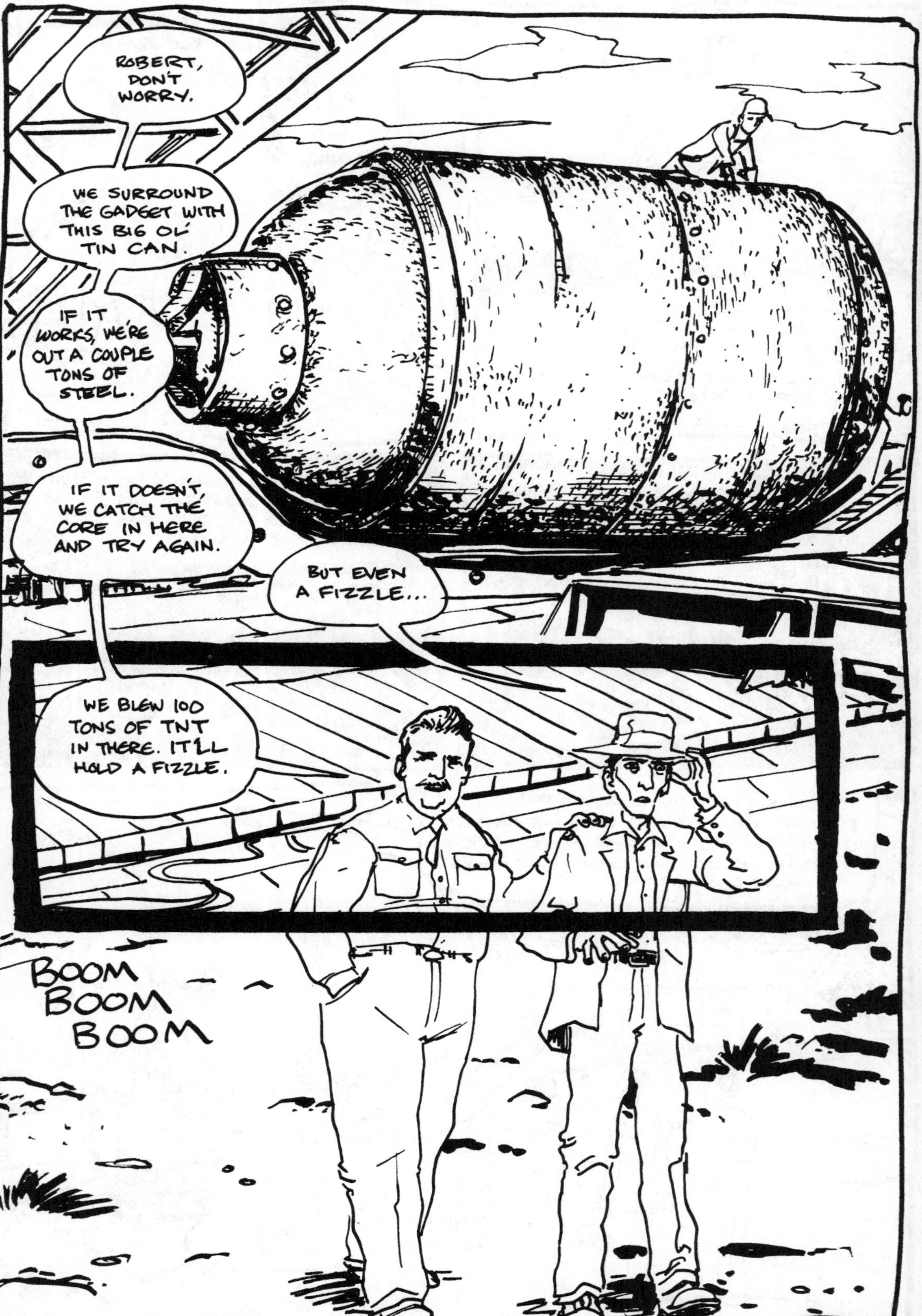
ROBERT, DON'T WORRY.
WE SURROUND THE GADGET WITH THIS BIG OL' TIN CAN.
IF IT WORKS, WE'RE OUT A COUPLE TONS OF STEEL.
IF IT DOESN'T, WE CATCH THE CORE IN HERE AND TRY AGAIN.
BUT EVEN A FIZZLE...
WE BLEW 100 TONS OF TNT IN THERE. IT'LL HOLD A FIZZLE.
BOOM
BOOM
BOOM

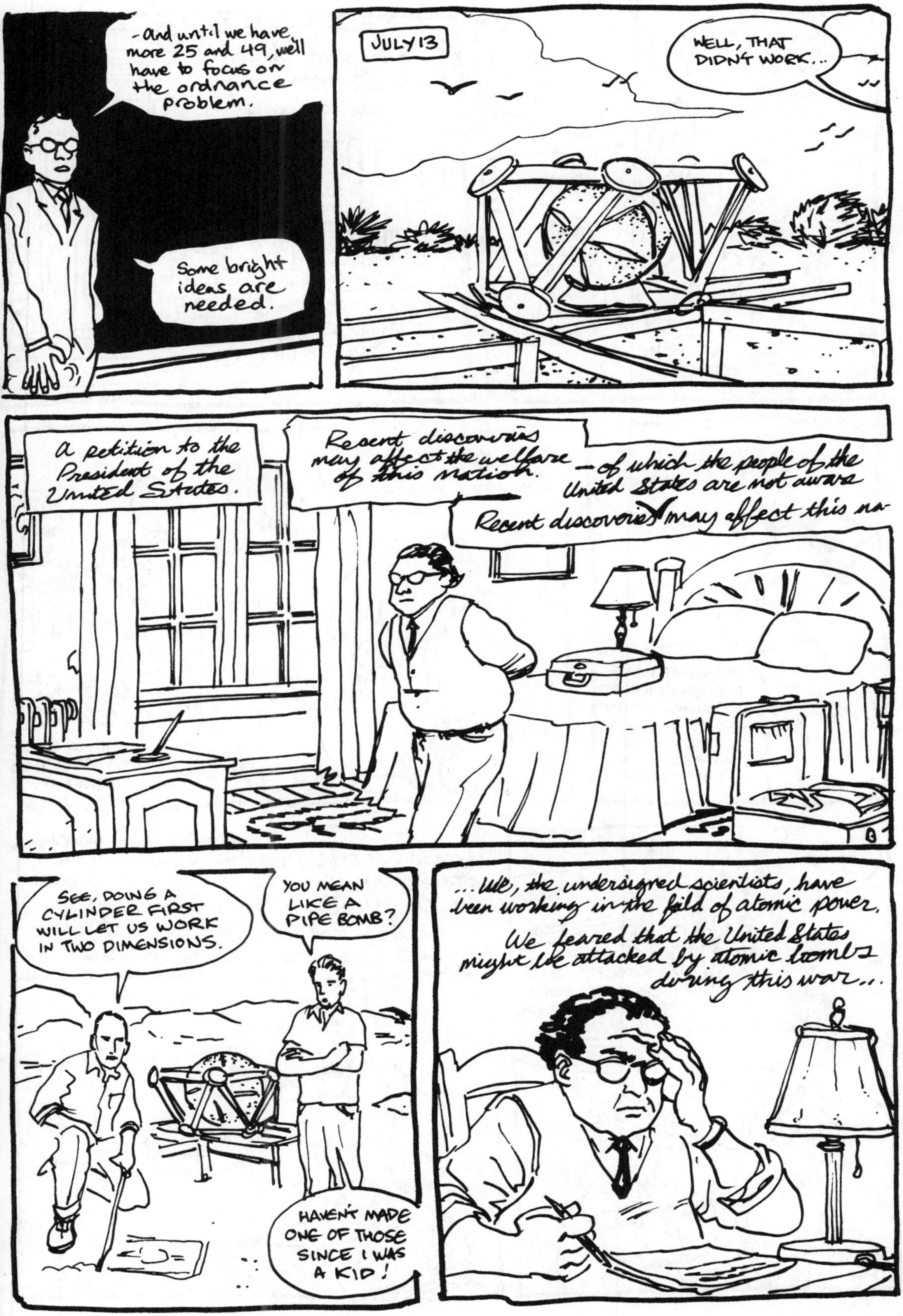
- and until we have more 25 and 49, we'll have to focus on the ordnance problem.
Some bright ideas are needed.
JULY 13
WELL, THAT DIDN'T WORK...
A petition to the President of the United States.
Recent discoveries may affect the welfare of this nation
— of which the people of the United States are not aware
Recent discoveries may affect this na-
SEE, DOING A CYLINDER FIRST WILL LET US WORK IN TWO DIMENSIONS.
YOU MEAN LIKE A PIPE BOMB?
HAVEN'T MADE ONE OF THOSE SINCE I WAS A KID!
...We, the undersigned scientists, have been working in the field of atomic power.
We feared that the United States might be attacked by atomic bombs during this war...

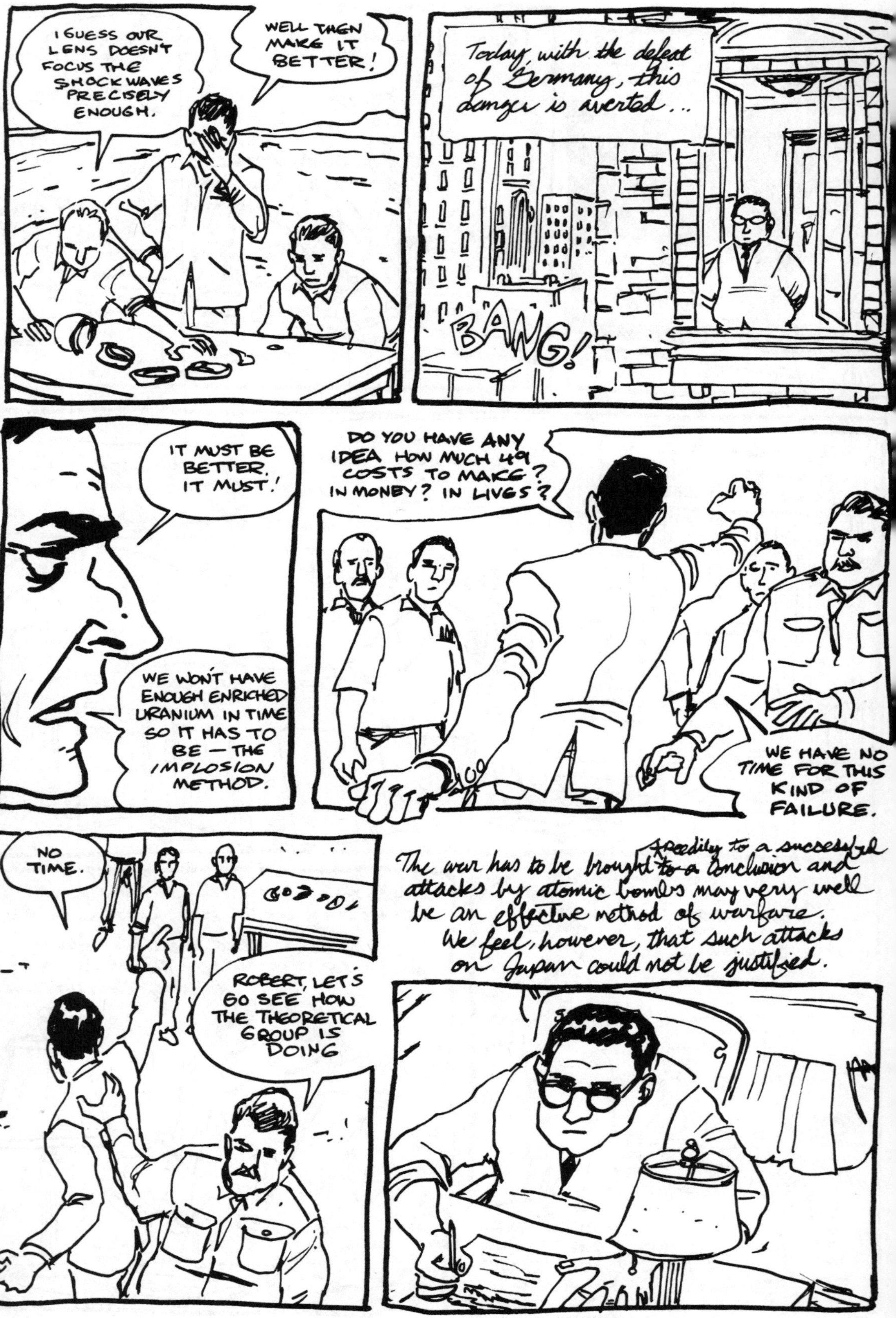
I GUESS OUR LENS DOESN'T FOCUS THE SHOCKWAVES PRECISELY ENOUGH.
WELL THEN MAKE IT BETTER!
Today with the defeat of Germany, this danger is averted...
BANG!
IT MUST BE BETTER. IT MUST!
WE WON'T HAVE ENOUGH ENRICHED URANIUM IN TIME SO IT HAS TO BE — THE IMPLOSION METHOD.
DO YOU HAVE ANY IDEA HOW MUCH 49 COSTS TO MAKE? IN MONEY? IN LIVES?
WE HAVE NO TIME FOR THIS KIND OF FAILURE.
NO TIME.
ROBERT, LET'S GO SEE HOW THE THEORETICAL GROUP IS DOING
The war has to be brought speedily to a successful conclusion and attacks by atomic bombs may very well be an effective method of warfare. We feel, however, that such attacks on Japan could not be justified.

... at least not unless the terms which we will impose on Japan were made public in detail and Japan were given an opportunity to surrender.

Atomic power will provide the nations with new means of destruction.

The atomic bombs at our disposal represent only the first step in this direction...

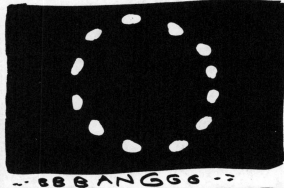

~ B B B A N G G G ->

: B B B A N G ...

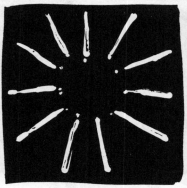

· B B B A N G :

B B B B B O O M :

EXCELLENT.

.. and there is almost no limit to the destructive power which will become available in the course of future development.

127

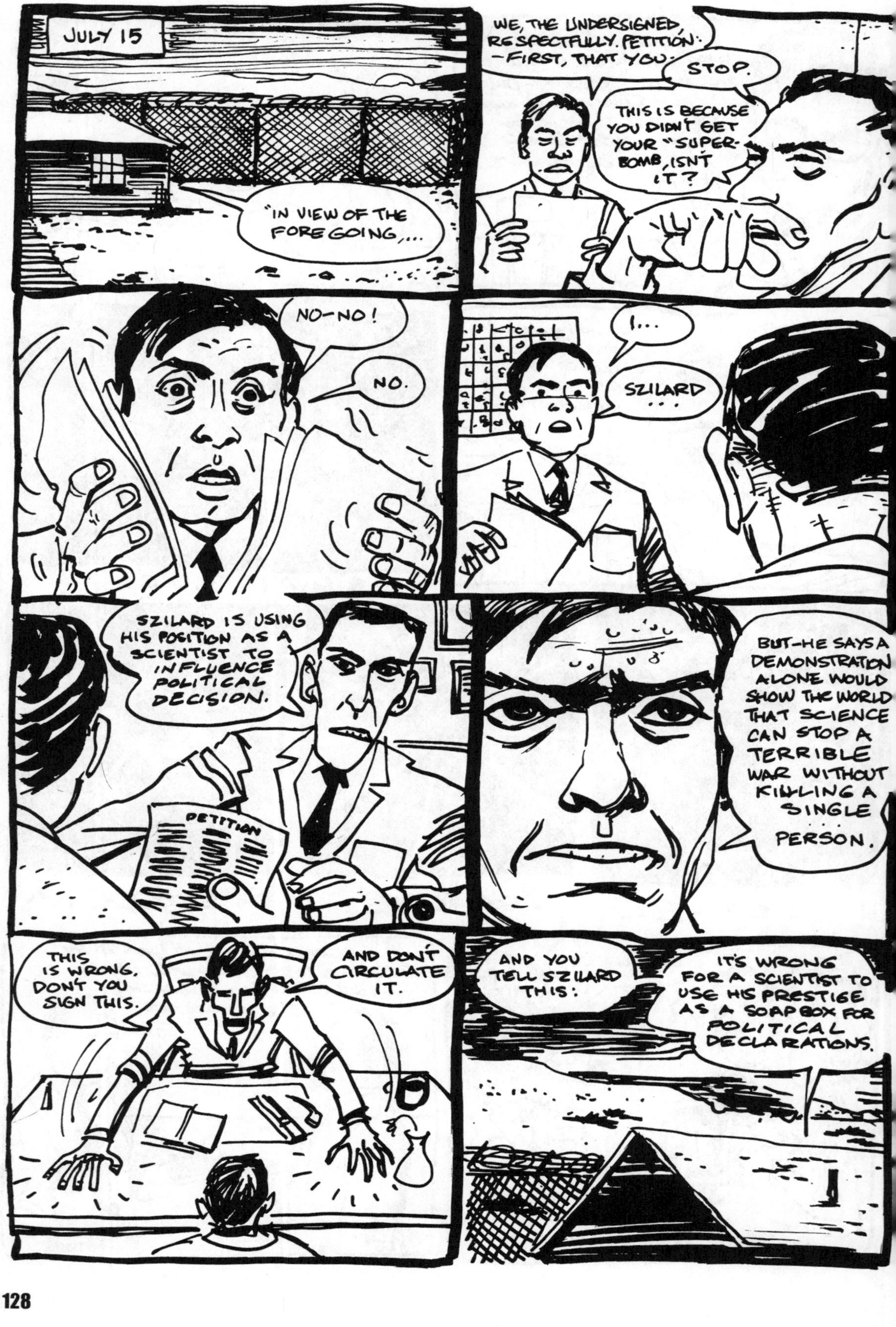
JULY 15
"IN VIEW OF THE FOREGOING,...
WE, THE UNDERSIGNED, RESPECTFULLY PETITION: -FIRST, THAT YOU-
STOP.
THIS IS BECAUSE YOU DIDN'T GET YOUR "SUPER-BOMB, ISN'T IT?
NO-NO!
NO.
I...
SZILARD ...
SZILARD IS USING HIS POSITION AS A SCIENTIST TO INFLUENCE POLITICAL DECISION.
PETITION
BUT-HE SAYS A DEMONSTRATION ALONE WOULD SHOW THE WORLD THAT SCIENCE CAN STOP A TERRIBLE WAR WITHOUT KILLING A SINGLE PERSON.
THIS IS WRONG. DON'T YOU SIGN THIS.
AND DON'T CIRCULATE IT.
AND YOU TELL SZILARD THIS:
IT'S WRONG FOR A SCIENTIST TO USE HIS PRESTIGE AS A SOAPBOX FOR POLITICAL DECLARATIONS.

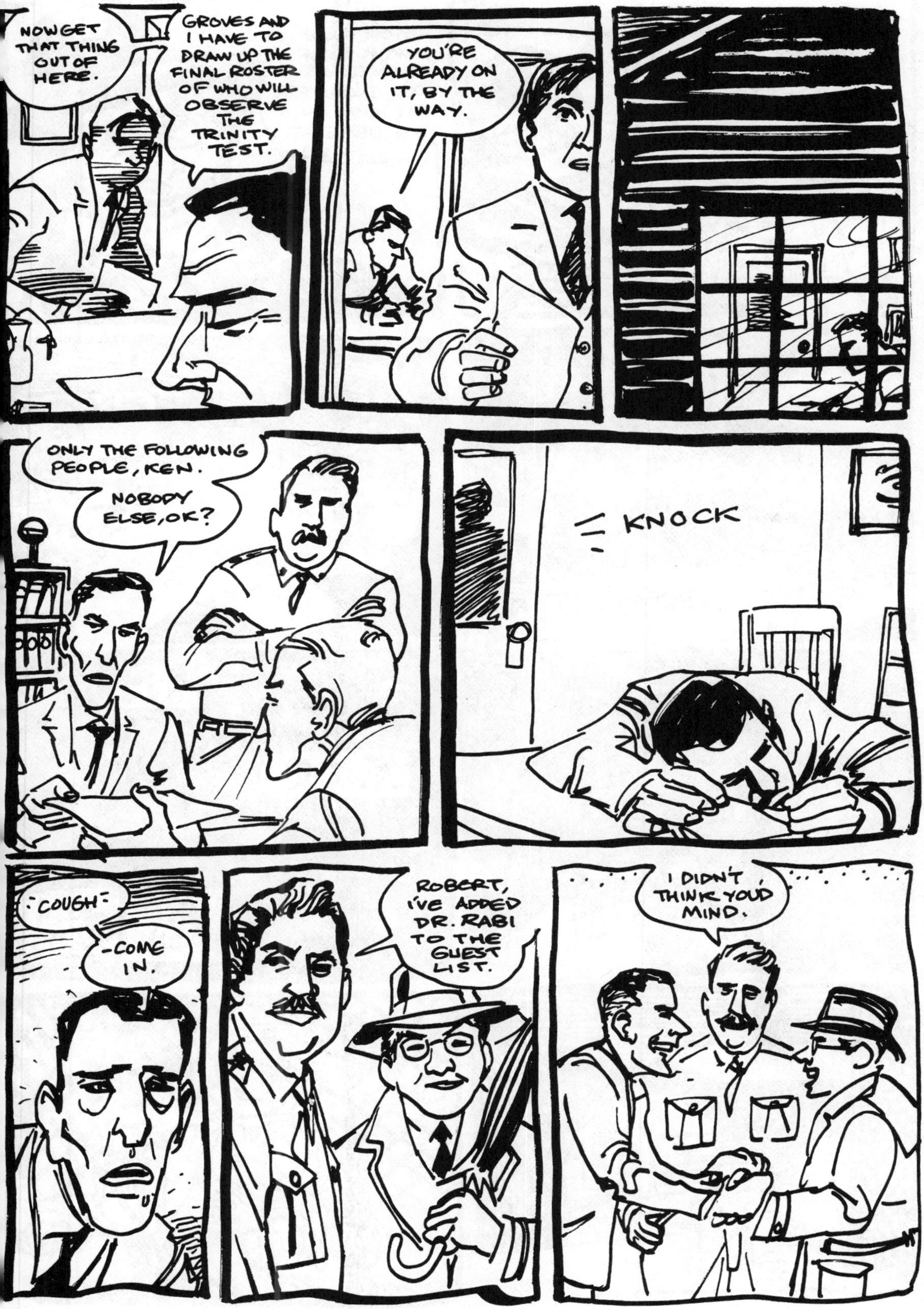
NOW GET THAT THING OUT OF HERE.
GROVES AND I HAVE TO DRAW UP THE FINAL ROSTER OF WHO WILL OBSERVE THE TRINITY TEST.
YOU'RE ALREADY ON IT, BY THE WAY.
ONLY THE FOLLOWING PEOPLE, KEN.
NOBODY ELSE, OK?
KNOCK
COUGH
-COME IN.
ROBERT, I'VE ADDED DR. RABI TO THE GUEST LIST.
I DIDN'T THINK YOU'D MIND.

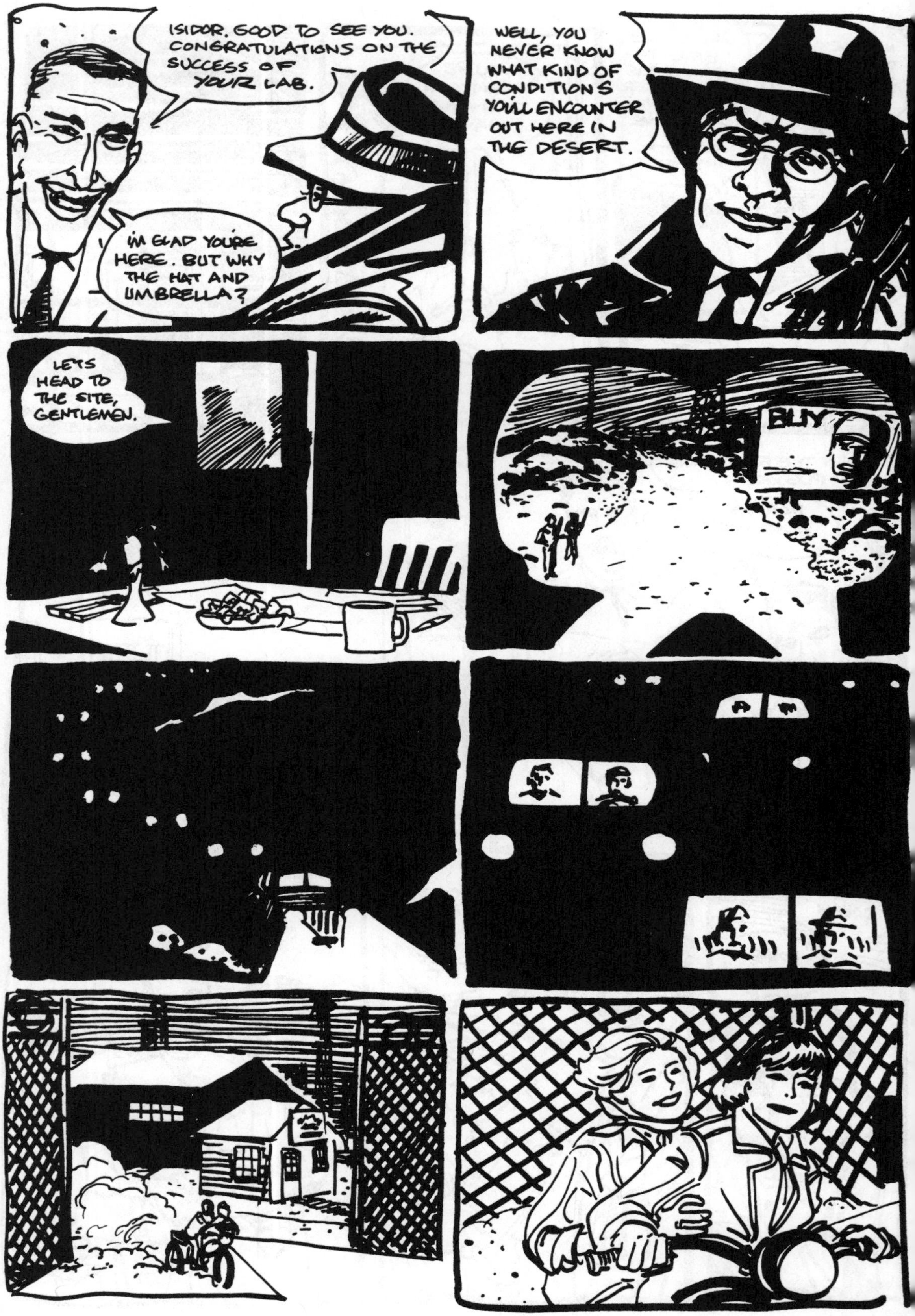
ISIDOR. GOOD TO SEE YOU. CONGRATULATIONS ON THE SUCCESS OF YOUR LAB.
I'M GLAD YOU'RE HERE. BUT WHY THE HAT AND UMBRELLA?
WELL, YOU NEVER KNOW WHAT KIND OF CONDITIONS YOU'LL ENCOUNTER OUT HERE IN THE DESERT.
LET'S HEAD TO THE SITE, GENTLEMEN.
BUY

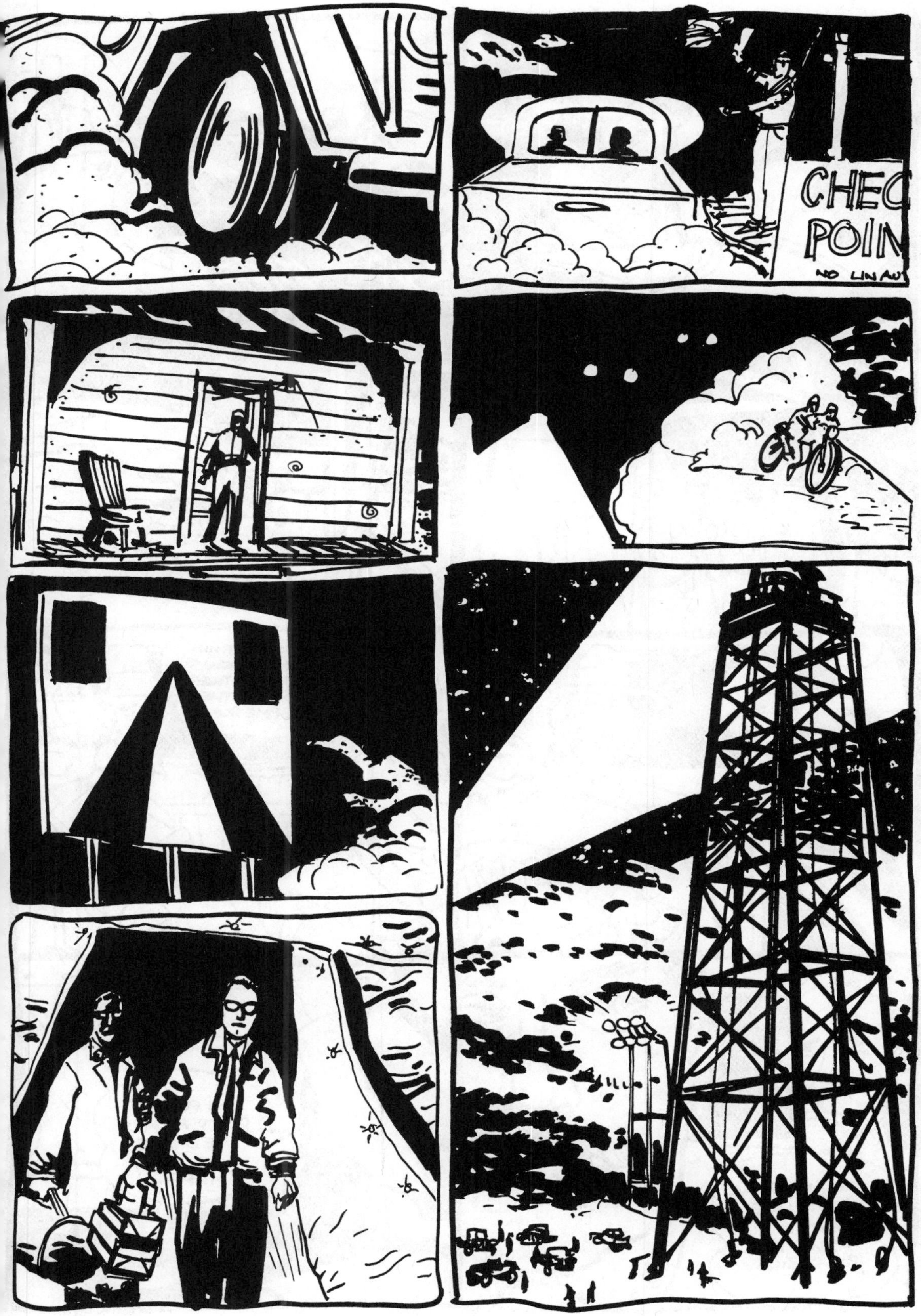
CHEC
POIN
NO UN AU

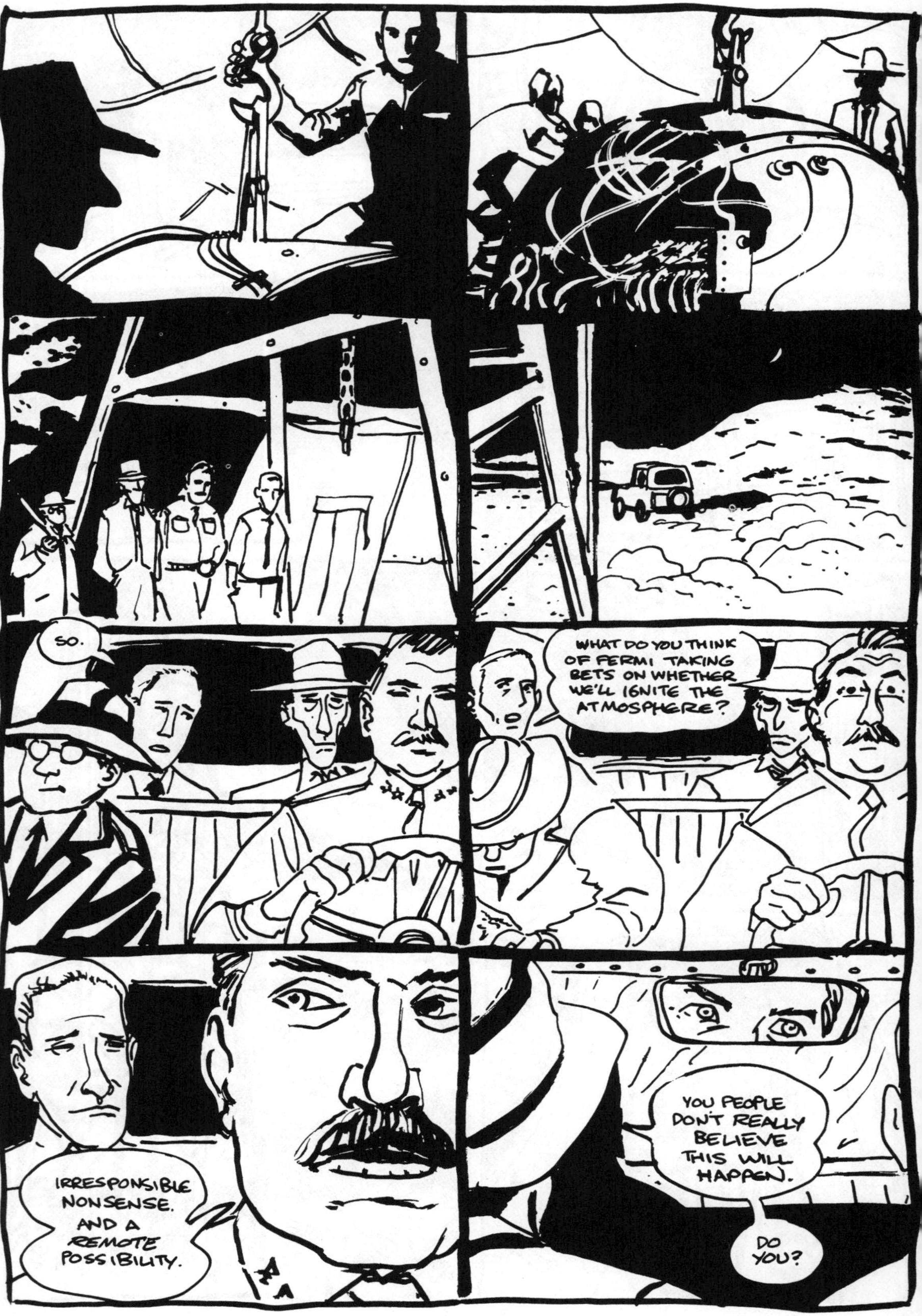
SO.
WHAT DO YOU THINK OF FERMI TAKING BETS ON WHETHER WE'LL IGNITE THE ATMOSPHERE?
IRRESPONSIBLE NONSENSE. AND A *REMOTE* POSSIBILITY.
YOU PEOPLE DON'T REALLY BELIEVE THIS WILL HAPPEN.
DO YOU?

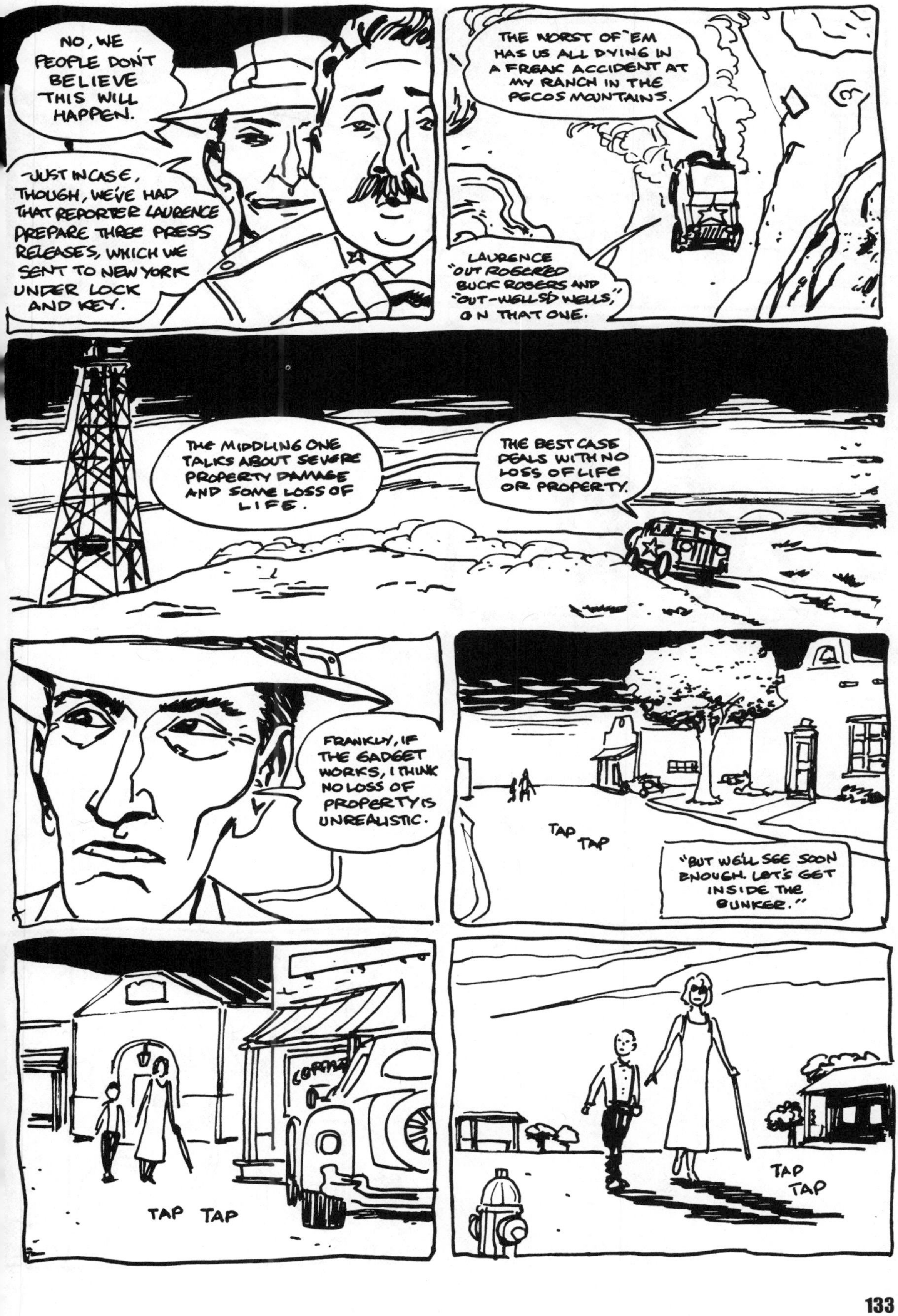
NO, WE PEOPLE DON'T BELIEVE THIS WILL HAPPEN.
-JUST IN CASE, THOUGH, WE'VE HAD THAT REPORTER LAURENCE PREPARE THREE PRESS RELEASES, WHICH WE SENT TO NEW YORK UNDER LOCK AND KEY.
THE WORST OF 'EM HAS US ALL DYING IN A FREAK ACCIDENT AT MY RANCH IN THE PECOS MOUNTAINS.
LAURENCE "OUT ROGERED" BUCK ROGERS AND "OUT-WELLSED WELLS," ON THAT ONE.
THE MIDDLING ONE TALKS ABOUT SEVERE PROPERTY DAMAGE AND SOME LOSS OF LIFE.
THE BEST CASE DEALS WITH NO LOSS OF LIFE OR PROPERTY.
FRANKLY, IF THE GADGET WORKS, I THINK NO LOSS OF PROPERTY IS UNREALISTIC.
TAP TAP
"BUT WE'LL SEE SOON ENOUGH. LET'S GET INSIDE THE BUNKER."
TAP TAP
TAP TAP

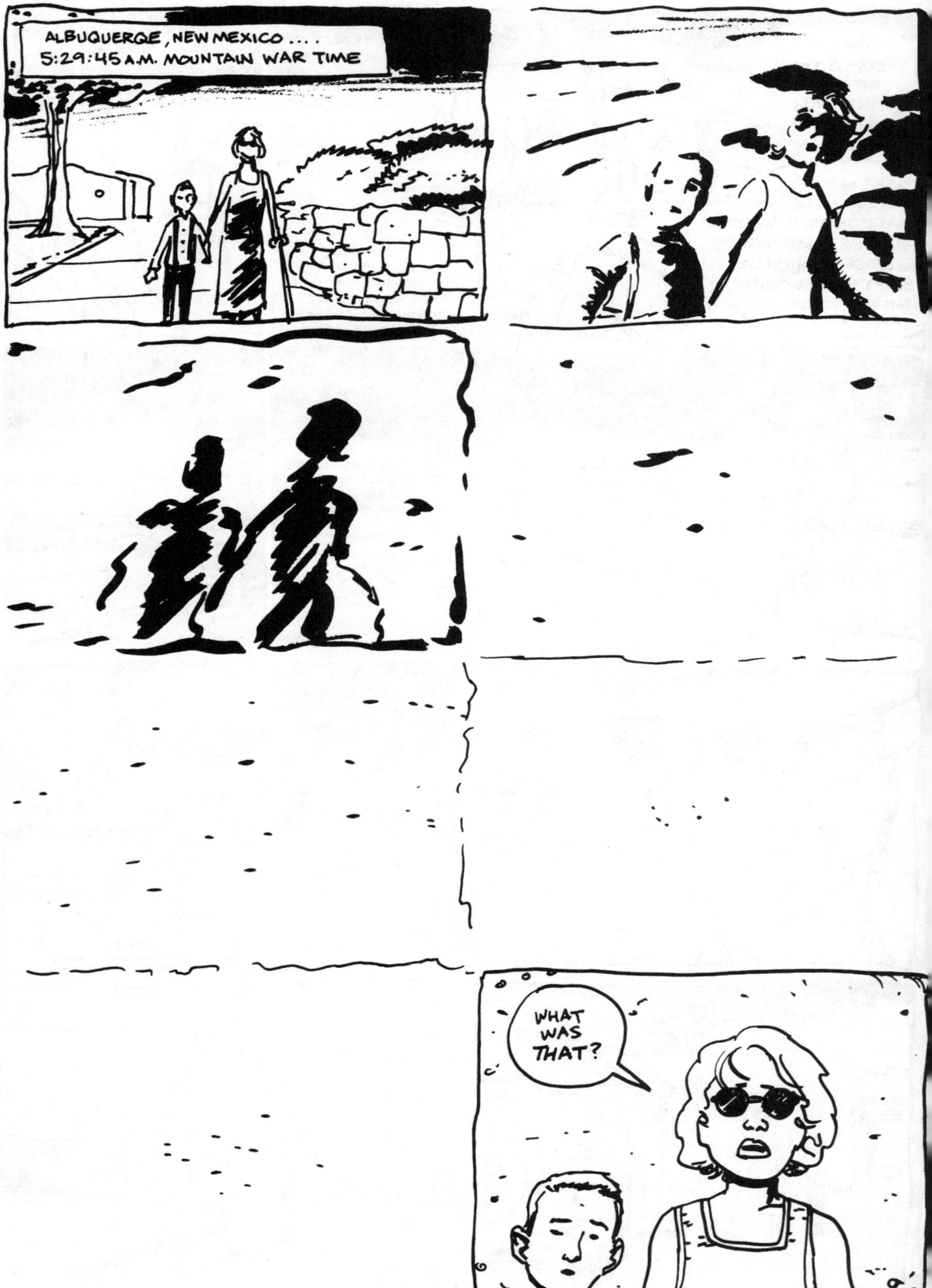
ALBUQUERQE, NEW MEXICO . . . .
5:29:45 A.M. MOUNTAIN WAR TIME
WHAT WAS THAT?

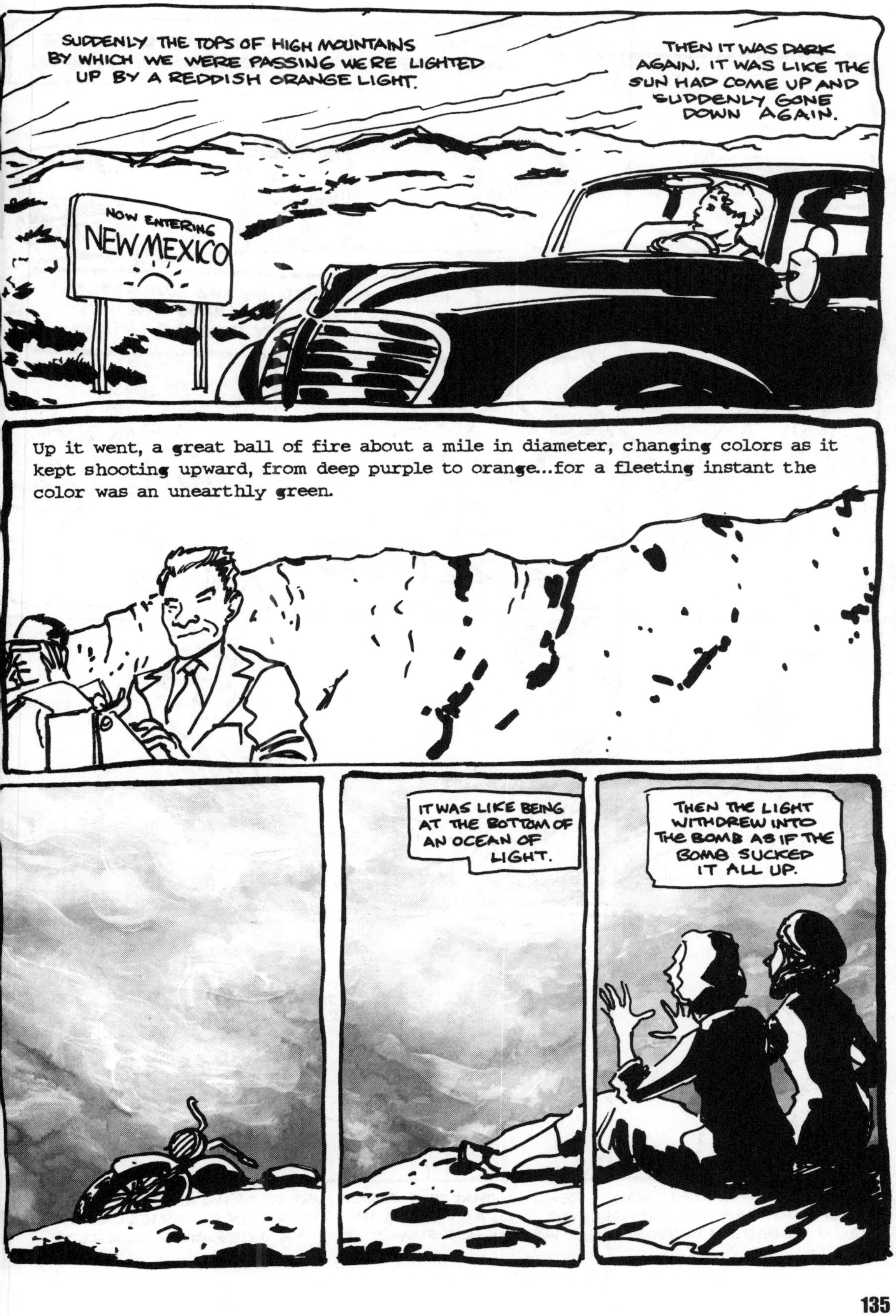
SUDDENLY THE TOPS OF HIGH MOUNTAINS BY WHICH WE WERE PASSING WERE LIGHTED UP BY A REDDISH ORANGE LIGHT.
THEN IT WAS DARK AGAIN. IT WAS LIKE THE SUN HAD COME UP AND SUDDENLY GONE DOWN AGAIN.
NOW ENTERING NEW MEXICO
Up it went, a great ball of fire about a mile in diameter, changing colors as it kept shooting upward, from deep purple to orange...for a fleeting instant the color was an unearthly green.
IT WAS LIKE BEING AT THE BOTTOM OF AN OCEAN OF LIGHT.
THEN THE LIGHT WITHDREW INTO THE BOMB AS IF THE BOMB SUCKED IT ALL UP.

THE CLOUD RESEMBLED A GIANT BRAIN, THE CONVOLUTIONS OF WHICH WERE CONSTANTLY CHANGING.

I WAS SURPRISED BY THE SHOCK WAVE'S COMPARATIVE GENTLENESS WHEN IT REACHED US FIFTY SECONDS LATER.

AS I LOOK BACK ON IT NOW, I REALIZE THAT THE SHOCK WAS VERY IMPRESSIVE, BUT THE LIGHT HAD BEEN SO MUCH GREATER THAN ANY HUMAN HAD PREVIOUSLY EXPERIENCED OR EVEN THAN WE HAD ANTICIPATED THAT WE DID NOT SHAKE OFF THE EXPERIENCE QUICKLY.

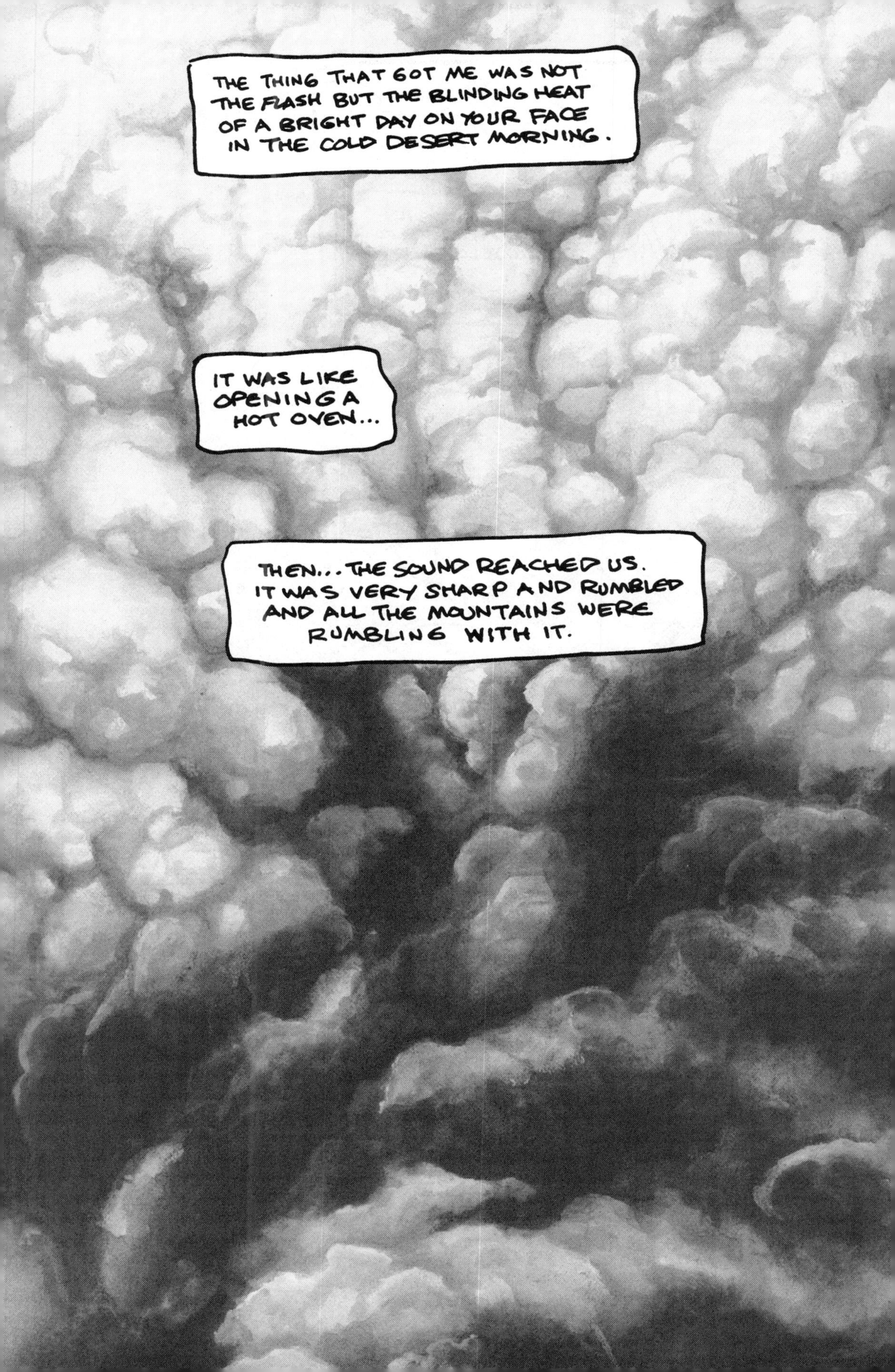
THE THING THAT GOT ME WAS NOT THE FLASH BUT THE BLINDING HEAT OF A BRIGHT DAY ON YOUR FACE IN THE COLD DESERT MORNING.
IT WAS LIKE OPENING A HOT OVEN...
THEN... THE SOUND REACHED US. IT WAS VERY SHARP AND RUMBLED AND ALL THE MOUNTAINS WERE RUMBLING WITH IT.

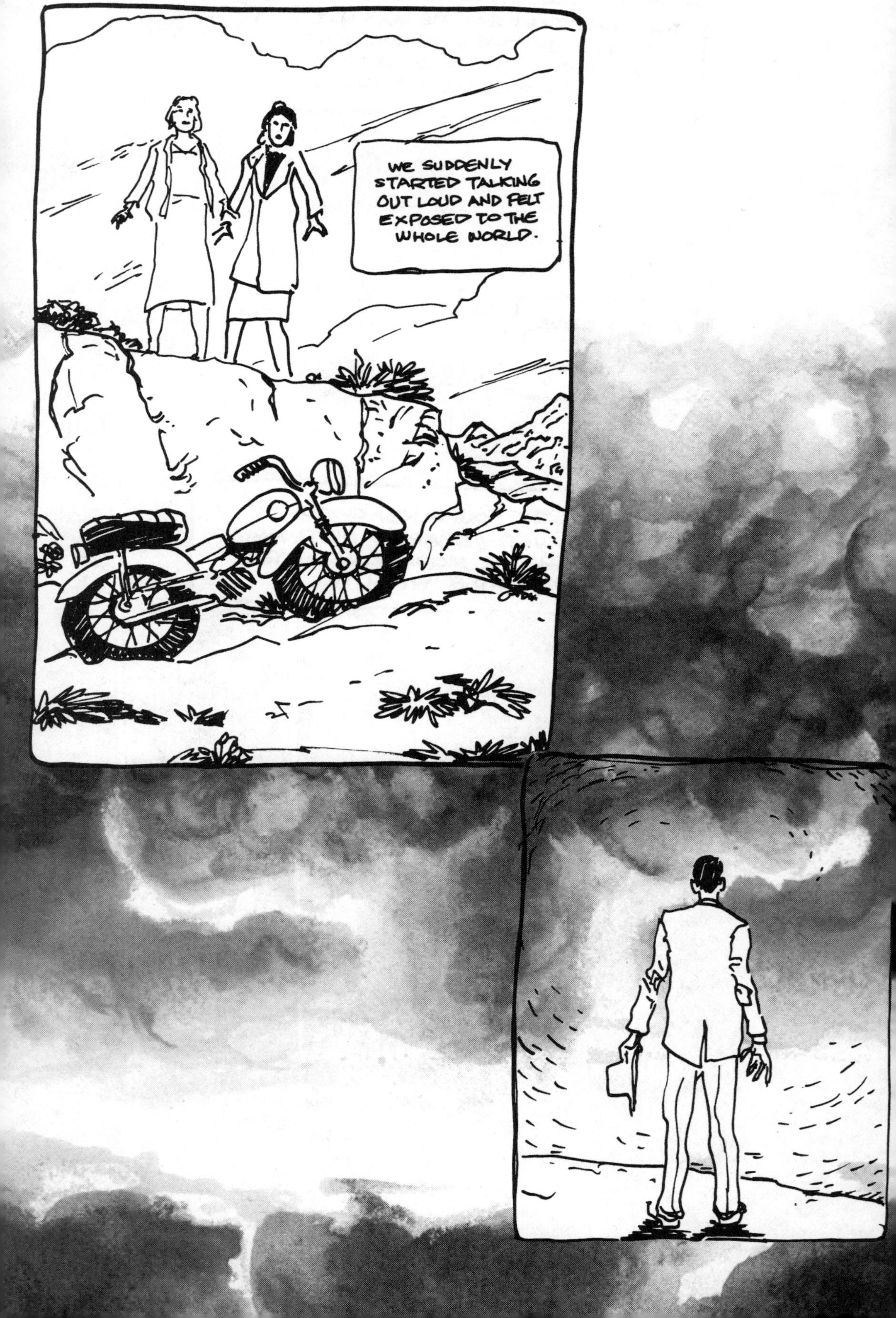
WE SUDDENLY STARTED TALKING OUT LOUD AND FELT EXPOSED TO THE WHOLE WORLD.

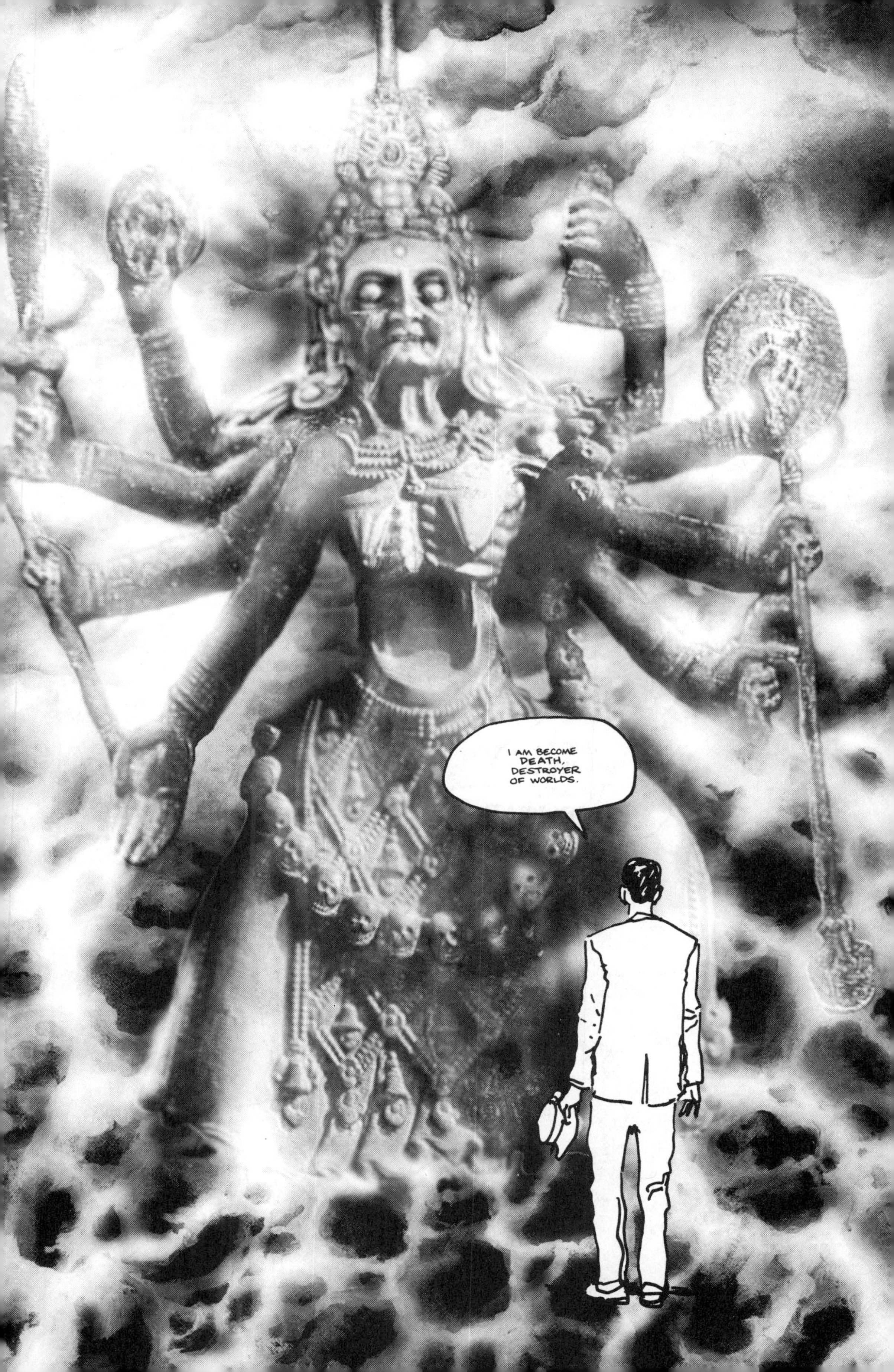
I AM BECOME DEATH, DESTROYER OF WORLDS.

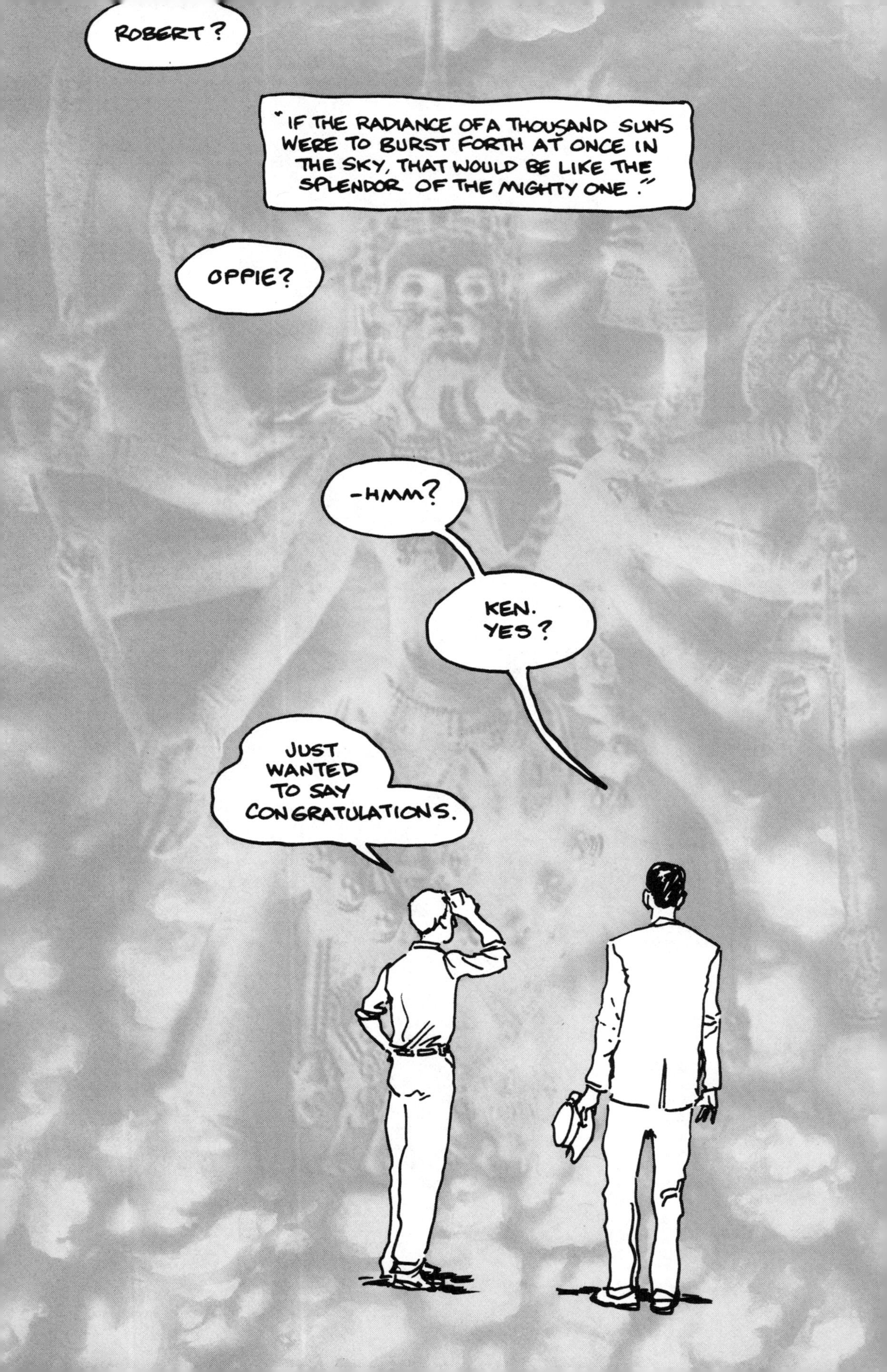
ROBERT?
"IF THE RADIANCE OF A THOUSAND SUNS WERE TO BURST FORTH AT ONCE IN THE SKY, THAT WOULD BE LIKE THE SPLENDOR OF THE MIGHTY ONE."
OPPIE?
-HMM?
KEN. YES?
JUST WANTED TO SAY CONGRATULATIONS.

NOW WE'RE ALL SONS OF BITCHES.

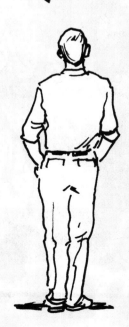

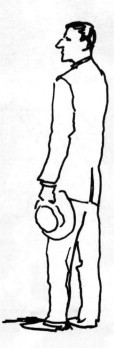

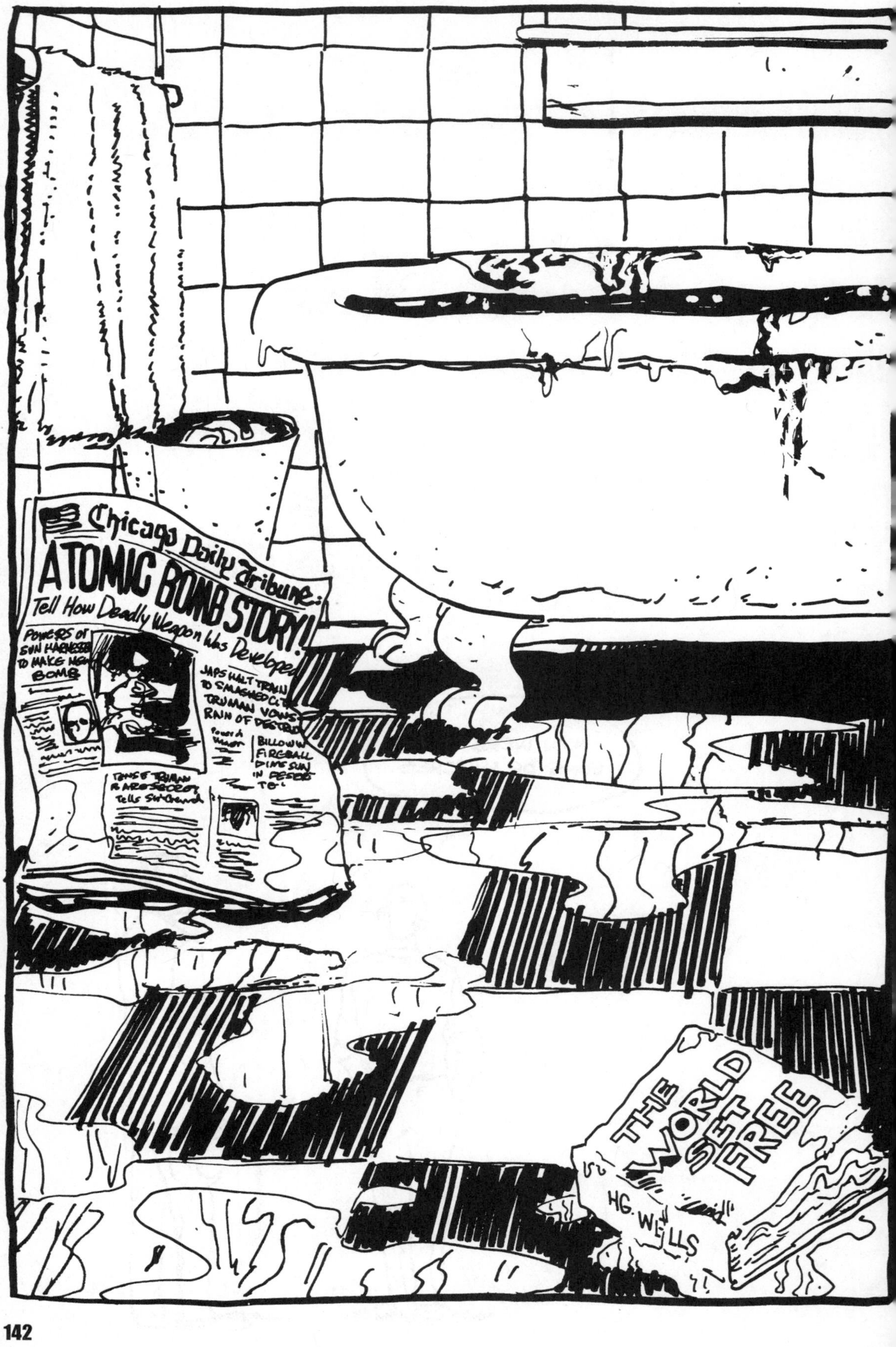
Chicago Daily Tribune
ATOMIC BOMB STORY!
Tell How Deadly Weapon Was Developed
THE WORLD SET FREE
H.G. WELLS

interlude

"The Beginning or the End"

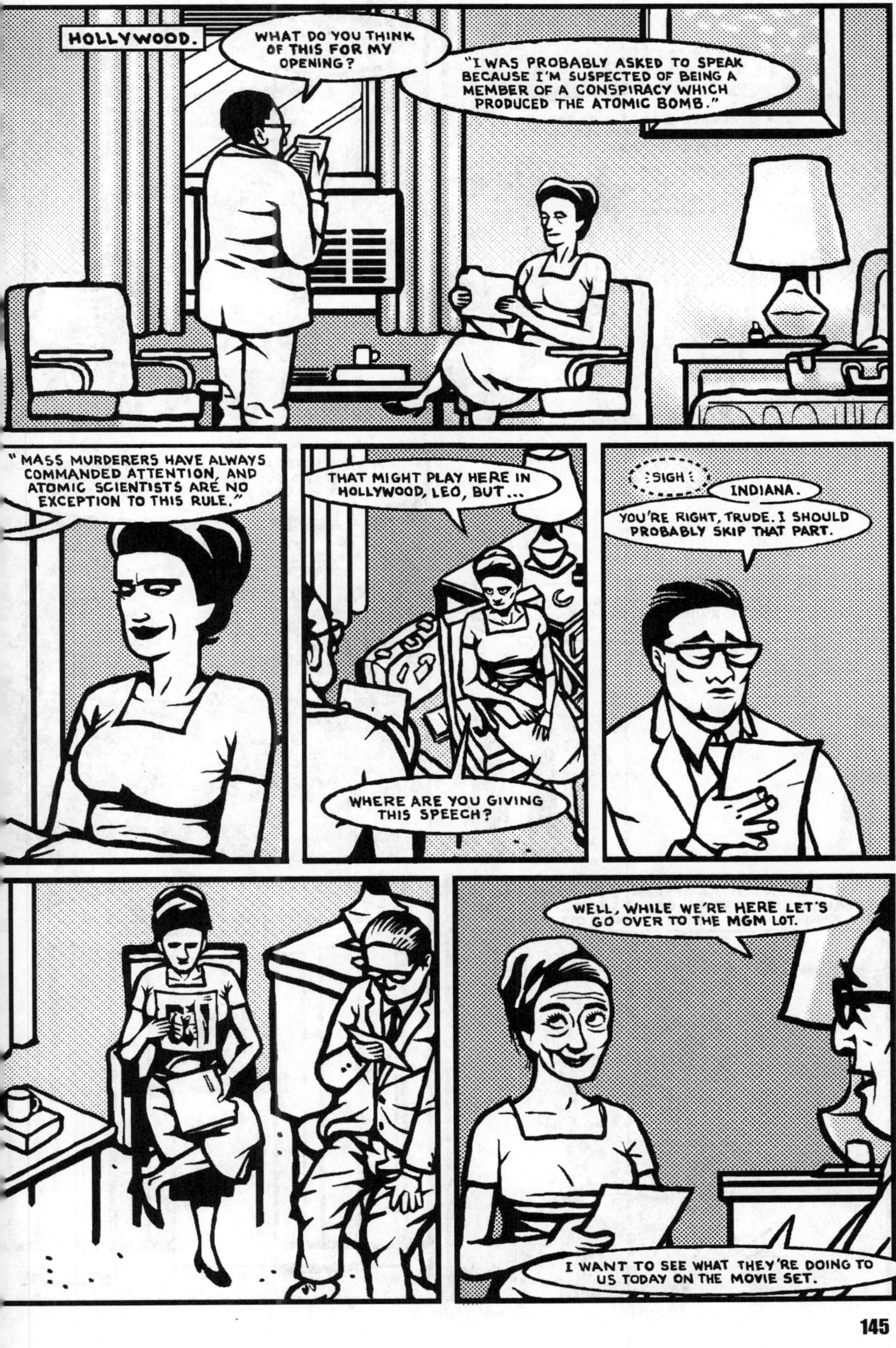
HOLLYWOOD.
WHAT DO YOU THINK OF THIS FOR MY OPENING?
"I WAS PROBABLY ASKED TO SPEAK BECAUSE I'M SUSPECTED OF BEING A MEMBER OF A CONSPIRACY WHICH PRODUCED THE ATOMIC BOMB."
"MASS MURDERERS HAVE ALWAYS COMMANDED ATTENTION, AND ATOMIC SCIENTISTS ARE NO EXCEPTION TO THIS RULE."
THAT MIGHT PLAY HERE IN HOLLYWOOD, LEO, BUT...
WHERE ARE YOU GIVING THIS SPEECH?
SIGH
INDIANA.
YOU'RE RIGHT, TRUDE. I SHOULD PROBABLY SKIP THAT PART.
WELL, WHILE WE'RE HERE LET'S GO OVER TO THE MGM LOT.
I WANT TO SEE WHAT THEY'RE DOING TO US TODAY ON THE MOVIE SET.

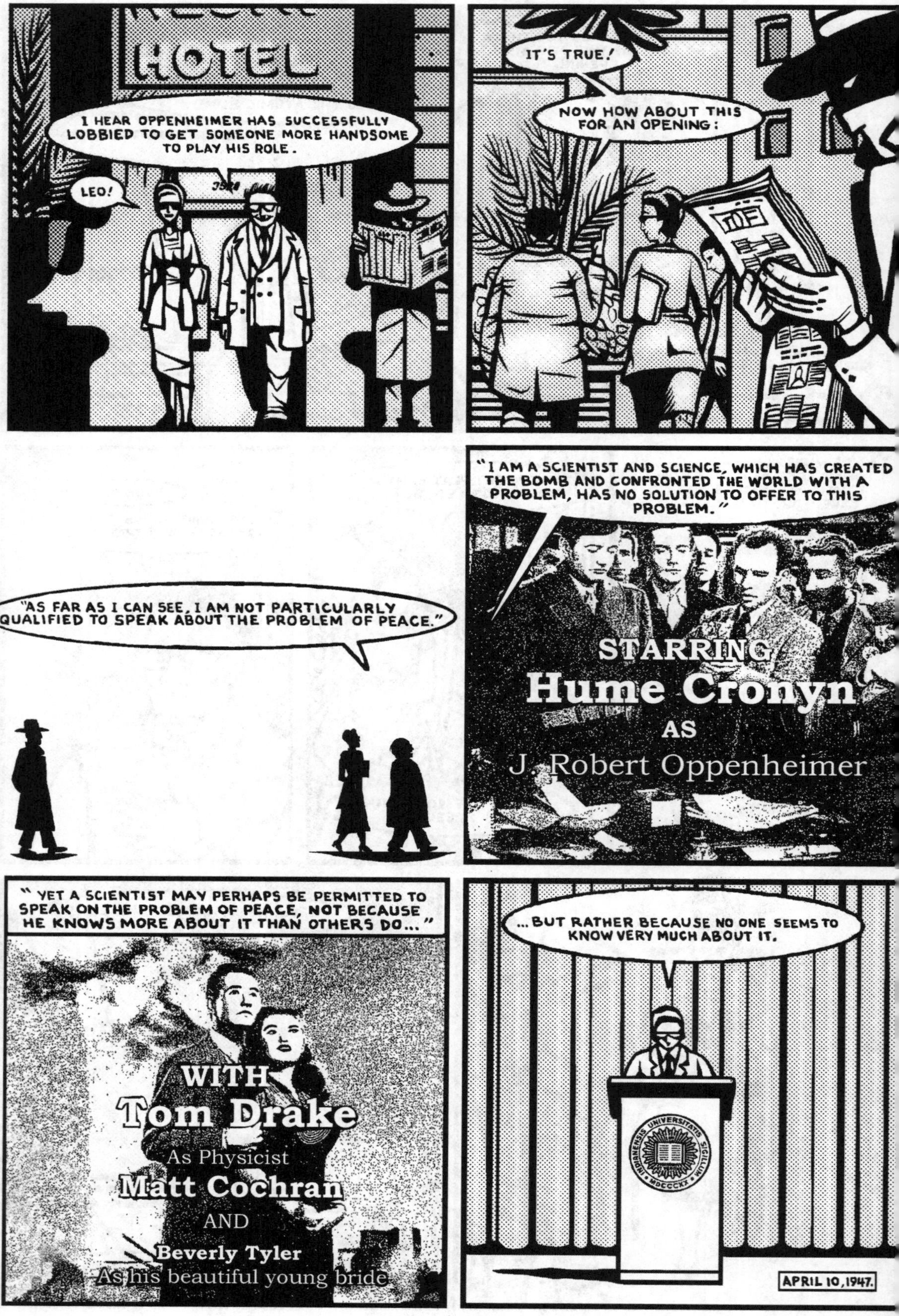
HOTEL
I HEAR OPPENHEIMER HAS SUCCESSFULLY LOBBIED TO GET SOMEONE MORE HANDSOME TO PLAY HIS ROLE.
LEO!
IT'S TRUE!
NOW HOW ABOUT THIS FOR AN OPENING:
"AS FAR AS I CAN SEE, I AM NOT PARTICULARLY QUALIFIED TO SPEAK ABOUT THE PROBLEM OF PEACE."
"I AM A SCIENTIST AND SCIENCE, WHICH HAS CREATED THE BOMB AND CONFRONTED THE WORLD WITH A PROBLEM, HAS NO SOLUTION TO OFFER TO THIS PROBLEM."
STARRING
Hume Cronyn
AS
J. Robert Oppenheimer
" YET A SCIENTIST MAY PERHAPS BE PERMITTED TO SPEAK ON THE PROBLEM OF PEACE, NOT BECAUSE HE KNOWS MORE ABOUT IT THAN OTHERS DO... "
WITH
Tom Drake
As Physicist
Matt Cochran
AND
Beverly Tyler
As his beautiful young bride
... BUT RATHER BECAUSE NO ONE SEEMS TO KNOW VERY MUCH ABOUT IT.
APRIL 10, 1947.

MOST PHYSICISTS BELIEVE THAT NOTHING SHORT OF A MIRACLE WILL BRING ABOUT A PERMANENT PEACE WITHOUT GOING THROUGH ANOTHER WORLD WAR.

BLOOMINGTON, INDIANA.

NOW, WE ARE QUITE WILLING TO SPEND AT PRESENT ABOUT TEN PERCENT OF OUR NATIONAL INCOME FOR THE ARMY AND NAVY.

I THEREFORE PROPOSE A CONSTITUTIONAL AMENDMENT FOR DEVOTING TEN PERCENT OF THE BUDGET TO HELPING OTHER COUNTRIES.

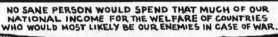

NO SANE PERSON WOULD SPEND THAT MUCH OF OUR NATIONAL INCOME FOR THE WELFARE OF COUNTRIES WHO WOULD MOST LIKELY BE OUR ENEMIES IN CASE OF WAR.

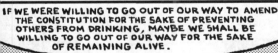

IF WE WERE WILLING TO GO OUT OF OUR WAY TO AMEND THE CONSTITUTION FOR THE SAKE OF PREVENTING OTHERS FROM DRINKING, MAYBE WE SHALL BE WILLING TO GO OUT OF OUR WAY FOR THE SAKE OF REMAINING ALIVE.

OBVIOUSLY THE ODDS ARE HEAVILY AGAINST US.

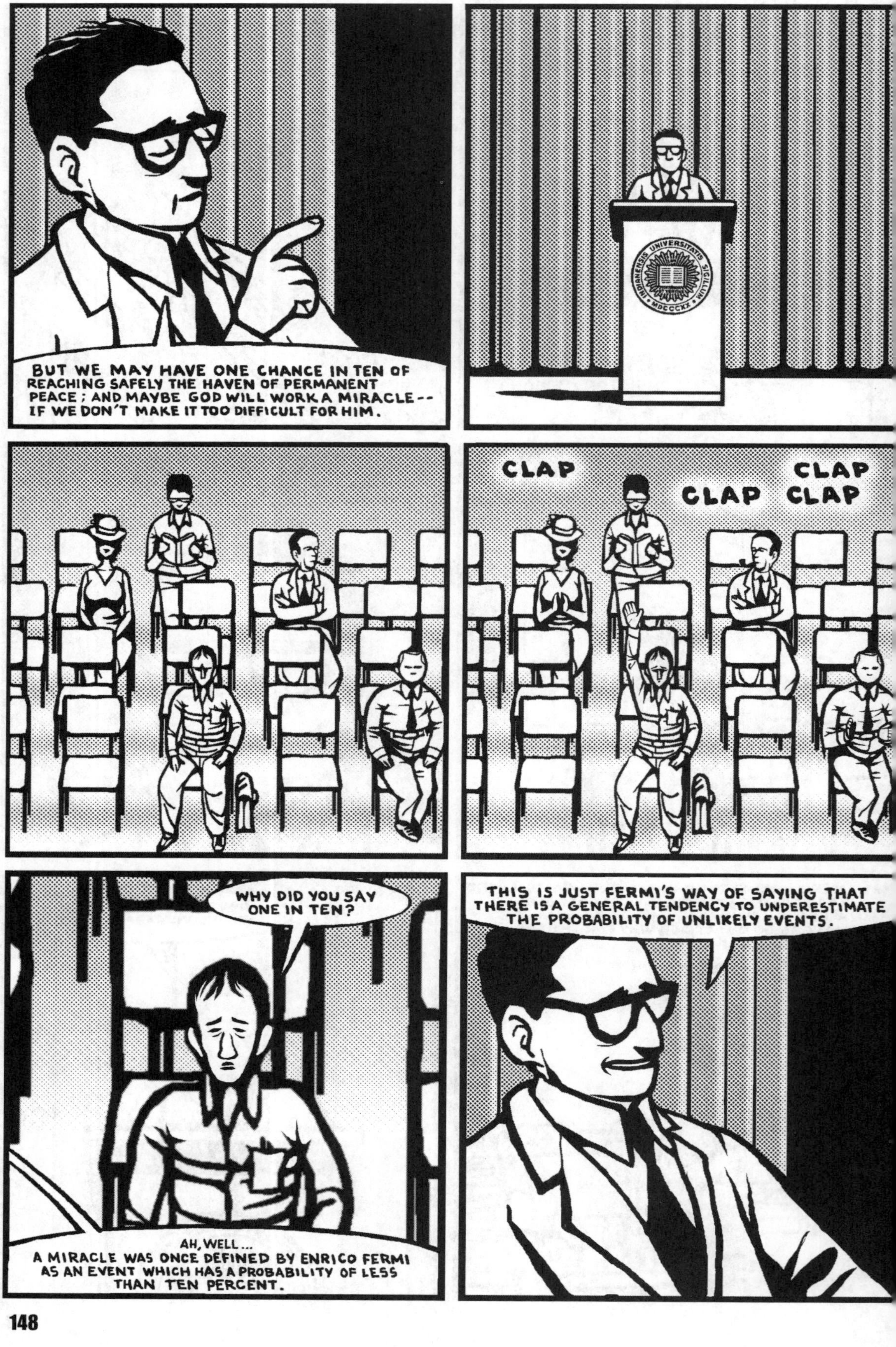
BUT WE MAY HAVE ONE CHANCE IN TEN OF REACHING SAFELY THE HAVEN OF PERMANENT PEACE ; AND MAYBE GOD WILL WORK A MIRACLE -- IF WE DON'T MAKE IT TOO DIFFICULT FOR HIM.
CLAP
CLAP
CLAP
CLAP
WHY DID YOU SAY ONE IN TEN?
AH, WELL ...
A MIRACLE WAS ONCE DEFINED BY ENRICO FERMI AS AN EVENT WHICH HAS A PROBABILITY OF LESS THAN TEN PERCENT.
THIS IS JUST FERMI'S WAY OF SAYING THAT THERE IS A GENERAL TENDENCY TO UNDERESTIMATE THE PROBABILITY OF UNLIKELY EVENTS.

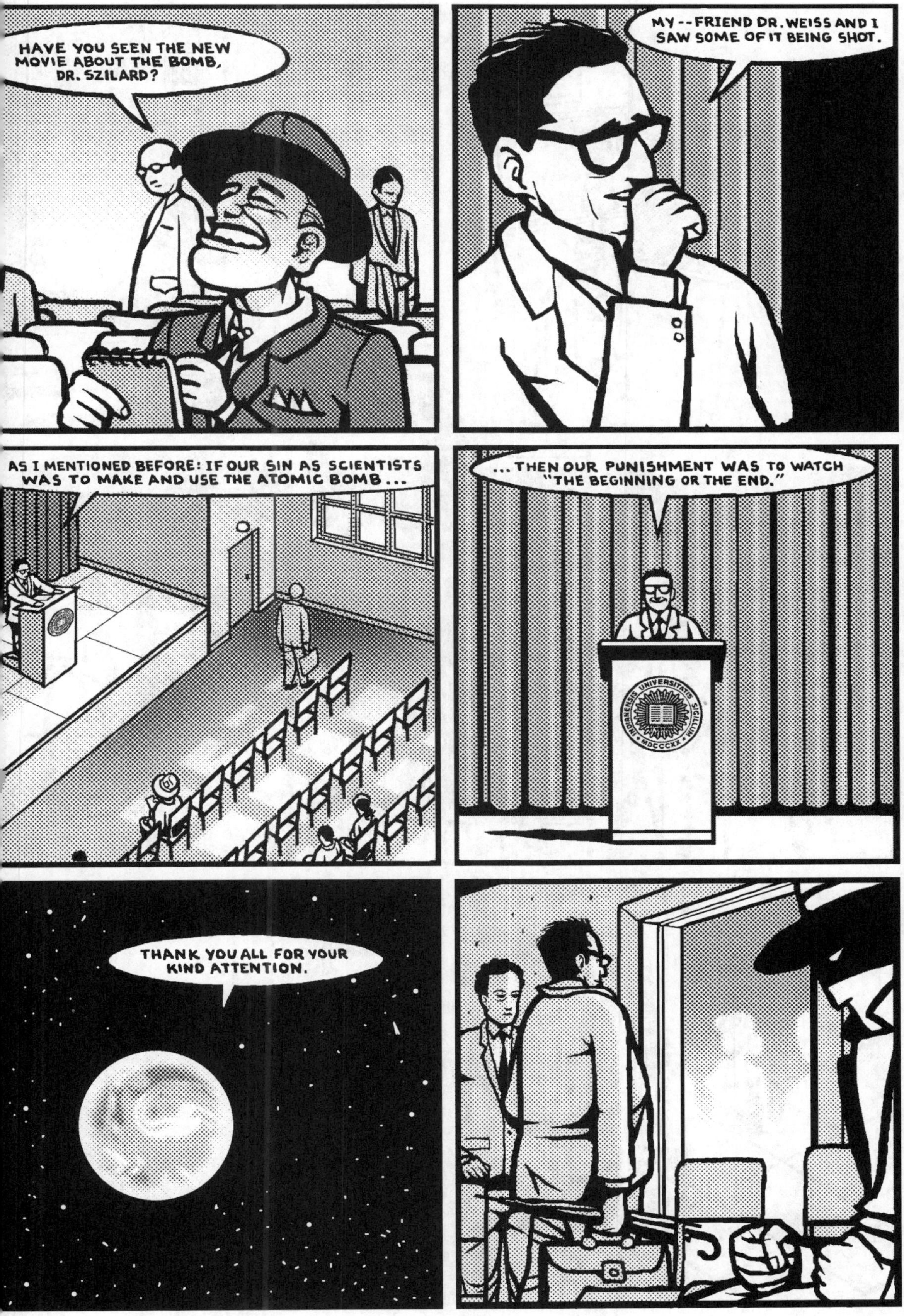
HAVE YOU SEEN THE NEW MOVIE ABOUT THE BOMB, DR. SZILARD?
MY -- FRIEND DR. WEISS AND I SAW SOME OF IT BEING SHOT.
AS I MENTIONED BEFORE: IF OUR SIN AS SCIENTISTS WAS TO MAKE AND USE THE ATOMIC BOMB ...
... THEN OUR PUNISHMENT WAS TO WATCH "THE BEGINNING OR THE END."
THANK YOU ALL FOR YOUR KIND ATTENTION.

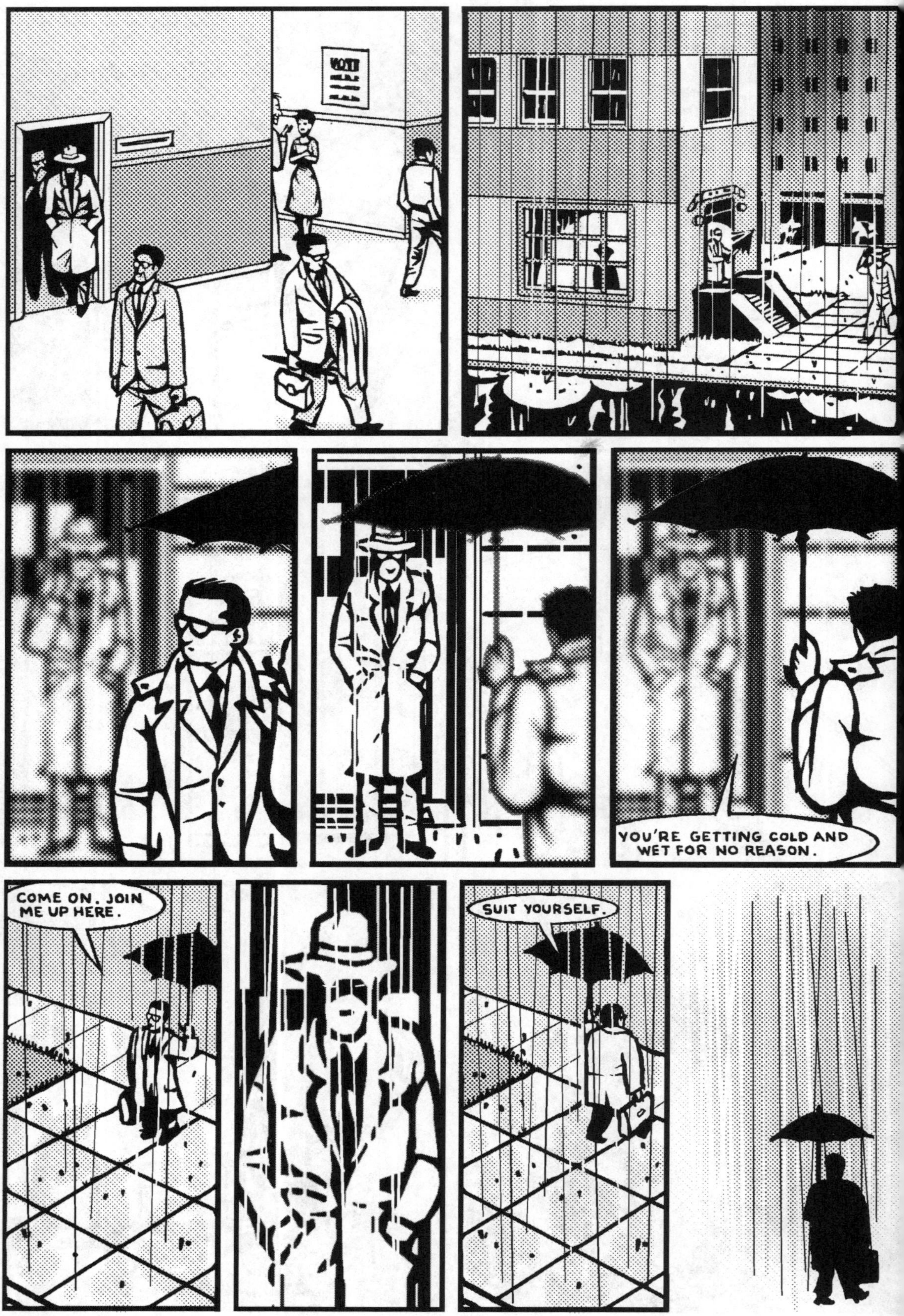
YOU'RE GETTING COLD AND WET FOR NO REASON.
COME ON. JOIN ME UP HERE.
SUIT YOURSELF.

death
(1954-)

People are cruel and stupid in a stupid age who might be gentle and splendid in a gracious one.

—H.G. Wells, *The World Set Free*

HM... SZILARD SAYS HERE THAT WITH ALL I KNOW...

"...WOULDN'T ARRESTING HIM AND SHOOTING HIM WITHOUT TRIAL BE THE ONLY PRUDENT COURSE OF ACTION FROM THE POINT OF VIEW OF 'NATIONAL SECURITY?'"

Washington D.C. April 12, 1954.

HE'S A LITTLE LESS FLIPPANT IN HIS CONCLUSION, AT LEAST...

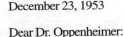

December 23, 1953

Dear Dr. Oppenheimer:

Section 10 of the Atomic Energy Act of 1946 places upon the Atomic Energy Commission the responsibility for assuring that individuals are employed by the Commission only when such employment will not endanger the common defense and security. In addition, Executive Order 10450 of April 27, 1953, requires the suspension of employment of any individual where there exists information indicating that his employment may not be clearly consistent with the interests of the national security.

As a result of additional investigation as to your character, associations, and loyalty, and review of your personnel security file, there has developed considerable question whether your continued employment will endanger the common defense and security and whether it is clearly consistent with the interests of the national security. This letter is to advise you of the steps which you may take to assist in the resolution of this question.

HE SAYS "CLASSING OPPENHEIMER AS A SECURITY RISK AND SUBJECTING HIM TO A FORMAL HEARING IS REGARDED BY SCIENTISTS IN THIS COUNTRY AS AN INDIGNITY AND AN AFFRONT TO ALL,"

"IT IS REGARDED BY OUR FRIENDS ABROAD AS A SIGN OF INSANITY-- WHICH IT PROBABLY IS,"

I DON'T THINK WE CAN USE IT.
I UNDERSTAND.
ANYWAY, I HEAR SZILARD'S HAVING TROUBLE WITH SECURITY AS WELL...
WRITING IN "BAITING THE BRASS" AS HIS HOBBY ON THAT CLEARANCE FORM PROBABLY DIDN'T HELP.
DR. OPPENHEIMER, PLEASE, FORGET SZILARD.

The substance of the information which raises the question concerning your eligibility for employment on Atomic Energy Commission work is as follows:

It was reported that in 1940 you were listed as a sponsor of the Friends of the Chinese People, an organization which was characterized in 1944 by the House Committee on Un-American Activities as a Communist-front organization. It was further reported that in 1940 your name was included on a letterhead of the American Committee for Democratic and Intellectual Freedom as a member of its national executive committee. It was characterized in 1942 by the House Committee on Un-American Activities as a Communist front which defended Communist teachers, and in 1943 it was characterized as subversive and un-American by a special subcommittee of the House Committee on Appropriations. It was further reported that you stated in 1943 that you were not a Communist, but had probably belonged to every Communist front organization on the west coast and had signed many petitions in which Communists were interested.

It was reported that your wife, Katherine Puening Oppenheimer, was formerly the wife of Joseph Dallet, a member of the Communist Party, who was killed in Spain in 1937 fighting for the Spanish Republican Army. It was further reported that during the period of her association with Joseph Dallet, your wife became a member of the Communist Party. The Communist Party has been designated by the Attorney General as a subversive organization which seeks to alter the form of Government of the United States by unconstitutional means, within the purview of Executive Order 9835…

It was reported that you were a subscriber to *The Daily People's World*, a West Coast Communist paper, in 1941 and 1942.

It was reported that you attended a housewarming party at the home of Kenneth and Ruth May on September 20, 1941, for which there was an admission charge for the benefit of *The People's World*…

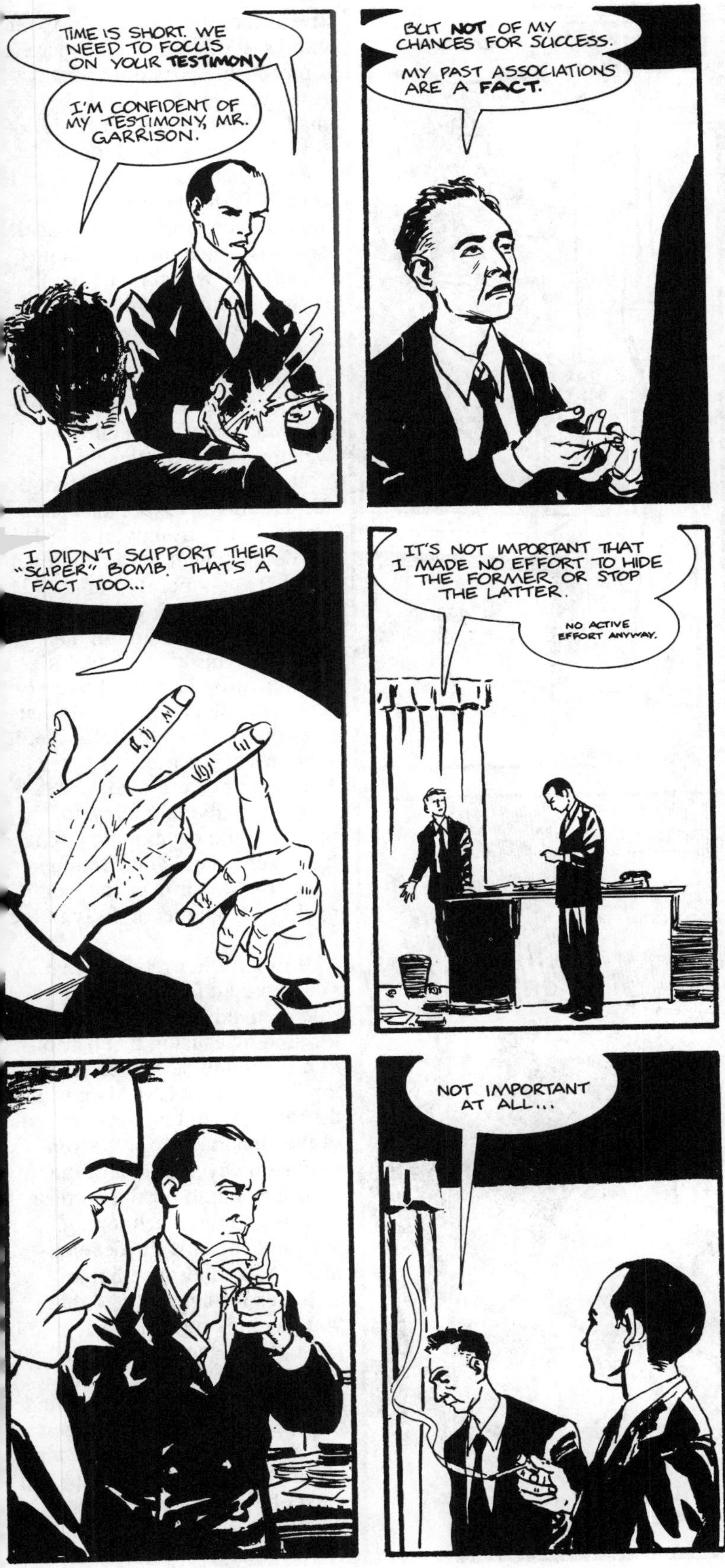

TIME IS SHORT. WE NEED TO FOCUS ON YOUR TESTIMONY
I'M CONFIDENT OF MY TESTIMONY, MR. GARRISON.
BUT NOT OF MY CHANCES FOR SUCCESS.
MY PAST ASSOCIATIONS ARE A FACT.
I DIDN'T SUPPORT THEIR "SUPER" BOMB. THAT'S A FACT TOO...
IT'S NOT IMPORTANT THAT I MADE NO EFFORT TO HIDE THE FORMER OR STOP THE LATTER.
NO ACTIVE EFFORT ANYWAY.
NOT IMPORTANT AT ALL...

It was reported that prior to March 1, 1943, possibly 3 months prior, Peter Ivanov, secretary of the Soviet consulate, San Francisco, approached George Charles Eltenton for the purpose of obtaining information regarding work being done at the Radiation Laboratory for the use of Soviet scientists; that George Charles Eltenton subsequently requested Haakon Chevalier to approach you concerning this matter; that Haakon Chevalier thereupon approached you, either directly or through your brother, Frank Friedman Oppenheimer, in connection with this matter; and that Haakon Chevalier finally advised George Charles Eltenton that there was no chance whatsoever of obtaining the information.

It was further reported that you did not report this episode to the appropriate authorities until several months after its occurrence; that when you initially discussed this matter with the appropriate authorities on August 26, 1943, you did not identify yourself as the person who had been approached, and you refused to identify Haakon Chevalier as the individual who made the approach on behalf of George Charles Eltenton; and that it was not until several months later, when you were ordered by a superior to do so, that you so identified Haakon Chevalier.

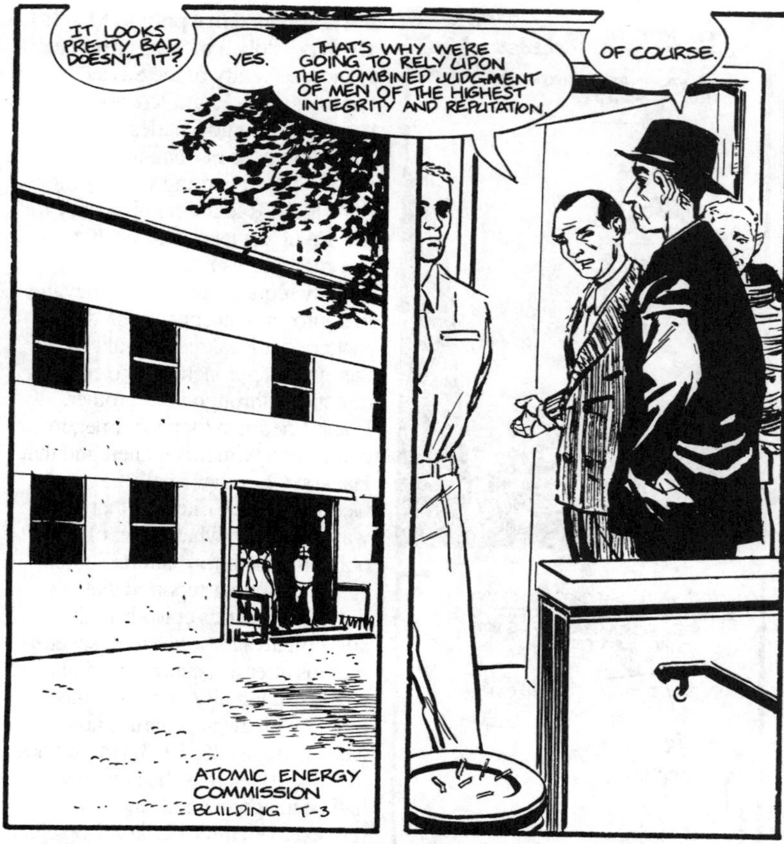
IT LOOKS PRETTY BAD DOESN'T IT?
YES.
THAT'S WHY WE'RE GOING TO RELY UPON THE COMBINED JUDGMENT OF MEN OF THE HIGHEST INTEGRITY AND REPUTATION.
OF COURSE.
ATOMIC ENERGY COMMISSION BUILDING T-3

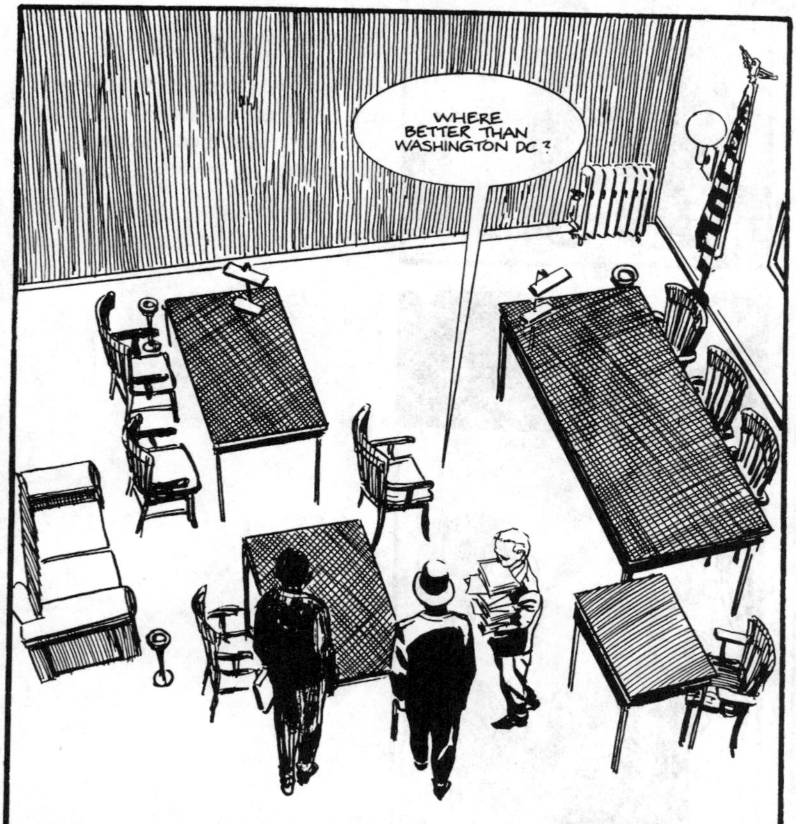
WHERE BETTER THAN WASHINGTON DC?

It was reported that in 1945 you expressed the view that "there is a reasonable possibility that it (the hydrogen bomb) can be made," but that the feasibility of the hydrogen bomb did not appear, on theoretical grounds, as certain as the fission bomb appeared certain, on theoretical grounds, when the Los Alamos Laboratory was started; and that in the autumn of 1949 the General Advisory Committee expressed the view that "an imaginative and concerted attack on the problem has a better than even chance of producing the weapon within 5 years."

It was further reported that in the autumn of 1949 and subsequently, you strongly opposed the development of the hydrogen bomb; (1) on moral grounds, (2) by claiming that it was not feasible, (3) by claiming that there were insufficient facilities and scientific personnel to carry on the development and (4) that it was not politically desirable. It was further reported that even after it was determined, as a matter of national policy, to proceed with development of a hydrogen bomb, you continued to oppose the project and declined to cooperate fully in the project.

It was further reported that you departed from your proper role as an adviser to the Commission by causing the distribution separately and in private, to top personnel at Los Alamos of the majority and minority reports of the General Advisory Committee on development of the hydrogen bomb for the purpose of trying to turn such top personnel against the development of the hydrogen bomb.

It was further reported that you were instrumental in persuading other outstanding scientists not to work on the hydrogen-bomb project, and that the opposition to the hydrogen bomb, of which you are the most experienced, most powerful, and most effective member, has definitely slowed down its development.

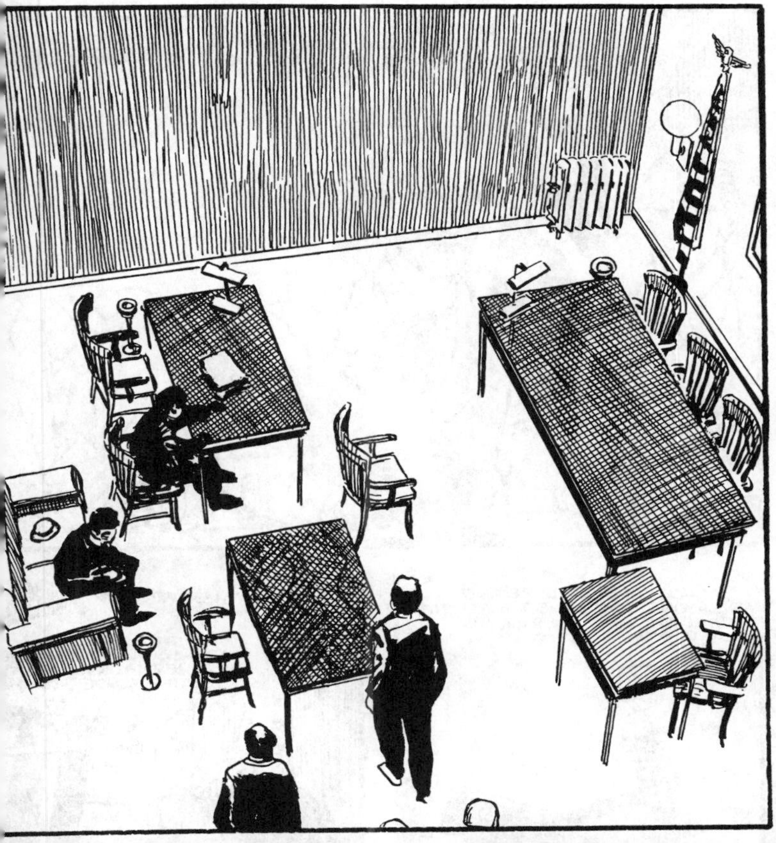

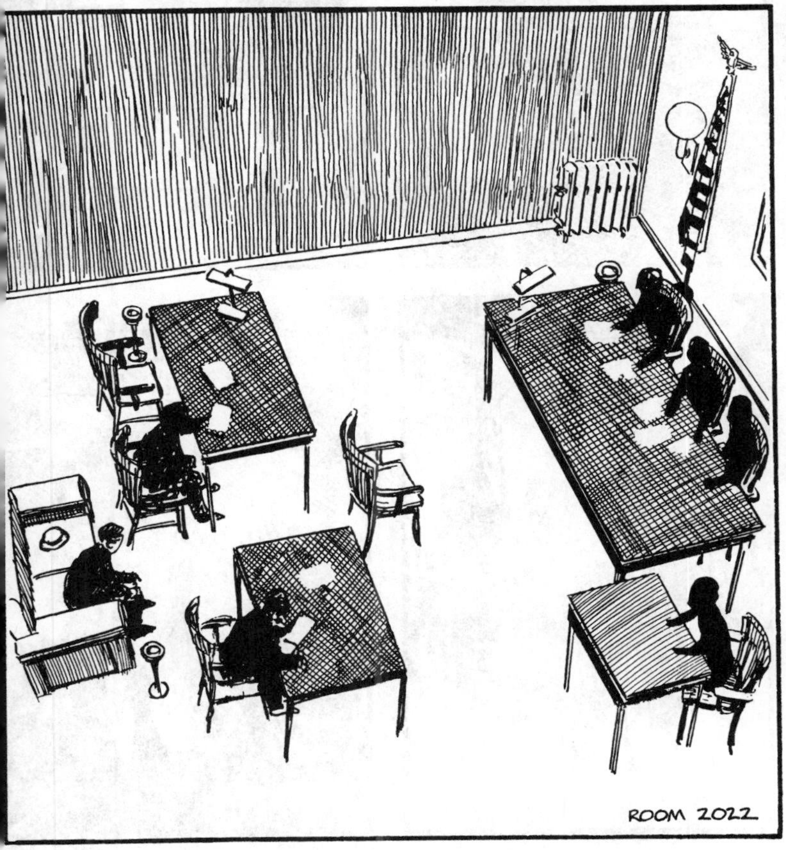
ROOM 2022

In view of your access to highly sensitive classified information, and in view of these allegations which, until disproved, raise questions as to your veracity, conduct and even your loyalty, the Commission has no other recourse, in discharge of its obligations to protect the common defense and security, but to suspend your clearance until the matter has been resolved.

Accordingly, your employment on Atomic Energy Commission work and your eligibility for access to restricted data are hereby suspended, effective immediately, pending final determination of this matter.

To assist in the resolution of this matter, you have the privilege of appearing before an Atomic Energy Commission personnel security board. To avail yourself of the privileges afforded you under the Atomic Energy Commission hearing procedures, you must, within 30 days following receipt of this letter, submit to me, in writing, your reply to the information outlined above and request the opportunity of appearing before the personnel security board. Should you signify your desire to appear before the board, you will be notified of the composition of the board and may challenge any member of it for cause. Such challenge should be submitted within 72 hours of the receipt of notice of composition of the board…

If a written response is not received from you within 30 days it will be assumed that you do not wish to submit any explanation for further consideration. In that event, or should you not advise me in writing of your desire to appear before the personnel security board, a determination in your case will be made by me on the basis of the existing record....

Very truly yours,
K. D. Nichols, General Manager,
Atomic Energy Commission

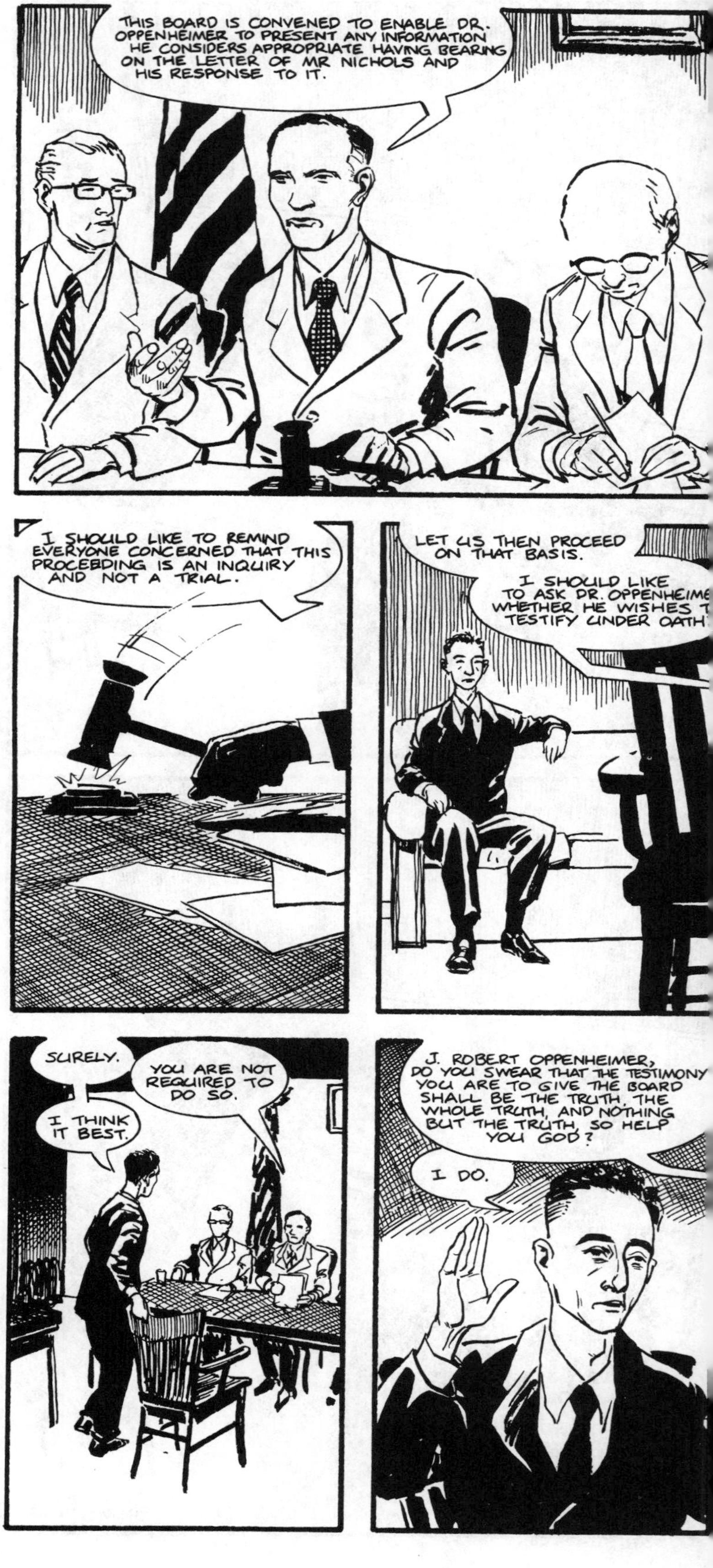
THIS BOARD IS CONVENED TO ENABLE DR. OPPENHEIMER TO PRESENT ANY INFORMATION HE CONSIDERS APPROPRIATE HAVING BEARING ON THE LETTER OF MR NICHOLS AND HIS RESPONSE TO IT.
I SHOULD LIKE TO REMIND EVERYONE CONCERNED THAT THIS PROCEEDING IS AN INQUIRY AND NOT A TRIAL.
LET US THEN PROCEED ON THAT BASIS.
I SHOULD LIKE TO ASK DR. OPPENHEIME WHETHER HE WISHES T TESTIFY UNDER OATH
SURELY.
YOU ARE NOT REQUIRED TO DO SO.
I THINK IT BEST.
J. ROBERT OPPENHEIMER, DO YOU SWEAR THAT THE TESTIMONY YOU ARE TO GIVE THE BOARD SHALL BE THE TRUTH, THE WHOLE TRUTH, AND NOTHING BUT THE TRUTH, SO HELP YOU GOD?
I DO.

Dear General Nichols:

This is in answer to your letter of Dec. 23, 1953, in which the question is raised whether my continued employment as a consultant of the Atomic Energy Commission work will "endanger the common defense and security and whether such continued employment is clearly consistent with the interest of the national security."

Though of course I would have no desire to retain an advisory position if my advice were not needed, I cannot ignore the question you have raised, nor accept the suggestion I am unfit for public service.

The items of so-called "derogatory" information set forth in your letter cannot be fairly understood except in the context of my life and work.

I was born in New York in 1904. My father had come to this country at the age of 17 from Germany. My mother was born in Baltimore and before her marriage was an artist and teacher of art.

I attended the Ethical Culture School and Harvard College, which I entered in 1922. I completed the work for my degree in the spring of 1925. I then left Harvard to study at Cambridge University and in Goettingen, where in the spring of 1927 I took my doctor's degree.

In the spring of 1929 I returned to the United States. I was homesick for this country and in fact I did not leave it again for over nineteen years.

I accepted concurrent appointments as Assistant Professor at the California Institute of Technology in Pasadena and at the University of California in Berkeley. For the coming twelve years I was to devote my time to these two faculties.

My friends, both in Pasadena and in Berkeley, were mostly faculty people, scientists, classicists, and artists. I studied and read Sanskrit with Arthur Rider. I read very widely, but mostly classics, novels, plays and poetry, and I read something of other parts of science. I was not interested in and did not read about economics or politics. I was almost wholly divorced from the contemporary scene in this country.

I never read a newspaper or a current magazine like Time *or* Harper's*; I had no radio, no telephone; I learned of the stock market crash in the fall of 1929 only long after the event; the first time I voted was in the Presidential election of 1936.*

To many of my friends my indifference to contemporary affairs seemed bizarre, ant they often chided me with being too much of a highbrow. I was interested in man and his experience; I was deeply interested in my science; but I had no understanding of the relations of man to his society.

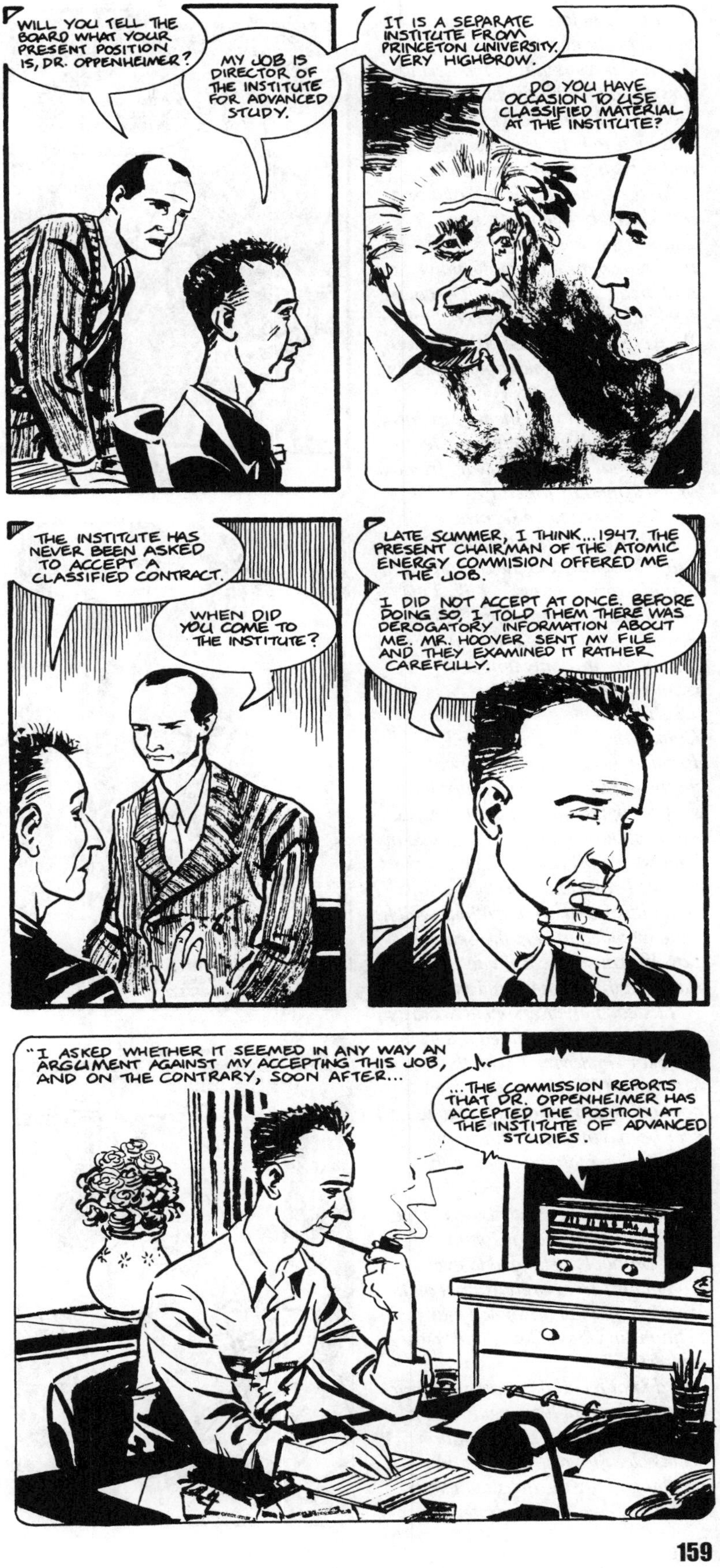

WILL YOU TELL THE BOARD WHAT YOUR PRESENT POSITION IS, DR. OPPENHEIMER?
MY JOB IS DIRECTOR OF THE INSTITUTE FOR ADVANCED STUDY.
IT IS A SEPARATE INSTITUTE FROM PRINCETON UNIVERSITY. VERY HIGHBROW.
DO YOU HAVE OCCASION TO USE CLASSIFIED MATERIAL AT THE INSTITUTE?
THE INSTITUTE HAS NEVER BEEN ASKED TO ACCEPT A CLASSIFIED CONTRACT.
WHEN DID YOU COME TO THE INSTITUTE?
LATE SUMMER, I THINK... 1947. THE PRESENT CHAIRMAN OF THE ATOMIC ENERGY COMMISION OFFERED ME THE JOB.
I DID NOT ACCEPT AT ONCE. BEFORE DOING SO, I TOLD THEM THERE WAS DEROGATORY INFORMATION ABOUT ME. MR. HOOVER SENT MY FILE AND THEY EXAMINED IT RATHER CAREFULLY.
"I ASKED WHETHER IT SEEMED IN ANY WAY AN ARGUMENT AGAINST MY ACCEPTING THIS JOB, AND ON THE CONTRARY, SOON AFTER...
...THE COMMISSION REPORTS THAT DR. OPPENHEIMER HAS ACCEPTED THE POSITION AT THE INSTITUTE OF ADVANCED STUDIES.

Beginning in late 1936, my interests began to change.

I had a continuing, smoldering fury about the treatment of Jews in Germany. I had relatives there, and was later to help in extricating them and bringing them to this country.

In the spring of 1936, I had been introduced by friends to Jean Tatlock, the daughter of a noted professor of English at the university; and in the autumn, I began to court her, and we grew close to each other. We were at least twice close enough to marriage to think of ourselves as engaged.

I should not give the impression that it was wholly because of Jean Tatlock that I made left-wing friends, or felt sympathy for causes which hitherto would have seemed so remote from me, like the Loyalist cause in Spain, and the organization of migratory workers… I liked the new sense of companionship, and at the time felt that I was coming to be part of the life of my time and country.

This was the era of what the Communists then called the United Front, in which they joined with many non-Communist groups in support of humanitarian objectives. Many of these objectives engaged my interest. I subscribed to The People's World; *I contributed to the various committees and organizations which were intended to help the Spanish Loyalist cause. I was invited to help establish the teacher's union…*

I listed, in the Personnel Security Questionnaire that I filled out in 1942 for employment with the Manhattan District, the very few political organizations of which I had ever been a member. I have no recollection of the Friends of the Chinese People.

The statement is attributed to me that, while I was not a Communist, I "had probably belonged to every Communist-front organization on the West Coast and had signed many petitions in which Communists were interested."

I do not recall this statement, nor to whom I might have made it, nor the circumstances. The quotation seems clear to me that, if I said anything along the lines quoted, it was a half-jocular overstatement.

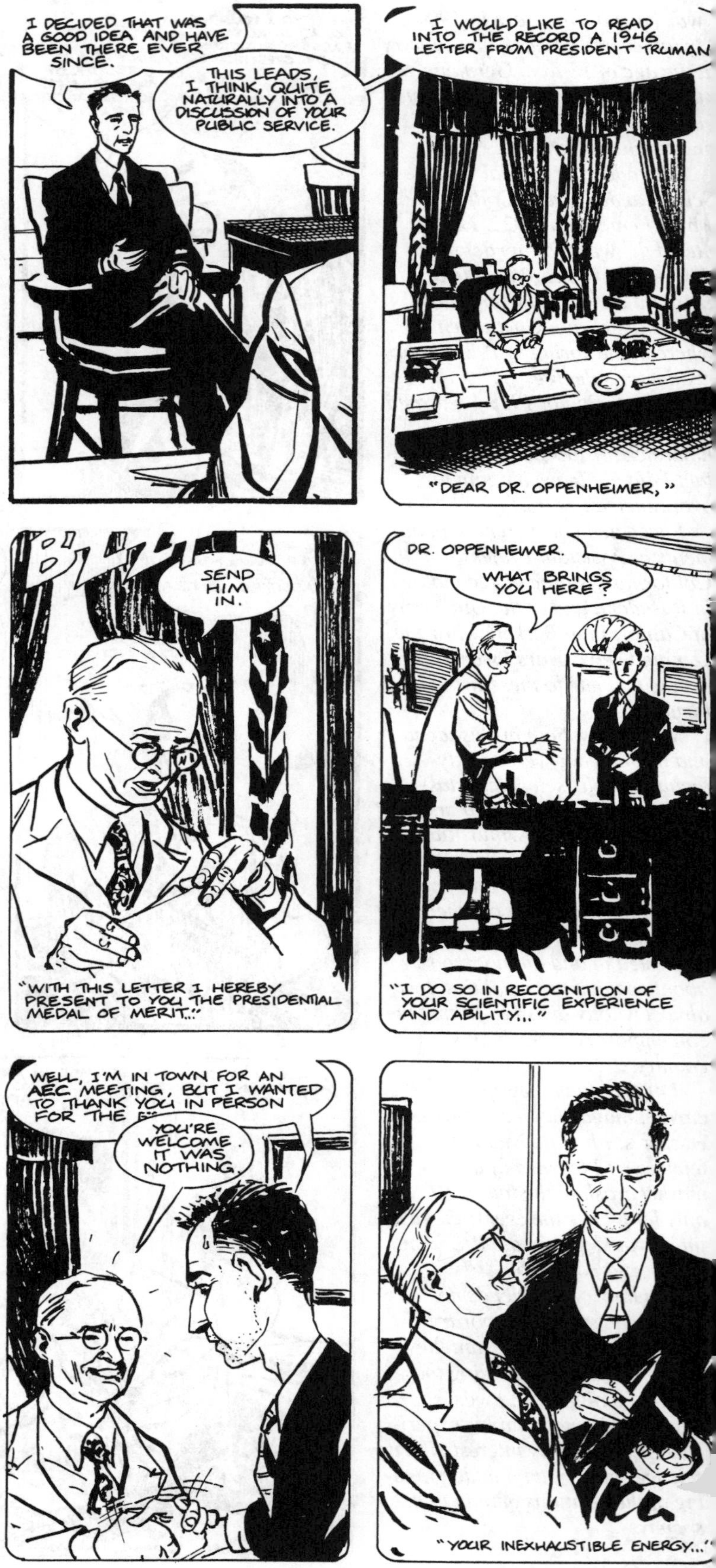

I DECIDED THAT WAS A GOOD IDEA AND HAVE BEEN THERE EVER SINCE.
THIS LEADS, I THINK, QUITE NATURALLY INTO A DISCUSSION OF YOUR PUBLIC SERVICE.
I WOULD LIKE TO READ INTO THE RECORD A 1946 LETTER FROM PRESIDENT TRUMAN
"DEAR DR. OPPENHEIMER,"
SEND HIM IN.
"WITH THIS LETTER I HEREBY PRESENT TO YOU THE PRESIDENTIAL MEDAL OF MERIT..."
DR. OPPENHEIMER.
WHAT BRINGS YOU HERE?
"I DO SO IN RECOGNITION OF YOUR SCIENTIFIC EXPERIENCE AND ABILITY..."
WELL, I'M IN TOWN FOR AN AEC MEETING, BUT I WANTED TO THANK YOU IN PERSON FOR THE
YOU'RE WELCOME. IT WAS NOTHING.
"YOUR INEXHAUSTIBLE ENERGY..."

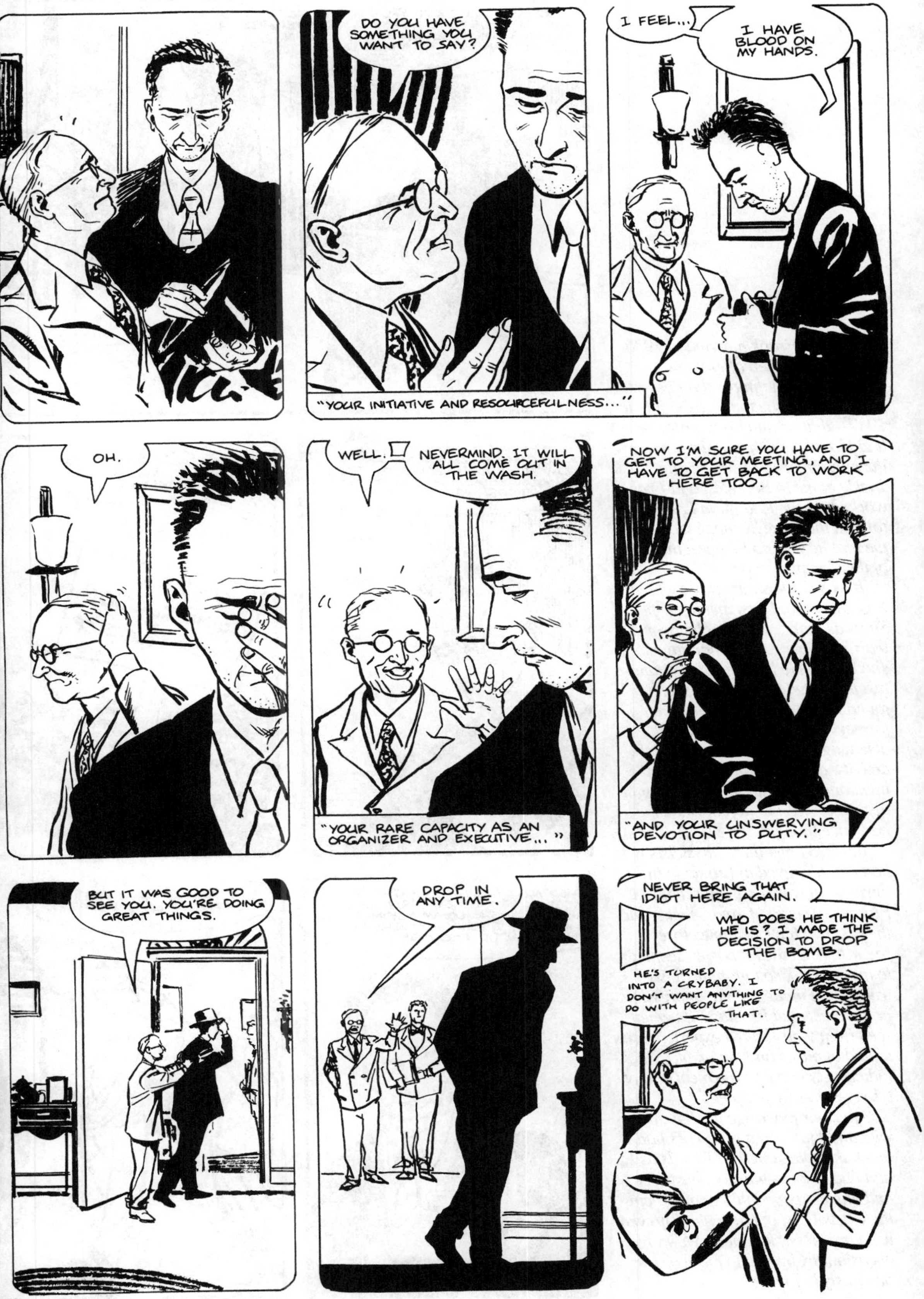
DO YOU HAVE SOMETHING YOU WANT TO SAY?
"YOUR INITIATIVE AND RESOURCEFULNESS..."
I FEEL...
I HAVE BLOOD ON MY HANDS.
OH.
WELL.
NEVERMIND. IT WILL ALL COME OUT IN THE WASH.
"YOUR RARE CAPACITY AS AN ORGANIZER AND EXECUTIVE..."
NOW I'M SURE YOU HAVE TO GET TO YOUR MEETING, AND I HAVE TO GET BACK TO WORK HERE TOO.
"AND YOUR UNSWERVING DEVOTION TO DUTY."
BUT IT WAS GOOD TO SEE YOU. YOU'RE DOING GREAT THINGS.
DROP IN ANY TIME.
NEVER BRING THAT IDIOT HERE AGAIN.
WHO DOES HE THINK HE IS? I MADE THE DECISION TO DROP THE BOMB.
HE'S TURNED INTO A CRYBABY. I DON'T WANT ANYTHING TO DO WITH PEOPLE LIKE THAT.

My brother Frank married in 1936. Our relations thereafter were inevitably less intimate than before. He told me at the time—probably in 1937—that he and his wife Jackie had joined the Communist party. In the autumn of 1941 Frank and Jackie came to Berkeley, and Frank worked for the Radiation Laboratory. At that time he made it clear to me that he was no longer a member of the Communist party.

It was in the summer of 1939 in Pasadena that I first met my wife. She was married to Dr. Harrison… I learned of her earlier marriage to Joe Dallet. He had been a Communist party member. When I met her I found in her a deep loyalty to her former husband, a complete disengagement from any political activity, and a certain disappointment and contempt that the Communist party was not in fact what she had once thought.

In 1938 I met three physicists who had actually lived in Russia in the thirties. All were eminent scientists, Placzek, Weisskopf, and Schein; and the first two have become close friends. What they reported seemed to me so solid, so unfanatical, so true, that it made a great impression; and it presented Russia, even when seen from their limited experience, as a land of purge and terror, of ludicrously bad management and of a long-suffering people.

After our marriage in 1940 my wife and I for about two years had much the same circle of friends as I had had before—mostly physicists and university people. Among them the Chevaliers, in particular, showed us many acts of kindness. We were occasionally invited to more or less obviously left-wing affairs.

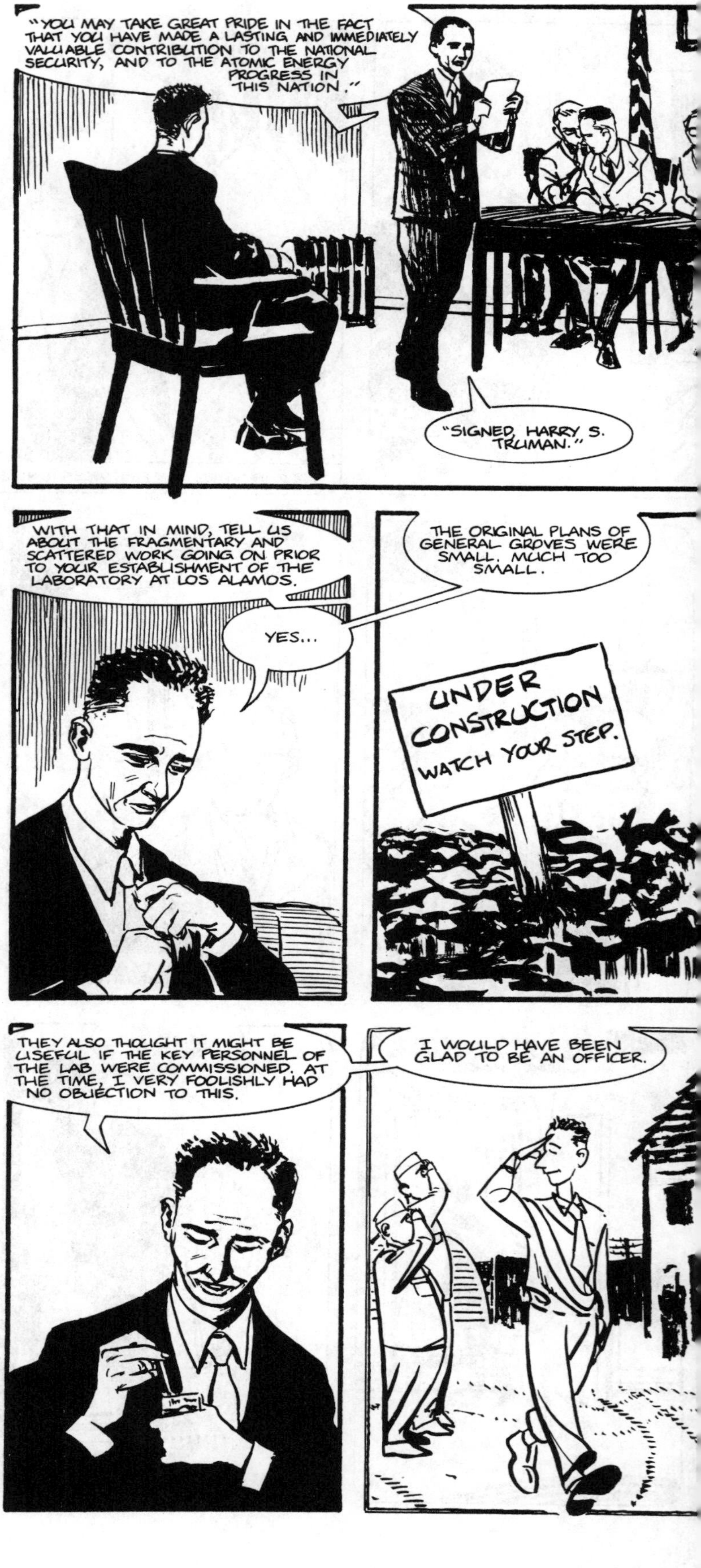
"YOU MAY TAKE GREAT PRIDE IN THE FACT THAT YOU HAVE MADE A LASTING AND IMMEDIATELY VALUABLE CONTRIBUTION TO THE NATIONAL SECURITY, AND TO THE ATOMIC ENERGY PROGRESS IN THIS NATION."
"SIGNED, HARRY S. TRUMAN."
WITH THAT IN MIND, TELL US ABOUT THE FRAGMENTARY AND SCATTERED WORK GOING ON PRIOR TO YOUR ESTABLISHMENT OF THE LABORATORY AT LOS ALAMOS.
YES...
THE ORIGINAL PLANS OF GENERAL GROVES WERE SMALL. MUCH TOO SMALL.
UNDER CONSTRUCTION WATCH YOUR STEP.
THEY ALSO THOUGHT IT MIGHT BE USEFUL IF THE KEY PERSONNEL OF THE LAB WERE COMMISSIONED. AT THE TIME, I VERY FOOLISHLY HAD NO OBJECTION TO THIS.
I WOULD HAVE BEEN GLAD TO BE AN OFFICER.

Because of these associations that I have described, and the contributions mentioned earlier, I might well have appeared at the time as quite close to the Communist Party—perhaps even to some people as belonging to it. As I have said, some of its declared objectives seemed to me desirable. But I never was a member of the Communist Party. I never accepted Communist dogma or theory; in fact, it never made sense to me.

There are two items of derogatory information on which I need to comment at this point. The first is that it was reported that I had talked the atomic bomb question over with Communist Party members during this period (1942-45). The second is that I was responsible for the employment on the atomic bomb project of individuals who were members of the communist party or closely associated with activities of the Communist party.

As to the first, my only discussion of matters connected with the atomic bomb were for official work or for recruiting the staff of the enterprise. So far as I knew none of these discussions were with Communist party members.

In order to bring responsible scientists to Los Alamos, I had to rely on their sense of the interest, urgency and feasibility of the Los Alamos mission. I had to tell them enough of what the job was, and give strong enough assurance that it might be successfully accomplished in time to affect the outcome of the war to make it clear that they were justified in leaving their other work to come to this job.

The notion of disappearing into the New Mexico desert for an indeterminate period and under quasi-military auspices disturbed a good many scientists, and the families of many more. But there was another side of it.

Almost everyone knew that this was a great undertaking. Almost everyone knew that if it were completed successfully and rapidly enough, it might determine the outcome of the war. Almost everyone knew that it was an unparalleled opportunity to bring to bear the basic knowledge and art of science for the benefit of his country. Almost everyone knew that this job, if it were achieved, would be a part of history.

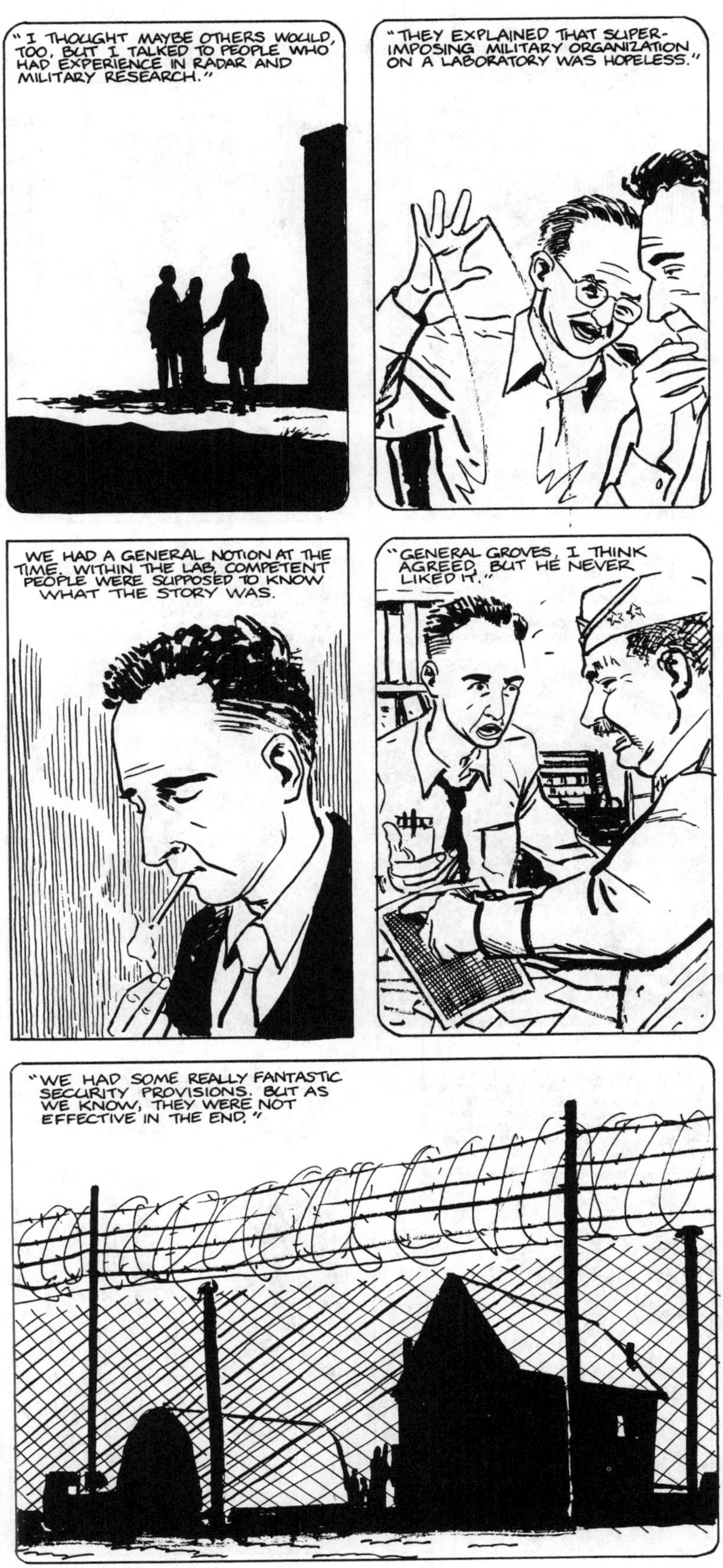
"I THOUGHT MAYBE OTHERS WOULD, TOO, BUT I TALKED TO PEOPLE WHO HAD EXPERIENCE IN RADAR AND MILITARY RESEARCH."
"THEY EXPLAINED THAT SUPER-IMPOSING MILITARY ORGANIZATION ON A LABORATORY WAS HOPELESS."
WE HAD A GENERAL NOTION AT THE TIME. WITHIN THE LAB, COMPETENT PEOPLE WERE SUPPOSED TO KNOW WHAT THE STORY WAS.
"GENERAL GROVES, I THINK AGREED, BUT HE NEVER LIKED IT."
"WE HAD SOME REALLY FANTASTIC SECURITY PROVISIONS. BUT AS WE KNOW, THEY WERE NOT EFFECTIVE IN THE END."

I HAD THE JOB OF DEVISING THESE IDIOTIC THINGS AND OF MAKING THE SCIENTISTS WELCOME.

FAMILIES COULD COME WITH THEIR HUSBANDS IF THEY WANTED TO BUT THEY WERE NOT ALLOWED TO LEAVE.

"THEY MONITORED ALL OUR PHONE CALLS."

CLICK
CLICK
CLI
CLI

"IT WAS ILLEGAL TO MAIL A LETTER EXCEPT IN THE AUTHORIZED DROPS. INGOING AND OUTGOING MAIL WAS CENSORED."

"A COUPLE PEOPLE DID LEAVE THE PROJECT, BUT THE ONUS AND PRESSURE AGAINST DOING THIS WAS VERY GREAT."

"PRESIDENT ROOSEVELT'S LETTER HELPED MAINTAIN THAT PRESSURE."

you ride
de with Hitler
Don't Let Ther Shadow Touch Them
Buy WAR BONDS
Join a
Car-Sharing Club
TODAY!
WOR
SLAVE
SACRIFICE FOR FREEDOM!

IN IT, HE STATED "--THE OUTCOME OF YOUR LABORS IS OF SUCH GREAT SIGNIFICANCE TO THE NATION, IT REQUIRES THAT THIS PROGRAM BE EVEN MORE DRASTICALLY GUARDED THAN OTHER HIGHLY SECRET WAR DEVELOPMENTS."

"YOU ARE FULLY AWARE OF THE REASONS WHY YOUR OWN ENDEAVOR AND THOSE OF YOUR ASSOCIATES MUST BE CIRCUMSCRIBED BY VERY SPECIAL RESTRICTIONS."

"NEVERTHELESS, I WISH YOU WOULD EXPRESS TO THE SCIENTISTS ASSEMBLED WITH YOU MY DEEPEST APPRECIATION OF THEIR WILLINGNESS TO UNDERTAKE THE TASKS WHICH LIE BEFORE THEM IN SPITE OF THE DANGERS AND PERSONAL SACRIFICES."

"WHATEVER THE ENEMY MAY BE PLANNING, AMERICAN SCIENCE WILL BE EQUAL TO THE CHALLENGE. WITH THIS THOUGHT IN MIND, I SEND THIS NOTE OF CONFIDENCE AND APPRECIATION."

HE CLOSED BY SAYING THAT THIS LETTER WAS SECRET, BUT THAT I COULD DISCLOSE IT TO MY ASSOCIATES UNDER A PLEDGE OF SECRECY.

*n 1943 when I was alleged to
ave stated that "I knew several
ndividuals then at Los Alamos
vho had been members of the
Communist Party," I knew of only
ne; she was my wife, of whose
lisassociation from the party, and
f whose integrity and loyalty to
he United States I had no
uestion. Later, in 1944 or 1945,
ny brother Frank, who had been
leared for work in Berkeley and
t Oak Ridge, came to Los Alamos
rom Oak Ridge with official
pproval.*

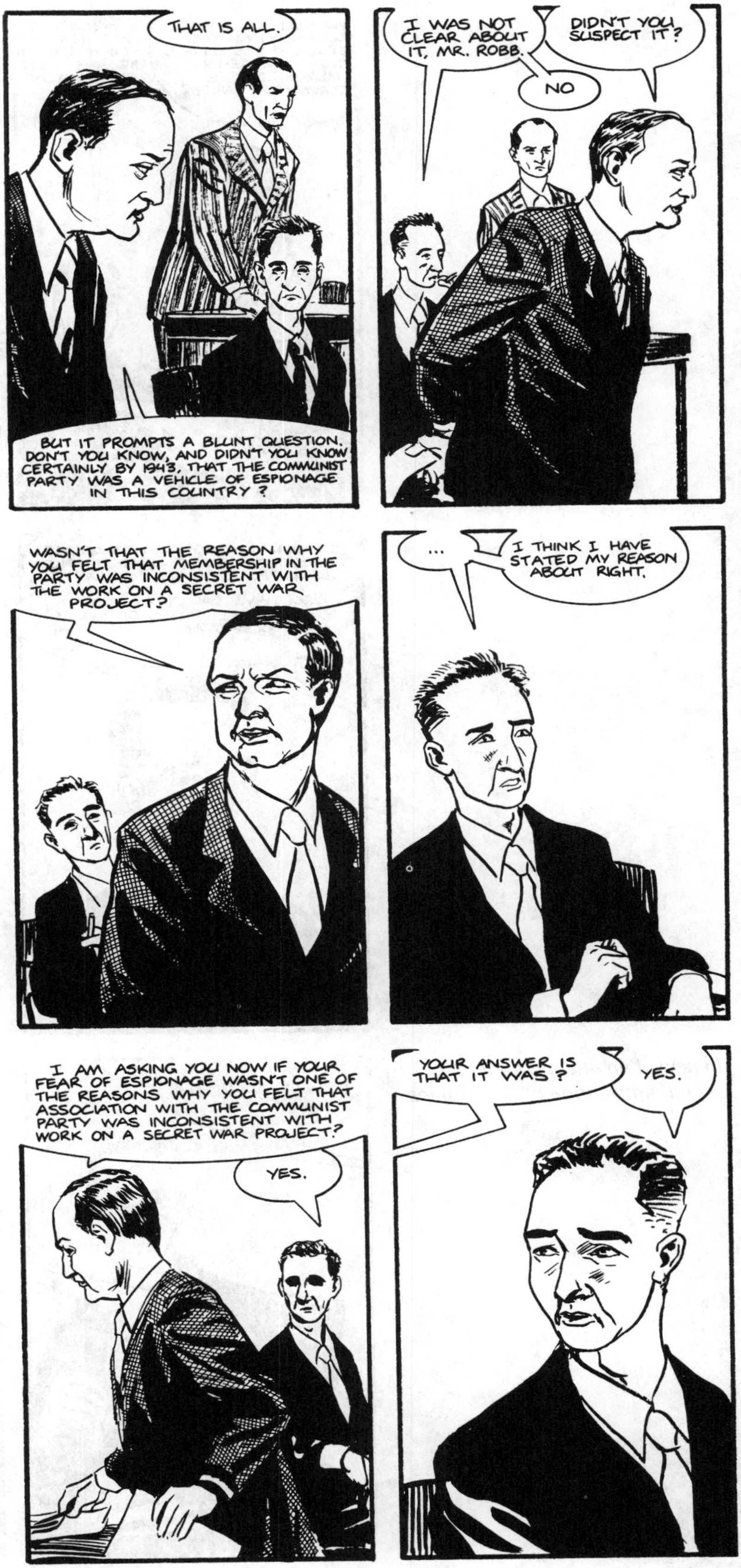

THAT IS ALL.
BUT IT PROMPTS A BLUNT QUESTION. DON'T YOU KNOW, AND DIDN'T YOU KNOW CERTAINLY BY 1943, THAT THE COMMUNIST PARTY WAS A VEHICLE OF ESPIONAGE IN THIS COUNTRY?
I WAS NOT CLEAR ABOUT IT, MR. ROBB.
DIDN'T YOU SUSPECT IT?
NO
WASN'T THAT THE REASON WHY YOU FELT THAT MEMBERSHIP IN THE PARTY WAS INCONSISTENT WITH THE WORK ON A SECRET WAR PROJECT?
...
I THINK I HAVE STATED MY REASON ABOUT RIGHT.
I AM ASKING YOU NOW IF YOUR FEAR OF ESPIONAGE WASN'T ONE OF THE REASONS WHY YOU FELT THAT ASSOCIATION WITH THE COMMUNIST PARTY WAS INCONSISTENT WITH WORK ON A SECRET WAR PROJECT?
YES.
YOUR ANSWER IS THAT IT WAS?
YES.

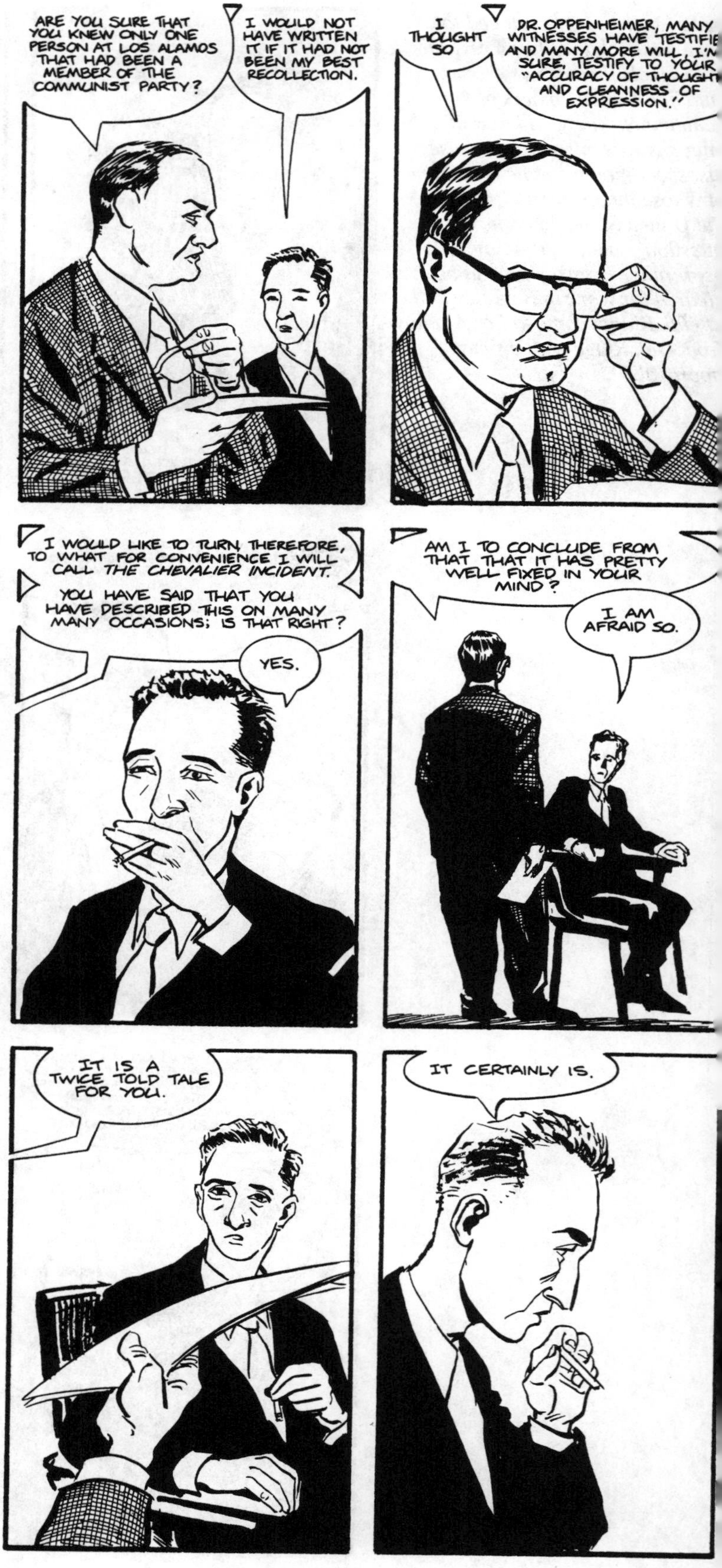

ARE YOU SURE THAT YOU KNEW ONLY ONE PERSON AT LOS ALAMOS THAT HAD BEEN A MEMBER OF THE COMMUNIST PARTY?
I WOULD NOT HAVE WRITTEN IT IF IT HAD NOT BEEN MY BEST RECOLLECTION.
I THOUGHT SO
DR. OPPENHEIMER, MANY WITNESSES HAVE TESTIFIE AND MANY MORE WILL, I'M SURE, TESTIFY TO YOUR "ACCURACY OF THOUGHT AND CLEANNESS OF EXPRESSION."
I WOULD LIKE TO TURN THEREFORE, TO WHAT FOR CONVENIENCE I WILL CALL *THE CHEVALIER INCIDENT.*
YOU HAVE SAID THAT YOU HAVE DESCRIBED THIS ON MANY MANY OCCASIONS; IS THAT RIGHT?
YES.
AM I TO CONCLUDE FROM THAT THAT IT HAS PRETTY WELL FIXED IN YOUR MIND?
I AM AFRAID SO.
IT IS A TWICE TOLD TALE FOR YOU.
IT CERTAINLY IS.

I knew of no attempt to obtain secret information at Los Alamos.

Prior to my going there my friend Haakon Chevalier with his wife visited us on Eagle Hill, probably in early 1943. During the visit, he came into the kitchen and told me that George Eltenton had spoken to him of the possibility of transmitting technical information to Soviet scientists. I made some strong remark to the effect that this sounded terribly wrong to me. The discussion ended there. Nothing in our long standing friendship would have led me to believe that Chevalier was actually seeking information; and I was certain that he had no idea of the work on which I was engaged.

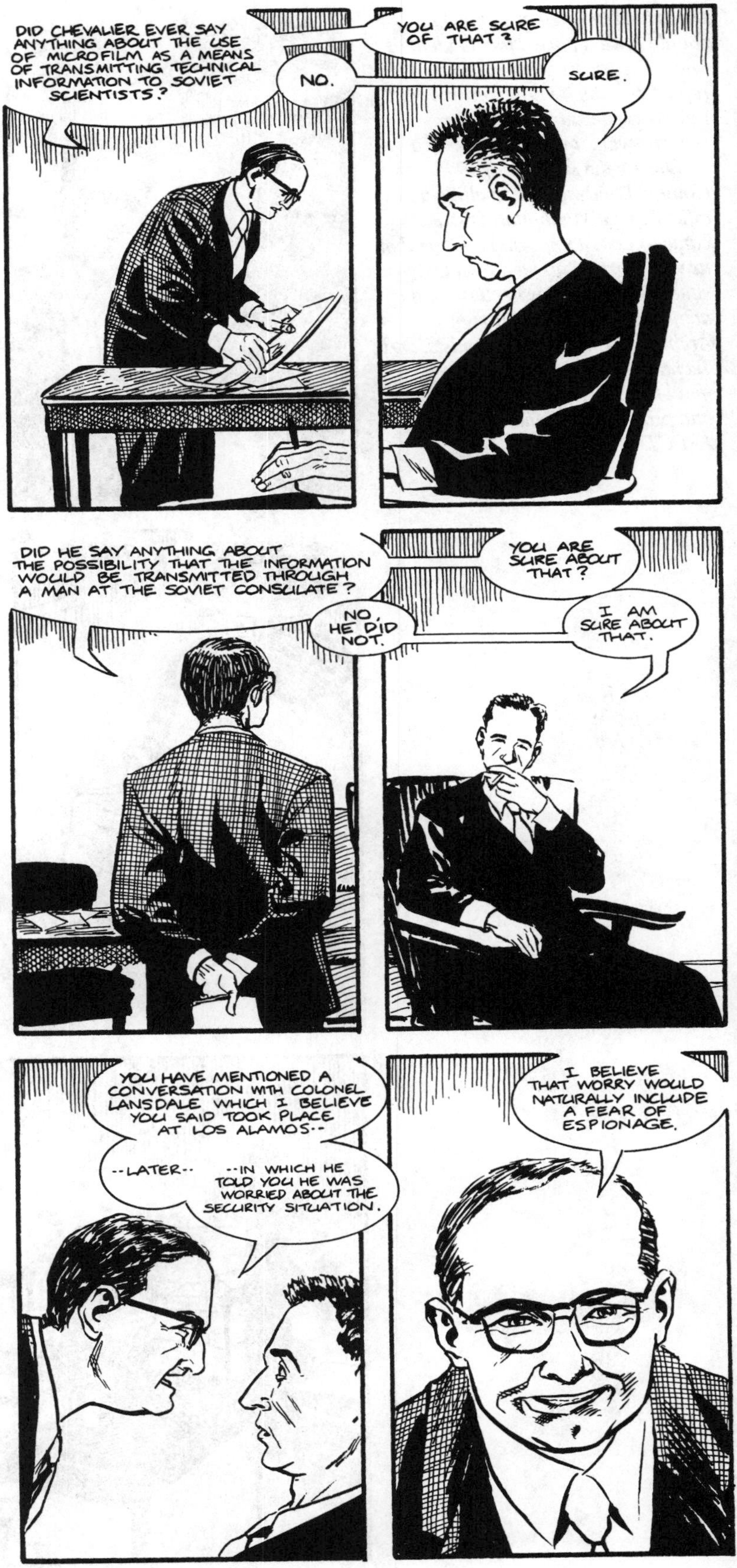

DID CHEVALIER EVER SAY ANYTHING ABOUT THE USE OF MICROFILM AS A MEANS OF TRANSMITTING TECHNICAL INFORMATION TO SOVIET SCIENTISTS?
NO.
YOU ARE SURE OF THAT?
SURE.
DID HE SAY ANYTHING ABOUT THE POSSIBILITY THAT THE INFORMATION WOULD BE TRANSMITTED THROUGH A MAN AT THE SOVIET CONSULATE?
NO, HE DID NOT.
YOU ARE SURE ABOUT THAT?
I AM SURE ABOUT THAT.
YOU HAVE MENTIONED A CONVERSATION WITH COLONEL LANSDALE WHICH I BELIEVE YOU SAID TOOK PLACE AT LOS ALAMOS--
--LATER--
--IN WHICH HE TOLD YOU HE WAS WORRIED ABOUT THE SECURITY SITUATION.
I BELIEVE THAT WORRY WOULD NATURALLY INCLUDE A FEAR OF ESPIONAGE.

It has long been clear to me that I should have reported the incident at once. The events that led me to report it—which I doubt ever would have become known without my report—were unconnected with it.

During the summer of 1943, Colonel Landsale, the intelligence officer of the Manhattan District, came to Los Alamos and told me that he was worried about the security situation in Berkeley because of the activities of the Federation of Architects, Engineers, Chemists, and Technicians. This recalled to my mind that Eltenton was a member and probably a promoter of the FAECT.

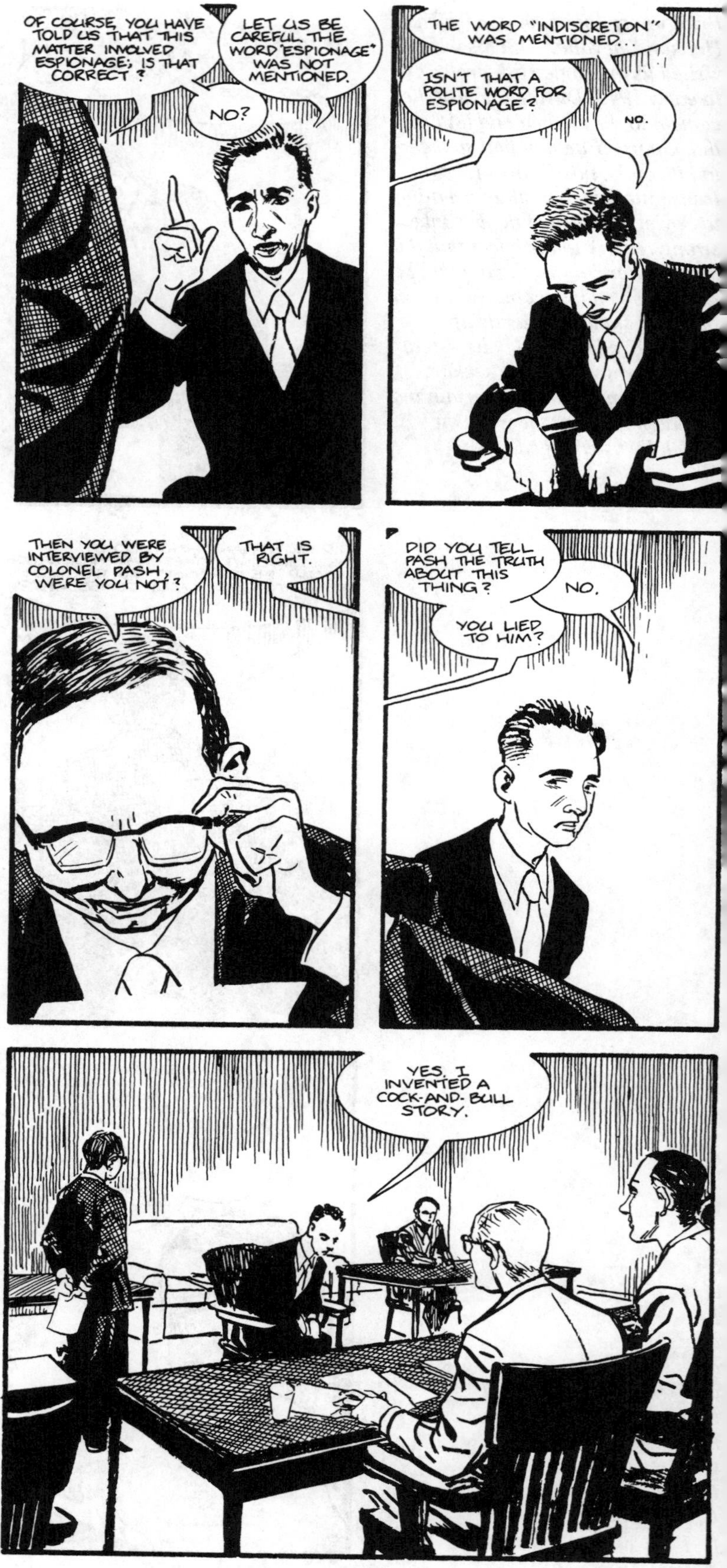

OF COURSE, YOU HAVE TOLD US THAT THIS MATTER INVOLVED ESPIONAGE; IS THAT CORRECT?
LET US BE CAREFUL. THE WORD "ESPIONAGE" WAS NOT MENTIONED.
NO?
THE WORD "INDISCRETION" WAS MENTIONED...
ISN'T THAT A POLITE WORD FOR ESPIONAGE?
NO.
THEN YOU WERE INTERVIEWED BY COLONEL PASH, WERE YOU NOT?
THAT IS RIGHT.
DID YOU TELL PASH THE TRUTH ABOUT THIS THING?
NO.
YOU LIED TO HIM?
YES. I INVENTED A COCK-AND-BULL STORY.

DID YOU TELL PASH THAT CHEVALIER-- LET'S CALL HIM X-- HAD APPROACHED THREE OTHER PERSONS ON THE MANHATTAN PROJECT?
I AM NOT CLEAR WHETHER I SAID THERE WERE THREE X'S OR THAT X APPROACHED THREE PEOPLE.
DIDN'T YOU SAY THAT "X" APPROACHED THREE PEOPLE?
PROBABLY
WHY DID YOU DO THAT DOCTOR?
BECAUSE I WAS AN IDIOT.
IS THAT YOUR ONLY EXPLANATION?
I WAS RELUCTANT TO MENTION CHEVALIER
NO DOUBT I WAS SOMEWHAT RELUCTANT TO MENTION MYSELF.
DIDN'T THAT MAKE IT WORSE FOR "X"?
I...
I DIDN'T MENTION CHEVALIER BY NAME.

Shortly thereafter, I was in Berkeley and I told the security officer that Eltenton would bear watching. When asked why, I said that Eltenton had attempted, through intermediaries, to approach people on the project, though I mentioned neither myself nor Chevalier. Later, when General Groves urged me to give the details, I told him of my conversation with Chevalier. I still think of him as a friend.

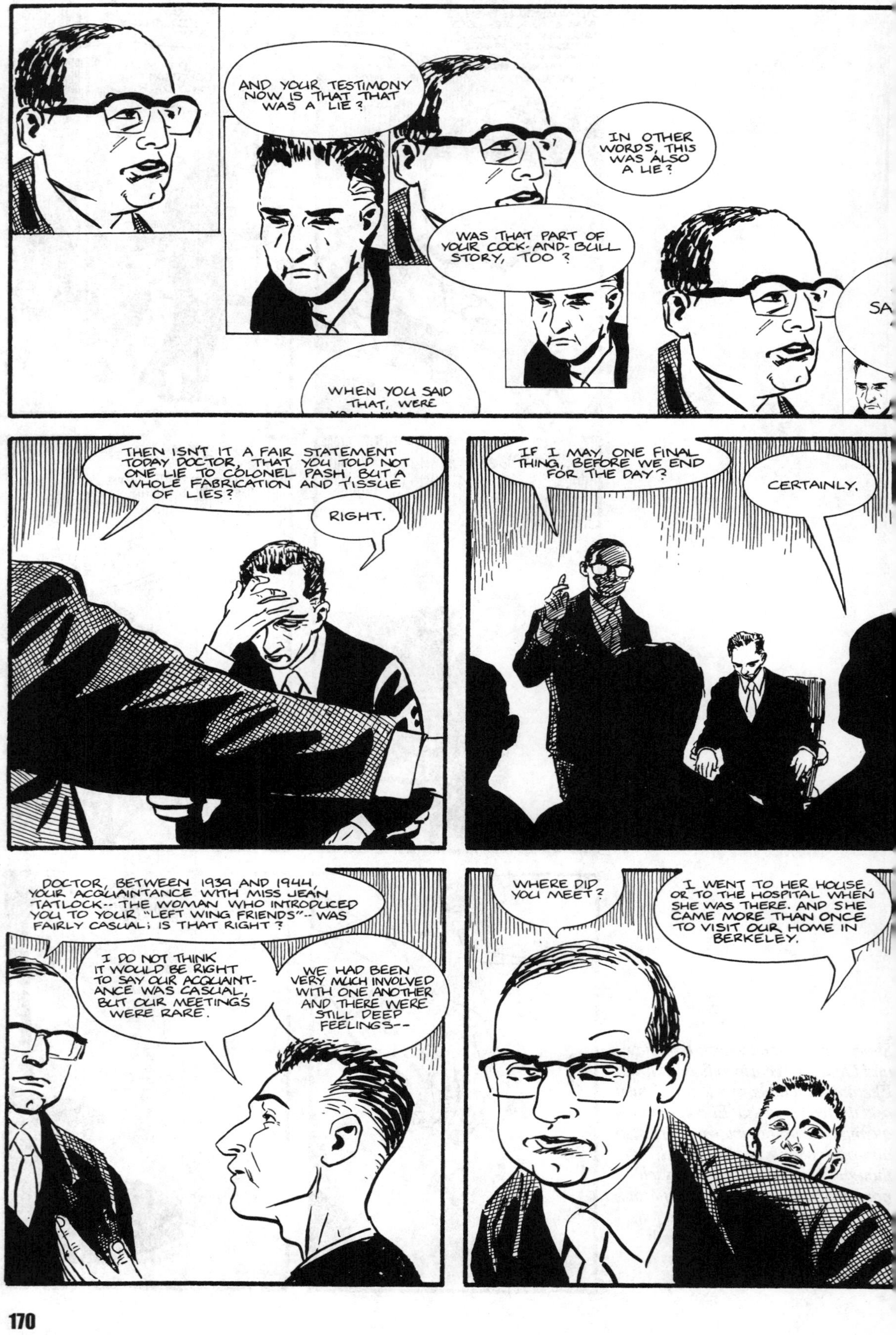
AND YOUR TESTIMONY NOW IS THAT THAT WAS A LIE?
IN OTHER WORDS, THIS WAS ALSO A LIE?
WAS THAT PART OF YOUR COCK-AND-BULL STORY, TOO?
WHEN YOU SAID THAT, WERE
THEN ISN'T IT A FAIR STATEMENT TODAY DOCTOR, THAT YOU TOLD NOT ONE LIE TO COLONEL PASH, BUT A WHOLE FABRICATION AND TISSUE OF LIES?
RIGHT.
IF I MAY, ONE FINAL THING, BEFORE WE END FOR THE DAY?
CERTAINLY.
DOCTOR, BETWEEN 1939 AND 1944, YOUR ACQUAINTANCE WITH MISS JEAN TATLOCK-- THE WOMAN WHO INTRODUCED YOU TO YOUR "LEFT WING FRIENDS"-- WAS FAIRLY CASUAL; IS THAT RIGHT?
I DO NOT THINK IT WOULD BE RIGHT TO SAY OUR ACQUAINT-ANCE WAS CASUAL, BUT OUR MEETINGS WERE RARE.
WE HAD BEEN VERY MUCH INVOLVED WITH ONE ANOTHER AND THERE WERE STILL DEEP FEELINGS--
WHERE DID YOU MEET?
I WENT TO HER HOUSE OR TO THE HOSPITAL WHEN SHE WAS THERE. AND SHE CAME MORE THAN ONCE TO VISIT OUR HOME IN BERKELEY.

"OUR HOUSE." YOUR AND MRS. OPPENHEIMER'S?"

"RIGHT. AND I VISITED HER IN JUNE OR JULY OF 1943."

"I BELIEVE YOU SAID IN CONNECTION TO THAT, THAT YOU HAD TO SEE HER. WHY?"

"SHE HAD INDICATED A GREAT DESIRE TO SEE ME BEFORE WE LEFT FOR LOS ALAMOS.

AT THAT TIME I COULDN'T GO, AND I WASN'T SUPPOSED TO SAY WHERE WE WERE HEADED. SHE WAS EXTREMELY UNHAPPY."

"DID YOU FIND OUT WHY SHE HAD TO SEE YOU?"

"BECAUSE SHE WAS STILL IN LOVE WITH ME."

"WAS SHE A COMMUNIST AT THE TIME?"

"WE DIDN'T EVEN TALK ABOUT IT. I DOUBT IT."

"YOU SPENT THE NIGHT WITH HER, DIDN'T YOU?"

"YES."

"WHEN YOU WERE WORKING ON A SECRET WAR PROJECT.?"

"YES."

"DID YOU THINK THAT WAS CONSISTENT WITH GOOD SECURITY?"

"..."

"IT **WAS**, AS A MATTER OF FACT. NOT A WORD--

(LONG PAUSE.)

"-- IT WAS NOT A GOOD PRACTICE."

MR. ROBB: It is half past four, Mr. Chairman.

MR. GRAY: All right. I should like to say before we recess that since there are so many references to other agencies, particularly the Defense Department, I am informed that it has been necessary to check not only with the security officers of the Commission but with other Departments. This in part explains why Dr. Oppenheimer's counsel has not been present for portions of the testimony.

MR. GARRISON: I am sure there is no "hidden agenda," Mr. Gray.

MR. GRAY: We will meet again at 9:30.

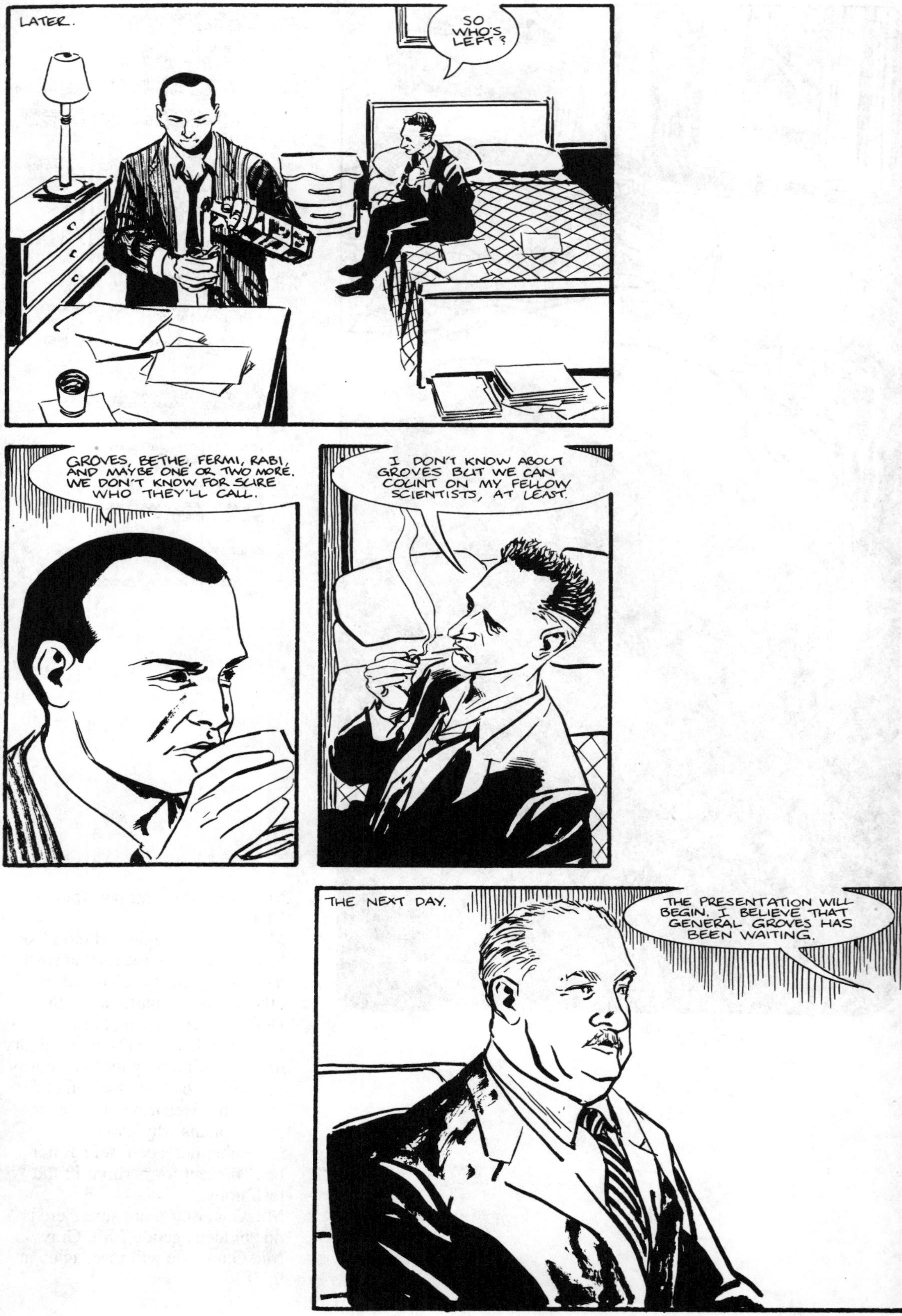
LATER.
SO WHO'S LEFT?
GROVES, BETHE, FERMI, RABI, AND MAYBE ONE OR TWO MORE. WE DON'T KNOW FOR SURE WHO THEY'LL CALL.
I DON'T KNOW ABOUT GROVES BUT WE CAN COUNT ON MY FELLOW SCIENTISTS, AT LEAST.
THE NEXT DAY.
THE PRESENTATION WILL BEGIN. I BELIEVE THAT GENERAL GROVES HAS BEEN WAITING.

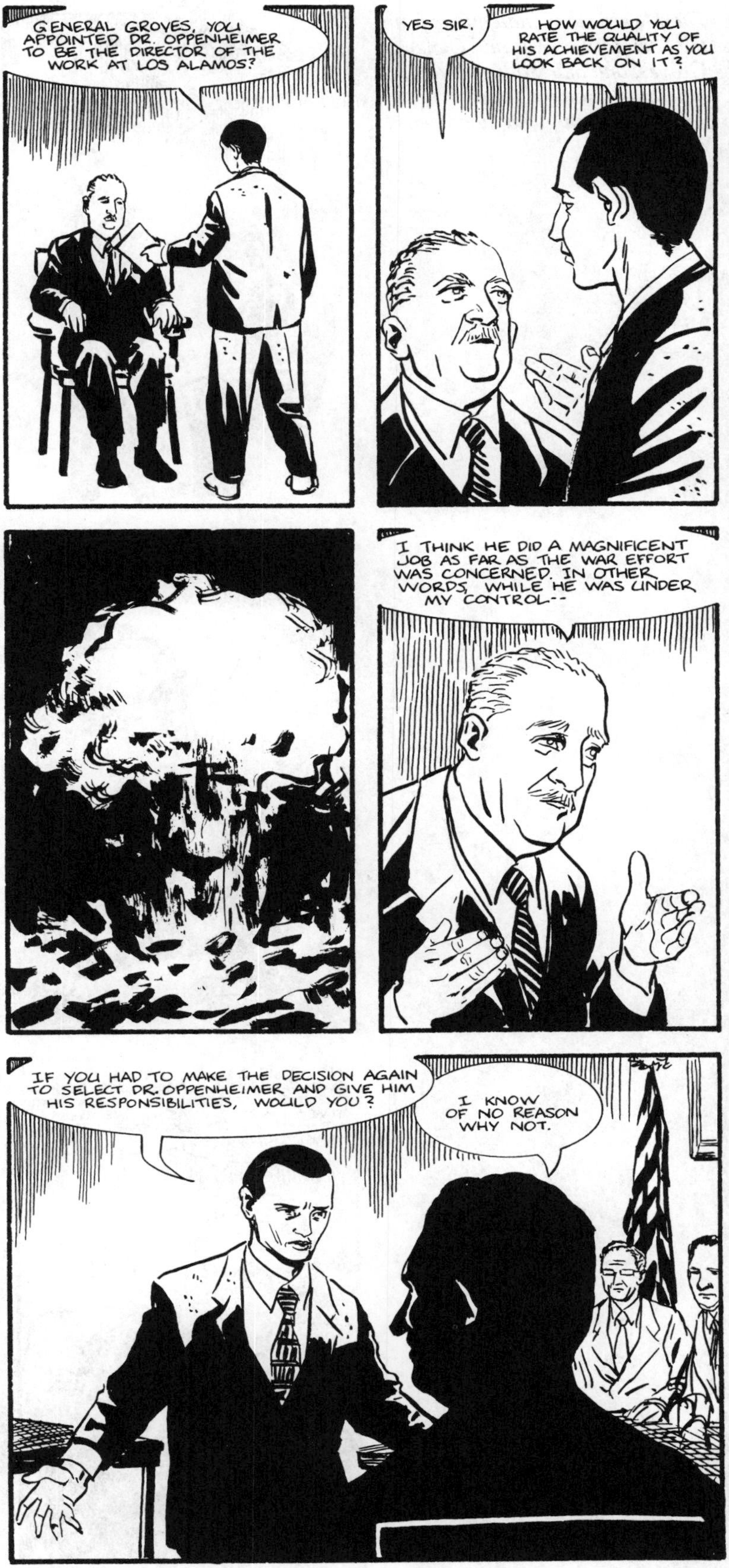
GENERAL GROVES, YOU APPOINTED DR. OPPENHEIMER TO BE THE DIRECTOR OF THE WORK AT LOS ALAMOS?
YES SIR.
HOW WOULD YOU RATE THE QUALITY OF HIS ACHIEVEMENT AS YOU LOOK BACK ON IT?
I THINK HE DID A MAGNIFICENT JOB AS FAR AS THE WAR EFFORT WAS CONCERNED. IN OTHER WORDS, WHILE HE WAS UNDER MY CONTROL--
IF YOU HAD TO MAKE THE DECISION AGAIN TO SELECT DR. OPPENHEIMER AND GIVE HIM HIS RESPONSIBILITIES, WOULD YOU?
I KNOW OF NO REASON WHY NOT.

Years of hard and loyal work of the scientists culminated in the test on July 16, 1945. It was a success.

I believe that in the eyes of the War Department, and other knowledgeable people, it was as early a success as they had thought possible, given all the circumstances, and a rather greater one.

There were many indications from the Secretary of War and General Groves, and many others that official opinion was one of satisfaction with what had been accomplished.

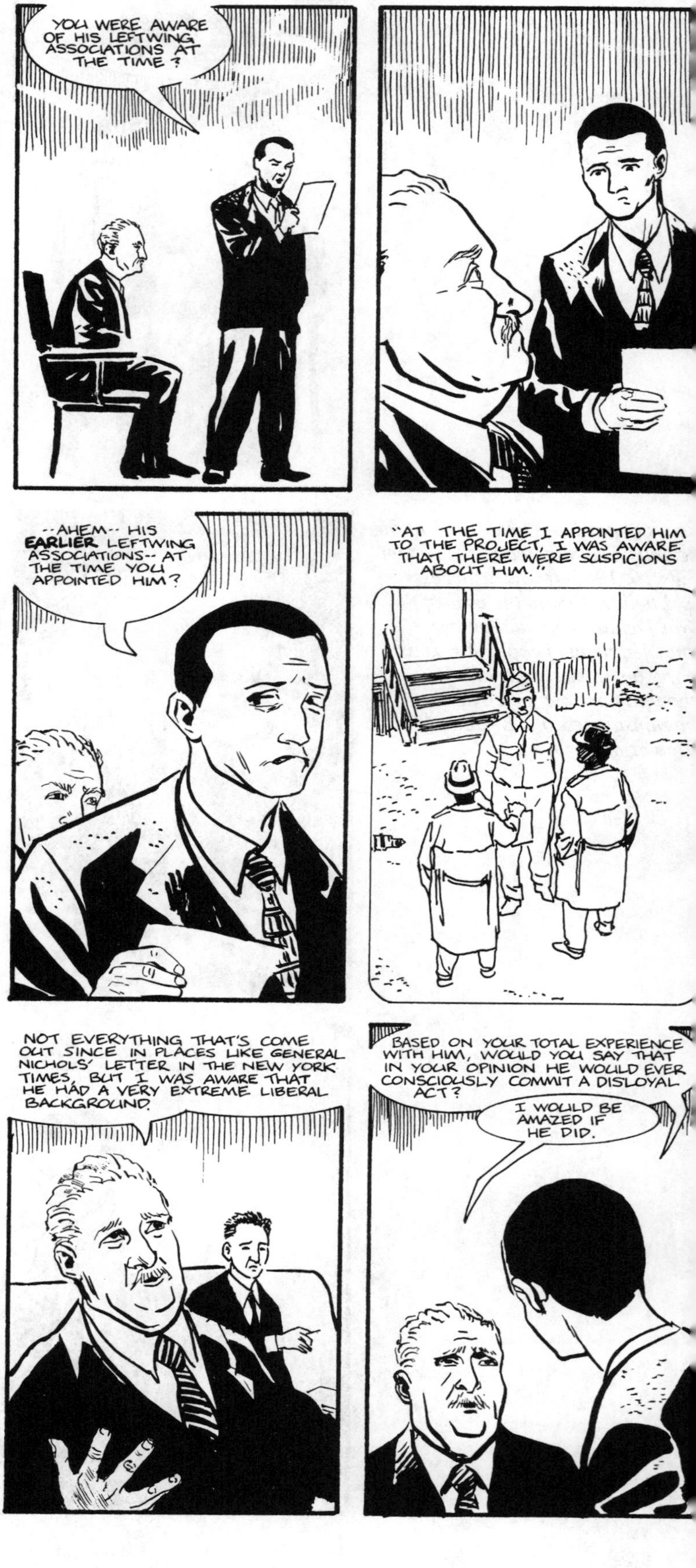
YOU WERE AWARE OF HIS LEFTWING ASSOCIATIONS AT THE TIME?
--AHEM-- HIS EARLIER LEFTWING ASSOCIATIONS-- AT THE TIME YOU APPOINTED HIM?
"AT THE TIME I APPOINTED HIM TO THE PROJECT, I WAS AWARE THAT THERE WERE SUSPICIONS ABOUT HIM."
NOT EVERYTHING THAT'S COME OUT SINCE IN PLACES LIKE GENERAL NICHOLS' LETTER IN THE NEW YORK TIMES, BUT I WAS AWARE THAT HE HAD A VERY EXTREME LIBERAL BACKGROUND.
BASED ON YOUR TOTAL EXPERIENCE WITH HIM, WOULD YOU SAY THAT IN YOUR OPINION HE WOULD EVER CONSCIOUSLY COMMIT A DISLOYAL ACT?
I WOULD BE AMAZED IF HE DID.

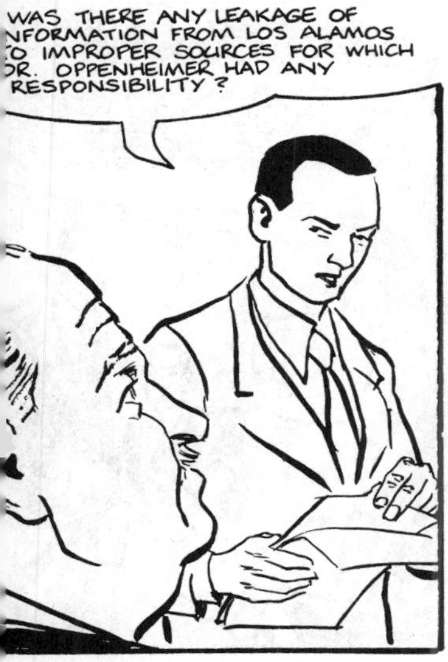
WAS THERE ANY LEAKAGE OF NFORMATION FROM LOS ALAMOS O IMPROPER SOURCES FOR WHICH R. OPPENHEIMER HAD ANY RESPONSIBILITY?

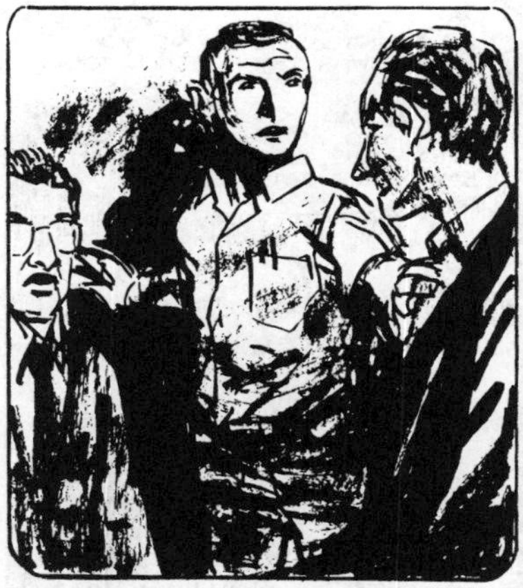

General Groves: That is a very difficult question, because it brings up the fact that scientists. . .were not in sympathy with the security requirements.

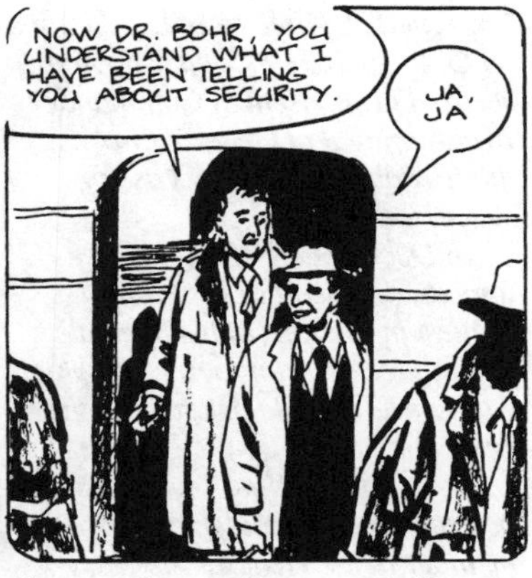
NOW DR. BOHR, YOU UNDERSTAND WHAT I HAVE BEEN TELLING YOU ABOUT SECURITY.
JA, JA

General Groves: For example, I got through talking to Niels Bohr on the train going to Los Alamos for the first time. I think I talked to him about 12 hours straight on what he was not to say.

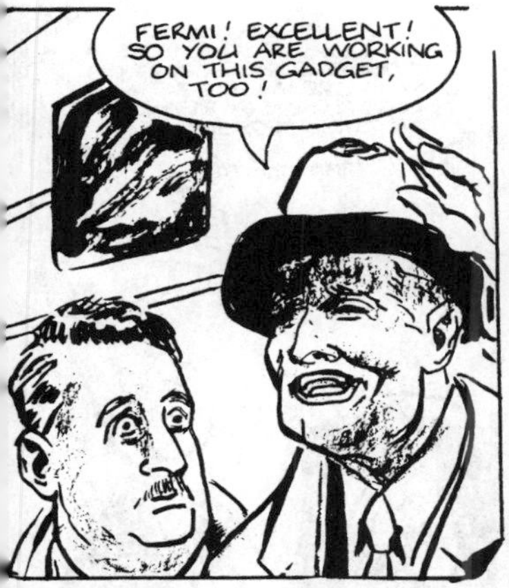
FERMI! EXCELLENT! SO YOU ARE WORKING ON THIS GADGET, TOO!

General Groves: I never held this against them, because I knew their whole lives had been based on the dissemination of knowledge.

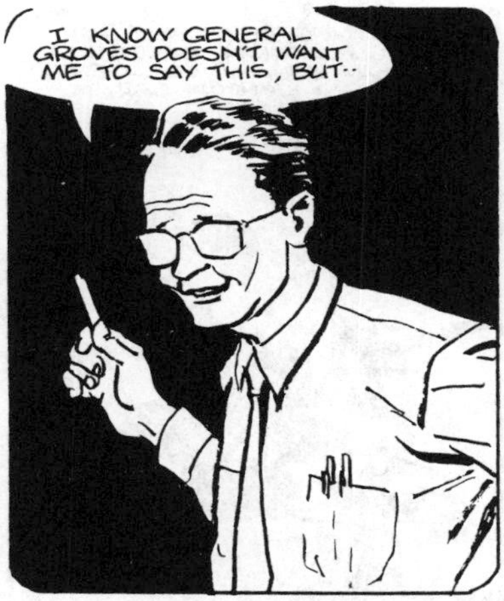
I KNOW GENERAL GROVES DOESN'T WANT ME TO SAY THIS, BUT..

General Groves: While I was always on the other side of the fence, it never surprised me when they broke the rules.

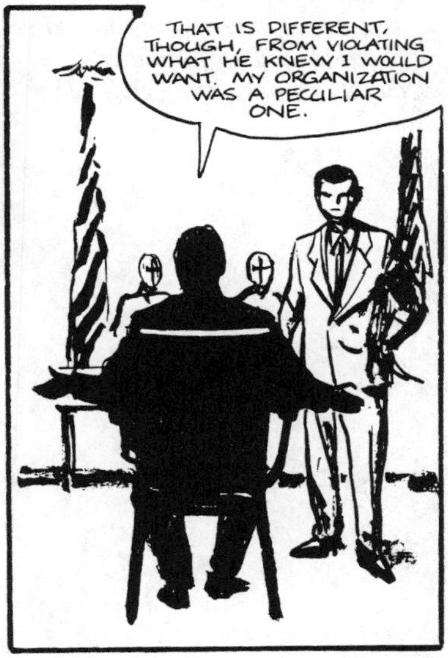
THAT IS DIFFERENT, THOUGH, FROM VIOLATING WHAT HE KNEW I WOULD WANT. MY ORGANIZATION WAS A PECULIAR ONE.

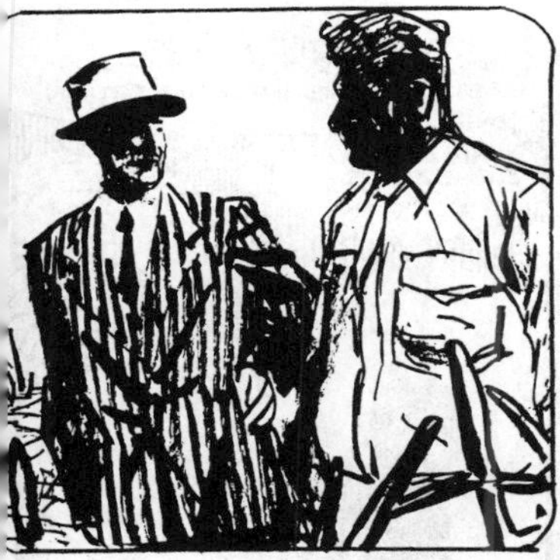

General Groves: They all knew the goal. They were the kind of men I wanted, and they were the kind of men that made the project a success. If I had a group of yes men we never would have gotten anywhere.

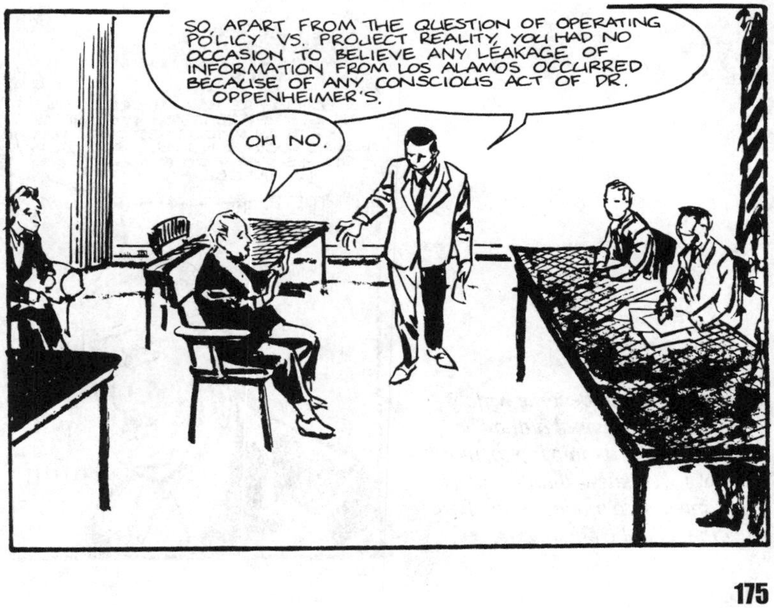
SO, APART FROM THE QUESTION OF OPERATING POLICY VS. PROJECT REALITY, YOU HAD NO OCCASION TO BELIEVE ANY LEAKAGE OF INFORMATION FROM LOS ALAMOS OCCURRED BECAUSE OF ANY CONSCIOUS ACT OF DR. OPPENHEIMER'S.
OH NO.

I resigned as Director of Los Alamos on October 16, 1945, after having secured the consent of Commander Bradbury and of General Groves that Bradbury should act as my successor.

In December, 1945, and later, I appeared at Senator McMahon's request in sessions of his Special Committee on Atomic Energy, which was considering legislation on the same subject.

At the end of 1946 I was appointed by the President as a member of the General Advisory Committee to the Atomic Energy Commission. At its first meeting I was elected chairman, and was reelected until the expiration of my term in 1952. This was my principal assignment during these years as far as the atomic energy program was concerned, and my principal occupation apart from academic work.

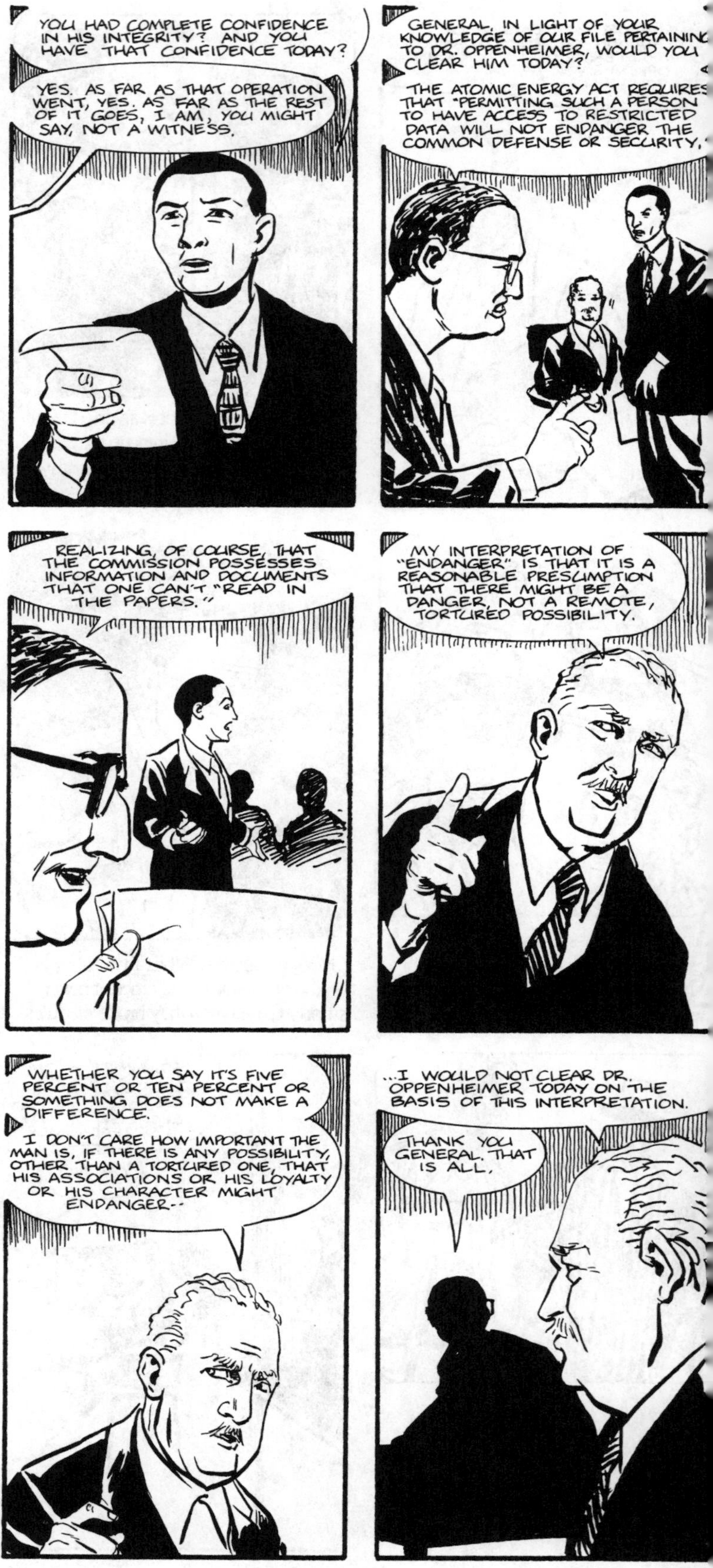

YOU HAD COMPLETE CONFIDENCE IN HIS INTEGRITY? AND YOU HAVE THAT CONFIDENCE TODAY?
YES. AS FAR AS THAT OPERATION WENT, YES. AS FAR AS THE REST OF IT GOES, I AM, YOU MIGHT SAY, NOT A WITNESS.
GENERAL, IN LIGHT OF YOUR KNOWLEDGE OF OUR FILE PERTAINING TO DR. OPPENHEIMER, WOULD YOU CLEAR HIM TODAY?
THE ATOMIC ENERGY ACT REQUIRES THAT "PERMITTING SUCH A PERSON TO HAVE ACCESS TO RESTRICTED DATA WILL NOT ENDANGER THE COMMON DEFENSE OR SECURITY,"
REALIZING, OF COURSE, THAT THE COMMISSION POSSESSES INFORMATION AND DOCUMENTS THAT ONE CAN'T "READ IN THE PAPERS."
MY INTERPRETATION OF "ENDANGER" IS THAT IT IS A REASONABLE PRESUMPTION THAT THERE MIGHT BE A DANGER, NOT A REMOTE, TORTURED POSSIBILITY.
WHETHER YOU SAY IT'S FIVE PERCENT OR TEN PERCENT OR SOMETHING DOES NOT MAKE A DIFFERENCE.
I DON'T CARE HOW IMPORTANT THE MAN IS, IF THERE IS ANY POSSIBILITY, OTHER THAN A TORTURED ONE, THAT HIS ASSOCIATIONS OR HIS LOYALTY OR HIS CHARACTER MIGHT ENDANGER--
...I WOULD NOT CLEAR DR. OPPENHEIMER TODAY ON THE BASIS OF THIS INTERPRETATION.
THANK YOU GENERAL. THAT IS ALL.

Meanwhile I had become widely regarded as principal author or inventor of the atomic bomb, more widely, I well knew, than the facts warranted. In a modest way I had become a public personage.

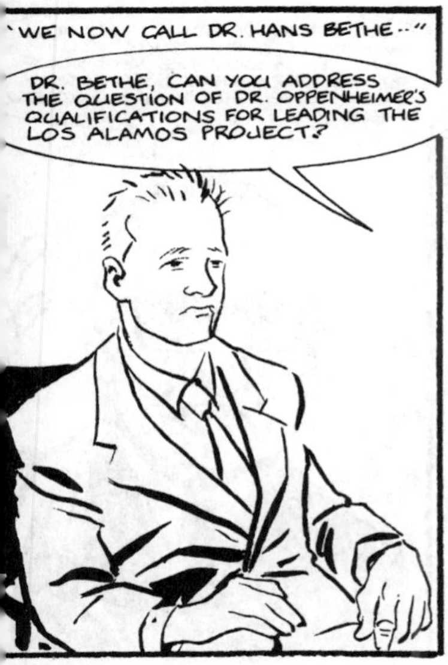
"WE NOW CALL DR. HANS BETHE..."
DR. BETHE, CAN YOU ADDRESS THE QUESTION OF DR. OPPENHEIMER'S QUALIFICATIONS FOR LEADING THE LOS ALAMOS PROJECT?

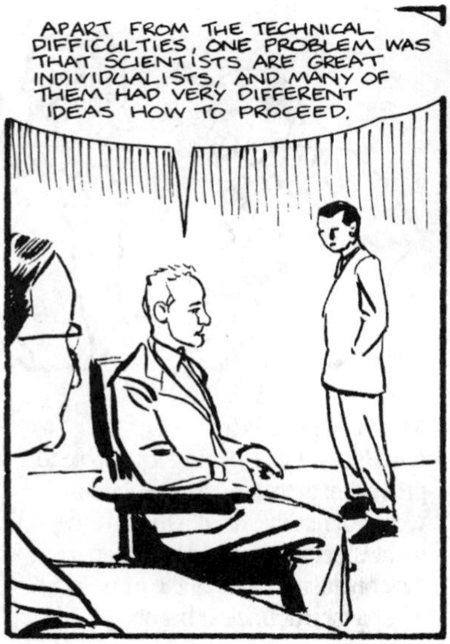
APART FROM THE TECHNICAL DIFFICULTIES, ONE PROBLEM WAS THAT SCIENTISTS ARE GREAT INDIVIDUALISTS, AND MANY OF THEM HAD VERY DIFFERENT IDEAS HOW TO PROCEED.

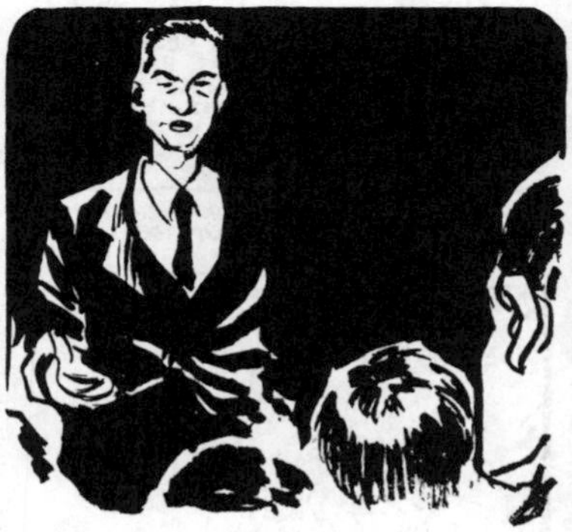

Dr. Bethe: We needed a unifying force and this unification could only be done by a man who really understood everything and was recognized by everybody as superior in judgment and knowledge to all of us. This was Oppenheimer.

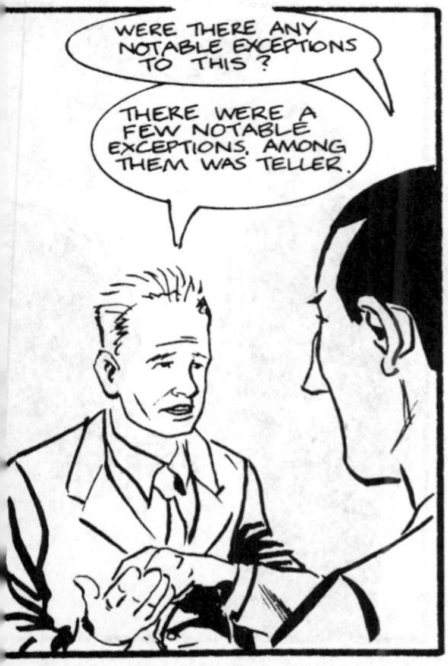
WERE THERE ANY NOTABLE EXCEPTIONS TO THIS?
THERE WERE A FEW NOTABLE EXCEPTIONS, AMONG THEM WAS TELLER.

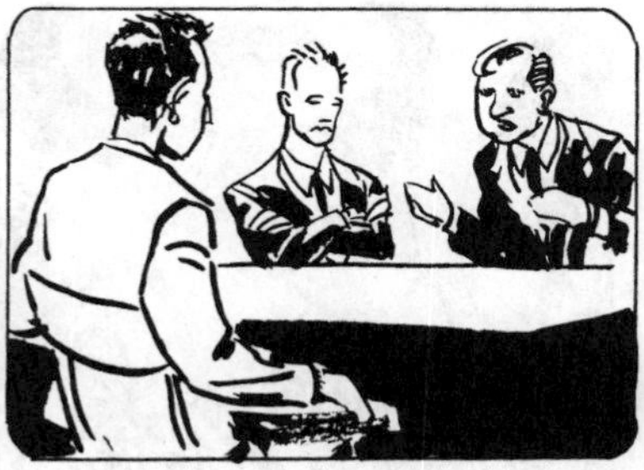

Mr. Garrison: He was on your staff?
Dr. Bethe: He was. I relied—and I hoped to rely heavily on him to help our work in theoretical physics. It turned out that he did not want to work on the agreed line of research that everybody else in the laboratory had agreed to.

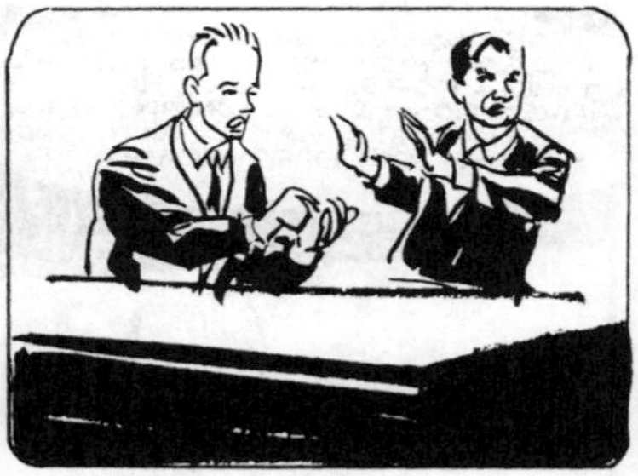

Dr. Bethe: So that in the end there was no choice but to relieve him of any work in the general line of development of Los Alamos, and to permit him to pursue his own ideas entirely unrelated to the World War II work.

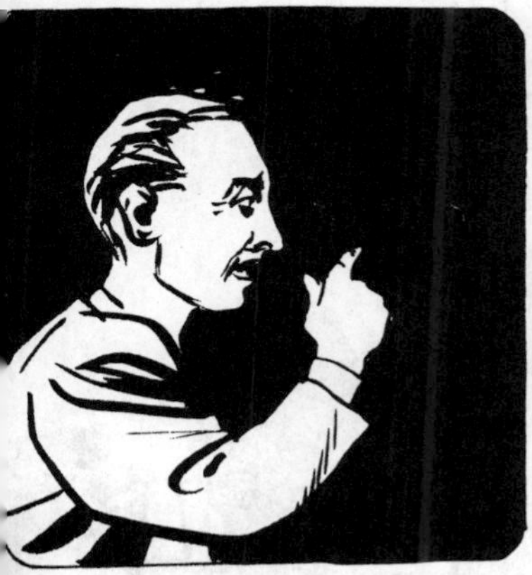

Mr. Garrison: Turning to another subject, what was the attitude of Dr. Oppenheimer with respect to the requirements of security at Los Alamos?

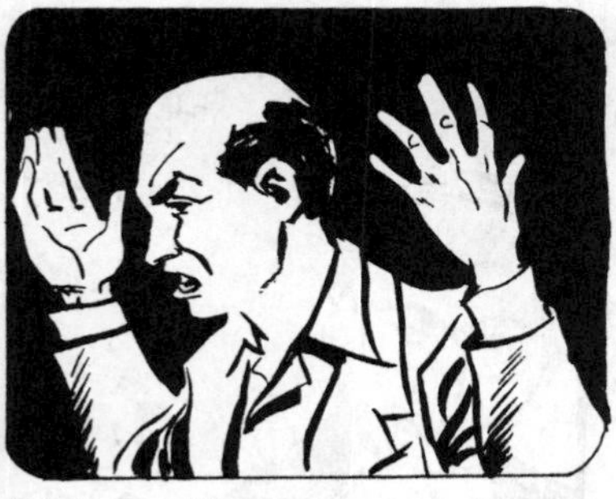

Dr. Bethe: He was very security minded compared to practically all the scientists. He occupied a position very much intermediate between the Army and the scientists and Dr. Oppenheimer was, I think, considerably more ready to see the need for strict requirements and to enforce security rules.

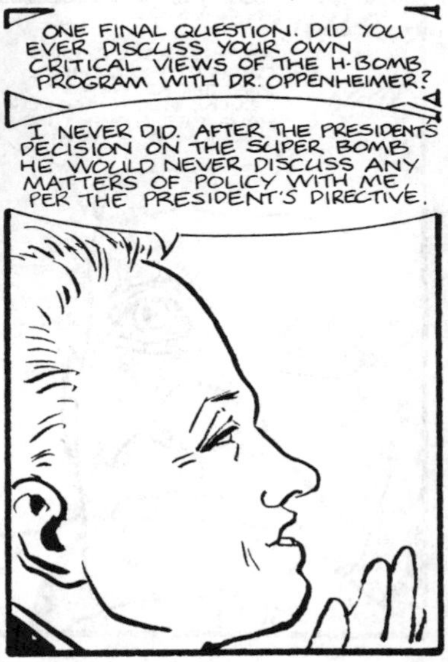
ONE FINAL QUESTION. DID YOU EVER DISCUSS YOUR OWN CRITICAL VIEWS OF THE H-BOMB PROGRAM WITH DR. OPPENHEIMER?
I NEVER DID. AFTER THE PRESIDENT'S DECISION ON THE SUPER BOMB HE WOULD NEVER DISCUSS ANY MATTERS OF POLICY WITH ME, PER THE PRESIDENT'S DIRECTIVE.

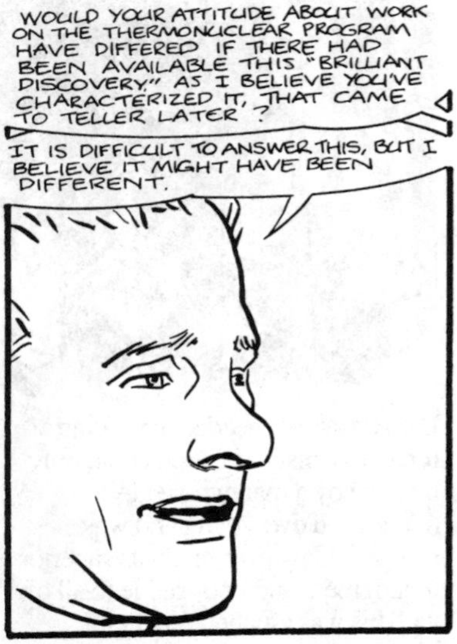
WOULD YOUR ATTITUDE ABOUT WORK ON THE THERMONUCLEAR PROGRAM HAVE DIFFERED IF THERE HAD BEEN AVAILABLE THIS "BRILLIANT DISCOVERY," AS I BELIEVE YOU'VE CHARACTERIZED IT, THAT CAME TO TELLER LATER?
IT IS DIFFICULT TO ANSWER THIS, BUT I BELIEVE IT MIGHT HAVE BEEN DIFFERENT.

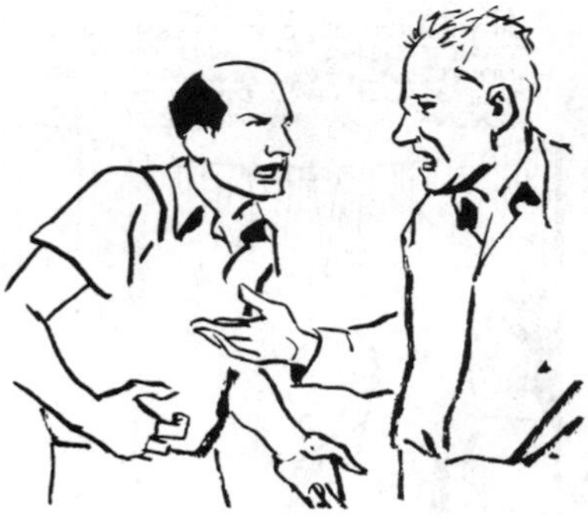

MR. GARRISON: Why?
DR. BETHE: I was hoping it possible to prove that thermonuclear reactions were not feasible at all. I thought the greatest security would have lain in the conclusive proof of the impossibility of a thermonuclear bomb.

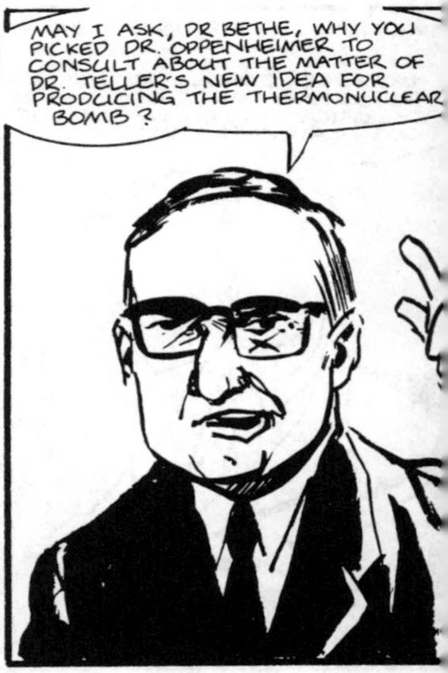
MAY I ASK, DR BETHE, WHY YOU PICKED DR. OPPENHEIMER TO CONSULT ABOUT THE MATTER OF DR. TELLER'S NEW IDEA FOR PRODUCING THE THERMONUCLEAR BOMB?

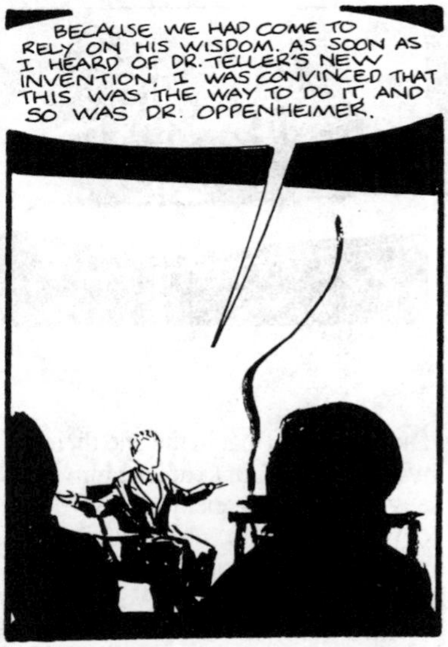
BECAUSE WE HAD COME TO RELY ON HIS WISDOM. AS SOON AS I HEARD OF DR. TELLER'S NEW INVENTION, I WAS CONVINCED THAT THIS WAS THE WAY TO DO IT, AND SO WAS DR. OPPENHEIMER.

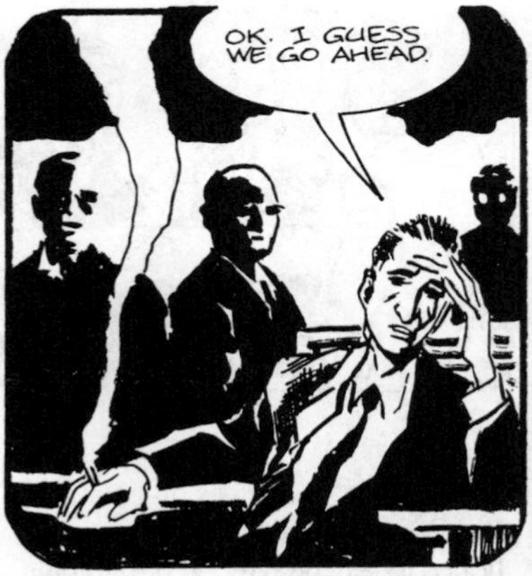
OK. I GUESS WE GO AHEAD.

DR. BETHE: At this meeting, which took place in 1951, in June, the final program for the thermonuclear bomb was set up. At this meeting Dr. Oppenheimer wholeheartedly supported the program.

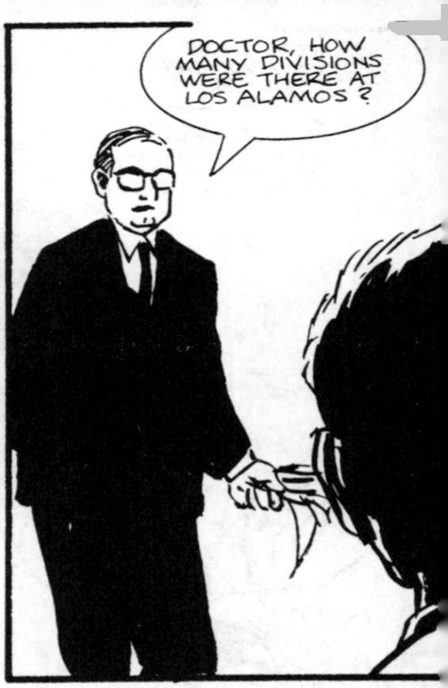
DOCTOR, HOW MANY DIVISIONS WERE THERE AT LOS ALAMOS?

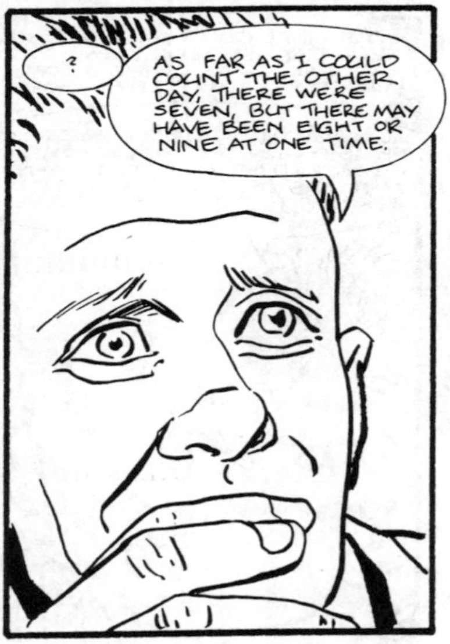
?
AS FAR AS I COULD COUNT THE OTHER DAY, THERE WERE SEVEN, BUT THERE MAY HAVE BEEN EIGHT OR NINE AT ONE TIME.

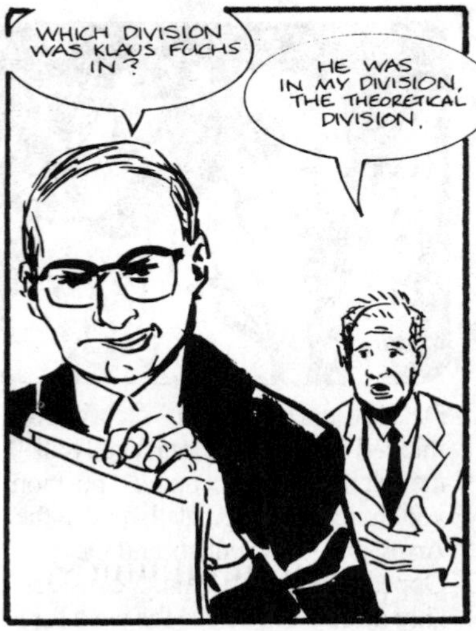
WHICH DIVISION WAS KLAUS FUCHS IN?
HE WAS IN MY DIVISION, THE THEORETICAL DIVISION.

KLAUS FUCHS WAS A RESPECTED PHYSICIST, AND RUSSIAN SPY, DURING WORLD WAR II.

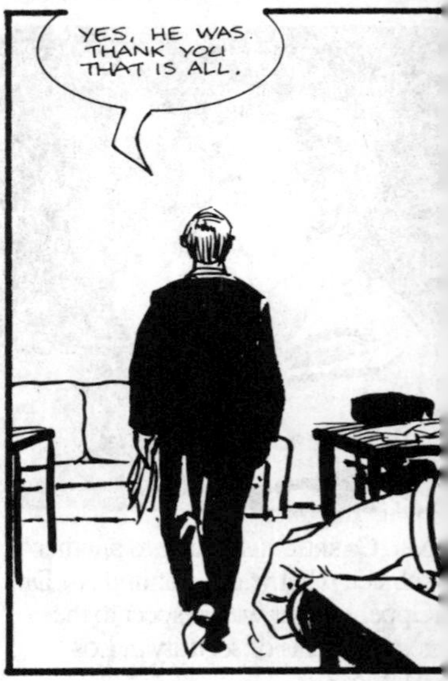
YES, HE WAS. THANK YOU THAT IS ALL.

Formulation of policy and the management of the vast atomic energy enterprise were responsibilities vested in the Commission itself. The General Advisory Committee had the role, which was fixed for it by statute, to advise the Commission.

During all the years that I served on the General Advisory Committee, its major preoccupation was with the production and perfection of atomic weapons. On the various recommendations there was never, so far as I can remember, any significant divergence of opinion among the members of the committee.

In that period the General Advisory Committee pointed out the still extremely unclear status of the problem from the technical standpoint, and urged encouragement of Los Alamos' efforts which were then directed toward modest exploration of the super and of thermonuclear systems. No serious controversy arose about the super until the Soviet explosion of an atomic bomb in the autumn of 1949.

Shortly after that event, in October 1949, the Atomic Energy Commission called a special session of the General Advisory Committee and asked us to consider and advise on two related questions:

First, whether in view of the Soviet success the Commission's program was adequate, and if not, in what way it should be altered or increased; second, whether a crash program for the development of the super should be a part of any new program.

As to the Super itself, the General Advisory Committee stated its unanimous opposition to the initiation by the United States of a crash program of the kind we had been asked to advise on. The report of that meeting, and the Secretary's notes, reflect the reasons which moved us to this conclusion.

It would have been surprising if eight men considering a problem of extreme difficulty had each had precisely the same reasons for the conclusion in which we joined. But I think I am correct in asserting that the unanimous opposition we expressed to the crash program was based on the conviction, to which technical considerations as well as others contributed, that because of our overall situation at that time such a program might weaken rather than strengthen the position of the United States.

"--DR. ENRICO FERMI--"

DR. FERMI, AS A MEMBER OF THE GENERAL ADVISORY YOU PARTICIPATED IN THE DELIBERATIONS CONCERNING THE ADVICE TO THE COMMISSION ON THE THERMONUCLEAR PROGRAM.

YES.

WOULD YOU TELL US BRIEFLY, IN AN UNCLASSIFIED WAY, ABOUT THOSE DELIBERATIONS, THE POSITIONS TAKEN, THE REASONS FOR THEM?

DR. FERMI: As far as I could see, I had the concern that pressure for this development was extremely inordinate. I was concerned that it might weaken development of conventional atomic weapons and set it back for what seemed to me at the time a not quite decided advantage on the other side.

MY OPINION AT THE TIME WAS THAT ONE SHOULD TRY TO OUTLAW THE THING BEFORE IT WAS BORN.

FAILING THAT, ONE SHOULD, WITH CONSIDERABLE REGRET, GO AHEAD.

ONE FINAL QUESTION. WHAT OPPORTUNITY DID DR. OPPENHEIMER AFFORD TO THE OTHER MEMBERS OF THE COMMITTEE TO FULLY EXPRESS THEIR VIEWS AND TO EXERT THEIR INFLUENCE?

DR. FERMI: Perfect opportunity. Of course, he's a person who knows a great deal about these things and knows how to express it with extreme efficacy, so he would naturally take a leading role. But everybody had perfect freedom to act with his own mind and according to his conscience on any issue.

DR ISIDOR I. RABI,...

I KNEW ALL THE REST. WHO'S THIS ONE?

RABI. RADAR STAYED AT M.I.T. RATHER THAN GO TO LOS ALAMOS.

SO WHY'S HE HERE?

OPPENHEIMER ASKED HIM TO BE ASSOCIATE DIRECTO[R] TURNED HIM DOWN

ACTED AS A VISITING CONSULTANT TO THE MANHATTAN PROJECT WAS ON THE ADVISORY COMMITTEE WITH OPPENHEIMER.

THAT SORT OF THING.

"VISITING CONSULTANT?" HOW'D GROVES LET HIM GET AWAY WITH THAT?

DR.--

RABI.

YES, DR RABI. LET'S GET RIGHT TO IT.

THERE HAVE BEEN THOSE WHO TESTIFIED--MEN OF CHARACTER AND STANDING AND LOYALTY-- THAT THE CHEVALIER EPISODE SHOULD SIMPLY BE DISREGARDED.

DO YOU FEEL THAT THIS IS A MATTER OF NO CONSEQUENCE.

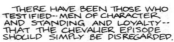

I DO NOT THINK ANY OF IT IS OF NO CONSEQUENCE. I THINK YOU HAVE TO TAKE THE MATTER IN ITS WHOLE CONTEX[T]

I.I. RABI: The country has been divided into sheep and goats. There are the people who are cleared and those who are not cleared. It is really a question of in one's personal life, should you refuse to enter a room in which a person is present against whom there is derogatory information? Of course, if you are extremely prudent and want your life circumscribed that way, no question would ever arise. If you feel that you want to live a more normal life and have confidence in your own integrity then you might act more freely.

ROBB: Let me say this. I think there is not anybody who is prepared to testify that he can spot a Communist with complete infallibility. I know that there have been people who surprised me...and witnesses including Dr. Oppenheimer himself have testified that there were people who later turned out to be Communists, to their surprise, who they identified.

ROBB: So can we afford to make it a matter of individual judgment as to whether a person is dangerous, in this case Mr. Chevalier. Even though the Chevalier incident did not, as I understand it, involve the disclosure of information, I believe you said you would expect Dr. Oppenheimer to follow a different course today.

I.I. RABI: I can't say anything but yes. We have all learned a whole lot since that time. You have to become accustomed to this kind of life when you are involved in this kind of information.

ROBB: You are saying that in your judgment Dr. Oppenheimer has changed?

I.I. RABI: I think he was always a loyal American. But he has learned more the way you have to live in the world as it is now.

ROBB: Dr. Rabi, if you were approached by someone attempting to secure from you security information, would you report it immediately, or would you consider it for quite a long time.

I.I. RABI: Are you talking about today?

ROBB: Oh, no.

I.I. RABI: What are you talking about?

ROBB: I am talking about the Chevalier Incident, late 1942 or early 1943.

I.I. RABI: I would like the question put more fully so I can answer the point rather than make up the question, so to speak.

ROBB: You're giving me a big job, aren't you?

I.I. RABI: This is not child's play, here.

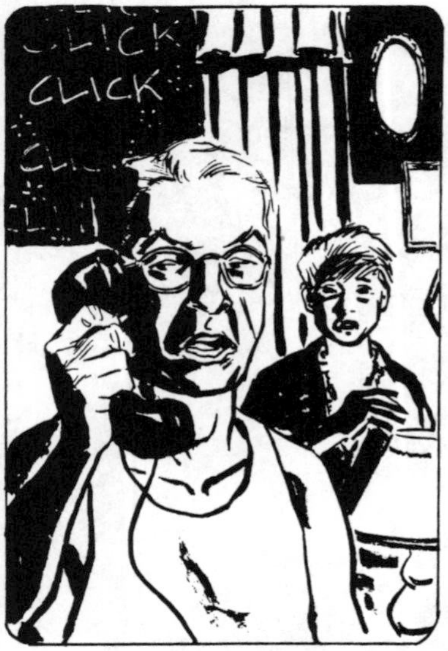
CLICK
CLICK

ROBB: If you had been working on security material, and someone came to you and told you that they had a way of getting that material to the Russians, what would you have done immediately?
I.I. RABI: I would have tried to see that the proper authorities found out what these people meant to do. I know a number of times during the war I heard funny noises in my telephone and got the security officers after it.

ROBB: Of course, Doctor, you don't know what Dr. Oppenheimer's testimony before this board about this incident may have been, do you?
I.I. RABI: No.
ROBB: And the board may be in possession of information which is not now available to you about the incident.

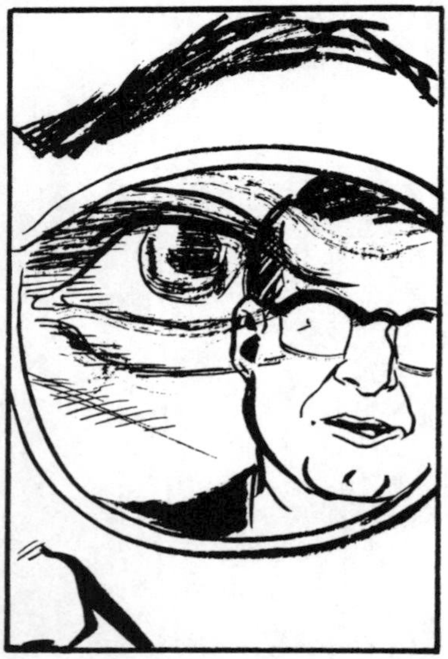

I.I. RABI: It may be. On the other hand, I am in possession of long experience with this man, going back to 1929, which is 25 years. In other words, I might even venture to differ from the judgment of the board without impugning their integrity at all.
ROBB: But it may well be that the board is now in a better position than you, so far as that incident is concerned, to evaluate it?
I.I. RABI: I can't say they are not. But on the other hand you have to take the whole story.

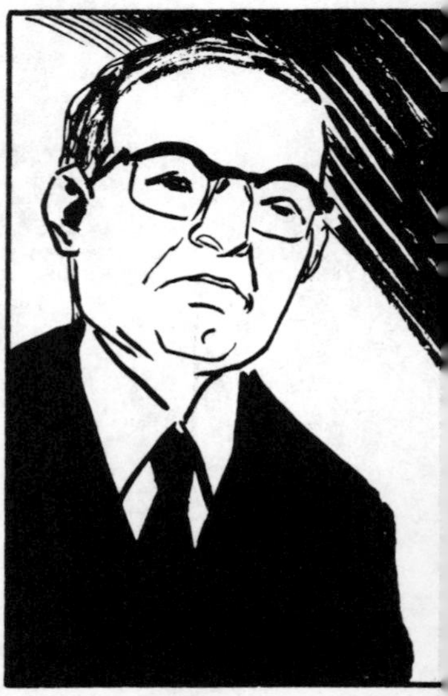

ROBB: Of course.
I.I. RABI: That is what novels are about. There is a dramatic moment; and the history of the man; what made him act, what he did, and what sort of person he was. That is what you are doing here. You are writing a man's life.
ROBB: But suppose the board was not satisfied that he had told the truth or the whole truth on some material matter; what would you say then?
I.I. RABI: It would depend on the nature of the material matter.
ROBB: Wouldn't you feel that you couldn't clear him, or would you rather not answer that?
I.I. RABI: It is the sort of hypothetical which to me goes under the terms of a meaningless question. If you want to set me up on the board, then I would come up with an answer after weighing this thing with the other members of the board.

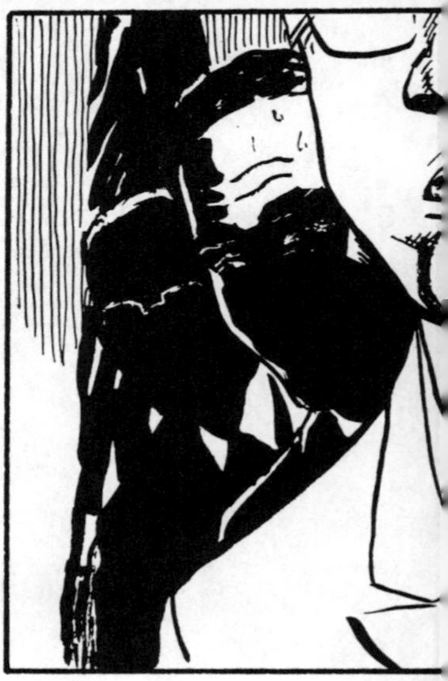

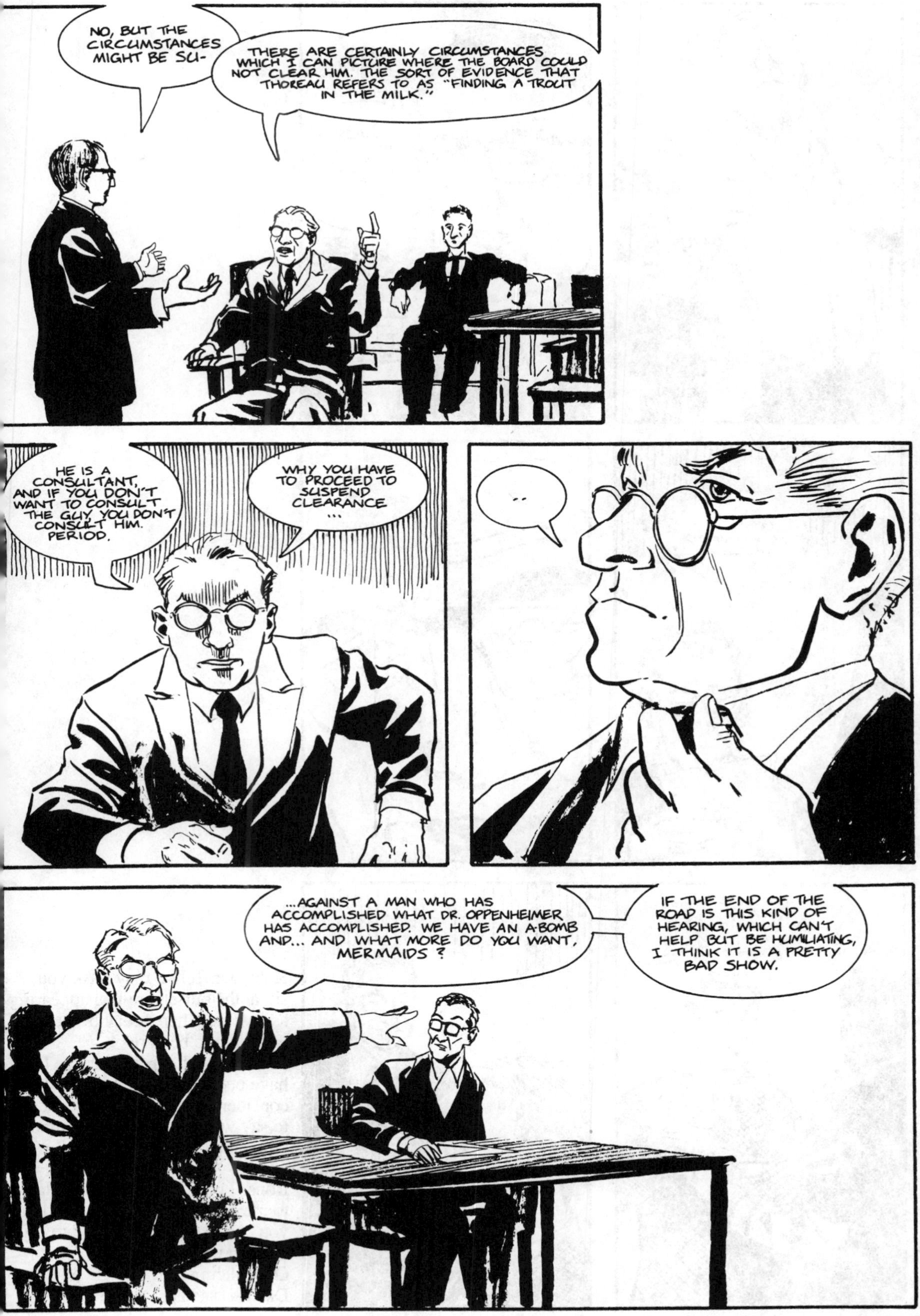
NO, BUT THE CIRCUMSTANCES MIGHT BE SU-
THERE ARE CERTAINLY CIRCUMSTANCES WHICH I CAN PICTURE WHERE THE BOARD COULD NOT CLEAR HIM. THE SORT OF EVIDENCE THAT THOREAU REFERS TO AS "FINDING A TROUT IN THE MILK."
HE IS A CONSULTANT, AND IF YOU DON'T WANT TO CONSULT THE GUY, YOU DON'T CONSULT HIM. PERIOD.
WHY YOU HAVE TO PROCEED TO SUSPEND CLEARANCE ...
..
...AGAINST A MAN WHO HAS ACCOMPLISHED WHAT DR. OPPENHEIMER HAS ACCOMPLISHED. WE HAVE AN A-BOMB AND... AND WHAT MORE DO YOU WANT, MERMAIDS ?
IF THE END OF THE ROAD IS THIS KIND OF HEARING, WHICH CAN'T HELP BUT BE HUMILIATING, I THINK IT IS A PRETTY BAD SHOW.

WHO'S NEXT?

PLEASE TELL ME NOT ANOTHER ONE OF THOSE.

WELL, YES.

IT'S...UM... DR. EDWARD TELLER.

AH.

THEN IT'S "YES AND NO" TO ANOTHER ONE OF THOSE.

WE MET LAST NIGHT.

ROBB: Dr. Teller, may I ask you, sir, at the outset, are you appearing as a witness here today because you want to be here?

DR. TELLER: I appear because I have been asked and because I consider it my duty upon request to say what I think in the matter. I would have preferred not to appear.

ROBB: I believe, sir, that you stated to me some time ago that anything you had to say, you wished to say in the presence of Dr. Oppenheimer?

DR. TELLER: That is correct.

ROBB: When did you begin to work on the atomic bomb program?

DR. TELLER: I am not sure I can answer simply. I became aware of the atomic bomb program early in 1939. I have been close to it ever since.

ROBB: To simplify the issues here, perhaps, let me ask you this: Is it your intention in anything you are about to testify to, to suggest that Oppenheimer is disloyal to the United States?

DR. TELLER: I know Oppenheimer as an intellectually alert and a very complicated person, and I think it would be presumptuous and wrong on my part if I would try in any way to analyze his motives.

DR. TELLER: But I have always assumed, and I now assume, that he is loyal to the United States.

ROBB: Now, a question which is the corollary of that. Do you or do you not believe Oppenheimer is a security risk?

DR. TELLER: In a great number of cases I have seen Oppenheimer act—I understood that he acted—in a way which for me was exceedingly hard to understand. I thoroughly disagree with him in numerous issues and his actions frankly appeared to be confused and complicated. To this extent I feel that I would like to see the vital interests of this country in hands which I understand better, and therefore trust more.

IT'S WRONG FOR A SCIENTIST TO USE HIS PRESTIGE AS A SOAPBOX FOR POLITICAL DECISIONS.

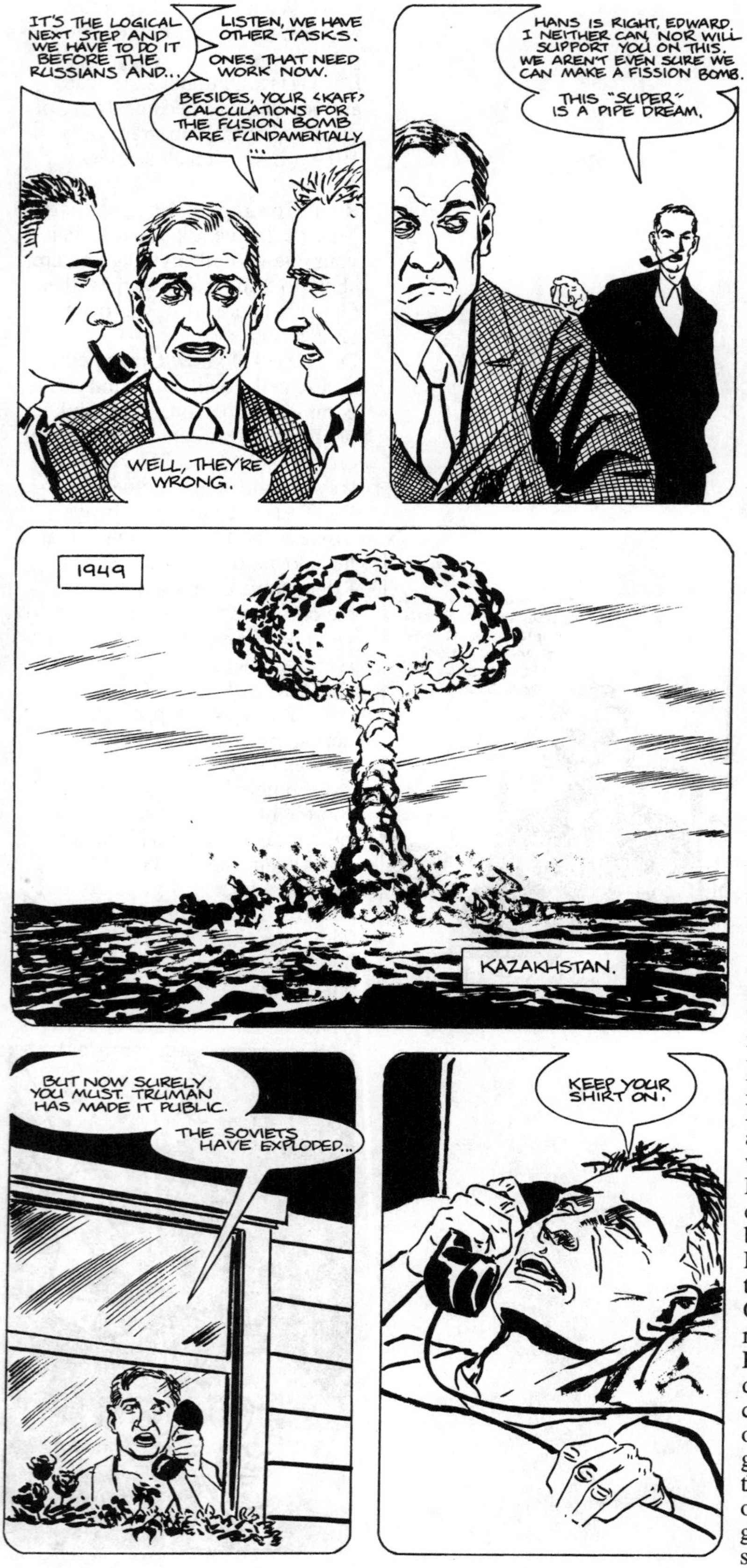
IT'S THE LOGICAL NEXT STEP AND WE HAVE TO DO IT BEFORE THE RUSSIANS AND...
LISTEN, WE HAVE OTHER TASKS.
ONES THAT NEED WORK NOW.
BESIDES, YOUR <KAFF> CALCULATIONS FOR THE FUSION BOMB ARE FUNDAMENTALLY ...
WELL, THEY'RE WRONG.
HANS IS RIGHT, EDWARD. I NEITHER CAN, NOR WILL SUPPORT YOU ON THIS. WE AREN'T EVEN SURE WE CAN MAKE A FISSION BOMB.
THIS "SUPER" IS A PIPE DREAM.
1949
KAZAKHSTAN.
BUT NOW SURELY YOU MUST. TRUMAN HAS MADE IT PUBLIC.
THE SOVIETS HAVE EXPLODED...
KEEP YOUR SHIRT ON.

ROBB: What was the nature of your work at Los Alamos?

DR. TELLER: It was theoretical work. Generally speaking I was more interested by choice and also by directive in advanced development, s my work shifted from what happene at Alamogordo into fields which wer not to bear fruition until much later.

ROBB: What was Oppenheimer's opinion during those years about the feasibility of producing a thermonuclear weapon?

DR. TELLER: I think his opinions shifte with the shifting evidence. I clearly remember that toward the end of the war he encouraged me to go ahead with thermonuclear investigations. I further remember that it was generally understood at Los Alamos that we are going to develop thermonuclear bom in a vigorous fashion and that quite a number of people, such as the most outstanding, like Fermi and Bethe, would participate in it.

DR. TELLER: I also know that very shortly after the dropping of bombs o Japan this plan was changed and to th best of my belief it was changed at least in good part because of the opinion of Oppenheimer that this is n the time to pursue this program any further. He argued that this is not the time at which to pursue the business further, that it would be a wonderful thing if we could pursue it in a really peaceful world under international cooperation, but that under the present setup this was not a good idea to go on

ROBB: Skipping ahead, then, Doctor, the record shows that in October, 1949 the General Advisory Committee held its meeting, and thereafter reported its views on the thermonuclear program. Did you later see a copy of the report?

DR. TELLER: I did. After the passage of a little while—I would say roughly tw weeks—the secretary of the GAC, Dr. Manley, who was also associate director in Los Alamos, showed me both the majority and minority reports. He used words which I at least that time interpreted as meaning that Oppenheimer wanted me to see these reports, which I thought was kind.

DR. TELLER: Of course I was just most dreadfully disappointed about the contents. I also should say that in my opinion the work in Los Alamos was going to be most seriously affected by the action of the GAC, not only as an official body, but because of the very great prestige of the people who were sitting on it.

After the report was submitted to the Commission, it fell to me as chairman of the committee to explain our position on several occasions, once at a meeting of the joint Congressional Committee on Atomic Energy. All this, however, took place prior to the decision by the President to proceed with the thermonuclear program.

This is the full story of my "opposition to the hydrogen bomb." It can be read in the records of the general transcript of my testimony before the joint congressional committee. It is a story which ended once and for all when in January 1950 the President announced his decision to proceed with the program.

I never urged anyone not to work on the hydrogen bomb project. I never made or caused any distribution of the GAC reports except to the Commission itself. As always, it was the Commission's responsibility to determine further distribution.

In summary, in October 1949, I and the other members of the General Advisory Committee were asked questions by the Commission to which we had a duty to respond, and to which we did respond with our best judgment in the light of evidence then available to us.

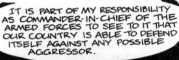

IT IS PART OF MY RESPONSIBILITY AS COMMANDER-IN-CHIEF OF THE ARMED FORCES TO SEE TO IT THAT OUR COUNTRY IS ABLE TO DEFEND ITSELF AGAINST ANY POSSIBLE AGGRESSOR.

1950

ACCORDINGLY, I HAVE DIRECTED THE ATOMIC ENERGY COMMISSION TO CONTINUE ITS WORK ON ALL FORMS OF ATOMIC WEAPONS, INCLUDING THE SO-CALLED HYDROGEN OR SUPER-BOMB.

ROBB: Doctor, in what way did you think that the work would be affected by the report?

DR. TELLER: I would say that I thought that this definitely was the end of any thermonuclear effort in Los Alamos. Actually I was completely mistaken. The report produced precisely the opposite effect.

ROBB: Why?

DR. TELLER: I think the strongest point was this: Not only to me, but to very many others who said this to me spontaneously, the report meant that as long as you people go ahead and make minor improvements and work very hard and diligently at it, you are doing a fine job, but if you succeed in making a great piece of progress, then you are doing something that is immoral.

DR. TELLER: The result was that I think the feelings of people turned more toward the thermonuclear development than away from it.

ROBB: You mean it made then mad.

DR. TELLER: Yes.

ROBB: Doctor, in the absence of the President's decision in January of 1950, would that anger have been effective?

DR. TELLER: No.

In the spring of 1951 work had reached a stage at which far-reaching decisions were called for with regard to the commission's whole thermonuclear program. In consultation with the Commission, I called a meeting in Princeton in the late spring of that year, which was attended by all members of the commission and several members of its staff, by members of the General Advisory Committee, by Dr. Bradbury and staff of the Los Alamos Laboratory, by Bethe, Teller, Bacher, Fermi, von Neumann, Wheeler and others responsibly connected with the program. The outcome of the meeting, which lasted for two or three days, was an agreed program and a fixing of priorities and effort both for Los Alamos and for other aspects of the commission's work. This program has been an outstanding success.

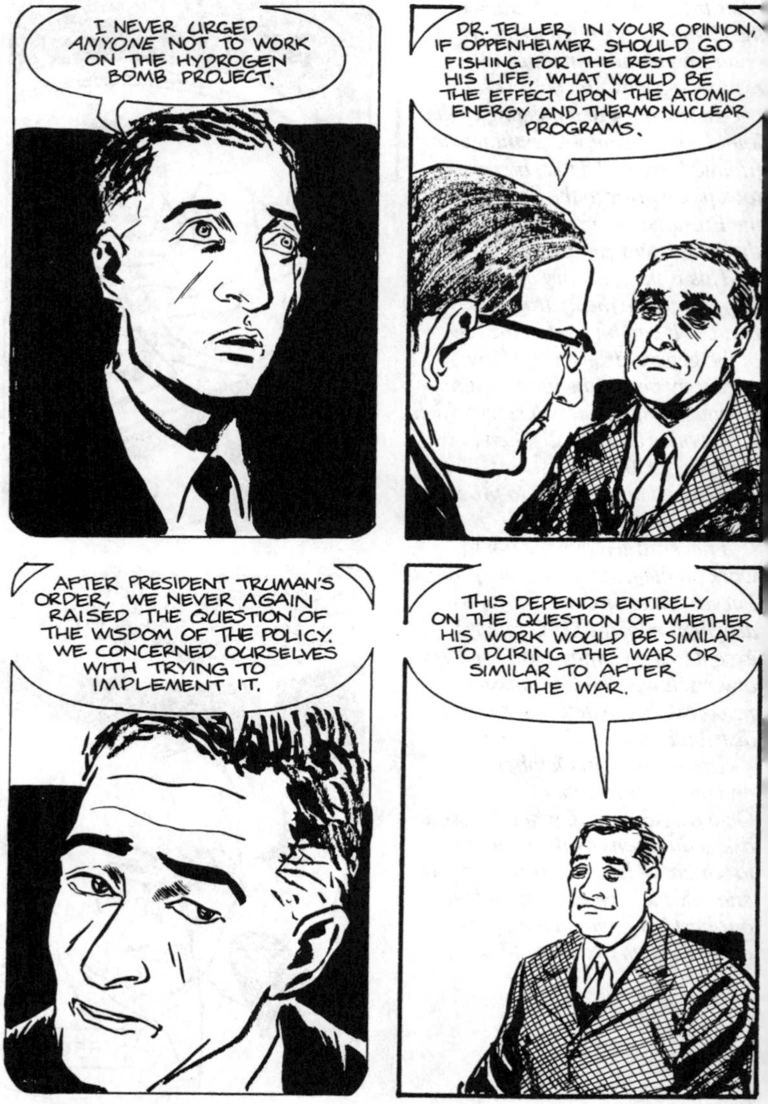

I NEVER URGED ANYONE NOT TO WORK ON THE HYDROGEN BOMB PROJECT.
DR. TELLER, IN YOUR OPINION, IF OPPENHEIMER SHOULD GO FISHING FOR THE REST OF HIS LIFE, WHAT WOULD BE THE EFFECT UPON THE ATOMIC ENERGY AND THERMONUCLEAR PROGRAMS.
AFTER PRESIDENT TRUMAN'S ORDER, WE NEVER AGAIN RAISED THE QUESTION OF THE WISDOM OF THE POLICY. WE CONCERNED OURSELVES WITH TRYING TO IMPLEMENT IT.
THIS DEPENDS ENTIRELY ON THE QUESTION OF WHETHER HIS WORK WOULD BE SIMILAR TO DURING THE WAR OR SIMILAR TO AFTER THE WAR.

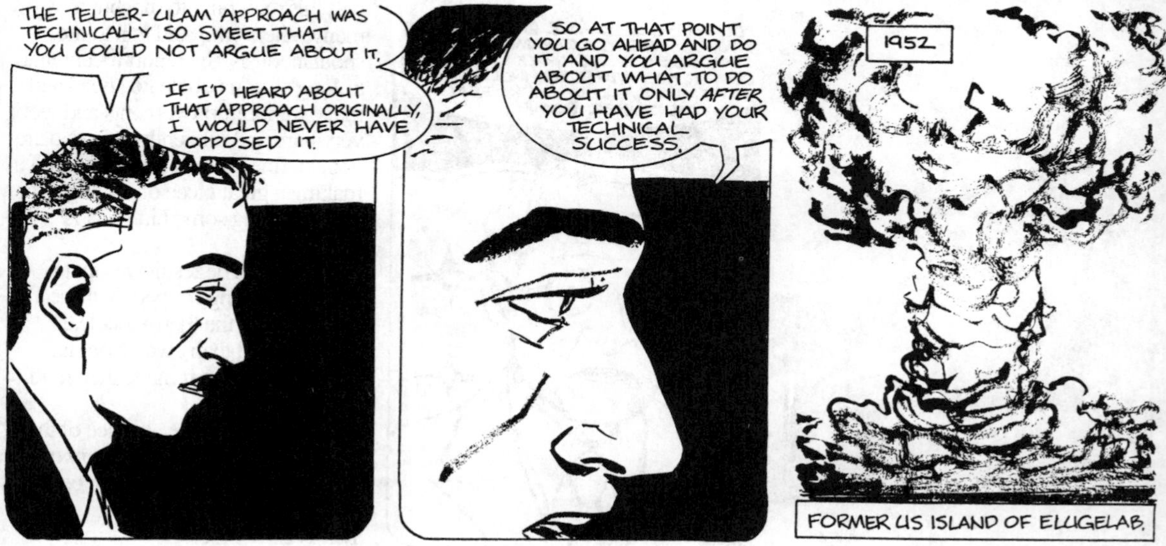

THE TELLER-ULAM APPROACH WAS TECHNICALLY SO SWEET THAT YOU COULD NOT ARGUE ABOUT IT.
IF I'D HEARD ABOUT THAT APPROACH ORIGINALLY, I WOULD NEVER HAVE OPPOSED IT.
SO AT THAT POINT YOU GO AHEAD AND DO IT AND YOU ARGUE ABOUT WHAT TO DO ABOUT IT ONLY AFTER YOU HAVE HAD YOUR TECHNICAL SUCCESS.
1952
FORMER US ISLAND OF ELUGELAB.

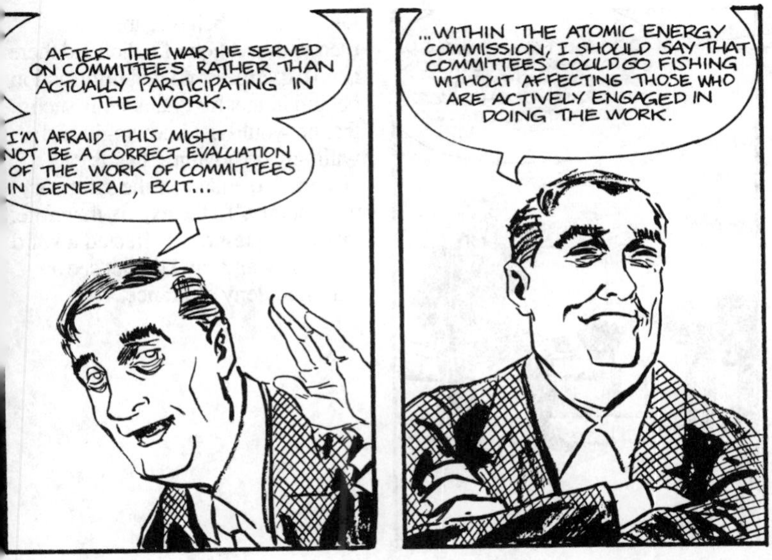
AFTER THE WAR HE SERVED ON COMMITTEES RATHER THAN ACTUALLY PARTICIPATING IN THE WORK.
I'M AFRAID THIS MIGHT NOT BE A CORRECT EVALUATION OF THE WORK OF COMMITTEES IN GENERAL, BUT...
...WITHIN THE ATOMIC ENERGY COMMISSION, I SHOULD SAY THAT COMMITTEES COULD GO FISHING WITHOUT AFFECTING THOSE WHO ARE ACTIVELY ENGAGED IN DOING THE WORK.

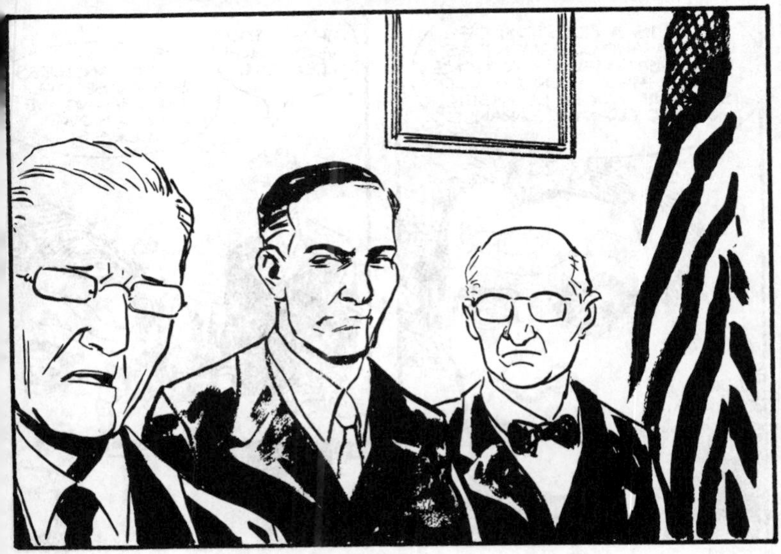

DR. TELLER: In particular, however, the general recommendations that I know have come from Oppenheimer were more frequently and I mean not only and not even particularly the thermonuclear case, but other cases, more frequently a hindrance than a help, and therefore, if I look into the continuation of this and assume that it will come in the same way, I think that further work of Oppenheimer on committees would not be helpful.

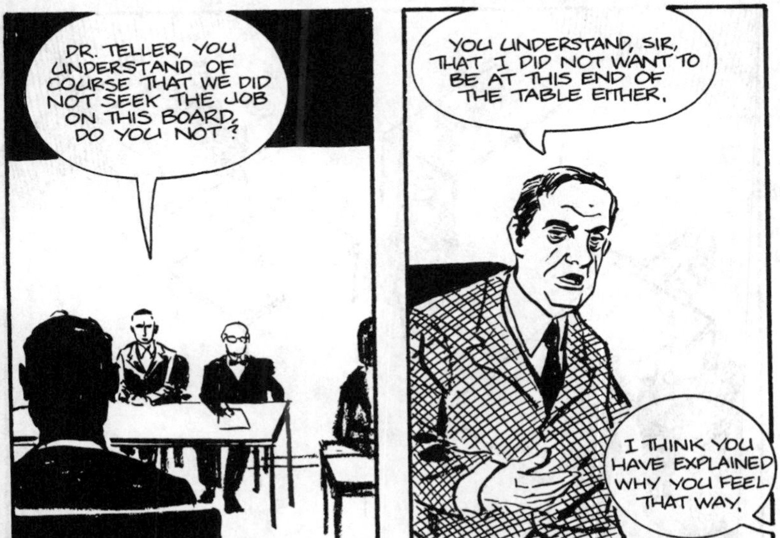
DR. TELLER, YOU UNDERSTAND OF COURSE THAT WE DID NOT SEEK THE JOB ON THIS BOARD, DO YOU NOT?
YOU UNDERSTAND, SIR, THAT I DID NOT WANT TO BE AT THIS END OF THE TABLE EITHER.
I THINK YOU HAVE EXPLAINED WHY YOU FEEL THAT WAY.

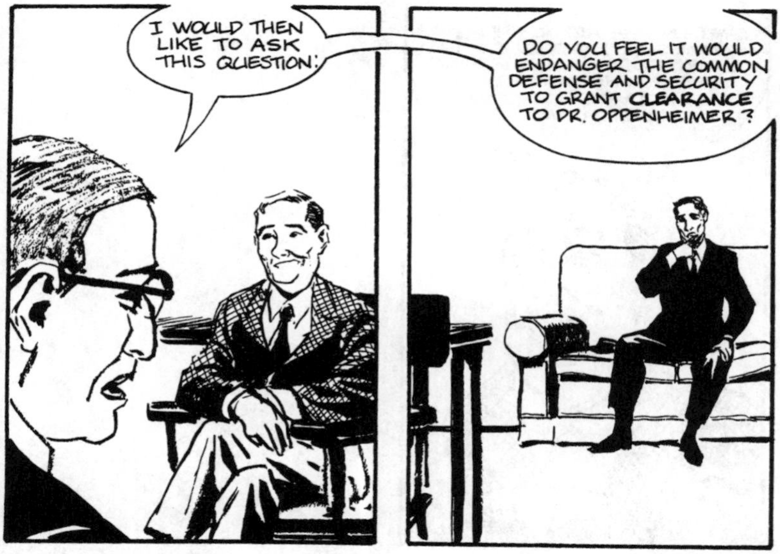
I WOULD THEN LIKE TO ASK THIS QUESTION:
DO YOU FEEL IT WOULD ENDANGER THE COMMON DEFENSE AND SECURITY TO GRANT **CLEARANCE** TO DR. OPPENHEIMER?

DR. TELLER: I believe, and it is merely a question of belief and there is no expertness, no real information behind it, that his character is such that he would not knowingly and willingly do anything that is designed to endanger the safety of this country. To the extent, therefore, that your question is directed toward intent, I would say I do not see any reason to deny clearance.

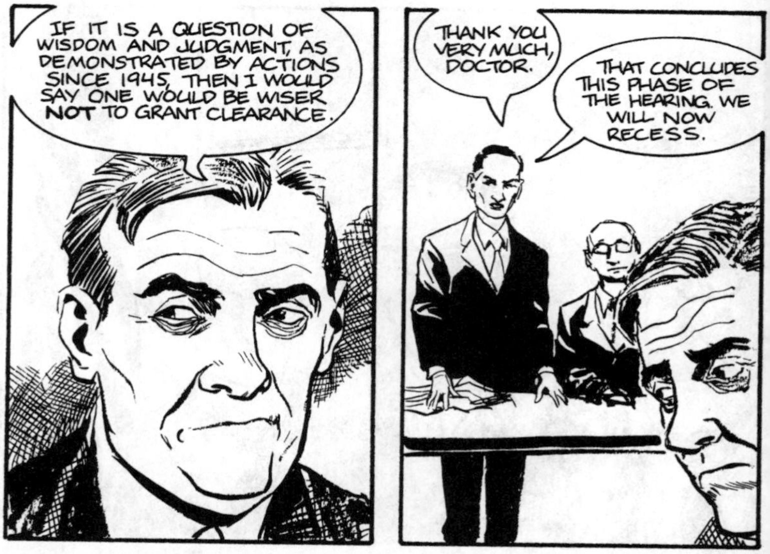
IF IT IS A QUESTION OF WISDOM AND JUDGMENT, AS DEMONSTRATED BY ACTIONS SINCE 1945, THEN I WOULD SAY ONE WOULD BE WISER **NOT** TO GRANT CLEARANCE.
THANK YOU VERY MUCH, DOCTOR.
THAT CONCLUDES THIS PHASE OF THE HEARING. WE WILL NOW RECESS.

In preparing this letter, I have reviewed two decades of my life. I have recalled instances where I acted unwisely. What I have hoped was, not that I could wholly avoid error, but that I might learn from it. What I have learned has, I think, made me more fit to serve my country.

Very truly yours,

J. Robert Oppenheimer

Princeton, NJ, March 4, 1954

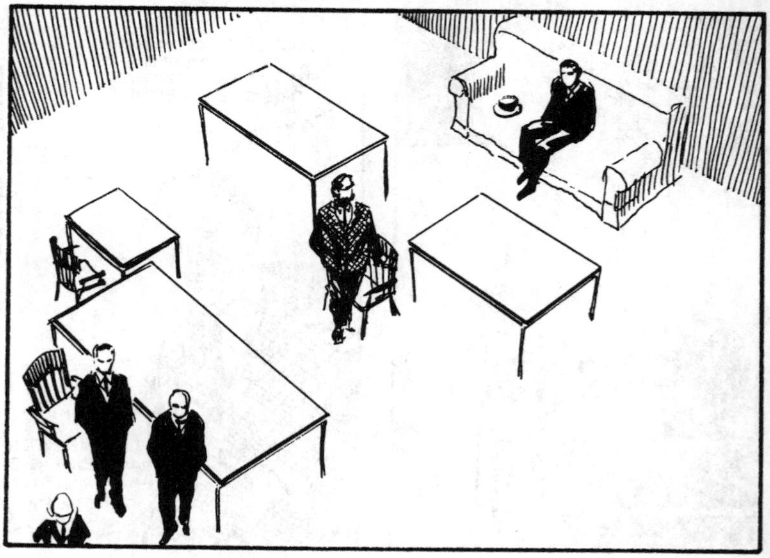

I'M SORRY.

AFTER WHAT YOU'VE JUST SAID, I DON'T KNOW WHAT YOU MEAN.

AND SO...

PRESIDENT OPPENHEIMER TRIAL TAKE

LATER

COMMUNIST

EVEN LATER...

Washington, D. C., May 27, 1954

Subject: Findings and recommendation of the Personnel Security Board in the case of Dr. J. Robert Oppenheimer.

Mr. K.D. Nichols, General Manager, U. S. Atomic Energy Commission 1901 Constitution Avenue NW., Washington 25, D.C.

Dear General Nichols:

On December 23, 1953, Dr. J. Robert Oppenheimer was notified by letter that his security clearance had been suspended. He was furnished a list of items of derogatory information and was advised of his rights to a hearing under AEC procedures. On March 4, 1954, Dr. Oppenheimer requested that he be afforded a hearing. A hearing has been conducted by the Board appointed by you for this purpose, and we submit our findings and recommendation.

Dr. Ward V. Evans dissents from the recommendation of the majority of the Board, and his minority report is attached.

The facts referred to in your letter fall clearly into two major areas of concern. The first of these, which is represented by items 1 through 23, involves primarily Dr. Oppenheimer's Communist connections in the earlier years and continued associations arising out of those connections.

The second major area of concern is related to Dr. Oppenheimer's attitudes and activities with respect to the development of the hydrogen bomb.

The Board has found the allegations in the first part of the Commission letter to be substantially true, and attaches the following significance to the findings: There remains little doubt that, from late 1936 or early 1937 to probably April 1942, Dr. Oppenheimer was deeply involved with many people who were active Communists. The record would suggest that the involvement was something more than an intellectual and sympathetic interest in the professed aims of the Communist Party. Although Communist functionaries during this period considered Dr. Oppenheimer to be a Communist, there is no evidence that he was a member of the party in the strict sense of the word.

…

The Board takes a most serious view of these earlier involvements. Had they occurred in very recent years, we would have found them to be controlling and, in any event, they must be taken into account in evaluating subsequent conduct and attitudes.

…

The Board believes, however, that there is no indication of disloyalty on the part of Dr. Oppenheimer by reason of any present Communist affiliation, despite Dr. Oppenheimer's poor judgment in continuing some of his past associations into the present. Furthermore, the Board had before it eloquent and convincing testimony of Dr. Oppenheimer's deep devotion to his country in recent years and a multitude of evidence with respect to active service in all sorts of governmental undertakings to which he was repeatedly called as a participant and as a consultant.

We feel that Dr. Oppenheimer is convinced that the earlier involvements were serious errors and today would consider them an indication of disloyalty. The conclusion of this Board is that Dr. Oppenheimer is a loyal citizen.

June 1, 1954

Mr. K. D. Nichols
General Manager,
U. S. Atomic Energy Commission
1901 Constitution Avenue NW.,
Washington 25, D.C.

Dear General Nichols:

Dr. Oppenheimer has received your letter of May 28, 1954, in which you enclosed a copy of the "Findings and Recommendation of the Personnel Security Board" dated May 27. In this document the Board unanimously found that Dr. Oppenheimer was a loyal citizen, but by a 2 to 1 vote, Dr. Ward V. Evans dissenting, recommended that Dr. Oppenheimer's clearance should not be reinstated. Dr. Oppenheimer has asked me to send you this reply on his behalf.

[W]e think it fitting to identify for the Commission what we conceive to be certain issues of basic importance which are presented by the majority and minority opinions.

To begin with, the majority's conclusion not to recommend the reinstatement of Dr. Oppenheimer's clearance stands in such stark contrast with the Board's findings regarding Dr. Oppenheimer's loyalty and discretion as to raise doubts about the process of reasoning by which the conclusion was arrived at. All members of the Board agreed:

(1) That the Nation owed scientists "a great debt of gratitude for loyal and magnificent service" and that "This is particularly true, with respect to Dr. Oppenheimer."

(2) That "we have before us much responsible and positive evidence of the loyalty and love of country of the individual concerned," and "eloquent and convincing testimony of Dr. Oppenheimer's deep devotion to his country in recent years and a multitude of evidence with respect to active service in all sorts of governmental undertakings to which he was repeatedly called as a participant and as a consultant."

(3) That "even those who were critical of Dr. Oppenheimer's judgment and activities or lack of activities, without exception, testified to their belief in his loyalty."

(4) That "we have given particular attention to the question of his loyalty, and we have come to a clear conclusion, which should be reassuring to the people of this country, that he is a loyal citizen. If this were the only consideration, therefore, we would recommend that the reinstatement of his clearance would not be a danger to the common defense and security."

(5) That "It must be said that Dr. Oppenheimer seems to have had a high degree of discretion reflecting in unusual ability to keep to himself vital secrets"

In spite of these findings of loyalty and discretion in the handling of classified data, the majority of the Board reached the conclusion that Dr. Oppenheimer's clearance should not be reinstated. How can this be?

1954

IN CLOSING, THE CASE STANDS OUT IN SHARP FEATURE RATHER SIMPLY THIS WAY:

THESE DEROGATORY ITEMS IN THE FILE MOSTLY HAVE TO DO WITH ACTIVITIES OF DR. OPPENHEIMER THAT GO BACK 12 TO 15 YEARS AGO.

With respect to the second portion of your letter, the Board believes that Dr. Oppenheimer's opposition to the hydrogen bomb and his related conduct in the postwar period until April 1951, involved no lack of loyalty to the United States or attachment to the Soviet Union. The Board was impressed by the fact that even those who were critical of Dr. Oppenheimer's judgment and activities or lack of activities, without exception, testified to their belief in his loyalty.

The Board confirms that in 1945 Dr. Oppenheimer expressed the view that there is reasonable possibility that it (the hydrogen bomb) can be made, but that the feasibility of the hydrogen bomb did not appear, on theoretical grounds, as certain as the fission bomb appeared certain, on theoretical grounds, when the Los Alamos Laboratory was started; and that in August of 1949, the General Advisory Committee expressed the view that "an imaginative and concerted attack on the problem has a better than even chance of producing the weapon within 5 years."

With respect to Dr. Oppenheimer's attitude and activities in relation to the hydrogen bomb in World War II, the evidence shows that Dr. Oppenheimer during this period had no misgivings about a program looking to thermonuclear development and, indeed, during the latter part of the war, he recorded his support of prompt and vigorous action in this connection. When asked under cross examination whether he would have opposed dropping an H-bomb on Hiroshima, he replied that "It would make no sense," and when asked "Why?" replied, "The target is too small." He testified further under cross examination that he believed he would have opposed the dropping of an H-bomb on Japan because of moral scruples although he did not oppose the dropping of an A-bomb on the same grounds. During the postwar period, Dr. Oppenheimer favored, and in fact urged, continued research in the thermonuclear field and seemed to express considerable interest in results that were from time to time discussed with him…

n the case of Dr. Oppenheimer's so-
alled disturbing conduct in the hydrogen
omb program the Board's unanimous
indings of fact again stand in stark
contrast with the conclusion of the
najority. Thus the Board unanimously
ound:

(1) That Dr. Oppenheimer's
pposition to the H-bomb program
'involved no lack of loyalty to the United
States or attachment to the Soviet
Jnion."

(2) That his opinions regarding the
levelopment of the H-bomb "were
hared by other competent and devoted
ndividuals, both in and out of Govern-
nent."

(3) That it could be assumed that
hese opinions "were motivated by deep
noral conviction."

(4) That after the national policy to
proceed with the development of the H-
omb had been determined in January
1950, he "did not oppose the project in a
ositive or open manner, nor did he
lecline to cooperate in the project."

(5) That the allegations that he urged
other scientists not to work on the
hydrogen bomb program were
unfounded.

(6) That he did not, as alleged,
distribute copies of the General Advisory
Report to key personnel with a view to
turning them against the project, but that
on the contrary this distribution was
made at the Commission's direction.

In short, all the basic allegations set forth in General Nichols' letter to Dr. Oppenheimer on December 23, 1953, regarding any improper action by him in the H-bomb problem were disproved.

In the face of these unanimous findings, the majority then conclude that "the security interests of the United States were affected" by Dr. Oppenheimer's attitude toward the hydrogen bomb program. Why? Because, according to the majority:

"We believe that, had Dr. Oppenheimer given his enthusiastic support to the program, a concerted effort would have been initiated at an earlier date.

"Following the President's decision, he did not show the enthusiastic support for the program which might have been expected of the chief atomic adviser to the Government under the circumstances. Indeed, a failure to communicate an abandonment of his earlier position undoubtedly had an effect upon other scientists."

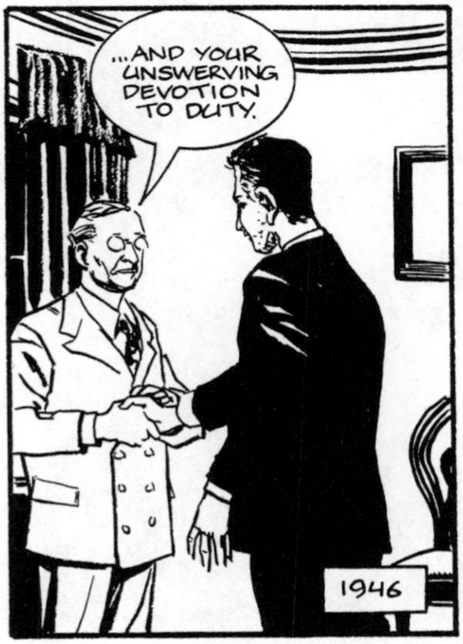

...AND YOUR UNSWERVING DEVOTION TO DUTY.
1946

The Board finds further that in the autumn of 1949, and subsequently, Dr. Oppenheimer strongly opposed the development of the hydrogen bomb on moral grounds; on grounds that it was not politically desirable: he expressed the view that there were insufficient facilities and scientific personnel to carry on the development without seriously interfering with the orderly development of the program for fission bombs; and until the late spring of 1951, he questioned the feasibility of the hydrogen bomb efforts then in progress.

...

The Board further concludes that after it was determined, as a matter of national policy (January 31, 1950) to proceed with development of a hydrogen bomb, Dr. Oppenheimer did not oppose the project in a positive or open manner, nor did he decline to cooperate in the project. However...the Board finds, that if Dr. Oppenheimer had enthusiastically supported the thermonuclear program either before or after the determination of national policy, the H-bomb project would have been pursued with considerably more vigor, thus increasing the possibility of earlier success in this field.

The Board does not find that Dr. Oppenheimer urged other scientists not to work on the program. However, enthusiastic support on his part would perhaps have encouraged other leading scientists to work on the program.

Because of technical questions involved, the Board is unable to make a categorical finding as to whether the opposition of the hydrogen bomb "has definitely slowed down its development." The Board concludes that the opposition to the H-bomb by many persons connected with the atomic energy program, of which Dr. Oppenheimer was the "most experienced, most powerful, and most effective member" did delay the initiation of concerted effort which led to the development of a thermonuclear weapon.

We believe that, had Dr. Oppenheimer given his enthusiastic support to the program, a concerted effort would have been initiated at an earlier date.

Without taking into account the factual evidence, which in our opinion should have led the Board to an opposite conclusion, we submit that the injection into a security case of a scientist's alleged lack of enthusiasm for a particular program is fraught with grave consequences to this country. How can a scientist risk advising the Government if he is told that at some later day a security board may weigh in the balance the degree of his enthusiasm for some official program? Or that he may be held accountable for a failure to communicate to the scientific community his full acceptance of such a program?

In addition to Dr. Oppenheimer's alleged lack of "enthusiasm," there are indications that the majority of the Board may also have been influenced in recommending against the reinstatement of Dr. Oppenheimer's clearance by judgments they had formed as to the nature and quality of the advice he gave to the AEC. While the majority of the Board stated—with sincerity, we are sure—that "no man should be tried for the expression of his opinions,", it seems to us that portions of the majority opinion do just that.

...

This poses a serious issue. If a scientist whose loyalty is unquestioned may nevertheless be considered a security risk because in the judgment of a board he may have given advice which did not necessarily reflect a bare technical judgment, or which did not accord with strategical considerations of a particular kind, then he is being condemned for his opinions. Surely our security requires that expert views, so long as they are honest, be weighed and debated and not that they be barred.

We quite agree with the Board's view that, "because the loyalty or security risk status of a scientist or any other intellectual may be brought into question, scientists and intellectuals are ill-advised to assert that a reasonable and sane inquiry constitutes an attack upon scientists and intellectuals generally." This statement, however, begs the fundamental question as to what are the appropriate limits of a security inquiry under existing statutes and regulations, and under a government of laws and not of men—a question of concern not merely to scientists and intellectuals but to all our people.

Following the President's decision, he did not show the enthusiastic support for the program which might have been expected of the chief atomic adviser to the Government under the circumstances. Indeed, a failure to communicate an abandonment of his earlier position undoubtedly had an effect upon other scientists. It is our feeling that Dr. Oppenheimer's influence in the atomic scientific circle with respect to the hydrogen bomb was far greater than he would have led this Board to believe in his testimony before the Board.

The Board has reluctantly concluded that Dr. Oppenheimer's candor left much to be desired in his discussions with the Board of his attitude and position in the entire chronology of the hydrogen-bomb problem.

RECOMMENDATION

In arriving at our recommendation we have sought to address ourselves to the whole question before us and not to consider the problem as a fragmented one either in terms of specific criteria or in terms of any period in Dr. Oppenheimer's life, or to consider loyalty, character, and associations separately.

However, of course, the most serious finding which this Board could make as a result of these proceedings would be that of disloyalty on the part of Dr. Oppenheimer to his country. For that reason, we have given particular attention to the question of his loyalty, and we have come to a clear conclusion, which should be reassuring to the people of this country, that he is a loyal citizen. If this were the only consideration, therefore, we would recommend that the reinstatement of his clearance would not be a danger to the common defense and security.

We have, however, been unable to arrive at the conclusion that it would be clearly consistent with the security interests of the United States to reinstate Dr. Oppenheimer's clearance and, therefore, do not so recommend.

...

Respectfully submitted,

GORDON GRAY, Chairman.
THOMAS A. MORGAN.

BEFORE WE ADJOURN, I WOULD LIKE TO SAY-- AND I AM SURE THIS IS THE SENSE OF ALL WHO ARE HERE-- I HAVE NOTED FOR SOME TIME THE WORK DONE BY DR. OPPENHEIMER AND I THINK WE HAVE ALL BEEN TREMENDOUSLY IMPRESSED WITH HIM AND ARE MIGHTY HAPPY WE HAVE HIM IN THE POSITION HE HAS IN OUR PROGRAM.

1949

We wish to make two more observations of a general character.

First, we trust that the Commission in weighing the evidence, including the instances of alleged lack of candor, will take into account certain procedural difficulties which beset the presentation of Dr. Oppenheimer's case. Weeks before the hearing commenced we asked you and the Commission's general counsel for much information which we thought relevant to our case but which was denied us—documents and minutes concerning Dr. Oppenheimer's 1947 clearance and a variety of other material. Much of this information did come out in the hearings but usually only in the course of cross-examination when calculated to cause the maximum surprise and confusion and too late to assist us in the orderly presentation of our case. Some of the information which was denied to us before the hearing was declassified at the moment of cross-examination or shortly before and was made available only during cross-examination or after.

It is true that Dr. Oppenheimer was accorded the privilege of reexamining, prior to the hearings, reports and other material in the preparation of which he had participated. But he was not given access to the broad range of material actually used and disclosed for the first time at the hearings by the Commission's special counsel who had been retained for the case. And of course Dr. Oppenheimer was not given access to the various documents which, according to the Board's report "under governmental necessity cannot be disclosed, such as reports of the Federal Bureau of Investigation."

The voluminous nature of this undisclosed material appears from the Board's report. It notes that in our hearings the Board heard 40 witnesses and compiled over 3,000 pages of testimony; and we then learn from the report that "in addition" the Board has "read the same amount of file material." We can only speculate as to the contents of this "file material." We cannot avoid the further speculation as to how much of this material might have been disclosed to Dr. Oppenheimer in the interests of justice without any real injury to the security interests of the Government if established rules of exclusion, which the Board felt bound to apply and we to accept, had not stood in the way.

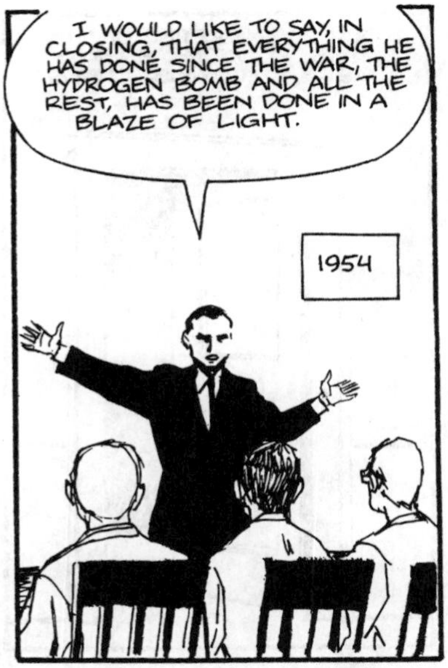
I WOULD LIKE TO SAY, IN CLOSING, THAT EVERYTHING HE HAS DONE SINCE THE WAR, THE HYDROGEN BOMB AND ALL THE REST, HAS BEEN DONE IN A BLAZE OF LIGHT.
1954

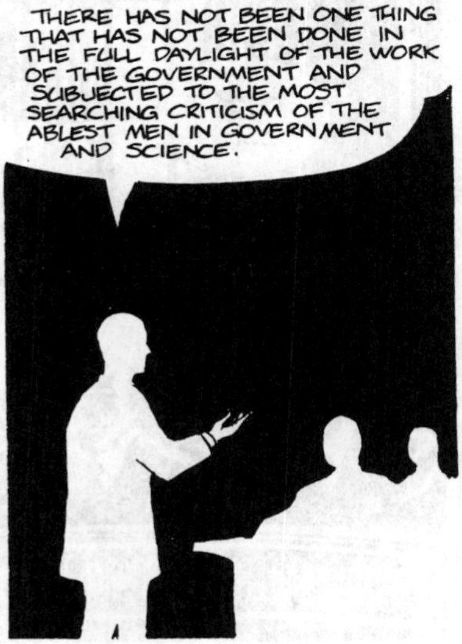
THERE HAS NOT BEEN ONE THING THAT HAS NOT BEEN DONE IN THE FULL DAYLIGHT OF THE WORK OF THE GOVERNMENT AND SUBJECTED TO THE MOST SEARCHING CRITICISM OF THE ABLEST MEN IN GOVERNMENT AND SCIENCE.

Having in mind the difficulties and handicaps which have been recounted above, we urge upon the Commission as strongly as possible the following:

(1) That in weighing the testimony, and particularly those portions where documents were produced on cross-examination in the manner described above, the Commission should constantly bear in mind how, under such circumstances, the natural fallibility of memory may easily be mistaken for disingenuousness;

(2) That in the consideration of documentary material not disclosed to Dr. Oppenheimer, the Commission should be ever conscious of the unreliability of ex parte reports which have never been seen by Dr. Oppenheimer or his counsel or tested by cross-examination; and

(3) That if in the course of the Commission's deliberations the Commission should conclude that any hitherto undisclosed documents upon which it intends to rely may be disclosed to us without injury to what may be thought to be overriding interests of the National Government, they should be so disclosed before any final decision is made.

…

[A]ll the witnesses testified to Dr. Oppenheimer's loyalty and the Board unanimously found him to be loyal… Every one of them had served with Dr. Oppenheimer, either at Los Alamos or on the many governmental boards and committees to which he was later appointed. They saw him on the job and off the job, and in their varied testimony about their contacts with him over many years they helped to fill in the picture of the "man himself" which the Atomic Energy Commission, in its 1948 opinion in Dr. Frank Graham's case, said should be considered in determining whether an individual is a good or bad security risk.

Because we believe that the "man himself" can only be understood, and therefore fairly judged, by the closest attention to the testimony of those who have known him and worked intimately with him, as well as to his own testimony, we are particularly hopeful that the Commission will permit us to file a brief and to be heard.

Very truly yours,

Lloyd K. Garrison

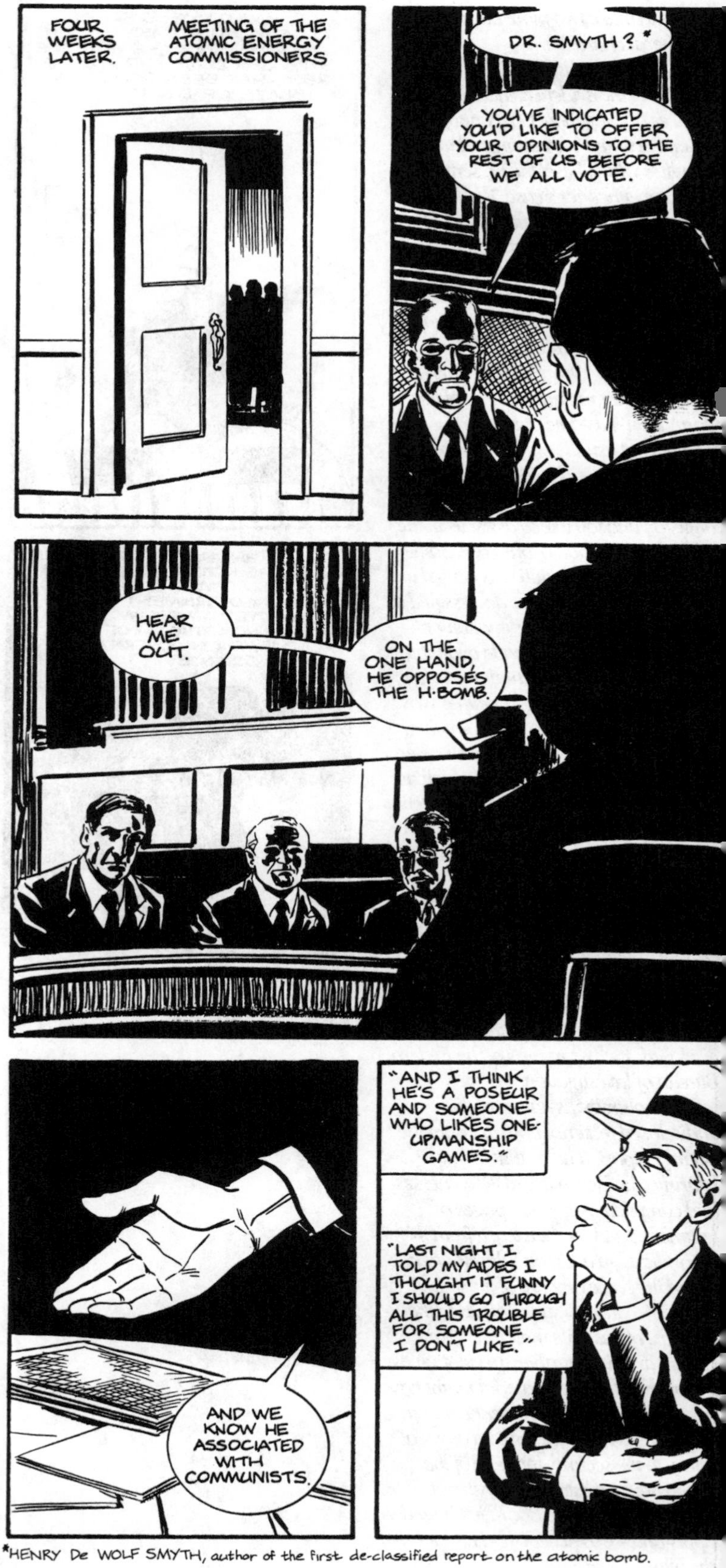
FOUR WEEKS LATER.
MEETING OF THE ATOMIC ENERGY COMMISSIONERS
DR. SMYTH?*
YOU'VE INDICATED YOU'D LIKE TO OFFER YOUR OPINIONS TO THE REST OF US BEFORE WE ALL VOTE.
HEAR ME OUT.
ON THE ONE HAND, HE OPPOSES THE H-BOMB.
AND WE KNOW HE ASSOCIATED WITH COMMUNISTS.
"AND I THINK HE'S A POSEUR AND SOMEONE WHO LIKES ONE-UPMANSHIP GAMES."
"LAST NIGHT I TOLD MY AIDES I THOUGHT IT FUNNY I SHOULD GO THROUGH ALL THIS TROUBLE FOR SOMEONE I DON'T LIKE."

*HENRY De WOLF SMYTH, author of the first de-classified report on the atomic bomb.

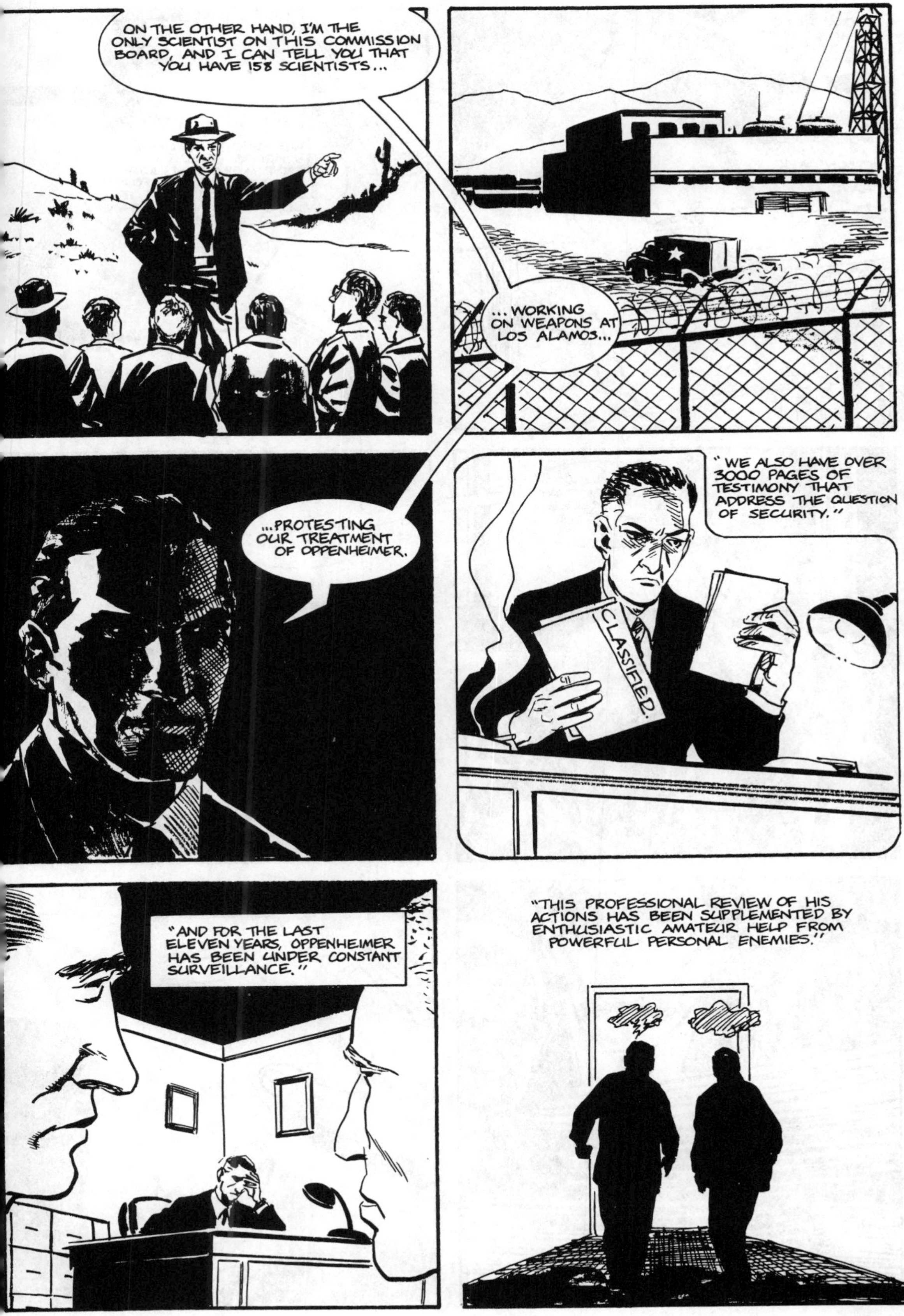
ON THE OTHER HAND, I'M THE ONLY SCIENTIST ON THIS COMMISSION BOARD, AND I CAN TELL YOU THAT YOU HAVE 158 SCIENTISTS...
...WORKING ON WEAPONS AT LOS ALAMOS...
...PROTESTING OUR TREATMENT OF OPPENHEIMER.
"WE ALSO HAVE OVER 3000 PAGES OF TESTIMONY THAT ADDRESS THE QUESTION OF SECURITY."
CLASSIFIED
"AND FOR THE LAST ELEVEN YEARS, OPPENHEIMER HAS BEEN UNDER CONSTANT SURVEILLANCE."
"THIS PROFESSIONAL REVIEW OF HIS ACTIONS HAS BEEN SUPPLEMENTED BY ENTHUSIASTIC AMATEUR HELP FROM POWERFUL PERSONAL ENEMIES."

AND WHAT DO WE HAVE AFTER ALL OF THIS?

NO EVIDENCE THAT HE HAS EVER DIVULGED SECRET INFORMATION TO PERSONS WHO SHOULD NOT HAVE IT.

WE ALSO HAVE ONLY 36 HOURS BEFORE OPPENHEIMER'S CONSULTANCY RUNS OUT, AT WHICH POINT OUR JURISDICTION, IF YOU WILL, ENDS, AND WE CAN DO NOTHING.

I WOULD SUGGEST THAT THIS IS PRECISELY WHAT WE SHOULD DO.

NOTHING.

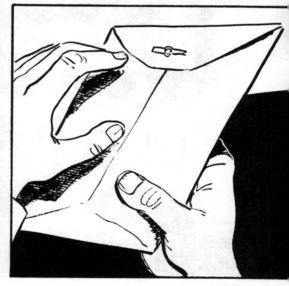

J. RO
OPPE
CLE
ERT
NHEIMER
ARANCE
ALAMO
NIED

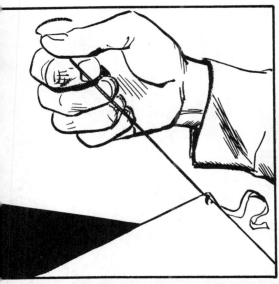

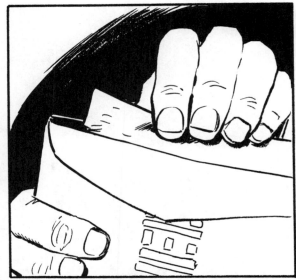

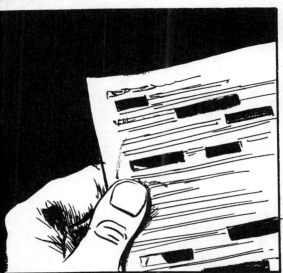

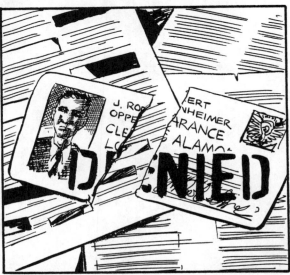

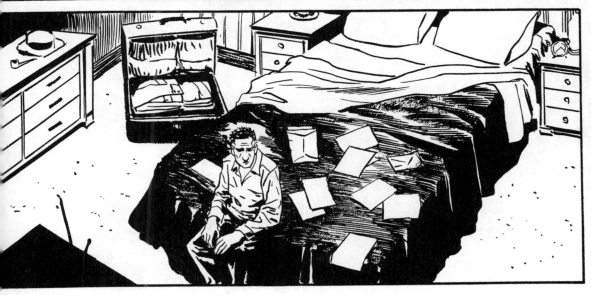

epilogue
(1960)

Lüge nicht ohne Notwendigkeit.
          —Zehn Gebote von Leo Szilard, 30. Oktober 1940
[Do not lie without need.
          —Ten Commandments by Leo Szilard, 30 October 1940]

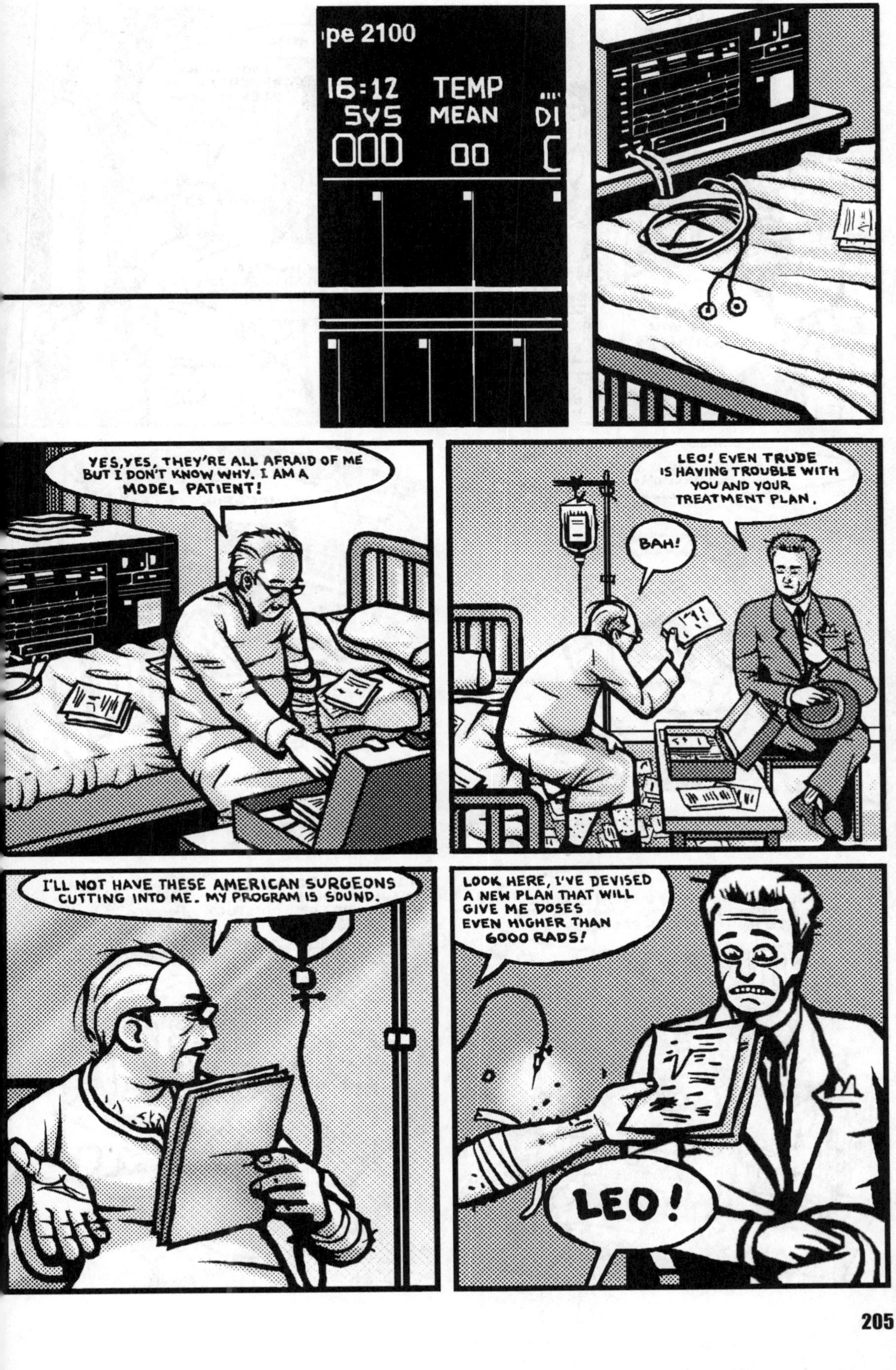
pe 2100
16:12 TEMP
SYS MEAN DI
000 00
YES, YES, THEY'RE ALL AFRAID OF ME BUT I DON'T KNOW WHY. I AM A MODEL PATIENT!
LEO! EVEN TRUDE IS HAVING TROUBLE WITH YOU AND YOUR TREATMENT PLAN.
BAH!
I'LL NOT HAVE THESE AMERICAN SURGEONS CUTTING INTO ME. MY PROGRAM IS SOUND.
LOOK HERE, I'VE DEVISED A NEW PLAN THAT WILL GIVE ME DOSES EVEN HIGHER THAN 6000 RADS!
LEO!

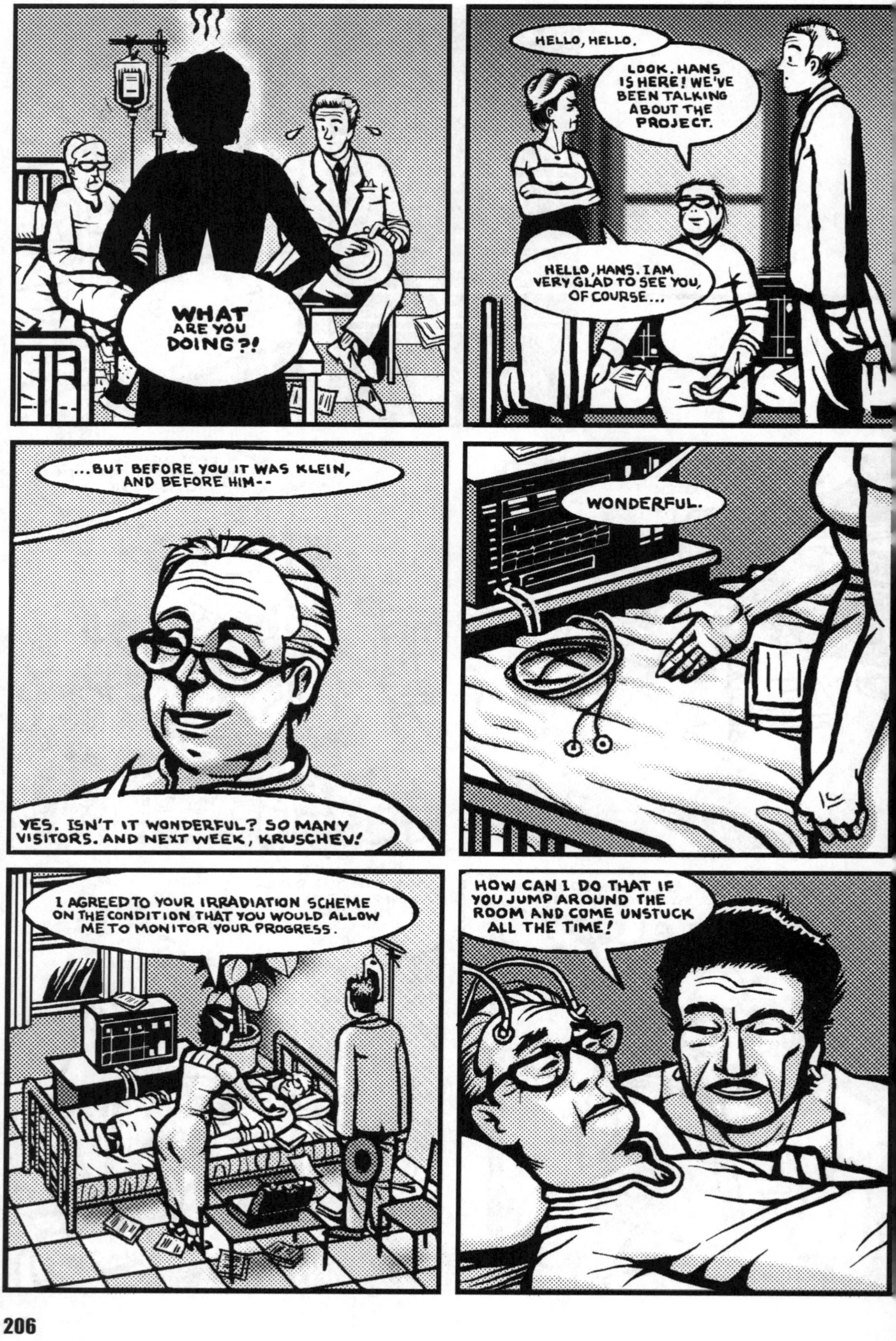
WHAT ARE YOU DOING?!
HELLO, HELLO.
LOOK. HANS IS HERE! WE'VE BEEN TALKING ABOUT THE PROJECT.
HELLO, HANS. I AM VERY GLAD TO SEE YOU, OF COURSE...
...BUT BEFORE YOU IT WAS KLEIN, AND BEFORE HIM--
YES. ISN'T IT WONDERFUL? SO MANY VISITORS. AND NEXT WEEK, KRUSCHEV!
WONDERFUL.
I AGREED TO YOUR IRRADIATION SCHEME ON THE CONDITION THAT YOU WOULD ALLOW ME TO MONITOR YOUR PROGRESS.
HOW CAN I DO THAT IF YOU JUMP AROUND THE ROOM AND COME UNSTUCK ALL THE TIME!

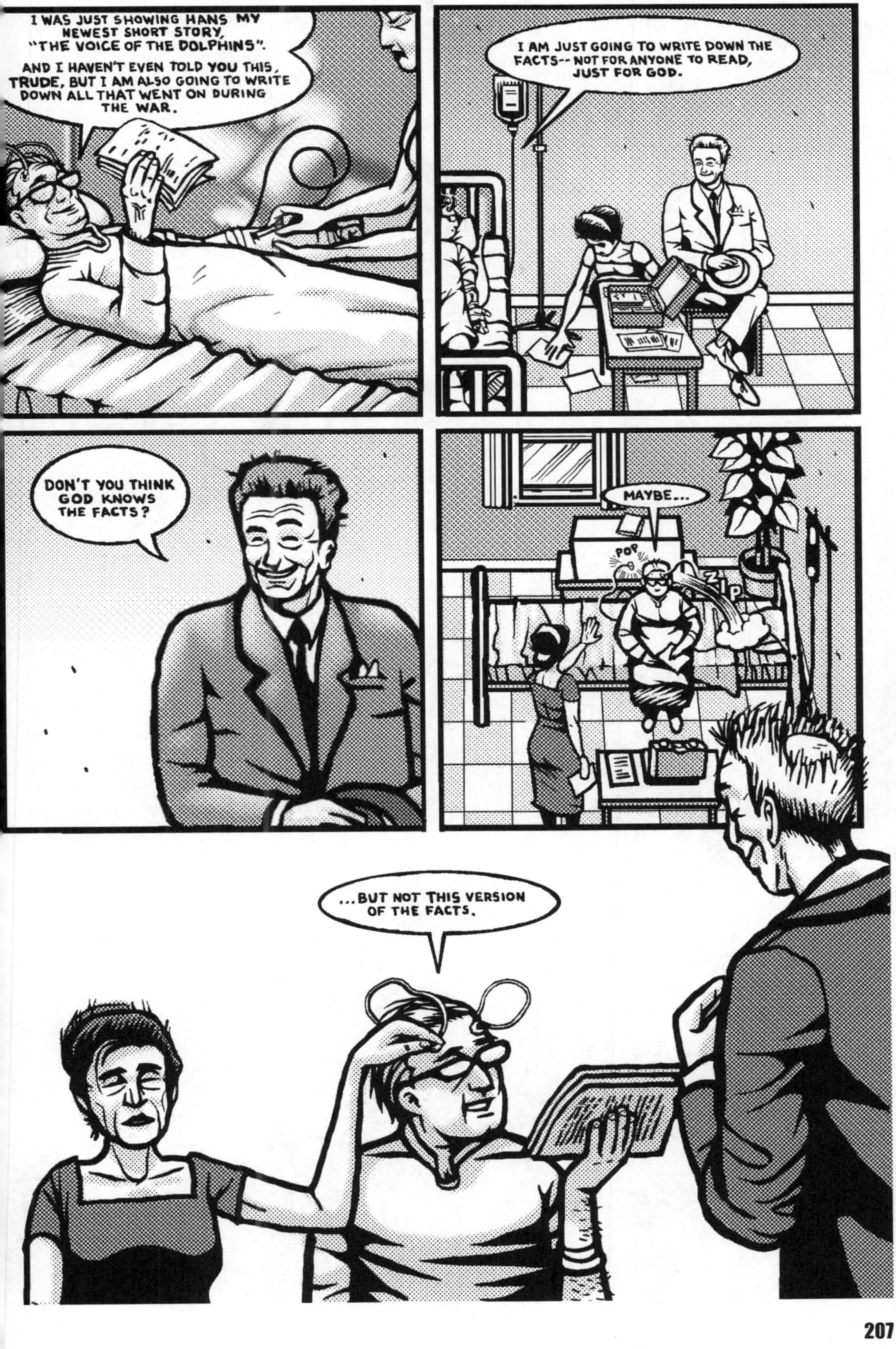
I WAS JUST SHOWING HANS MY NEWEST SHORT STORY, "THE VOICE OF THE DOLPHINS".
AND I HAVEN'T EVEN TOLD YOU THIS, TRUDE, BUT I AM ALSO GOING TO WRITE DOWN ALL THAT WENT ON DURING THE WAR.
I AM JUST GOING TO WRITE DOWN THE FACTS-- NOT FOR ANYONE TO READ, JUST FOR GOD.
DON'T YOU THINK GOD KNOWS THE FACTS?
MAYBE...
POP
ZIP
...BUT NOT THIS VERSION OF THE FACTS.

notes and
references

A man will turn over half a library to make one book.
　　　　—Samuel Johnson, entry for 6 April 1775
　　　　in *Life of Johnson* by James Boswell, 1791

prologue

PAGE 13

When I first saw it, I assumed that Peter Sellers' scientist character (he also plays two other roles, including the President of the United States) in the movie *Dr. Strangelove, or: How I Learned to Stop Worrying and Love the Bomb* was based on the German rocket scientist Werner von Braun. (The reflexive salute was the main reason for making that connection.) Teller it is, though. He has lived with the comparison ever since, and remains notoriously touchy about the subject of the Sellers role.

Note: Except when referring to reference works difficult to obtain from a visit to a library—such as the Leo Szilard Papers found only at the University of California, San Diego, noted by their box/folder number as MSS 32: xx/yy—these notes won't usually cite specific sources.

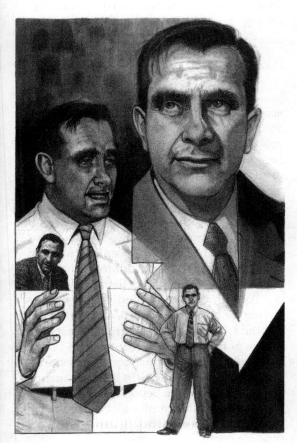

birth

PAGES 17-18

For this morning's soak—a ritual he indulged in whenever he could—Szilard is reading *The World Set Free* by H.G. Wells, one of two books he credited for shaping his world view. (The other is *Tragedy of Man* by Imre Madách, which he refers to on page 25.)

PAGES 18-20

This is not the first place Szilard settled in London. His first residence was the Imperial, in the heart of London's Bohemian Bloomsbury neighborhood, whose facade was decorated in Edwardian Gothic style, and probably reminded him of Vienna. His second stop was a boarding house at 97 Cromwell Road, but he didn't stay there long before packing up his two suitcases (all he brought with him when he left Hungary, and setting a pattern for his travels from then on) and moving back into a hotel, this time The Strand Palace which, though it sounds quite fancy, wasn't. Szilard rented a room that had once been a maid's closet, and he took his customary multi-hour soak in the shared bath down the hall. His meeting with Beveridge actually occurred while he was staying at the Imperial.

PAGE 20

Panels 2-4: The London we see here is in the throes of the global depression, which ran through the beginning of the war.

PAGE 21

The son of a British civil servant in India, Sir William Beveridge was educated at Oxford. After serving as subwarden of Toynbee Hall, a London settlement house and then a director of Labour Exchanges, he became permanent secretary of the Ministry of Food in 1919. He directed the London School of Economics and Political Science from 1919 to 1937, when he was elected master of University College, Oxford. He served as a Liberal member of Parliament from 1944-1945, and it was during this period he helped work out the blueprints of the new British welfare state.

PAGE 22

Panels 2-3: Szilard would later make light of his good luck, and his prescience, by saying "To succeed in this world you don't have to be much cleverer than others; you just have to be one day earlier."

Panel 5: Szilard actually said this to Max Planck. If anything, doing so required even more *chutzpah* than saying it to Einstein, since when Szilard began his studies Planck was considered the intellectual founder (though he was reluctant to be known as such) of quantum theory. Einstein would have been just coming into his own fame at this point.

PAGE 23

Szilard's monologue here comes mainly from letters he sent to Beveridge and other scholars at the time he was working to help set up the Academic Assistance Council (AAC).

Panel 4: Einstein actually expressed his thoughts on this more strongly, telling Szilard that "Your plan doesn't really set me on fire."
(Regarding Szilard's Jewish heritage, ever the pragmatist, he had applied in his neighborhood to change his religion from "Israelite" to "Calvinist.")

PAGE 24

Panel 4: Stanley Baldwin preceded the more notorious appeaser Neville Chamberlin as Prime Minister of Great Britain.
Panel 6: See the note for page 22, panels 2-3 for the actual quote.

PAGE 25

Panel 2: Szilard was premature in many things. I gave him this particular line think-

ing about the aforementioned *Tragedy of Man*. It's apparently a tough slog for adults, and he read it when he was only 10. But from it he learned the notion quoted here.

PAGES 26-27

Sources for the quotes and thoughts here include *Genius, His Version of the Facts*, and the Szilard archives [MSS 32:42/25].
Szilard told the story of how quickly (and exactly where) his inspiration about the chain reaction occurred in a couple of different ways over the years. I've chosen the version where the vision occurs to him the same day he read about Rutherford's dismissal of atomic energy.

PAGE 26

Szilard missed Rutherford's talk because of a bad cold the day before we see him here. The paper in which the transcript appeared, *The Times*, didn't run headlines, so we take the liberty of using the *Evening Standard* instead.

PAGE 28

James Chadwick discovered the neutron about a year before Szilard's insight. The atomic model of a spherical nucleus surrounded by a solar system of electrons, used here for simplicity, is actually an anachronism: Physicists had begun to think of the atom as something far more complicated. However, this popular shorthand for describing what an atom looks like and how fission occurs persists, and works well enough for our purpose here. For a closer look at how fission works you may want to read about Lise Meitner in *Dignifying Science*.
As with the atomic model, the graphics shown for chain reactions is commonly used, but the specific reference for this depiction comes from a serialized feature called "The Story of the Atom" which appeared, courtesy of the NEA Service, Inc., in 17 installments from September 4 to September 21, 1945— just days after the bombing of Japan. (Thanks to Don Mangus for sending copies of this obscure comic strip.)

From the last panel of page 28 through to page 36 we have excerpts from Wells' *The World Set Free*, as it might have filtered through Szilard's vivid imagination…an imagination so vivid that I've taken the poetic license of tinkering with Wells' work by having Szilard insert himself into the narrative.

PAGE 38

I have Szilard overstating his role in influencing Meitner, Hahn, and Strassman in panels 6 and 7 (they didn't waste their time testing all 70 known elements), the Curies in panel 8, and Niels Bohr in the last panel, but by the same token I greatly compress (and thus understate and diminish) Szilard's efforts along those same experimental lines.

PAGE 39

Panel 2: Fermi, as we see later in the story, was in many ways Szilard's polar opposite. In other words, he was a brilliant experimentalist, a thorough, careful and somewhat conservative scientist, and almost totally oblivious to (or at least uninterested in) the political implications of the work he did.

Panels 4-6: This statement comes from a recollection made much later by Szilard, reverse-engineering the reasoning behind his decision to approach Einstein.

PAGE 40

Panel 1: The first letter Einstein and Szilard wrote together was actually to the Belgian government, warning of the danger of allowing the Nazis to get hold of the uranium supplies in Belgian Congo (now the Democratic Republic of Congo).

Panels 2-4: Einstein pauses for three beats here to consider the problem on scientific, philosophical, and political grounds:

First, he wasn't entirely immune to worrying about being thought a fool. His famous mass-energy equation was, up until then, only a theory for him—Szilard was making it a reality. Second, he was an avowed pacifist, so advocating something as terrible as weapons research was bound to cause him discomfort. But the third consideration, and the one that I think overcame the first two, was the risk of doing nothing.

Panel 7: Einstein did indeed go sailing right after this meeting, and Szilard did indeed use his economic contacts to hook up with Alexander Sachs. Though this provides our story with a convenient parallel to his meeting with Beveridge, I don't believe there's any actual connection.

PAGE 41

Panels 2-4: Yes, this is a real quote from Sach's interoffice communication (bizarrely) titled "Notes on Imminence World War in Perspective Accrued Errors and Cultural Crisis of the Inter-War Decades." And yes, there was no intended audience for the memo other than himself. You can't make some of this stuff up!

Panel 5: This quote comes from a letter Szilard wrote to Einstein months after they had sent their letter to Roosevelt—in other words it's out of context here, but nonetheless likely to reflect his thoughts about Sachs.

Panel 6: Enter Teller, sitting across from Sachs, in on the earliest days of the bomb almost by accident. Since Szilard didn't drive, Teller took him to Einstein's cottage on Long Island, serving as his second chauffeur in doing so.

Sachs was perhaps involved in an early draft of Szilard's letter, a draft that proved over-long and needlessly detailed. (What a surprise.) Einstein was probably not around for this, so this scene compresses that initial draft and Szilard's more direct collaboration with Einstein.

PAGE 42

Panel 1: These are again Sachs' own words (paraphrased, of course, since you can't fit

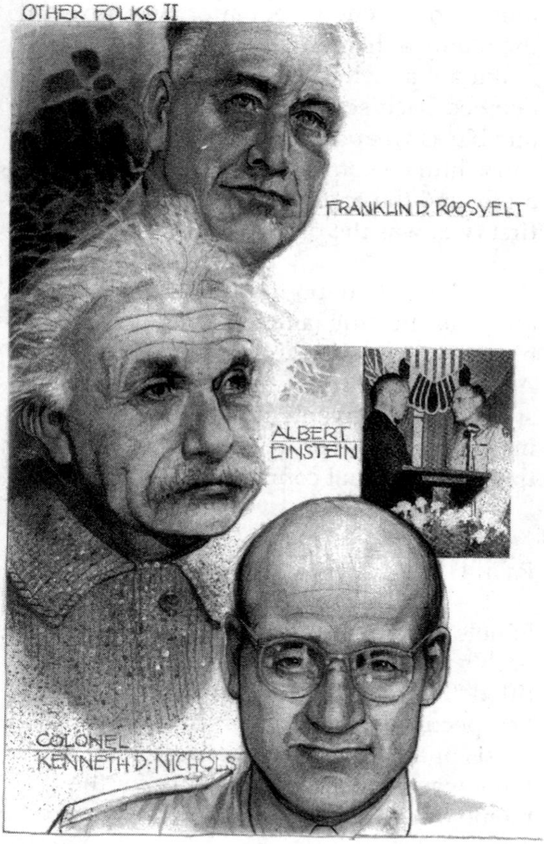
OTHER FOLKS II
FRANKLIN D. ROOSVELT
ALBERT EINSTEIN
COLONEL KENNETH D. NICHOLS

the whole thing into an industry standard word balloon), written well after the fact and without a hint of irony.

Panel 8: Again, the evidence suggests that Einstein didn't do much writing, at least of the first draft. He does in this version since I don't like the almost complete detachment from the process of setting the bomb in motion that having Szilard work on it alone would imply.

Einstein's quote about rational thought is genuine, but the quote about selling the idea rather than explaining it is paraphrased from Sachs. It's too plain-spoken for the Sachs persona created for this story, though, so I give the lines to Einstein instead.

Page 43

Panels 3, 5, and 7: These panels combine text from two letters from Szilard to Einstein (written in the opposite order shown) to emphasize Szilard's continued misgivings regarding Sachs. These misgivings weren't so much in terms of his confidence in Sachs' ability to convince Roosevelt as much as his ability to actually get an audience with him.

Szilard did consider Lindbergh as an emissary, though he quickly abandoned that idea based on Lindbergh's increasingly rabid position regarding U.S. neutrality.

I further have Szilard writing three times since that's the number of times he composed letters intended for delivery to the President.

Panel 9: More labored prose from Sachs here and in the first panel of the next page. This bit is taken out of context from a much later meeting of the Uranium Committee. (I just can't cut this guy a break.)

Pages 44-45

From panel 8 on we, for the most part, hear Sachs read The Letter. Not all of it, since it's longer than you—not to mention President Roosevelt—would have patience for. (And easy to find in many of the references, if you're so inclined.) But he read it aloud, all the way through. As presented here, parts of Sachs' speech to Roosevelt come from an October 11, 1939 letter Sachs wrote to the President. The remainder come from Szilard and Einstein's letter. I've rearranged and condensed it, but not so much (I hope) that you miss out on the density—not to mention the content—of his presentation.

Page 46

Panel 7: Standing in the doorway we have Roosevelt's secretary, General Edwin M. "Pa" Watson. And though Roosevelt reacted favorably—and immediately—to Einstein's letter, as indicated in both the interlude and by the gap of three years between the end of this section and the beginning of the next, it took a while for the government bureaucracy to spring into action on this.

interlude

Panel 2: The government initially only appropriated $6,000 to research, and did so only starting in 1940, many months after the close of the previous section. More money became available later in the year—$100,000 at about the time the German army entered Paris. Another letter from Einstein (again via Szilard) prompted a meeting with Szilard, Fermi, Teller, Wigner and government officials where Sachs argues effectively on behalf of the physicists for greater funding and against "bit-a-bit procedures."

The U.S. only committed to full-scale pursuit of military applications of nuclear chain reactions on December 6, 1941...one day before the attack on Pearl Harbor.

Panel 3 on: As mentioned before, Fermi and Szilard couldn't have taken a more different approach to science and their lives. Fermi was the "scientist's scientist." (When playing "Who do you want to be on your day off"—a party game of amateur psychoanalysis—Oppenheimer chose Fermi.)

PAGE 52

Panel 6: In case you want to look it up, "Divergent Chain Reactions in Systems Composed of Uranium and Carbon," was eventually published as Report A-55 of the Uranium Committee, and declassified in November 1946 as MDDC-446 (1940). It begins: "As early as 1913 H.G. Wells forecast the discovery of induced radioactivity for the year 1933 and described the advent of nuclear transmutations on an industrial scale." True to his word, Szilard cites Wells' book properly in his first footnote.

school

Panel 1: Oppenheimer joined the bomb project (not yet called the Manhattan Project at this point) in February of 1942. He took it over, largely by default, from Gregory Breit in May. At this point in our story he wasn't director and Bainbridge wasn't his assistant, though, so in that sense this scene is anachronistic.

The flowers aren't, though. They're here, and in the rest of the book as both an icon and as a reference to a story told by his brother Frank in *The Day After Trinity*:

> Everything Robert did would sort of be special. If he went off in the woods to take a leak he'd come back with a flower. Not to disguise the fact that he'd made a leak, but just to make it an occasion, I guess.

Oppenheimer, though often called the father of the atom bomb, didn't match the picture people who grew up with the Cold War might have of him. He was of course a brilliant physicist. But he was also a poet, self-educated in the arts, fluent in many languages (both living and dead), and sensitive in the pre-1960s meaning of the word.

Panels 4-5: Agents Pash and Lansdale probably did not interview Oppenheimer at this time, but since they figure into later investigations we use them here as well.

PAGE 56

The misspellings and other excerpts from the reports are real. However, while having Oppenheimer act so supercilious is in character at this point in his political career, it's also unlikely that he did so in exactly this way.

PAGE 57

Panel 2: One of Oppenheimer's first tasks was to step up the caliber of scientist working on the bomb project. The Manhattan Project was slow to gain momentum, and early on—before the U.S. became engaged in the war—the very top physicists were not involved. (With a few notable, and previously noted, exceptions.) For instance, early on I.I. Rabi's radar group at MIT had more and better scientists

Panel 5: Ironically, Oppenheimer began to reduce his involvement with political groups sharply at the time he took on a more active role in the bomb project. (My presumption, as indicated here, is that he did this both because of time constraints and the sense that war work took precedence over ideology.)

PAGE 59

Panel 1: Oppenheimer refers to Fermi's fondness for slang, which, as we saw in the previous interlude, he took pains to use often.

Panel 3: It seems likely that at this point, Oppenheimer would not have thought of himself as an administrator, hence his desire to gloss over personnel and budget and get right to the science.

Panels 4-5: Six was the first guess regarding the size of the initial group of scientists who would move out to Los Alamos. Even 600 was low—the Manhattan Project employed nearly 7,000 people by the end of the war.

PAGE 60

Panel 1: Lawrence is angry because he thought he should head the project. General Groves, who hasn't entered the scene yet in this version of the narrative, thought otherwise. Lawrence held a grudge against Groves (and probably Oppenheimer) for a long time after.

Panel 2: It turned out that Lawrence's favored method of electromagnetic separation did not prove feasible. In other words, what worked great for producing a few micrograms of weapons grade uranium worked poorly for producing kilograms. (For one thing, there wasn't enough copper in the U.S. to construct the necessary magnets.)

The gaseous diffusion method, on the other hand, proved more successful in exploiting the slight mass differences between the type (isotope) of uranium the bomb required and the far more common type that was merely in the way. The largest gaseous diffusion operation during the war took place in Oak Ridge, Tennessee—newspaper comics fans will recognize "Dogpatch," the workers' nickname for the place, as coming from Al Capp's *Li'l Abner*.

PAGE 62

Panel 1: The graphite blocks are 4x4 in. (10x10 cm) bricks with holes drilled in them to hold lumps of uranium oxide, and the physicists and their assistants stacked them in 4x10 ft. (1.2x3 m) piles in Columbia. Most wore dust masks and food service-like cloth caps. After a few hours of work the only white you could see on them were from their eyes and teeth.

Panel 3: The impurity was boron, the chemical equivalent of a neutron sponge. The first shipments of graphite that Fermi and Szilard used were laced with it, and its presence ruined their initial experiments.

Panel 4: The quotation about "remote possibility," though indeed from a conversation about the bomb with Fermi, is taken far (in both time and space) out of context. The real conversation occurred in 1939 between Fermi and I.I. Rabi, where Fermi considers the probability that "neutrons may be emitted in the fission of uranium and then of course a chain reaction can be made" unlikely.

PAGES 63-74

Szilard's talent, as indicated in the previous section, ran more along the lines of instigating fruitful lines of research and working behind the scenes to make that research possible. (He wasn't particularly good at doing the work needed to turn his ideas into reality.) These pages show an amalgamation of Szilard's efforts in pursuit of neutron fission, which included getting funding to rent some radium from The Radium Chemical Company of New York and Chicago—a subsidiary of a company in the soon-to-be-overrun-by-the-Nazis Belgium, securing boron-free graphite, and borrowing uranium oxide, free of charge, from the Eldorado Radium Corporation.

Szilard on Fermi from MSS 32: 40/4, "Book": "I doubt that he ever understood that some people live in two worlds like I do. A world, and science is a part of this one, in which we have to predict what is going to happen, and another world in which we try to forget these predictions in order to be able to fight for what we would like to happen."

PAGE 63

Panel 7: For all the bluster shown here, Fermi did value Szilard's abilities along these lines, saying "He did a marvelous job which later on was taken over by a more powerful organization than was Szilard himself, although to match Szilard it takes a few able-bodied customers."

PAGE 64

Panel 1: Fermi was actually present at this luncheon as well, but I left him out for the sake of clarity and to contrast the type of work he typically did with that of Szilard.

PAGE 65

Panels 1-2: Though plans were drawn up to can and vacuum pack the first reactor, the specifications were exacting and especially troublesome because the only contractor skilled enough to meet them didn't speak English.

Panel 5: The reference to the Metallurgical Lab is probably anachronistic, since I don't believe this was the name of Fermi's group until it moved to the University of Chicago.

PAGES 66-67

About those "feetballers" Szilard refers to: By this point the University had volunteered the services of the football team to do the heavy lifting for the scientists. As indicated previously, building the piles was tough work. Herbert Anderson had this to say:

> We were reasonably strong, but I mean we were, after all, thinkers. So Dean Pegram…looked around and said that seems to be a job a little bit beyond your feeble strength, but there is a football squad at Columbia that contains a dozen or so of very husky boys who take jobs by the hour just to carry them through college. Why don't you hire them?

> And it was a marvelous idea; it was really a pleasure for once to direct the work of these husky boys…handling packs of 50 or 100 pounds with the same ease as another person would have handled three or four pounds. Fermi tried to do his share of the work. [H]e donned a lab coat and pitched in to do his stint with the football men, but it was clear that he was out of his class. The rest of us found a lot to keep us busy with measurements and calibrations that suddenly seemed to require exceptional care and precision.

PAGE 67

Panels 7-8: Szilard did indeed say…and do…these things.

Panel 8: "I hear they're moving us soon" is fabrication, though Szilard was more likely to know this than Fermi.

PAGE 68

Panels 1-5: This briefing actually happened, though in reality Groves wasn't there with the Navy admiral. Just before Fermi entered the room, he heard his presence announced as "There's a wop outside." This no doubt added to his willingness to give an overly conservative assessment of the likelihood of producing a workable nuclear weapon.

PAGE 69

Panel 4: Note that the quoted phrase from Fermi may be something Rhodes (in *The*

Making of the Atomic Bomb, p. 295) inferred from his research, but even though I couldn't verify it using other sources it's a good and appropriate one, so I've used it.

PAGE 70

Panel 6: Eugene Wigner, also Hungarian, was the third strong proponent of secrecy about nuclear fission. On voting, see for example, MSS 32:40/4: "Book", p. X.

PAGE 71

Note that Compton (one of the few scientists who got along with Groves) probably didn't—and in fact probably wouldn't—consult or even tell Oppenheimer about this, since Oppenheimer was still working at the periphery of the project at this point.

PAGE 72

Panel 2: Here I give Szilard Fermi's speech pattern, for two reasons: First, I initially wrote this scene with Fermi doing the lecturing, but then realized that a) he probably wouldn't have taken the time to explain what he was doing to a non-scientist, and b) at this point in the story I needed Szilard to get in trouble with Groves, not Fermi. Second, and the after-the-fact rationalization for leaving it be, is because I liked the idea of suggesting that Fermi rubbed off on Szilard more than Szilard let on.

Panel 4: As I checked to make sure that the balloon was actually silk, I ran across the fact that it was custom-made by Goodyear, who later went on to bigger and better balloons…

PAGES 73-74

Groves and Szilard clashed from the very beginning. Though both advocated secrecy, Szilard only wanted to keep the results away from the Nazis. Groves' military background made his security concerns more restrictive. He favored compartmentalization of the various U.S. scientific groups, and considered Szilard the only villain of the Project. Szilard in turn thought Groves its biggest fool.

In MSS 32: 114/13 you can find a July 4, 1945 letter Groves wrote to Lord Cherwell of the British War Cabinet stating "Frankly, Dr. Szilard has not, in our opinion, evidenced wholehearted cooperation in the maintenance of security." Groves actually had no evidence of this, despite continued surveillance of Szilard. In reply, Cherwell wrote:

> I am sorry to hear that Szilard has been indiscreet. …As you know he worked in my laboratory at Oxford and always had rather a bee in his bonnet about the awful international implications of these matters…
> When I spoke to Szilard in Washington in 1943, he was, so far as I can remember, mainly concerned with a topic which has inflamed so many scientists' minds, namely what sort of arrangements could be made to prevent an arms race with all the disastrous consequences to which this would lead. I do not recall that he offered any solution… My impression is that his security was good to the point of brusqueness. He did, I believe, complain that compartmentalism was carried to undue lengths in America.

PAGE 74

Panel 2: This quote from Groves, though real enough, is taken out of context…but I've softened it as well. After giving a lecture to Compton, Fermi, Szilard, and others on security that clearly went in one ear and out the other, Groves made this comment in regards to the security of the scientists themselves: "General, what would you think if someone threw a hand grenade through that window?" "It'd be a damn good thing. There's too much hot air in here."

Panel 3: Per MSS 32: 5/21, September 8, 1945 letter from Szilard to Bush, Szilard actually said this to Vannevar Bush, not Groves, but it fits perfectly here.

PAGE 76

On this and the next two pages we build the CP-1 (Chicago Pile One) reactor from the bottom up, adding seven layers of graphite and uranium in each panel.

Panel 1: Pile height = 12 layers. As mentioned before, the element boron is a neutron absorber. So while it's a "poison" for reactors, it's actually great to use in a detector, since that absorption property is just what you'd want. To count neutrons you need to capture them—it's not like you can watch 'em as they go by!

Panel 2: Pile height = 22 layers. Szilard was indeed working on CP-2 (Chicago Pile 2), a reactor designed to try and produce plutonium, something never done in quantity before.

PAGE 77

Panel 1: Pile height = 32 layers. Wigner teases Fermi about his definition of a remote possibility.

PAGE 78

Panel 1: Pile height = 52 layers. Woods' detectors and calculations show that the pile will reach critical mass sooner than anyone expected…

Panel 2: …so they won't have to vacuum-pack it to achieve the first self-sustaining nuclear reaction. (Pile height = 57 layers.)

PAGE 80

Panel 2: Raccoon coats? Rifles? What's going on? A cold winter, an under-funded project, and a lab built beneath the stands of what used to serve as the University of Chicago's football stadium resulted in this unusual variation on the military dress code.

PAGE 81

Panel 2: Though I use Woods here, Szilard actually invited Heinrich Kluver (a friend from another academic department) out for his second dinner of the day. Woods makes a

good stand-in, since in many respects she too was an outsider, even though she was very much in the know and part of the team. (Note that Woods, like many of her colleagues, thought Szilard was rich.)

Panel 5: Szilard's fears foreshadow those of the Trinity scientists who speculated on the atmosphere igniting upon explosion of the first atomic bomb.

PAGES 83-85

Most of what follows comes from Woods' description of the first criticality experiment given in her book *The Uranium People*.

PAGE 83

Panels 1-2: The cadmium nitrate (a neutron absorber) and zip rod are primitive versions of a method for "scramming" a reactor—the term used for shutting down the nuclear reaction abruptly in case of emergencies. We don't rely on people standing near the core with buckets any more, though.

PAGE 84

The instrumentation to record the experiment was "glowing and winking and radiating some gratefully received heat"—for all its potential to do so the reactor itself didn't generate much warmth.

PAGE 85

Panel 7: Fermi didn't really pull out the wires himself. A scientist named Volney Wilson took care of the control circuits, but since Fermi did let the alarms ring for a while—in an uncharacteristic break with his usual caution—I let him take control of stopping them as well.

PAGE 86

The beverage on hand was a bottle of chianti, which wouldn't have popped like champagne. But since it was a celebratory wine,

interlude

and given their budget for this sort of thing was probably small, it's reasonable to give it some fizz.

Page 88

Panel 1: I've manufactured the telegram Oppenheimer receives from a phone call between Compton and Conant. As noted, and in a classic good news/bad news sort of situation, Fermi reached critical mass with the pile sooner than he had expected. That's the good news. But it was bad news as well, since it probably led the U.S. team to believe that the Nazis had an easy time as well.

Fortunately, achieving criticality was by no means trivial, and building a bomb proved even less so.

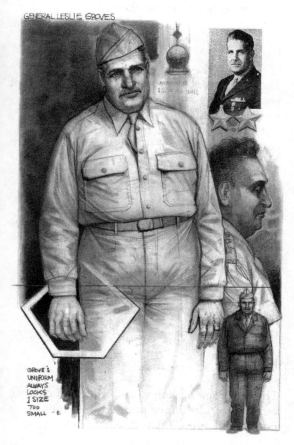

GENERAL LESLIE GROVES

GROVE'S
UNIFORM
ALWAYS
LOOKS
1 SIZE
TOO
SMALL -t

Page 93

Panel 3: Groves' dialogue comes from a different (and earlier) meeting with scientists than the one presented here, borrowed because it fits well with the tone and mood of this anecdote.

Page 94

Panel 5: This turn of phrase comes from my high school physics teacher, Mr. Valentine, who would often call some subtle principle or elusive phenomenon "intuitively obvious to even the most casual observer."

Panel 6: Phrases such as "atomic energy," "atomic fission," and "uranium" disappear from news reports in the U.S. in June, 1943.

Page 95

Panel 2: Renan also wrote "O Lord, if there is a Lord, save my soul, if I have a soul." (*Prière d'un Sceptique*), a phrase just as likely to have come to Oppenheimer's mind—though perhaps later in the project.

Panel 6: Oppenheimer probably coined the term "gadget."

Page 96

Groves' speech didn't occur in this exact context, but it's appropriate to place it at the first large gathering of scientists in Los Alamos.

Panels 4-6: Also in the audience during Grove's embarrassing speech were Hans Bethe, Nobel Prize winner in 1967, Harold Urey (1934) and James Franck (1925). Otto Frisch, who along with Lise Meitner was the first to correctly interpret Hahn and Strassman's fission experiments, may have been there too.

(Oppenheimer never won a Nobel.)

work

Much of what Robert Serber says here is quoted or paraphrased from Report LA-1, also known as "The Los Alamos Primer." I've moved things around to better serve the narrative, and omitted a great deal of material in the process, but what you get in this section is the state-of-the-art knowledge on how to build an atomic bomb. State of the art circa the 1940s, that is. (Did you really think you were going to learn how to make an atomic bomb from a comic book?)

And just as I haven't given the scientists accents (the melting pot theory of the United States was never tested more severely than at Los Alamos!), I've omitted Serber's lisp. Feel free to imagine it if you like.

PAGE 102

Panel 3: Fermi's quote comes from MSS 32: 40/4, "Book" p. 6.

Panel 5: Here, and throughout the rest of the story, I have "normalized" the units, using the English more often than the metric system, since foots and pounds were in more common use than meters and kilograms. The Primer itself mixes and matches the two systems, though, and that mixture occasionally creeps into our story as well.

PAGE 103

Panel 1: Soviet troops liberated Auschwitz on this date.

Panel 6: Contrast this with Oppenheimer's testimony in "Death."

PAGE 104

Panel 6: The Hanford reservation in Washington was the other major source for weapons-grade material. It was a tough town. According to Leona Woods: "There was nothing to do except fight, with the result that occasionally bodies were found in garbage cans the next morning."

PAGE 105

Panel 1: Emphasis on "interesting" here is mine. The prose style of the Primer is uniformly flat.

PAGE 106

Panel 1: In February regular shipments of plutonium began to arrive at Los Alamos. And on this particular date U.S. troops land on Iwo Jima.

Panels 2-4: We're following Richard Feynman as he makes his way back into the compound after sneaking out through a hole in the fence. See the chapters titled "Los Alamos from Below" and "Safecracker Meets Safecracker" in *Surely You're Joking, Mr. Feynman!* for a complete account of his shenanigans. (For more about Feynman in comics form, including the safecracker story, see *Two-Fisted Science*, the first of G.T. Labs' books about scientists.)

PAGE 107

Panels 6-7: The analogies of a baseball and a watermelon are suggested by Richard Rhodes in *The Making of the Atomic Bomb*.

PAGE 108

Panel 1: On this date, within 24 hours of Roosevelt's death, Harry Truman received his first briefing on what the Manhattan Project was all about. He had tried to learn about it on his own as chairman of the Senate Committee to Investigate the National Defense Program, but Secretary of War Henry Stimson had persuaded him to call off the investigation.

Panel 5: Teller's advocacy of a super (what we now call a thermonuclear/hydrogen) bomb, and desire to work on it before anybody even knew how or whether they could make even a wimpy little fission bomb caused friction between him and his superiors well before the scene depicted here.

It's hard to understand why he or anyone would think this was a good idea. Many have written about him (and he's spoken for himself too, naturally) and through my reading I've come to believe that his actions come from a combination of his deep-seated fears of the Russian juggernaut and his awareness of how huge the territory Russia would likely control after the war, for which "mere" fission bombs wouldn't be enough. These fears had some basis in reality, but not enough to justify the destructive courses he has advocated—from the hydrogen bomb to the Strategic Defense Initiatives. (I view him more as a broken figure than an evil one. But just as you would never want to use a damaged part in a complex and dangerous machine, I wish Teller was never part of what Eisenhower called the military-industrial complex.)

Panel 6: Very early on, Niels Bohr and John Wheeler believed, correctly, that only a particularly rare variety of uranium could be used effectively in the creation of an atomic explosion. Bohr said this uranium isotope could not be separated from common uranium except by turning the country into a gigantic factory… Years later, when Bohr came to Los Alamos, Wheeler was prepared to say "You see…" but before he could open his mouth, Bohr said "You see, I told you it couldn't be done without turning the whole country into a factory. You have done just that."

PAGE 109

Panel 1: Klaus Fuchs, the notorious spy for the Russians, did indeed report to Bethe. Though he fooled everyone—from security personnel to his colleagues—for years, this came back to haunt Bethe.

Panel 3: VE (Victory in Europe) Day was May 8, 1945.

Panels 5-7: Actual quotes by Oppenheimer, taken in context.

PAGE 112

To keep the cast of characters from growing too large I again make a substitution, replacing Otto Frisch with Fermi. Frisch actually performed this experiment, but Fermi also used the lab here so it's not too much of a stretch to keep the cast of characters smaller by switching them.

PAGE 114

Panel 5: Fermi's referring to the controlled experiments done at CP-1.

PAGE 115

Panel 3: In June a civilian advisory group to President Truman called the Interim Committee recommended that "the bomb should be used against Japan as soon as possible; that it be used on a war plant surrounded by workers' homes; and that it be used without warning." A separate Target Committee was at work at the same time.

PAGES 117-127

On these pages I paraphrase and quote from Szilard's draft of "The Story of a Petition" dated July 28, 1946, from MSS 32: 40/15, marked as "Not For Release." I place the actual events a little out of sequence here for dramatic effect, since Szilard didn't circulate the petition until right after the Trinity test.

The 'bang' and 'boom' sound effects on these pages are there to indicate both the constant explosives testing and also the celebrations (p. 126) throughout the U.S.

PAGE 117

Panel 8: Here Szilard refers to the March bombing of Tokyo, where the resultant firestorm killed an estimated 124,000 in a single night.

Page 120

Panel 3: This, known for obvious reasons as the gun method for assembly, was the mechanism used by the Hiroshima bomb, also known as "Little Boy."

Page 121

Panels 4-7: Fermi's actions are shown out of context here—he wouldn't have performed such an imprecise measurement of the blast effects under laboratory (well, "laboratory") conditions. He did, on the other hand, use just this method to estimate the explosive force of the Trinity test.

As he tells it, and other accounts confirm, he Trinity's light but didn't hear the explosion, since at that point he was busy estimating the bomb's yield by noting how far little bits of paper he dropped were kicked away from him by the wind. Unlike what we show here, he measured the scraps traveled with his shoes (which he knew were nine inches long). He then consulted a chart he'd prepared in advance and predicted 20 kilotons—as good a figure for the yield as the one obtained by the sophisticated instrumentation set up at the site.

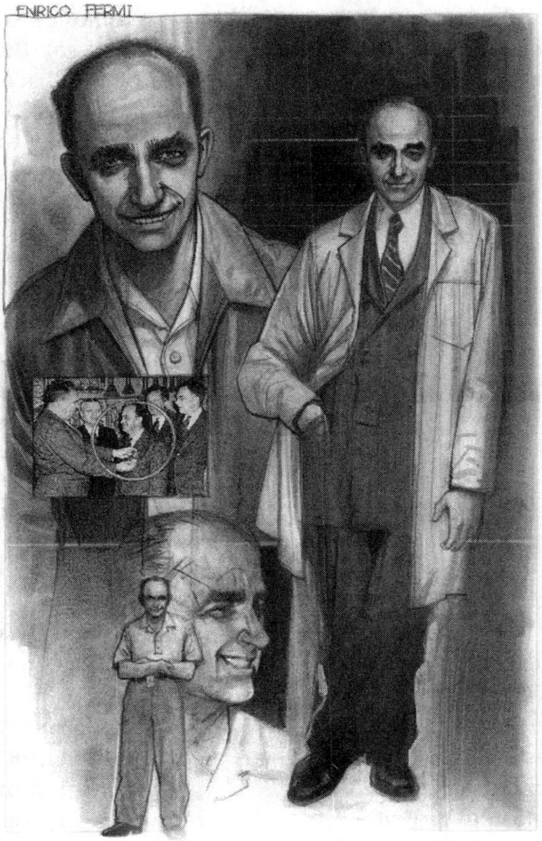
ENRICO FERMI

Pages 122-123

The work on the implosion method began well before the time you see here—George Kistiakowsky came to Los Alamos in January 1944 to begin work on the implosion method for detonating a plutonium bomb. The problem proved difficult, though, and the work continued at a frantic pace right up to Trinity.

Page 124

Oppenheimer, at over 6 feet (1.8 m) tall, weighed approximately 100 lb. (45 kg) by the time of the test, partly because he was recovering from chicken pox at the time, but mostly because of nerves. By the time of the Trinity test the scientists had enough confidence that they didn't use Jumbo, but moved it about a half mile away from ground zero. It remains there to this day.

Page 126

Panel 6: The strikethrough in this passage is in the original petition draft, and shows one of Szilard's rare concessions to political reality.

Page 127

Assembling a core, using either the gun or implosion method, is extremely difficult. Recall that you must put it together with almost perfect precision (or you get a fizzle), very fast (or you get a fizzle), and that you must have a neutron source there to initiate the chain reaction at just the right time (or you get a fizzle).

The basic research behind the implosion method shown here required massive computational power and prompted the development—almost from scratch—of modern computational fluid dynamics.

The petition scene is presented one day before the test rather than when it actually occurred, which is one day after. I did this mainly because I wanted to close this section with the immediate reactions to the first atomic bomb, all of which are reported accurately based on eyewitness accounts—except for Szilard's, which is fiction.

About this meeting, Teller later said: "I made the great mistake of feeling relieved of my responsibility" and "The chance to show the world that science can stop a terrible war without killing a single person was lost." The quotes from Oppenheimer are real and were probably said without much irony.

Panel 1: As noted earlier, Rabi worked on the development of radar at MIT's Radiation Laboratory.

Panel 3: Two versions of the origin of the name "Trinity" exist: One attributes the name to Oppenheimer, who based it on the four-teenth Holy Sonnet by John Donne, a 16th century English poet and sermon writer. The sonnet starts "Batter my heart, three-personed God." The other comes from Szasz in *The Day the Sun Rose Twice*, where he quotes Robert W. Henderson (head of the Engineering Group in the Explosives Division). According to Henderson, he and Major W. A. (Lex) Stevens were at the test site discussing the best way to haul Jumbo (see above) the thirty miles from the closest railway siding to the test site. "A devout Roman Catholic, Stevens observed that the railroad siding was called 'Pope's Siding.' He [then] remarked that the Pope had special access to the Trinity, and that the scientists would need all the help they could get to move the 214 ton Jumbo to its proper spot."

Regardless, in reality Oppenheimer and all the other invitees went out to the site well before the eve of the test…

Panels 7-8: …though Leona Woods and Joan Hinton did sneak out via motorcycle in the early morning hours on the day of the test.

Panels 1-3: I couldn't find all the contingency press releases written by NYT reporter William Laurence. All I know is "they were safely filed in New York. One dealt with no loss of life or property; the second discussed severe damage to property; the third detailed the obituaries of all the famous men in the immediate area, including himself…" and "Laurence enjoyed concocting this version of the explosion—all the people supposedly died from a freak accident at Oppenheimer's ranch in the Pecos Mountains."

As he recalled years later, he "out Roger'd Buck Rogers" and "out Wells'd H.G. Wells."

Albuquerque is roughly 100 miles away from the Trinity test's ground zero. Though Georgia Green (the blind woman we see here) is real, as was her experience, the actual setting for "What was that?" was in a car her brother was driving. They were on their way from her home in Socorro to the University of New Mexico where she was a music student. And though none of the rest were blind like Ms. Green, people in three states saw the first blast (not knowing what it was). Other reactions included:

> A sheep herder who lay sleeping on a cot about 15 miles from ground zero was awakened by the flash and blown off his cot.

> An old man at a crossroads store commented to two of the scientific observers who passed by on the way to a measurement site: "You boys must have been up to something this morning. The sun came up in the west and went down again."

> Suddenly, there was an enormous flash of light… It blasted; it pounced; it bored its way right through you.
> —I.I. Rabi

> It was golden, purple, violet, gray and blue. Atomic fission…was

almost full grown at birth.
—General T.F. Farrell

[The cloud] resembled a giant brain, the convolutions of which were constantly changing.
—Dr. Charles A. Thomas

Then as a climax, which was exceedingly impressive in spite of the fact that the blinding brightness had subsided, the top of the slenderer column seemed to mushroom out into a thick parasol of a rather bright but spectral blue…
—D.R. Inglis, ballistics expert

I can still hear it.
—Otto Frisch

PAGE 135

Panel 1: This quote comes from a Mrs. H.E. Weiselman, who saw the explosion while driving into New Mexico.

Panel 2: William Laurence's description.

Panels 4-5: Joan Hinton's description. (Hinton's words also appear on page 137, panel 3 and page 138, panel 1.)

PAGE 136

Panels 4-5: Leslie Groves' description.

PAGE 137

Panel 2: Philip Morrison's description.

PAGE 139

Oppenheimer is quoting from and visualizing a passage from the *Bhagavad Gita* where Vishnu tries to persuade the Prince that he should do his duty and, to impress him, takes on his many-armed form.

PAGE 142

Fiction, as far as I know. I place Wells' book in the scene since he described a nuclear explosion proceeding more along the runaway lines of what some scientists initially feared (as mentioned on page 132) this way in *The World Set Free*:

CHAPTER THE FOURTH
THE NEW PHASE

It is a remarkable thing that no complete contemporary account of the explosion of the atomic bombs survives. There are, of course, innumerable allusions and partial records, and it is from these that subsequent ages must piece together the image of these devastations.

The phenomena, it must be remembered, changed greatly from day to day, and even from hour to hour, as the exploding bomb shifted its position, threw off fragments or came into contact with water or a fresh texture of soil. Barnet, who came within forty miles of Paris early in October, is concerned chiefly with his account of the social confusion of the country-side and the problems of his command, but he speaks of heaped cloud masses of steam. 'All along the sky to the south-west' and of a red glare beneath these at night. Parts of Paris were still burning, and numbers of people were camped in the fields even at this distance watching over treasured heaps of salvaged loot…'

Other descriptions agree with this; they all speak of the 'continuous reverberations,' or of the 'thudding and hammering,' or some such phrase; and they all testify to a huge pall of steam, from which rain would fall suddenly in torrents and amidst which lightning played. Drawing nearer to Paris an observer would have found the salvage camps increasing in number and blocking up the villages, and large numbers of people, often starving and ailing, camping under improvised tents because there was no place for them to go. The sky became more and more densely overcast until at last it blotted out the light of day and left nothing but a dull red glare 'extraordinarily depressing to the spirit.' In this dull glare, great numbers of people were still living, clinging to their houses and in many cases subsisting in a state of partial famine upon the produce in their gardens and the stores in the shops of the provision dealers.

…

If our spectator could have got permission to enter it, he would have entered also a zone of uproar, a zone of perpetual thunderings, lit by a strange purplish-red light, and quivering and swaying with the incessant explosion of the radio-active substance. Whole blocks of buildings were alight and burning fiercely, the trembling, ragged flames looking pale and ghastly and attenuated in comparison with the full-bodied crimson glare beyond. The shells of other edifices already burnt rose, pierced by rows of window sockets against the red-lit mist.

Every step farther would have been as dangerous as a descent within the crater of an active volcano. These spinning, boiling bomb centres would shift or break unexpectedly into new regions, great fragments of earth or drain or masonry suddenly caught by a jet of disruptive force might come flying by the explorer's head, or the ground yawn a fiery grave beneath his feet. Few who adventured into these areas of destruction and survived attempted any repetition of their experiences. There are stories of puffs of luminous, radio-active vapour drifting sometimes scores of miles from the bomb centre and killing and scorching all they overtook. And the first conflagrations from the Paris centre spread westward half-way to the sea.

Moreover, the air in this infernal inner circle of red-lit ruins had a peculiar dryness and a blistering quality, so that it set up a soreness of the skin and lungs that was very difficult to heal…

Even a casual browse of your local library's or bookstore's shelves will present scores of books about atomic weapons. These notes and references offer a starting point for histories, but don't mention others, except as follows:

In prose, my favorite cautionary tale on science and war is *A Canticle for Leibowitz* by Walter M. Miller, Jr. In comics, the famous "Gen" series by Keiji Nakazawa (beginning with *Barefoot Gen*) offers a cartoon history of the Hiroshima bombing and its aftermath. It spends only two panels on the explosion itself, appropriately focusing on the people it affected. Many editions are available, as it goes in and out of print on an irregular basis. Also noteworthy is the 1953 Harvey Kurtzman/Wally Wood collaboration "Atom Bomb" from *Two-Fisted Tales* #33, available from Gemstone Publishing. Much shorter and much less complex than Nakazawa's story, this tale is still noteworthy not only for its graphic excellence, but also for its rather daring approach, appearing as it did during the height of U.S. fervor for these weapons.

Finally, though our story here doesn't touch at all upon the other major horror of the time, any book done in comics that deals with World War II must mention Art Spiegelman's *Maus*—if you read only one of the books recommended in this paragraph, please make it this one.

And as for Szilard himself, I found no documentation of his immediate reaction to the bombing of Hiroshima, or the setting in which he first heard about it. Perhaps because this was one of the first scenes I visualized, I didn't try all that hard.

interlude

PAGES 145-148

The text of the speech excerpted here comes from MSS 32: 42/13, "Bloomington Speech."

PAGE 145

Panel 1: Here's the first we see of Dr. Trude Weiss, Szilard's friend since 1929. They kept in close touch from then until they married in 1951.

Their relationship was never conventional. They lived apart for many years after their wedding, but were almost constant companions for many years before. They also (probably at Szilard's insistence) didn't formally announce their marriage. Further, he sometimes forgot to introduce her as his wife. So having him hesitate here, while perhaps not likely in this instance/context, is certainly in character.

Panel 6: Szilard wasn't in Hollywood to hobnob with the stars, but rather to act as script doctor. (His reaction to the first shooting script was "It stinks.") So he remained on hand to rewrite some of the scenes to more accurately portray his meetings with Einstein.

PAGE 146

Panel 1: This is an overstatement. (Probably.) But Oppenheimer did appear to be pleased that the actor chosen to portray him was the most handsome and famous of all of those in the film.

PAGES 147-148

I have no idea about the real size of the crowds Szilard spoke to, or whether he made this speech indoors. But given the tenor of the times it's safe to assume that he was not telling people what they wanted to hear, and that people received his lectures with limited enthusiasm and in small numbers.

PAGE 150

Like many others involved with the bomb—though especially true for troublemakers like him—Szilard remained under almost constant surveillance for years. It wasn't done subtly, since it was intended to intimidate as well as to gather information. So Szilard did indeed know his shadows, and did indeed offer to share umbrellas and cabs with them.

death

The sidebar text in this section comes from *In the Matter of J. Robert Oppenheimer*, heavily edited from its original 992 pages. I've used the words verbatim when possible, but in cases where people were either so long-winded or used such tortured sentence construction that readers wouldn't believe anybody would ever actually talk that way, I've paraphrased their speech.

PAGE 155

Panel 1: Lloyd Garrison and Oppenheimer never became friends, or even friendly. Said Garrison: "He never went out of his way to thank us at all although we were doing all this without fee and at vast personal cost." Garrison also noted later that "…he may well have thought that I wasn't adequate for the occasion. Never a word of that was suggested to me, but he might well have felt that."

PAGES 160-161

This sequence with Harry Truman is inserted into a place where it doesn't belong in terms of strict chronology and testimony.

Though the quoted letter from Truman is real, the actual letter Garrison reads into testimony here was the one Oppenheimer sent to Lewis Strauss, head of the AEC:

Dear Lewis:

Yesterday, when you asked to see me, you told me for the first time that my clearance by the Atomic Energy Commission was about to be suspended. You put to me as a possibly desirable alternative that I request termination of my contract as a consultant to the Commission, and thereby avoid an explicit consideration of the charges…

I have thought most earnestly of the alternative suggested. Under the circumstances this course of action would mean that I accept and concur in the view that I am not fit to serve this Government, that I have now swerved for some 12 years. This I cannot do.…If I were thus unworthy I could hardly have served our country as I have tried, or have spoken, on more than one occasion, in the name of science and our country.

And of course Truman's reaction to Oppenheimer's hand-wringing doesn't appear in the testimony at all.

PAGE 162

Panel 5: In fact, Philip Morrison, Robert Serber, Luis Alvarez, and a number of other scientists were given field commissions as uniformed officers when it came time for them to assemble the bombs.

PAGE 164

Panel 3: Richard Feynman and his wife Arline enjoyed baiting the brass as much as Szilard did, and got into just as much trouble for doing so.

PAGE 166

Panel 2: Robb is quoting from the testimony of Marvin Kelly here.

PAGE 171

Sidebar text: Garrison's actual words were "I am sure there is no 'design,' Mr. Gray." But out of context from the paragraphs I removed this turn of phrase probably wouldn't make sense, so I've changed it to the more contemporary 'hidden agenda.'

PAGE 176

Panel 2: Groves, rather than Robb, actually made the statement in the second word balloon.

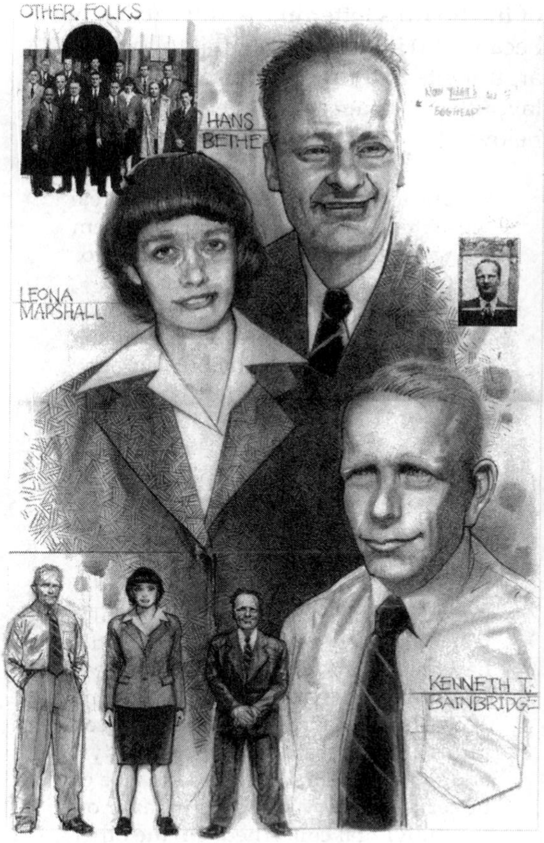
OTHER FOLKS
HANS BETHE
LEONA MARSHALL
KENNETH T. BAINBRIDGE

PAGE 177

Bethe's questioner was one of Oppenheimer's co-counsels named Marks, but for the sake of not introducing yet another character I use Garrison here instead.

PAGE 179

Panel 4: Note that Fermi is careful to call these non-scientific judgments "opinions."

PAGE 184

Panel 5: Robb and Teller had met the night before, where Teller had initially opined that Oppenheimer wasn't a security risk.

Sidebar text: This is the last use of the word "Dr." when referring to Oppenheimer. This is something of a cheat on my part, since they did use the honorific occasionally. But because this is the testimony that destroys Oppenheimer (politically) and Teller (socially, at least with many of his peers) I chose to emphasize how Robb and Teller drop the pretense of respect for Oppenheimer's status.

PAGE 185

Panel 2: This is how Teller recollected their conversation in the 1960s.

PAGE 186

Sidebar text: To editorialize, Teller's saying he was "just most dreadfully disappointed" in his otherwise stone cold testimony brings to mind the snifflingly excessive sincerity of some corrupt version of *Little Women*.

PAGE 188

Panel 5: Teller still bridles when Ulam's name gets mentioned in conjunction with the design of the hydrogen ("super") bomb. In a recent article in the *New York Times* (April 24, 2001, Late Edition - Final, Section F, Page 1, "Who Built The H-Bomb? Debate Revives," by William J. Broad) he credits Dick Garwin for the first design. Along with himself, of course. Teller has long been silent about Garwin's role. He makes no mention of him in his books, perhaps because like many others Garwin is now an advocate of arms control, saying "If I could wave a wand [and make the hydrogen bomb go away] I would do that."

PAGES 192-197

The text in the right-hand sidebars is distilled from the Boards' findings based on General Nichols' recommendations, and in the left-hand sidebars you see a condensation of Lloyd Garrison's response.

Right sidebar: I initially included almost all of the Board's letter in the story itself, but because (a) it wasn't essential to the board's arguments and (b) it did bad things to the layout of the pages, I deleted the chunks below:

> We are acutely aware that in a very real sense this case puts the security system of the United States on trial, both as to procedures and as to substance. This notion has been strongly urged upon us by those who recommended clearance for Dr. J. Robert Oppenheimer, and no doubt a similar view is taken by those who feel he should not be cleared.
>
> If we understand the two points of view, they may be stated as follows: There are those who apprehend that our program for security at this point in history consists of an uneasy mixture of fear, prejudice, and arbitrary judgments. They feel that reason and fairness and justice have abdicated and their places have been taken by hysteria and repression. They, thus, believe that security procedures are necessarily without probity and that national sanity and balance can be served only by a finding in favor of the individual concerned. On the other hand, there is a strong belief that in recent times our government has been less than unyielding toward the problem of communism, and that loose and pliable attitudes regarding loyalty and security have prevailed to the danger of our society and its institutions. Thus, they feel that this proceeding presents the unrelinquishable opportunity for a demonstration against communism, almost regardless of the facts developed about the conduct and sympathies of Dr. Oppenheimer.
>
> We find ourselves in agreement with much that underlies both points of view. We believe that the people of our country can be reassured by this proceeding that it is possible to conduct an investigation in calmness, in fairness, in disregard of public clamor and private pressures, and with dignity. We believe that it has been demonstrated that the Government can search its own soul and the soul of an individual whose relationship to his Government is in question with full protection of the rights and interests of both. We believe that loyalty and security can be examined within the frameworks of the traditional and inviolable principles of American justice...

Gratitude from a young California Congressman named Richard M. Nixon...

Panel 2: I switched the words "science" and "government" from the original to add emphasis and provide a smoother transition to the scene on the next page.

Panel 2: Here are highlights from the complete text of Ward Evans' minority report, referred to by Smyth. Since there is little within it that isn't in Garrison's letter, I only used a few pieces of it in the story pages:

> I have reached the conclusion that Dr. J. Robert Oppenheimer's clearance should be reinstated and am submitting a minority report in accordance with AEC procedure.
>
> ...
>
> I am in perfect agreement with the majority report of its "findings" with respect to the allegations in Mr. Nichols' letter and I am in agreement with the statement of the Board concerning the significance of its "findings" to the end of page 32. I also agree with the last paragraph of this section in which the Board makes a final comment on Mr. Nichols' letter. I do not, however, think it necessary to go into any philosophical discussion to prove points not found In Mr. Nichols' letter.
>
> The derogatory information in this letter consisting of 24 items has all been substantiated except for one item. This refers to a Communist meeting held in Dr. Oppenheimer's home, which he is supposed to have attended.

On the basis of this finding, the Board would have to say that Dr. Oppenheimer should not be cleared.

But this is not all.

Most of this derogatory information was in the hands of the Commission when Dr. Oppenheimer was cleared in 1947. They apparently were aware of his associations and his left-wing policies; yet they cleared him. They took a chance on him because of his special talents and he continued to do a good job. Now when the job is done, we are asked to investigate him for practically the same derogatory information. He did his job in a thorough and painstaking manner. There is not the slightest vestige of information before this Board that would indicate that Dr. Oppenheimer is not a loyal citizen of his country. He hates Russia. He had communistic friends, it is true. He still has some. However, the evidence indicates that he has fewer of them than he had in 1947. He is not as naive as he was then. He has more judgment; no one on the Board doubts his loyalty—even the witnesses adverse to him admit that—and he is certainly less of a security risk than he was in 1947, when he was cleared. To deny him clearance now for what he was cleared for in 1947, when we must know he is less of a security risk now than he was then, seems to be hardly the procedure to be adopted in a free country.

...

His judgment was bad in some cases, and most excellent in others but, in my estimation, it is better now than it was in 1947 and to damn him now and ruin his career and his service, I cannot do it.

His statements in cross examination show him to be still naive, but extremely honest and such statements work to his benefit in my estimation. All people are somewhat of a security risk. I don't think we have to go out of our way to point out how this man might be a security risk.

Dr. Oppenheimer in one place in his testimony said that he had told "a tissue of lies." What he had said was not a tissue of lies; there was one lie...
He did not hinder the development of the H-bomb and there is absolutely nothing in the testimony to show that he did.

First he was in favor of it in 1944. There is no indication that this opinion changed until 1945. After 1945 he did not favor it for some years perhaps on moral, political or technical grounds. Only time will prove whether he was wrong on the moral and political grounds. After the Presidential directive of January 31, 1950, he worked on this project. If his opposition to the H-bomb caused any people not to work on it, it was because of his intellectual prominence and influence over scientific people and not because of any subversive tendencies.

I personally think that our failure to clear Dr. Oppenheimer will be a black mark on the escutcheon of our country. His witnesses are a considerable segment of the scientific backbone of our Nation and they endorse him. I am worried about the effect an improper decision may have on the scientific development in our country. Nuclear physics is new in our country. Most of our authorities in this field came from overseas. They are with us now. Dr. Oppenheimer got most of his education abroad. We have taken hold of this new development in a very great way. There is no predicting where and how far it may go and what its future potentialities may be. I would very much regret any action to retard or hinder this new scientific development.

This is my opinion as a citizen of a free country.

I suggest that Dr. Oppenheimer's clearance be restored.

[signed]
WARD V. EVANS

epilogue

PAGE 205

Panels 3-6: True to form, Szilard devised his own treatment for his bladder cancer, which, along with his unorthodox ways, did not endear him to the staff doctors.

All of the books on Szilard make note of this, but I'm particularly grateful to Dr. Anders Barany of the Nobel Museum in Stockholm for sending me "Leo Szilard Plays Chess with Death," by George Klein. This article provided many insights—not only into this particular scene, but into Szilard's character in general.

The dose Szilard chose is tremendously high, but it worked to kill Szilard's cancer. It also destroyed his bladder.

PAGE 206

Panel 3: Szilard had to visit Khrushchev rather than the other way around. At their meeting, Szilard brought a Schick Injector razor and extra blades as a gift. "If you like the razor, I will send you fresh blades from time to time. But this I can do, of course, only as long as there is no war." Khrushchev replied "If there is a war I will stop shaving."

PAGE 207

Panels 2-5: "I am just going to write…this version of the facts." comes from MSS 32: 40/4: "Book."

references

BOOKS AND MANUSCRIPTS

"Leo Szilard Papers" at the University of California, San Diego. MSS 32: various boxes/folders as per the notes.

The primary source for some of the most telling story elements in this book.

The very first thing I saw when I opened the very first folder I wanted was a signed letter from Niels Bohr, which gave me a physical jolt not unlike an electric shock. I owe thanks to the archives staff at the Geisel Library.

(Yes, the Geisel we all know better as Dr. Seuss...the original cover art to *The Lorax* was in the display case right outside the Special Collections section.)

Atomic Quest, by Arthur Holly Compton (NY: Oxford University Press, 1956).

The source for some of the quotes and observations on the Trinity test, as well as background for the Oppenheimer hearings.

Atoms in the Family, by Laura Fermi (Chicago: University of Chicago Press, 1954).

Fermi's life from his wife's perspective, which for me added depth to the characterization of him, his colleagues, and the environment in which they worked.

The Collected Papers of Enrico Fermi, Volume 2, edited by Emilio Segré (Chicago: University of Chicago Press, 1965).

My source for Fermi's perspective on both the early days of reactor research and Szilard.

The Collected Works of Leo Szilard: Scientific Papers, Volume I, edited by Bernard T. Feld and Gertrude Weiss Szilard (Cambridge, MA: The MIT Press, 1972).

Here you can read many of Szilard's papers in facsimile form, including his patent documents and the technical papers referred to in the story.

Critical Assembly: A Technical History of Los Alamos during the Oppenheimer Years, 1943-1945, by Lillian Hoddeson, Paul W. Henriksen, Roger A. Meade, and Catherine Westfall (Cambridge: Cambridge University Press, 1993).

This goes well beyond the "Los Alamos Primer" to provide both the physical context and a technical description of the weapons work done during the war.

Dawn Over Zero: The Story of the Atomic Bomb, by William L. Laurence (NY: Alfred A. Knopf, 1946).

One of the first books written about the Manhattan Project, by the reporter given exclusive rights to cover the story.

The Day the Sun Rose Twice, by Ferenc Morton Szasz (Albuquerque: University of New Mexico Press, 1985).

A detailed account of the happenings on the day of the first nuclear explosion. One of the many books that provided a source for impressions this event made on observers.

Genius in the Shadows: A Biography of Leo Szilard, by William Lanouette with Bela Szilard (Chicago: The University of Chicago Press, 1992).

The best biography I read on Leo Szilard.

Hitler's Uranium Club: The Secret Recordings at Farm Hall, by Jeremy Bernstein (Woodbury, NY: American Institute of Physics, 1996).

Though not directly referenced in the story you just read, this book will give you background on Germany's wartime efforts in the field of nuclear fission. The naiveté (for lack of a better word) of the German scientists is one of the most notable things that come through in the transcripts of the tapes made while Heisenberg and his colleagues were interred in Britain.

In the Matter of J. Robert Oppenheimer: Transcript of Hearing before Personnel Security Board, Washington D.C. April 12, 1954 through May 6, 1954 (Washington: Government Printing Office, 1954).

Almost 1000 pages of small print, at least in the edition I worked from. Excruciating and fascinating in more ways than one.

J. Robert Oppenheimer: Shatterer of Worlds, by Peter Goodchild (Boston: Houghton Mifflin, 1981).

A companion volume to the BBC television series of the same name, this book offers a thorough overview of Oppenheimer's life and features illustrations and photographs on almost every page.

Lawrence and Oppenheimer, by Nuel Pharr Davis (NY: Simon and Schuster, 1968).

Though the story you just read paints Teller as Oppenheimer's most vocal and damaging political opponent, as you saw from his behavior Oppenheimer had no trouble getting on someone's bad side. Ernest Lawrence and he clashed over policy (in no small part out of jealousy on Lawrence's part, in my opinion) from very early on, and this book provides a detailed account of the situation.

The Legacy of Hiroshima, by Edward Teller (NY: Macmillan, 1962).

The source for the quote by Niels Bohr about turning the whole country into a factory, it also provides insight into Teller's way of thinking at the time he recommended Oppenheimer for the Fermi Medal.

Leo Szilard: His Version of the Facts, Volume II of the Collected Works of Leo Szilard, edited by Spencer R. Weart and Gertrud Weiss Szilard (Cambridge, MA: The MIT Press, 1978).

Here you can find Szilard's Ten Commandments, personal recollections and letters, and the anecdote that inspired our epilogue.

Leo Szilard: Science as a Mode of Being, by David A. Grandy (Lanham, MD: University Press of America, Inc., 1996).

This book helped to round out the portrait of Szilard that I constructed from Lanouette's and Rhodes' work. Though short, it offers valuable insights into the cultural context in which Szilard lived and worked.

The Making of the Atomic Bomb, by Richard Rhodes (NY: Simon and Schuster, 1986).

Rhodes won the Pulitzer Prize, the National Book Award, and the National Book Critics Circle Award for this work of history and literature. If you read no other book about the development of the first atomic bombs, please read this one.

Men and Decisions, by Lewis L. Strauss (NY: Doubleday & Company, 1962).

Strauss' cold-blooded account of the Oppenheimer hearings are a perfect match with the self-important title of his book.

Now It Can Be Told, by Leslie R. Groves (NY: Harper & Brothers, 1962).

The title says a great deal about the tone of the book, but Groves' point of view is an important one to hear regardless of how he presents it.

Picturing the Bomb: Photographs from the Secret World of the Manhattan Project, by Rachel Fermi and Esther Samra (NY: Harry N. Abrams, 1995).

Hundreds of superb pictures that provided reference for what you saw here, including the images that served as the basis for the inside front and back covers.

Robert Oppenheimer: Letters and Recollections, edited by Alice Kimball Smith and Charles Weiner (Cambridge, MA: Harvard University Press, 1980).

Letters to and from Oppenheimer, with the majority of the correspondence predating the Los Alamos period.

Science and the Common Understanding and *The Open Mind*, by J. Robert Oppenheimer (NY: Simon and Schuster, 1954 and 1955, respectively).

Philosophical writings by Oppenheimer, touching on the role of science and politics. Copyright dates notwithstanding, all were written before Oppenheimer's political downfall.

"Surely You're Joking, Mr. Feynman!", by Richard P. Feynman (as told to Ralph Leighton (NY: W.W. Norton & Company, 1985).

The "Dragon's Tail" experiment is

described here, as are the incidents with the censors and an excellent example of Feynman's capacity for mischief regarding the strict security—a capacity we've only alluded to in the story. See "Los Alamos From Below" for all this and more.

Their Day in the Sun: Women of the Manhattan Project, by Ruth H. Howes and Caroline L. Herzenberg (Philadelphia: Temple University Press, 1999).

Important to the story you just read for its outsider view of the Trinity test and the scene of Hinton and Woods hopping on a motorcycle to crash the party.

Toward a Livable World: Leo Szilard and the Crusade for Nuclear Arms Control, Volume III of the Collected Works of Leo Szilard, edited by Helen S. Hawkins, G. Allen Greb, and Gertrud Weiss Szilard (Cambridge, MA: The MIT Press, 1987).

More writing by Szilard, this time on political matters.

The Uranium People, by Leona Marshall Libby (NY: Crane, Russak & Company, 1979).

You know her in this story as Dr. Woods, but she married fellow scientist John Marshall soon after the CP-1 experiment. This book was an excellent source for details about the first atomic pile and the people who worked on it.

The Voice of the Dolphins and Other Stories, by Leo Szilard (Stanford, CA: Stanford University Press, 1961).

I'm not fond of Szilard as a prose writer, but the introduction makes this book worth picking up. And though I don't think his estate is likely to land a major motion picture based on any of the stories printed here, Szilard's intellectual range and great imagination are evident, and impressive.

What Little I Remember, by Otto Frisch (London: Cambridge University Press, 1979).

The source for Frisch's "I can still hear it." quote, along with the a more accurate account of the Dragon's Tail experiment than you read here.

The World Set Free, by H.G. Wells (1914, accessible from Project Gutenberg at *ftp://sailor.gutenberg.org/pub/gutenberg/etext97/twsfr10.txt*).

The inspiration for Szilard, and though not Wells' best by far, it still contains many prescient details and some vivid writing.

ARTICLES

"Did Bohr Share Nuclear Secrets?," by Hans Bethe, Kurt Gottfried and Roald Z. Sagdeev and "What Did Heisenberg Tell Bohr About the Bomb?" by Jeremy Bernstein in *Scientific American*, vol. 272, no. 5, May 1995, 83-97.

The short answer: "No." Excellent articles that put Bohr's sometimes difficult to understand actions and philosophy in context.

"Dr. Oppenheimer Suspended by A.E.C. in Security Review; Scientist Defends Record," by James Reston, with letters from K.D. Nichols and J. Robert Oppenheimer in the *New York Times*, vol. 103, no. 35143, April 13, 1954, 1,16-19.

Breaking news, as the hearings began. It's all there in excruciating detail.

"The German Uranium Project," by Hans Bethe in *Physics Today*, vol. 53, no. 7, July 2000, 34-36.

A brief look at what Heisenberg and his fellow scientists did (and mostly didn't) know during the war.

"Infamy and Honor at the Atomic Café," by Gary Stix in *Scientific American*, vol. 281, no. 4, October 1999, 42-44.

The source of the "infamous" Teller quote, and a superb portrait of Teller in his later years.

"J. Robert Oppenheimer: Before the War," by John S. Rigden in *Scientific American*, vol. 273, no. 1, 76-81.

A quick overview of Oppenheimer's achievements in building an "American School" of physics that would rival the great European schools that dominated the world scene until World War II.

"Leo Szilard Plays Chess With Death," by George Klein in the Eötvös Physical Society's *Leo Szilard Centenary Volume* (ed. George Marx, Budapest: Eötvös Physical Society, 1998), 169-175.

> As noted above, this is the source for the details about Szilard's self-designed and administered radiation treatment.

"The Odd Couple of the Bomb," by William Lanouette in *Scientific American*, vol. 283, no. 5, November 2000, 104-109.

> Like his book on Szilard, you'll find Lanouette provides an excellent portrait of Fermi and Szilard and their uneasy liaison in this article.

"Physicists in Wartime Japan," by Laurie M. Brown and Yochiro Nambu in *Scientific American*, vol. 279, no. 6, December 1998, 96-103.

> Though it has nothing about bomb development, since there was none in Japan, this article points out some of the excellent science done during the war despite difficult conditions and almost complete isolation.

"A Reporter at Large: The Contemporaneous Memoranda of Dr. Sachs," by Geoffrey T. Hellman in *The New Yorker*, vol. 21, no. 32, December 1, 1945, 73-81.

> The tortured syntax of Alexander Sachs comes through loud, clear, and quotable in this hot-from-today's-headlines article.

"Teller Deplores Secret Research," by J.N. Wilford in *The New York Times*, vol. 120, no. 41246, December 28, 1970, 1, 25 and "Political Science 1970," in *Newsweek*, vol. 77, no. 2, January 11, 1971, 78.

> In both Teller describes presenting Oppenheimer with Szilard's petition. In the latter you can read about his refusal to accept the Public Health Research Institute's "Dr. Strangelove Award."

CD-ROMs

Critical Mass: America's Race to Build the Atomic Bomb produced and directed by Lisa C. Anderson (Seattle: Corbis, 1996).

> An overview of the Manhattan Project

and biographical sketches of Bohr, Fermi, Feynman, and Oppenheimer.

The Day After Trinity: J. Robert Oppenheimer and the Atomic Bomb, a film by Jon Else (1980, CD-ROM version by NY: Voyager, 1995).

> Seek it out as a film, but the CD makes a fine substitute because of its elegantly presented supplementary material.

WEBSITES

"Historical Nuclear Weapons Test Films," *http://www.nv.doe.gov/news%26pubs/ photos%26films/testfilms.htm*.

> I don't have any direct experience to compare with, but I doubt these will give you much of a sense of what an actual explosion is like. Thank goodness we currently have no live alternative.

"LANL Research Library: Laboratory Publications: History: Los Alamos 50 Years Ago," *http://lib-www.lanl.gov/pubs/lanl50th/ Homepage.htm*, updated 27 November 2000, ©2000, University of California.

> The highlight of this site is the detail unavailable elsewhere, especially in such a condensed but readable form.

"Los Alamos Primer" (also known as "Los Alamos Technical Report LA-1"), *http://lib-www.lanl.gov/la-pubs/00349710.pdf*.

> Rough going unless you have a good technical background, but reading the Primer today does a great job of transporting you back to the early days of the Manhattan Project.

"Truman and the Bomb, a Documentary History, Chapter 10: War Department Press Release C. August 6, 1945," edited by Robert H. Ferrell, *http://www.whistlestop.org/ study_collections/bomb/small/mb11.htm*.

> The first public announcement of the atomic bomb.

"G.T. Labs: Fallout," *http://www.gt-labs.com/ fallout.html*.

> Visit the G.T. Labs site for live links, downloadable notes and references, color versions of some of the images from the book, and other extras.

the artists

JANINE JOHNSTON ("Birth" and visions of Trinity in "Work") lives in Victoria, British Columbia. When not doing artwork of various sorts, she's usually found gardening, cycling, taking photos, gathering more reference books, and enjoying life. She would like to give special thanks to Michael Kaluta for his amazing search skills and Jo-Lee Bertrand for printing out all those images, which made getting this project done on time that much easier.

JEFFREY JONES (cover) was born and raised in Atlanta, Georgia, and his passion for drawing seemed born with him. An interest in art and science got him through childhood, and he entered college majoring in physics. He soon switched to art, but dissatisfied with the curriculum he moved to New York City where he learned to paint during visits to the Metropolitan Museum of Art. Books of his work have been translated into eight languages and he has won many international awards. Now female, Jeffrey lives with her wife Maryellen in the Catskill Mountains of Woodstock, New York. Find out more at *www.jeffreyjones.com*.

CHRIS KEMPLE (Szilard's visions of *The World Set Free* in "Birth") currently resides in Durham, NC with his wife Krista, 2 dogs, and his soon-to-be-born daughter. In addition to freelancing, Chris is an artist in the video game industry as well as creator, artist and writer of his own comic, the 1950's adventure character "Red Vengeance", recently in development as a cartoon at FoxKids. Contact Chris via email at *chriskemple@ipass.net*.

STEVE LIEBER ("Death"), Eisner award winning artist of *Whiteout* and *Whiteout: Melt*, makes his home in Portland, Oregon. He has toiled for all of the major comics publishers and many of the minor ones as well. Look for *Morning Dragons* (with Warren Ellis), scheduled for release in 2002. For more about Steve and his work, visit *www.unrewarding.com/steve*.

VINCE LOCKE ("School") is the creator of *Deadworld* and has illustrated *Sandman, Saint*

Germaine, and the original graphic novel *A Brief History of Violence*. He lives in Michigan. Nate Pride assisted him on the lettering.

BERNIE MIREAULT (prologue, interludes, and epilogue) is the mastermind behind *MacKenzie Queen, Dr. Robot, The Jam, Isaac vs. Eli* (which you can find on the web at *www3.sympatico.ca/ bem69*) and more innovative art and coloring jobs than you can imagine. He gets old-fashioned mail at his home in Montreal, Quebec and on the net at *bem69@sympatico.ca*.

EDDY NEWELL (the model sheets you see interspersed throughout these notes) has won critical acclaim for his moody work on *Black Lightning, Batman, Daredevil*, and for numerous illustration projects, from fashion on out. He lives in Ohio, on the shores of Lake Erie.

TOM ORZECHOWSKI (letterer, "Birth") has worked for a variety of comic book publishers on titles ranging from *X-Men* to *Captain Carrot and His Amazing Zoo Crew*. Over the years he has received every major professional and fan award, but is proudest to have been a contributor to *Neal Adams' Skateman*, known in the industry as the World's Worst Comic Book. You can contact him by email at *SouthHill@aol.com*.

JEFF PARKER ("Work") earns his daily bread in Los Angeles doing storyboard and animation work. Keep an eye out for his own series, *The Interman*, coming soon. He lives near Hollywood, and nearer still to the beach.

ROBIN THOMPSON (layouts for "Birth") currently writes and draws his own independent titles *Captain Space Man* and *Knuckles Malone: Private Gut Buster*. A graduate of the Ontario College of Art in Toronto, he currently lives in Victoria, British Columbia.

JIM OTTAVIANI's first career was as a nuclear engineer. He currently works as a librarian and writes comics about scientists. Contact him via either *www.gt-labs.com* or G.T. Labs, P.O. Box 8145, Ann Arbor, MI 48107.

LEO SZILARD

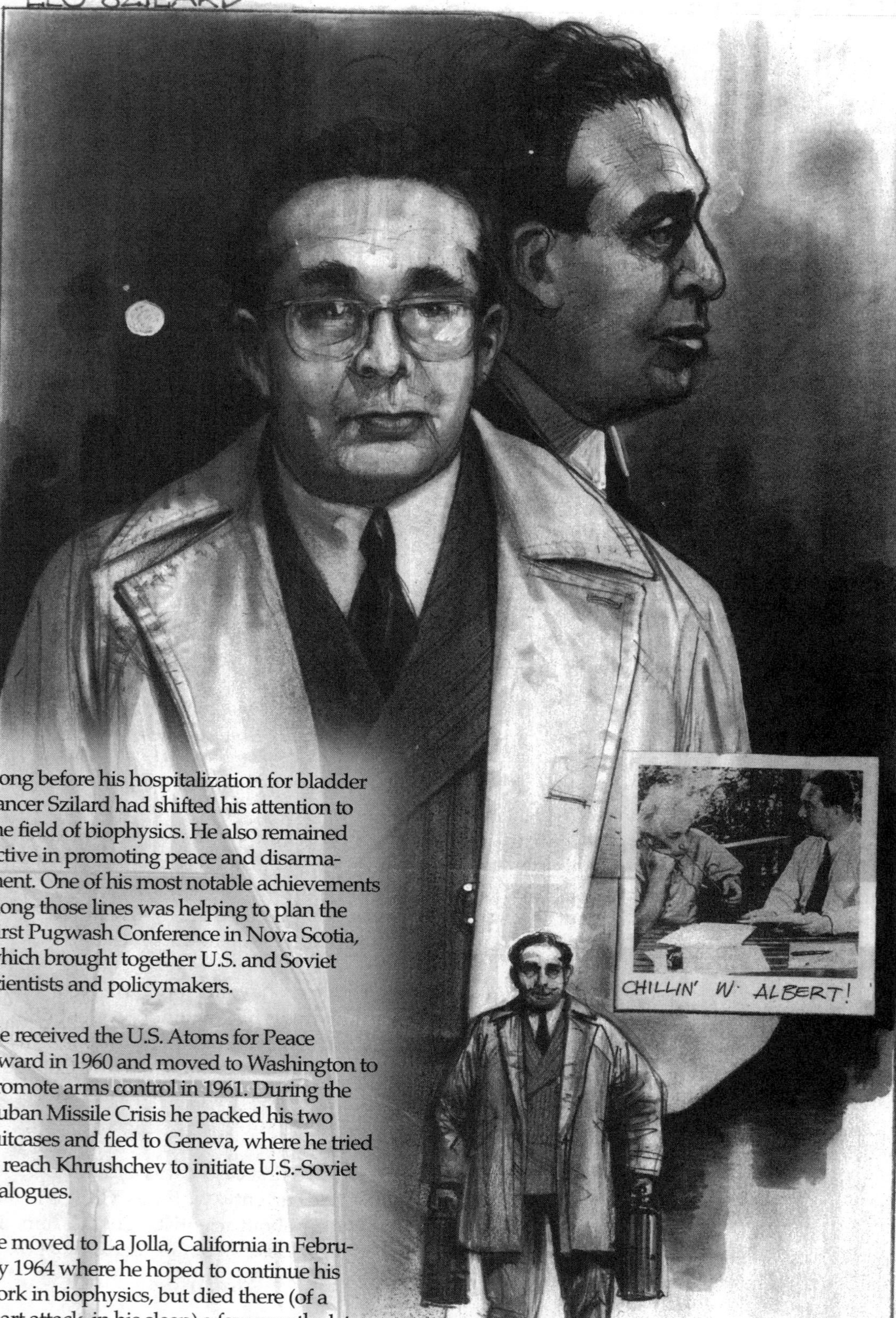
CHILLIN' W. ALBERT!

Long before his hospitalization for bladder cancer Szilard had shifted his attention to the field of biophysics. He also remained active in promoting peace and disarmament. One of his most notable achievements along those lines was helping to plan the First Pugwash Conference in Nova Scotia, which brought together U.S. and Soviet scientists and policymakers.

He received the U.S. Atoms for Peace Award in 1960 and moved to Washington to promote arms control in 1961. During the Cuban Missile Crisis he packed his two suitcases and fled to Geneva, where he tried to reach Khrushchev to initiate U.S.-Soviet dialogues.

He moved to La Jolla, California in February 1964 where he hoped to continue his work in biophysics, but died there (of a heart attack, in his sleep) a few months later.

J. ROBERT OPPENHEIMER

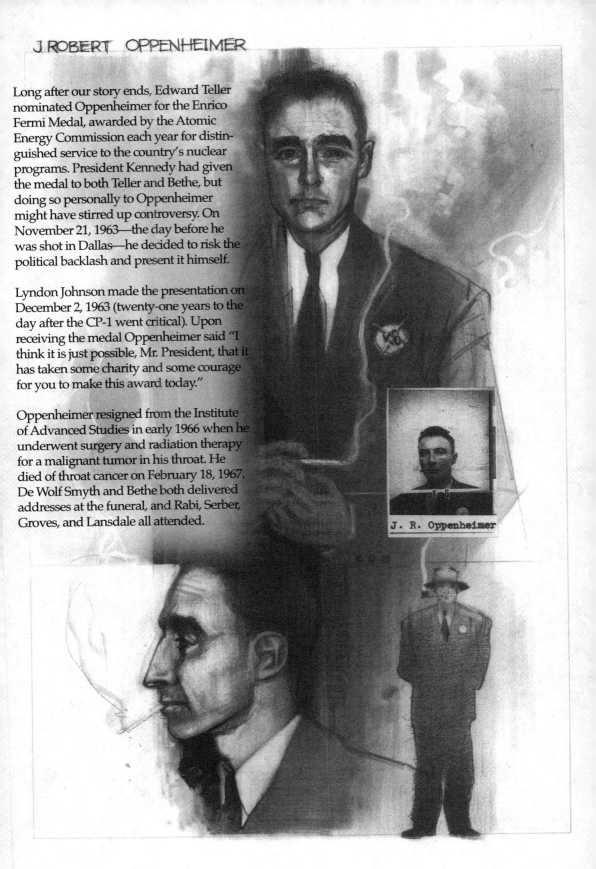

Long after our story ends, Edward Teller nominated Oppenheimer for the Enrico Fermi Medal, awarded by the Atomic Energy Commission each year for distinguished service to the country's nuclear programs. President Kennedy had given the medal to both Teller and Bethe, but doing so personally to Oppenheimer might have stirred up controversy. On November 21, 1963—the day before he was shot in Dallas—he decided to risk the political backlash and present it himself.

Lyndon Johnson made the presentation on December 2, 1963 (twenty-one years to the day after the CP-1 went critical). Upon receiving the medal Oppenheimer said "I think it is just possible, Mr. President, that it has taken some charity and some courage for you to make this award today."

Oppenheimer resigned from the Institute of Advanced Studies in early 1966 when he underwent surgery and radiation therapy for a malignant tumor in his throat. He died of throat cancer on February 18, 1967. De Wolf Smyth and Bethe both delivered addresses at the funeral, and Rabi, Serber, Groves, and Lansdale all attended.

J. R. Oppenheimer

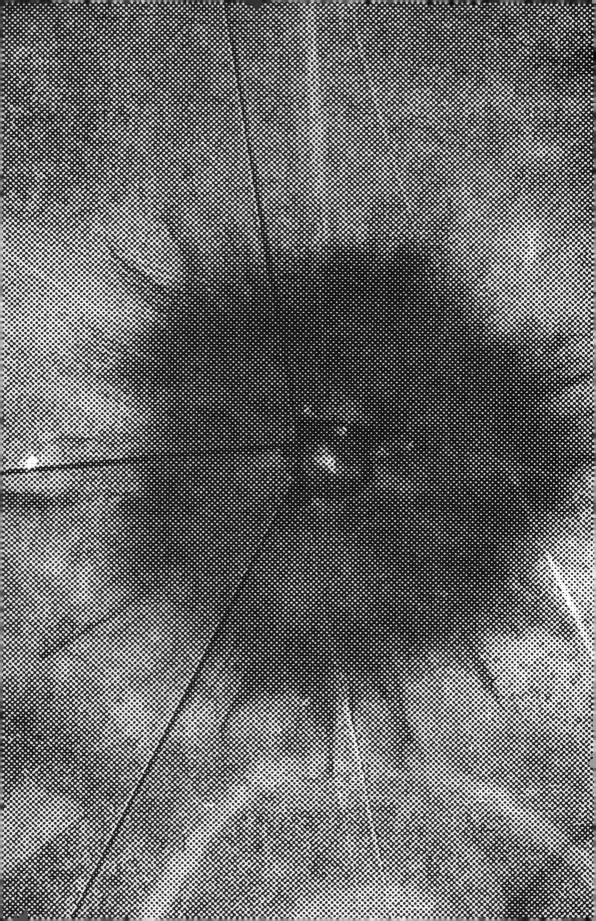